THE COMMAND OF WORDS

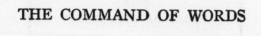

THE COMMAND OF WORDS

BY

S. STEPHENSON SMITH
University of Oregon

THOMAS Y. CROWELL COMPANY
PUBLISHERS : : NEW YORK

Fourth Printing
1939

PREFACE

This work is meant for the reader who wants to build a wide vocabulary and have it under ready and sure command. I hope it will not tempt anyone to become word-drunk. Compression, pace, and continuous forward drive are requisites in modern speaking and writing. At their best, the radio speaker, the writer of talkie dialogue, and the journalist possess these virtues; but they could do with a chaster diction, and so could the amateur of words who is exposed to their influence. The ideal is a vocabulary large enough to permit judicious discarding.

Gains in vocabulary should come step by step with increasing sureness in the use of words. To acquire a sense of their right use, words should be studied in context, in the light of their relations to each other. The spelling bee, the game of anagrams, and the cross word puzzle are not enough. They deal with words as isolated odds and ends, as counters in a game. To be sure, an interest in problem-solving and zeal in competition are good sauce to word-study. These motives are enlisted in the verbal recreations and exercises which make up half this book. I hope that at least half the examples show due deference to the American comic spirit, and that the rest are not too sawdusty. Word-study should belong to the gayer arts, not to the dismal sciences. Yet it has its serious side. In language, as in gunnery, range without precision will never do. Words should hit the mark.

The problem of meaning is central in systematic vocabulary-building. English is rich in single words with many meanings, and richer yet in many words to express different shades of a single meaning. Sometimes this wealth of words is embarrassing; but it can be shared round to advantage, if the law of parsimony is applied to diction. A large vocabulary permits a more judicious selection of words to express one's meaning. The fewer words the better, if only they are to the point. But a truly laconic style comes from a plenty, not from a paucity, of words.

In building vocabulary, what words should first be added to an existing stock? Clearly, those words, beyond the ordinary range, which the reader is most apt to encounter, or the writer to want. E. L. Thorndike has determined, by their rank in thousands, the

25,000 English words in most common use,—an invaluable service to the vocabulary-builder. Professor Thorndike and the Scott Foresman Company, publishers of the *Thorndike Century Junior Dictionary*, have kindly permitted the use of his frequency numbers after the words in vocabulary lists in this book. The vocabulary tests are also made, in part, from Thorndike's list as a reservoir. After taking these tests, the reader can tell at a glance whether a word is beyond his ordinary range, and hence calls for especial attention. C. K. Ogden and the Orthological Institute, inventors of Basic English, have also granted permission to use their findings as to the indispensable ideas for which terms are required in civilized communication. While Basic English, with its 850 words, aims at shrinking vocabulary, it is useful in providing, to head synonym-lists in standard English, words of widest generality, key-symbols of fundamental ideas. Scientific studies of word-frequency and meaning (semantics and general linguistics) are an admirable supplement to the traditional methods of vocabulary-building, which are here treated at length.

Slang has been treated, not as casting a social stigma on its user, but as language in the making. Slang is fascinating material for the student of language and social history, and should not be dismissed with mere tut-tutting. The best way to avoid it is to know all about it, and to extract to the full its humorous possibilities. Jargon is in like case with slang. Instead of muttering vague cautions against it, in the manner of the Alexandrian grammarians, who are not all dead yet, I have treated the varieties of learned jargon under the heading Special and Technical Vocabularies.

Since a word is not really a part of the vocabulary unless it is ready on the tongue or pen, chapters have been added on the art of conversation, on diction in informal speaking, and on the vexed problem, when to write as you talk. Finally, since the work is designed to aid the writer with his problems of diction, a device has been appended for quick check on the correctness of any written work,—a kind of slide rule for writers.

My debts to the standard treatises on words, those of Trench, Greenough and Kittredge, Ernest Weekley, the Fowlers, and G. P. McKnight, are apparent throughout; while the OED has been a constant resource and a court of last resort.

                  S. S. S.

University of Oregon,
September 7, 1935.

CONTENTS

CHAPTER   PAGE

I. A READY, WIDE, AND SURE VOCABULARY 1

II. TIME-HONORED MODES OF BUILDING VOCABULARY . . . 31

III. THE USE OF THE DICTIONARY 42

IV. WORD-FAMILIES AND WORD-BUILDING 60

V. WORD-MEANINGS—PAST AND PRESENT 112

VI. THE FINE SHADES OF MEANING: SYNONYMS 131

VII. WORDS UNDER SUSPICION: SLANG AND JARGON 165

VIII. SPECIAL AND TECHNICAL VOCABULARIES 181

IX. THE ART OF CONVERSATION 215

X. THE AFTER-DINNER TOUCH 234

XI. WHEN TO WRITE AS YOU TALK 239

STYLE RULE 251

A DESK-SET FOR THE STUDENT OF WORDS 265

BIBLIOGRAPHY 266

KEYS TO EXERCISES 267

INDEX 281

THE COMMAND OF WORDS

CHAPTER I

A READY, WIDE, AND SURE VOCABULARY

How ready, wide, and sure is your vocabulary? It takes a minimum of from five to fourteen thousand words to read an ordinary newspaper. The figure depends somewhat on how ordinary the newspaper is, and how much of it you read. The jargons of the sport and fashion pages will raise the number. The figure varies also, depending on which vocabulary expert you believe. Probably nine thousand is nearer the mark, for the average *passive* or reading vocabulary. Most persons use actively in conversation or letter-writing less than half the words they know in print. This *active* vocabulary is rather hard to test. But it is fairly easy to find the range of your reading vocabulary.

RANGE

Journalists since Defoe have been interested in writing in a language that everybody could read. The novelist who wants to sell by the hundred thousand must use everyday words. Radio announcers usually succeed in hitting a low common denominator of language. But just what words are included in this common range? It is only in the last fifteen years that the facts have been ascertained. E. L. Thorndike, with his assistants, has counted ten million running or consecutive words in English and American works commonly read, and has picked out the words which occur most frequently. In the list of 20,000 and the dictionary of 25,000, each word has after it a number indicating in which thousand it is found. The word *coalesce* is followed by the number 16, meaning it is in the sixteenth thousand for frequency, well above the extreme newspaper range. The word *escape* is followed by the number 1 to

1

indicate that it is in the most common thousand. Is it clear from these examples that the higher the number which follows a word the less frequently does that word occur? Given these frequencies, it is interesting to note how accurately Defoe hit upon words in commonest use. Hazlitt and Emerson, too, kept close to the everyday run of language. This knowledge of word-frequency is indeed invaluable for estimating the difficulty of a given piece of prose. But there are other uses for these figures.

By using Thorndike's list, and similar reservoirs of selected words, it is easy to compile tests which will show the range of an individual vocabulary. Samples are taken from each thousand. If you know the meaning of thirty samples from a given thousand, it is quite probable that you know all the words in that thousand. Wherever in the scale you begin to encounter words that keep you guessing, the chances are that at that point you need to begin to build up your vocabulary. Judging by the following test, where should you start?

1) The words occurring in the first column and numbered from 1—10 are from the first 1000, 11—20 from the second 1000, in Thorndike's list [1] of 20,000 words in most common use, etc. Place in the parentheses the number of the word or phrase closest in meaning to the initial word:

1. ( ) escape (1) get away (2) exit (3) runway (4) back door.
2. ( ) oak (1) sturdy (2) full-grown acorn (3) vine (4) all right.
3. ( ) row (1) group (2) paddle (3) line (4) squad.
4. ( ) object (1) idiot (2) wretch (3) apology (4) thing.
5. ( ) crown (1) king's head-covering (2) hit someone (3) wreath (4) jewels.
6. ( ) built (1) added to (2) well-formed (3) constructed (4) organized.
7. ( ) again (1) also (2) soon (3) once more (4) in opposition to.
8. ( ) surprise (1) shock (2) annoy (3) please (4) catch unprepared.
9. ( ) shore (1) land near sea (2) sand (3) marshy land (4) certain.
10. ( ) increase (1) plait (2) become greater (3) salary (4) fold tightly.

11. ( ) anxious (1) careful (2) unstrung (3) worried (4) fretful.
12. ( ) ashamed (1) brazen (2) bothered (3) moderate (4) mortified.
13. ( ) empire (1) forest reserve (2) eminent domain (3) crown colony (4) many states under one rule.
14. ( ) feather (1) cowardice (2) pillow (3) light, airy (4) plumage.
15. ( ) grade (1) a crossing (2) sign of efficiency (3) bad mark (4) slope.

[1] The Thorndike frequency numbers, here and elsewhere in this work, are used by the kind permission of Dr. E. L. Thorndike and Scott, Foresman and Company.

16. ( ) knight (1) a cavalier (2) fellow (3) slave (4) highwayman.
17. ( ) produce (verb) (1) bring forward (2) multiply (3) educate (4) lead astray.
18. ( ) rate (1) time (2) an increase (3) proportionate measure (4) outrank.
19. ( ) spent (1) shot (2) worked-out vein (3) consumed (4) bought.
20. ( ) constant (1) faithful (2) consistent (3) certain (4) foolish.

21. ( ) butterfly (1) cocoon (2) brightly-colored insect (3) specimen (4) churn.
22. ( ) confess (1) relate (2) lie (3) admit in confidence (4) to tell a true story.
23. ( ) convince (1) conquer (2) knock down (3) wreak (4) persuade fully.
24. ( ) dame (1) wench (2) lady (3) profane exclamation (4) hold back.
25. ( ) hawk (1) auctioneer (2) bird of prey (3) fly overhead (4) pawn.
26. ( ) lively (1) sparkling (2) healthy (3) animated (4) neat.
27. ( ) peasant (1) a rustic (2) oaf (3) American farmer (4) brute.
28. ( ) stuck (1) hung on (2) caught (3) adhered to (4) cheated.
29. ( ) poultry (1) cheap (2) hen-house (3) tame fowls (4) wild game.
30. ( ) abroad (1) widely (2) traveling (3) sailing (4) scandal.

31. ( ) fringe (1) shrink (2) border (3) cliff (4) support for door.
32. ( ) courtier (1) more polite (2) too clever (3) one at court (4) runner.
33. ( ) devour (1) pious (2) prayer (3) wildcat (4) eat up.
34. ( ) highway (1) robber's hangout (2) bypath (3) main road (4) elevated road.
35. ( ) philosopher (1) shrewd columnist (2) a theoretical thinker (3) one who denies God (4) an optimist.
36. ( ) resist (1) oppose (2) restrain (3) refrain (4) react.
37. ( ) transfer (1) wrench (2) hoist (3) forward (4) shift.
38. ( ) risk (1) rugged individualism (2) hazard (3) gossipy (4) naughty.
39. ( ) situation (1) fix (2) establishing a location (3) position (4) relationship.
40. ( ) vile (1) bass note (2) bass viol (3) unperfumed (4) base.

41. ( ) aware (1) cognizant of (2) wakeful (3) dish (4) open to.
42. ( ) carrier (1) guard (2) watchman (3) conveyer (4) hodman.
43. ( ) dispense (1) distribute (2) medicine (3) to give away liquor (4) pardon.
44. ( ) explanation (1) argument (2) explication (3) code (4) answer.
45. ( ) murderer (1) hangman (2) gangster (3) butcher (4) killer.
46. ( ) painful (1) mean (2) wretched (3) causing suffering (4) inhumane.

47. ( ) thaw (1) colder (2) grow warmer (3) late winter (4) melt.
48. ( ) turnip (1) cause to face up (2) wheel around (3) vegetable (4) whirling device.
49. ( ) extract (1) spice (2) shut out (3) drive out (4) pull out.
50. ( ) petition (1) charity (2) humble (3) fiat (4) request.

51. ( ) moisten (1) slipping (2) slick (3) wet (4) put a damper on.
52. ( ) puritan (1) pure food advocate (2) affecting great purity of life (3) censor (4) total abstainer.
53. ( ) statute (1) image in stone (2) a written law (3) offense against morals (4) bas-relief.
54. ( ) taint (1) pollution (2) treason (3) distaste (4) sourness.
55. ( ) zoological (1) fishy (2) aquarium (3) caged animals (4) pertaining to life sciences.
56. ( ) pestilence (1) meanness (2) tic (3) annoying (4) plague.
57. ( ) rung (1) cross-piece (2) circle (3) squeezed out (4) rib.
58. ( ) girt (1) chest measurement (2) kind of garter (3) belted (4) formed.
59. ( ) fraternal (1) brotherly (2) lodge (3) kindly (4) initiation.
60. ( ) edition (1) impression (2) revolt (3) form of publication (4) frolic.

61. ( ) alligator (1) one who alleges (2) saurian lizard (3) eel (4) jaw.
62. ( ) charitable (1) publican (2) faithful (3) hopeful (4) generous.
63. ( ) usher (1) porter (2) seat-holder (3) one who shows patrons to their seats (4) footman.
64. ( ) ethereal (1) anesthetic (2) heavenly (3) woebegone (4) samite.
65. ( ) upbraid (1) weave together (2) lift up (3) rise up (4) reprove.
66. ( ) decade (1) twenty years (2) pause (3) indefinite period of time (4) ten years.
67. ( ) impulse (1) seize by force (2) refusal (3) sudden inclination to act (4) full of holes.
68. ( ) clod (1) a moron (2) dull thump (3) lump of earth (4) obstruct.
69. ( ) assailant (1) drunkard (2) person who attacks (3) insurance agent (4) something which absorbs.
70. ( ) terminate (1) come to an end (2) railway station (3) a violent, scolding woman (4) tender.

71. ( ) ado (1) bother (2) acting (3) hurry (4) note in music.
72. ( ) bauble (1) crooked seam (2) showy trifle (3) pacifier (4) prattle.
73. ( ) bode (1) dwelling (2) hill-cave (3) mine (4) portend.
74. ( ) civic (1) of a city or citizen (2) a center (3) muskcat (4) perfume.
75. ( ) credulous (1) gullible (2) unbelieving (3) trustworthy (4) intoxicated.

76. ( ) flare (1) preference (2) explosive (3) mist (4) flame.
77. ( ) frugal (1) saving (2) fruity (3) wretched (4) stingy.
78. ( ) jingle (1) sleigh-bell (2) shiver (3) thick brush (4) clink.
79. ( ) massive (1) heavy (2) steep (3) slab-sided (4) pyramidal.
80. ( ) shingle (1) sheet of shale (2) layer of coal (3) a mound (4) roofing unit.

81. ( ) brigade (1) organized marching group (2) epaulet (3) billet (4) general.
82. ( ) dowry (1) legacy to a widow (2) marriage portion (3) money in litigation (4) a house.
83. ( ) inflammation (1) melt (2) reddening and swelling (3) heated (4) stirring.
84. ( ) neutrality (1) impartiality (2) favoring one side (3) hedging (4) the word *it*.
85. ( ) lecturer (1) organizer of bordom (2) formal expository speaker (3) reader (4) professor.
86. ( ) saber (re) (1) heavy sword (2) a tiger (3) German student (4) the act of rattling.
87. ( ) whiz (1) sizzle (2) go by fast with a hum (3) inexpert (4) old joke.
88. ( ) inveterate (1) a joker (2) forever (3) chronic (4) old soldier.
89. ( ) seafaring (1) steamer fare (2) ocean-going (3) old salt (4) Norseman.
90. ( ) disc (1) throw of dice (2) edged wheel (3) cookie (4) urn.

91. ( ) vindictive (1) justifying (2) vile (3) bearing a grudge (4) happy.
92. ( ) protestation (1) exhaustion (2) giving back (3) solemn declaration (4) making an offer.
93. ( ) seraph (1) pixie (2) angel (3) cupid (4) native of India.
94. ( ) industrial (1) hard-working (2) careful (3) pertaining to industry (4) factorial.
95. ( ) coincidence (1) chance (2) concurrence (3) peculiar (4) fall.
96. ( ) gauge (1) a gorge (2) lady's favor (3) measuring instrument (4) wide railway.
97. ( ) hostage (1) enemy (2) envoy (3) messenger (4) a person held as a guarantee.
98. ( ) inpenetrable (1) impervious (2) thick (3) a membrane (4) hide.
99. ( ) ploughshare (1) tenant's part of the crop (2) furrow (3) blade of a plough (4) treasue turned up by plough.
100. ( ) ungracious (1) snarling (2) uncivil (3) irreligious (4) mean.

101. ( ) abdicate (1) renounce (2) repeal (3) sentence (4) assign.
102. ( ) zest (1) amusing anecdote (2) a fanatic (3) keen enjoyment (4) oath.

103. ( ) cannonade (1) church laws (2) row of columns (3) awning (4) to attack with cannon.
104. ( ) wriggle (1) ridge (2) twist with force (3) turn and twist (4) fold of skin.
105. ( ) disintegrate (1) break up (2) free from illusion (3) fail to obey rules (4) shameful.
106. ( ) exhilarate (1) emit, as vapor (2) enliven (3) eradicate (4) deprive of virtue.
107. ( ) germination (1) making peculiarly German (2) sprouting (3) alliance (4) catching disease.
108. ( ) ignore (1) disregard wilfully (2) to be dishonorable (3) to kindle (4) phosphorescent light.
109. ( ) liability (1) illicit intimacy (2) a drink offering (3) lechery (4) accountability.
110. ( ) natal (1) pert. to one's birth (2) pert. to swimming (3) native sodium carbonate (4) pert. to the nose.

111. ( ) accountable (1) capable of accomplishment (2) responsible (3) necessary (4) additive.
112. ( ) barbarism (1) barber shop witticism (2) popular melody (3) uncivilized state (4) harsh-sounding.
113. ( ) carouse (1) merry-go-round (2) allegorical dance (3) stately carriage (4) drinking bout.
114. ( ) notary (1) public officer (2) worthy of notice (3) famous man (4) give notice to.
115. ( ) disparagement (1) lessening of esteem (2) distribution (3) inequality (4) dispossession.
116. ( ) expulsion (1) breathing out (2) outburst (3) driving out (4) partial excuse.
117. ( ) glutton (1) tough sticky substance in flour (2) greedy eater (3) sugar occurring in fruits (4) sparkle.
118. ( ) improbable (1) not likely to happen (2) resistant to attack (3) not useful (4) not excitable.
119. ( ) lingerie (1) one who is unwilling to leave (2) speaking several languages (3) outlandish speech (4) fine underclothes.
120. ( ) niche (1) recess in wall (2) famous resort in France (3) a notch (4) a vase.

121. ( ) affiliate (1) promise to marry (2) join with (3) courteous (4) genial.
122. ( ) bastion (1) illegitimate child (2) set of big guns (3) strip of iron (4) projecting part of fortification.
123. ( ) caucus (1) mountains in Eurasia (2) burns or destroys flesh (3) political meeting (4) like a tail.
124. ( ) turnpike (1) one who turns a roast of meat on a spit (2) deserter (3) jailer (4) originally a toll road.
125. ( ) doubly (1) man's close-fitting garment (2) Spanish gold coin (3) valiant (4) twice.

126. ( ) fastidious (1) finicky (2) imbecilic (3) quick to complain (4) fashionable.
127. ( ) haphazard (1) unfortunate (2) perhaps (3) at random (4) dangerous.
128. ( ) incantation (1) words used as a charm (2) glowing with heat (3) embodied in flesh (4) Jewish singing.
129. ( ) longitudinal (1) lengthwise (2) far-sighted (3) long-winded (4) moderately long.
130. ( ) nutritious (1) containing nitrogen (2) nourishing (3) meaty (4) full of flavor.

131. ( ) aggregation (1) annoyance (2) made greater (3) unjust injury (4) assemblage.
132. ( ) beldam (e) (1) beautiful woman (2) ugly old woman (3) madhouse (4) uproar, confusion.
133. ( ) chinchilla (1) Spanish dish (2) fur (3) cotton cloth (4) lap robe.
134. ( ) cultural (1) pert. to training of mind and morals (2) pert. to concentration in a chosen field (3) increased by addition (4) cunning.
135. ( ) drear (1) gloomy (2) frightful (3) fond (4) deathlike.
136. ( ) ferrule (1) metal ring on end of cane (2) ruler (3) prolific (4) pointer.
137. ( ) guilder (1) society for mutual aid (2) Dutch silver coin (3) a trickster (4) goldsmith.
138. ( ) inexhaustible (1) relentless (2) endless (3) not practicable (4) free from error.
139. ( ) lubricator (1) one who brings in money (2) ridiculous person (3) a mournful person (4) one who makes smooth or slippery.
140. ( ) orison (1) as far as eye can see (2) beginning (3) opening (4) prayer.

141. ( ) alleviate (1) relieve (2) tempt (3) indirectly refer to (4) form by deposit.
142. ( ) beshrew (1) curse (2) avoid (3) wed an ill-tempered woman (4) attack venomously.
143. ( ) unearth (1) subterranean (2) to immortalize (3) bury (4) dig up.
144. ( ) curvet (1) abrupt (2) curved design (3) bow (4) leap of a horse.
145. ( ) ducat (1) having title of a duke (2) coin (3) dukedom (4) tube or canal.
146. ( ) flagrant (1) sweet-smelling (2) broken off part (3) cheating (4) glaring.
147. ( ) halo (1) salutation (old Eng.) (2) make sacred (3) strong and well (4) ring of light.
148. ( ) insatiable (1) cannot be satisfied (2) hungry (3) mysterious (4) cannot be dissolved.

149. ( ) malefactor (1) mal-practicing physician (2) evil-doer (3) male factory-worker (4) capitalist.
150. ( ) palliate (1) roof of the mouth (2) touched or felt (3) beat rapidly (4) mitigate.

151. ( ) anarch (1) disbeliever in law and government (2) a solemn curse (3) imperfect curve (4) angel of higher rank.
152. ( ) bitch (1) a kind of tree (2) resinous gum (3) female dog (4) marsh bird.
153. ( ) cobalt (1) silver white metal (2) blueness of the sea (3) venomous snake (4) dried cocoanut meat.
154. ( ) decadence (1) decline (2) lack of rhythm (3) formal statement (4) deception.
155. ( ) educe (1) infer from a general principle (2) instruct, uplift (3) wear out (4) bring out, develop.
156. ( ) floral (1) pert. to flowers (2) Renaissance art (3) showy (4) grow in vigor.
157. ( ) hawser (1) short cannon (2) large rope (3) one who drives oxen (4) peddler.
158. ( ) interfuse (1) say no (2) throw into disorder (3) blend, permeate (4) vaporize.
159. ( ) mania (1) raving lunatic (2) man-like (3) a craze (4) madness afflicting dogs.
160. ( ) parody (1) model of perfection (2) apparent opposites making a near-truth (3) equity (4) ridicule by imitation.

161. ( ) anthrax (1) naphtha soap (2) infectious disease of animals (3) hair wash (4) pollen-bearing.
162. ( ) bowsprit (1) string of a bow (2) distance bow sends arrow (3) part of ship (4) sandbar revealed by tide.
163. ( ) comity (1) civility (2) amusing incident (3) equality (4) sweetmeat.
164. ( ) deleterious (1) failing to do a duty (2) becoming liquid by absorption (3) prepared, as of foods (4) harmful.
165. ( ) emblazon (1) set fire to (2) opening in a wall (3) adorn with coat of arms (4) to beautify.
166. ( ) formulary (1) set of words (2) matter of form (3) some time ago (4) hard to overcome.
167. ( ) helot (1) slave (2) vicious trouble-maker (3) fanatical partisan (4) courtezan.
168. ( ) intone (1) make amends (2) recite in a singing voice (3) to deal craftily (4) urge on.
169. ( ) matrix (1) mold for casting (2) mother (Lat.) (3) wife or widow (4) implement for digging or grubbing.
170. ( ) pelvis (1) large waterbird (2) a woman's long cloak (3) transparent, clear (4) bone formation of hip and back bones.

171. ( ) apposite (1) contrary (2) favorable (3) mixture (4) appropriate.
172. ( ) brigantine (1) brig with fore-and-aft mainsail (2) part of an army (3) native of Constantinople (4) pirate.
173. ( ) concerto (1) musical entertainment (2) fruit pectin (3) musical composition in which one instrument predominates (4) small accordion.
174. ( ) derangement (1) wrecking a train (2) mockery (3) impeachment (4) disorder.
175. ( ) energize (1) deprive of nerve (2) set free (3) give energy to (4) bring into being.
176. ( ) fountainhead (1) fountain (2) statue used as fountain (3) source of a stream (4) nozzle.
177. ( ) jaunt (1) a small part (2) combat between two mounted knights (3) close together (4) a short journey.
178. ( ) hobnail (1) bring together (2) crunch under foot (3) peg above a hearth (4) heavy shoe-nail.
179. ( ) mickle (1) five cents (2) much (3) the middle (4) small bone in knee joint.
180. ( ) philologist (1) stamp collector (2) lover of wisdom (3) benefactor (4) a linguistic scholar.

181. ( ) asinine (1) stupid, silly (2) coming from Asia (3) saline substance from acid (4) colorless gas.
182. ( ) bumpkin (1) squash-like fruit (2) lout (3) earthwork for defense (4) large crop.
183. ( ) conjoint (1) united, connected (2) harmonious (3) crooked gambling place (4) wed.
184. ( ) detritus (1) a belittling (2) a plan, or scheme (3) skill, cleverness (4) material worn away from a mass.
185. ( ) euphony (1) falsehood (2) speech of praise (3) mild, indirect statement (4) agreeable sound.
186. ( ) frustration (1) excitement (2) congratulation (3) haste (4) thwarting.
187. ( ) horny (1) callous (2) wearing horns (3) interfering (4) ancient.
188. ( ) joist (1) a tilt (2) amusing anecdote (3) small supporting beam (4) exactly.
189. ( ) modicum (1) consisting of two or more atoms (2) effeminate boy (3) small income (4) small quantity or portion.
190. ( ) plagiarism (1) quietude (2) literary theft (3) vexation (4) making a promise.

191. ( ) attaché (1) fastened to (2) member of ambassador's staff (3) brief case (4) wasted away.
192. ( ) caravansary (1) a kind of small ship (2) company of merchants (3) cooking seeds (4) hotel or inn.

193. ( ) consequential (1) important (2) congruous (3) coördinating (4) reasonable.
194. ( ) dilapidation (1) great pleasure (2) procrastination (3) outline (4) state of disrepair.
195. ( ) esoteric (1) known to an inner circle (2) pert. to sexual love (3) controversial (4) corroded.
196. ( ) galena (1) native lead sulphide (2) dress material (3) brilliant assemblage (4) turpentine resin.
197. ( ) hyperbolic (1) exaggerated (2) over-critical (3) far-sighted (4) dissembling.
198. ( ) laudation (1) expression of amusement (2) a cleansing (3) profuseness (4) praise.
199. ( ) monolith (1) a soliloquy (2) large single stone pillar (3) an exclusive possession (4) a souvenir.
200. ( ) scone (1) harm (2) an ugly old woman (3) wall bracketed candlestick (4) a thin Scotch cake.

(The key for this test and for all others which have definite answers will be found just before the index.)

To make the sampling complete, a list of four hundred words follows, twenty from each thousand of Thorndike's list of 20,000 words in most common use. Run over this list carefully, checking the words the meaning of which you do not know. That is, unless you feel certain that you would know the meaning of the word if you encountered it in print, check it off as belonging in the quota of words unfamiliar to you.

bone, nice, different, people, extend, sight, fix, some, moment, subject, did, cried, hope, grew, order, nose, story, smoke, able, yesterday

creep, copper, hardly, frighten, toss, oil, skirt, society, absolute, ye, accept, swell, effect, opportunity, proceed, urge, spite, utter, stuff, yonder

affect, reserve, devote, slumber, henceforth, thrust, moderate, vanish, proclaim, hither, annual, design, importance, bestow, passage, cordial, smith, flee, zone, smart

accord, beware, cathedral, delivery, flowery, girdle, liver, parson, sadness, testimony, van, substantial, perpetual, invade, grin, fluid, dainty, bowel, novelty, achieve

apparel, confuse, enrich, harlot, mercury, preside, sheath, timothy, utterance, voluntary, abate, beseech, confident, glade, insert, obscure, plunder, quoth, sable, trough

attest, casement, dimple, exempt, husk, molten, repentance, sooth, tenor, wreathe, abbey, blasphemy, caution, discreet, gnat, herein, pavilion, stave, truant, yew behavior, convene, eminence, grab, lamentable, penury, tragic, withstood, yore, zephyr, adversity, baffle, chanticleer, espouse, impulse, jig, knob, mourner, penance, refute

ally, calculate, conserve, doze, fundamental, irrigate, mart, recessive, tolerable, wile, agitate, bequeath, caramel, defer, gauze, paramour, precocious, revery, severity, woody

affront, belle, capricious, diversity, incomparable, lilac, ominous, preëminence, regime, similitude, akin, betake, choleric, delicacy, edging, intricate, plumage, outcry, scrim, trinity

assassinate, candor, evade, dissembler, insulator, medley, quince, tyrannous, ulster, veto, adjourn, ambiguous, elegance, funnel, imp, picket, reservoir, stench, tormentor, sentinel

abash, biography, convulsive, edict, glowworm, jailor, musty, perspiration, robust, subterranean, arid, cuticle, entail, grimace, incarnate, kodak, maneuver, outskirts, quay, sedition

wry, toboggan, shepherdess, provost, nocturnal, laggard, hag, equalize, crimp, breakwater, unsavory, worshipful, bedlam, dank, forefront, howbeit, lineal, neuter, pellet, revolutionist

adz, bricklayer, creosote, enshrine, haphazard, knightly, noisome, promoter, shellac, tolerance, tenacity, ventral, zebra, angler, entwine, gizzard, inoculate, kiln, messaline, sententious

ammonium, canto, debater, expostulation, hogshead, limber, optimism, rascally, slumberous, turbid, outset, quota, script, umbrage, woolly, biblical, debauchery, forager, homicide, jubilant

antagonism, celibacy, declamation, fanatical, hovel, liturgy, overarch, reassemble, solidity, unaccountable, licentiousness, nostrum, pictorial, reinstate, touchstone, vaccine, append, carboniferous, equivocation, generator

turpitude, beatitude, complaisance, dromedary, gala, insubstantial, modulation, plash, sanity, surcharge, incumbrance, knapsack, misnomer, oratorical, quasi, stricture, unpretending, watershed, yokefellow, boycott

wobble, thresher, shard, problematical, negligible, kinetic, guileless, encase, couplet, brae, disbursement, flighty, humpback, jennet, linguist, nominee, plaudit, reformatory, tripe, vociferous

ashy, chantry, detract, flashy, imminence, maidenly, patroon, repertoire, sponsor, unexceptionable, amidships, cocktail, emaciation, gristle, ichneumon, misconceive, obsidian, quadrate, speedometer, unlace bairn, cockerel, disputable, freedman, infantile, mediate, phaeton, rigmarole, subtrahend, vapory, wreckage, yawl, bondwoman, expositor, hypotenuse, juryman, limpet, nectarine, paternity, replica

yaw, titbit, shibboleth, proportionable, nominative, jingo, hanker, enzyme, coxswain, bream, radii, talc, valance, azalea, caravel, extortioner, generic, insincerity, margent, ossify

To make a rough estimate of your reading vocabulary, on the basis of these six hundred samples, carry forward your error score from the first part of the test. Add to this the number of words unknown to you in the last four hundred. What is your total error score? Subtract this from 600. Divide the result by three and multiply by 100. This last result represents the approximate number of words in your reading vocabulary. For example, if your total error score is 330, subtract this from 600, leaving a balance of 270 words which you know; divide this by 3 which gives 90; multiply by 100 and you get 9000 words as your approximate reading vocabulary.

You will naturally want to look up in the dictionary the words with which you are unfamiliar; and perhaps some of the "confusions," as the false definitions are commonly called by vocabulary-testers. In the first part of the test, in which thousand for frequency was the first word you missed? In which group did you first miss more than three? This is probably the point at which you need to begin building your vocabulary.

In the light of these facts as to your own stock of words, how has the myth arisen as to the poverty of the average vocabulary? Frequently the claim is made that in 95 per cent of telephone conversations, and in the bulk of business letters, only 700 different words are used. Frank Vizetelly, the editor of the *Standard Dictionary*, says that frequently statements are brought to his attention "that a workman who reads the newspapers may command from 700 to 1000 words; and that 5000 is a large number, even for an educated reader or speaker." These figures are far too low. It is true that the small change of language, used over and over, makes up a great proportion of both talk and print. Ten words, *the, of, and, to, a, in, that, it, is, I,* make up 25 per cent of current English writing. These ten words, repeated, make up about a quarter of Shakespeare and of the Bible. Add forty more, and the list comprises the number which make up half the total running words in most English and American writing. In a novel of 100,000 words, for example, 50,000 consist of these fifty words used again and again:

the, and, of, to, it, was, is, will, at, we, on, he, dear, from, are, all, has, very, were, been, I, a, in, that, you, for, as, have, not, with, be, your, by, but, my, this, his, which, me, so, one, if, they, had, would, she, or, there, her, an.

Clearly, any count of a short passage or a few conversations will show a great preponderance of these common words.

Ayres has also found that two thousand different words make up the number employed by most American adults in correspondence. But this is no adequate measure of their total vocabulary. One must double, perhaps quadruple, the number to get a measure of the *reading* vocabulary of these same persons. Most men have also a specialized stock of words peculiar to their trade or profession, and another sacred to their favorite sport. How could anyone, even a word-counter, limit a mule-skinner's vocabulary to three hundred words? Or an army general's to seven hundred? True, this does not argue as to their stock of English words in common and reputable use, which is the point in question. But all these facts argue that the low figures given for the average vocabulary are far under the mark. The consensus of opinion is that anyone with a high school education, or its equivalent in the school of experience, has a reading vocabulary of at least nine thousand words, and it may run to fourteen thousand.

2) How large a percentage of your *reading* vocabulary do you use in talk or writing? Check through the list above again (also those at the end of this chapter), to see how many of these words you employ in conversation or in letter-writing.

Logically, you should begin to build your vocabulary at whatever point these rough-and-ready measures show that your command of word-meanings begins to grow uncertain. Just as clearly, you should try to transplant into your active stock the words which you know only as you read them.

Not that all of the words recognized in print will be desirable for active use. Who wants to talk like a book? But a great proportion of the reading vocabulary gradually becomes available for active use, so soon as one decides to make these words do double duty.

No very intricate test is needed, as to whether words hitherto unfamiliar will pass muster in conversation and familiar writing. Your friends will tell you; or they will ask you to repeat, to be certain of the meaning; or they will smile at the polysyllable. If you use, as Bernard Shaw does, the word *eupeptic,* you may be able to put it into currency, as the ideal antonym for *dyspeptic*. But the chances are you will be credited with a coinage from *pep;* or will simply be labeled freakish. Such words are sometimes worth the risk. It may be suspected that *eupeptic* fills a real want in everyday language. John Evelyn used it, in 1699; Carlyle was fond of it, especially since he rarely enjoyed the state which the word describes. But *eupeptic* is certainly preferable to 'hopped-up,' or 'jazzed-up,' or 'full of pep': all slang phrases which attempt to supply this want of a familiar and reputable word for the state of euphoria and general well-being. When Jefferson remarked that he had been blessed with a digestion which could accept and concoct whatever his palate chose to consign to it, he laid the groundwork for the word *eupeptic*.

For the most part, there is no need of forcing words to run any such long gauntlet, in effecting a transfer from the passive to the active vocabulary. Once committed to a habit of expanding your word-range by this route, you soon become adept in trying out words which you have hitherto left to the authors you read. After all, this is only pioneering in a known country. You have in mind the new words which you want to acclimate. If the words are suitable to your habits of speech and writing, you will soon get them to settle down comfortably side by side with your old, familiar stock.

The situation is different when you have an idea in mind which can be best expressed by some word which you have almost, but not quite, learned. You are then trying to summon up from the shadowy fringes of memory some term or symbol which seems just to elude your grasp. It is as if you were trying to recall a foreign language equivalent for an English word. This common predicament suggests that it is essential not only to have a wide range of vocabulary, but also to have the stock of words under ready command.

READINESS

In fact, a wide-ranging vocabulary is only fully alive if it is ready on the tongue or pen. When Glendower boasted that he could call spirits up from out the vasty deep, Hotspur retorted, "Why so can I, or so can any man. But will they come?" So it is with words. Will they come? That is the question. The man is envied who can readily hit on the right word to clinch a point. What is the secret? It is not a flood of words which is wanted. We long for a Maxim silencer to stop a long-winded bore. What would be the effect on you, for instance, if you received the following letter? It is cited in a leading work on vocabulary-building, as a "literary gem, written by an art dealer, that illustrates the practical use of the *Beauty* vocabulary. Notice that the letter might refer to a beautiful vase, an oriental rug, or a valuable watch, etc." The words taken from the *Beauty* vocabulary are italicized:

"Dear Madam—A *Gloriously Beautiful Masterpiece* has been *Exquisitely Fashioned* for your enjoyment. Its *Delightful, Beauteous Grace* is *Indescribably Attractive.* You will be enraptured with its *Fascinating Charm* and its *Gracious Elegance.* We are happy to have you among the select few to whom we have written that this *Superbly Adorable* thing is now ready to add its *Bewitching Loveliness* to your personal *Dignity.* Please post card."

This shows readiness of a kind, but it has the air of being written by a person who is word-drunk. It lacks chastity and sobriety of language. If a wider range of words is to lead to this sort of fearful embroidery, it might be better to stay at home and cultivate one's own verbal backyard.

Mere verbal facility has, in fact, long been a subject for mockery. "They mistake words for things," Leonardo said of the Schoolmen. There lies the danger of verbalism. Yet the power to summon the words which are needed for a given occasion or purpose, is an enviable one. The words which are needed: no more, no less. That is the saving clause. For readiness need not imply a plethora of words. Wordiness is more apt to be due to lack of ability to command the word which will drive home a point.

Wit, for instance, depends for its form, though not for its ideas, on words which will fall into place with a click. So Pope writes, "At every word a reputation dies." Any change in the word order, or any substitution of a new word, would ruin the effect of the stroke. Lengthening would mar it still more. An attempted joke, long drawn out, is no laughing matter. When it is a matter of storytelling, everyone recognizes the need for a nimble and a ready power of phrase.

3) When you have an idea in mind, how readily can you call up words to express it?

Turning back to exercise 1 on page 2, test your readiness in summoning words by guessing the words which the makers of the test had in mind when they contrived the "confusions," or false definitions. As you probably noted when you took the test, most of the confusions were suggested by words which sound like the original word, but which have a very different meaning. For No. 160, *parody*, for example, (1) *model of perfection* is a confusion devised from *paragon;* (2) *apparent opposites making a near-truth* is a confusion from *paradox;* (3) *equality* is a confusion derived from *parity.*

4) Using the definitions below as cues, much as you would in solving a crossword puzzle, fill in the blanks in the following sentences with appropriate words.

1. The two lawyers reached an _____ on all points.
2. He could find no common basis for _____ between the two sets of data.
3. Rugged individualism implied stiff _____ between firms.
4. Consulting his compass, he decided in which _____ to go.
5. He was not sure just what _____ was mixed with tin to form bronze.
6. They did not engage in an angry argument, but were content with quiet _____.
7. The slaves in their underground pens were in a dreadful state of _____, both physical and mental.
8. The men-at-arms were hardy, but the Lily Maid was _____.
9. To the dragon-fly and other _____, a day may seem like a century; they live and move so fast.
10. _____ is based on written records, monuments, art objects, and to some extent on tradition embedded in linguistic usage.
11. Galileo made the _____ of the laws of falling bodies.
12. The delegation of employers made a civil _____ for a hearing.
13. By passing a magnet through a coil of wire in which an electric current was thus induced, Faraday rendered possible practically every _____ made by Thomas Edison.
14. The doctor had his _____ in his house.
15. He traced the stages in the _____ of language.
16. The outcome was _____, once the terms of the Treaty were settled.
17. "May I venture to make a _____?" said President Wilson.
18. A rise of one foot in five, gives a grade of twenty per cent, which is far too steep a _____ for heavy motor traffic.
19. The judge first summed up the law in the case, then left it to the jury to decide on the _____.
20. Macaulay had a superb _____, both for isolated facts and for systematically connected ideas.
21. They used the anchor as a _____ to pull up the buoy.
22. Is it possible to have poetic power without a creative _____?
23. He measured the speed of the _____ by noting how long it took a log to drift to a point a mile downstream.
24. Do you know of any _____ for rubber?

25. With the true governing man, talents for _____ and administration imply a feeling for human values.

The numbers of these definitions correspond to the numbers of the sentences in which the word defined is to be placed.

1. Act of settling on something which commands common consent.
2. Finding points in common between things.
3. The general term for personal or commercial rivalry.
4. General term embracing north, south, east, and west.
5. Class to which gold, silver, lead, copper, belong.
6. Act of talking subjects over calmly.
7. State of being wretched.
8. The opposite of hardy.
9. Class to which bees, ants, and wasps belong.
10. The record of the past.
11. Process of finding out something; and the thing found out.
12. To ask politely.
13. Making something new; and the new thing made.
14. Place where a professional man works and receives his clients.
15. Process of growth, of an institution, or character.
16. Fixed, sure, predictable.
17. Indirect or guarded presentation of a matter; a hint.
18. Rate of ascent or descent of a road or curve.
19. An actual, real thing, deed, or circumstance.
20. Faculty of recalling the past.
21. A grappling instrument.
22. Power by which we envisage things absent as if they were present.
23. Flow of a liquid.
24. Liquid in which a substance will dissolve.
25. Process of bringing about order and coherence among parts.

(See Keys before the index for correct list of words.)

Readiness depends primarily upon clarity of thought. Arnold Bennett says that no idea comes except in the form of words. This is perhaps putting it too strongly. It is possible to have a clear visual image, or a recollection of muscular motion or touch, without easily finding words to express it. For instance, where a paved highway has been tip-tilted at a curve, so that it is like an automobile racing track, what is the technical name for the tilting? Everyone who has driven a car around such a curve can visualize the scene, or recall his movements as he turned the car wheel. But it may be necessary to cudgel the memory to recall that the process of tip-tilting is called *banking* in the case of a road; although everyone would know what was meant by a *well-banked* road, if he saw the word in print.

There is a large range of words of this sort where it is necessary to learn, by sheer rote memory, the names of objects, processes, and the like. The names of flowers and animals, for example, or the terms for the parts of machines, must be acquired through gradually increasing familiarity with the objects represented by these words. We may sometimes know the thing when we see it, but fail to know its name. We use the term 'gadget,' or 'thing-um-a-jig,' or 'What-d'ye-call-it,' at the same time pointing. But suppose the object is not in sight? It behooves us then to command our stock of *general* words so that we can, if driven to it, describe or delimit these special things and processes, sufficiently to identify them for the specialist,—say an auto mechanic, a radio repair man, or a physician. We need to know the class to which an object or process belongs, so that we can find it under the right topic in a handbook or encyclopedia. But there is no substitute for extensive first-hand contact with concrete objects in learning this part of the vocabulary. Even in this sphere, however, there are devices which will help to fix these terms in the memory.

It was by an accident that a modern commercial teacher of languages discovered this truth. He and his partner wanted to go away on vacation. They had a large class of children taking French and German, and could get no one to supply instruction for them. One day they ran into a young Alsatian who had just taken his doctor's degree at the Sorbonne. He had landed in New York without money, so he was running an elevator for the time being. They talked with him in French, naturally. They did not think to ask him if he knew English—which he did not. So they left him in charge of the classes of American children. When they returned, several weeks later, they found he had installed long tables in the classroom, which were covered with hundreds of objects. He would point to a pen, or an apple, and give the French word for it, which the children would repeat after him. They had learned, in three weeks, to chatter French and German like magpies; more, indeed, than the regular teachers had accomplished by months of grammar and formal exercises.

This method of direct contact with the object or process is clearly the best way to acquire the nomenclature of the crafts, arts, or professions with which one may be casually concerned. If one keeps his eye on the object, there is little danger of coming under Leonardo's indictment by mistaking words for things.

Leonardo da Vinci, the most versatile genius of modern times, never, indeed, committed this sin for which he condemned the Schoolmen. He did not need to, for he commanded all the modes of expression. He filled a hundred notebooks, in a strange shorthand written from right to left on the page, so that it must be read with a mirror. In these private notes will be found sketches for projected inventions, anatomical drawings, rough cartoons for paintings or sculptures; there appear also da Vinci's daydreams, his household accounts, and his philosophical speculations. The great artist apparently hardly noticed whether he was drawing or writing. But he showed rare finesse in choosing the medium best suited to the particular matter in hand. When he wanted to show the direction of pull in a muscle, he used his drawing pen. With the mastery of significant line which he possessed, he could tell more of muscular tension and strain by a graphic, almost moving stroke, than he could have conveyed by a page of descriptive words. He could indicate, by lines and shading in the face, the whole psychological history of a character. To show a novel design for a war-tank, with scythe-like projections from the axles, he sketched. For equations, he used number and letter symbols. When he came to present specifications for materials, however, or to deal with qualities, or to set forth his philosophical ideas, he resorted to words as the most convenient symbols for his purpose. Did he want to talk of the possibility of flight in heavier-than-air machines? Did he feel moved to comment on the nature of force? Did he want to commend his theories on the significance of fossils? He used words. On these subjects, and on ordinary household matters, he wrote in plain and simple style. He abhorred the plastered-on verbal ornament so much in vogue with the humanists of Milan. In writing, as in drawing, he admired economy. In all his ventures, he had a feeling for rightness of accent which led him instinctively to choose the medium best suited to the matter in hand.

In general, it may be assumed from examining Leonardo's notebooks that the user of words needs a sense of their limitations. A writer should not try to employ words for work which can be better done by line-drawings. On the other hand, the experiments of modern writers have shown that it is possible to convey on the printed page the bodily movements, gestures, and attitudes which accompany lively talk. If one commands the tune of the spoken word, sufficiently to transfer it to the printed page, one may convey the nuances of tone, the pauses, and the peculiar accent of the speaker. A few novelists have reached the point where they can make us overhear thought itself. There is no limit, in fact, to what words can do—in a dramatic direction. But they should not be strained too far.

There is a realm where, as the Chinese say, one picture is worth ten thousand words. Everyone is annoyed by the use of verbal subtitles in a talkie. In such a case, the director was evidently too lazy to make his continuity clear by the use of pictorial shots and spoken dialogue; hence he resorted to the older device of the written word, which served as a makeshift in the days of the silent movies.

There are times, however, when a poet or novelist can evoke a whole picture by a few imaginative words. So Conrad writes, ". . . the evening star appeared, like a lamp hung over the grave of the sun." This summons up a tropical night, by a single stroke. The desire to convey such images has led all writers who take pride in their craft to set great store by the right word,—*le mot juste,* as Flaubert called it. He carried this care in the selection and ordering of words to a point almost beyond belief. He labored sometimes a day, even a week, on a single sentence. Writing out the tentative draft large on a piece of paper, and cutting it into bits containing single words, he would rearrange time after time, to find the best, the only, order. Often, too, he would substitute other words for those he had first set down, rewriting nine or ten times to find the *one* word which would suddenly, as if by magic, conjure up in the reader's mind the picture which was in the novelist's vision. Such a thirst for perfection is admirable. It led to a flawless style. Yet there is, in reading it, a sense of strain, and the feeling-tone is not always happy. Maupassant learned from Flaubert this labor of hard writing which makes easy reading; and Turgenev, Henry James, and Conrad followed him in search for perfection of phrasing.

5) What word or words did the author use?

Kipling—"Far out, a three-funnelled Atlantic transport with turtle bow and stern (waddled, sailed, struggled) in from the deep sea."

Stevenson—"Books are good enough in their own way, but they are a mighty (bloodless, dry, poor) substitute for life."

Stevenson—"It is a sore thing to have labored along and scaled the (difficult, weary, arduous) hilltops, and when all is done, find humanity indifferent to your (labors, achievement)."

Stevenson—"Many make a large fortune, who remain underbred and (tremendously, pathetically, habitually) stupid to the last."

Conrad—"The long, long stress of a gale does it; the suspense of the (never-ending, interminably culminating, gradually approaching) catastrophe; and there is a bodily fatigue in the mere holding on to existence within the (inordinate, excessive, immoderate) tumult; a searching and insidious fatigue that (enters, penetrates, goes) deep into a man's breast to cast down and (break, sadden, deaden) his heart, which is (incorrigible, unchanging, immortal) and of all the gifts of the earth—even before life itself—aspires to peace."

Stevenson—"It was September, 1429; the weather had fallen sharp; a flighty, piping wind, (filled with rain, laden with showers, damp with mist) beat about the township; and the dead leaves (ran riot, were whipped, scoured) along the streets."

It is easy to follow this quest for the most telling word in Conrad's manuscripts. He changes the single word or phrase in order to make the image clearer; in order to narrow his meaning; in order to improve the euphony; in order to condense or amplify the thought, whichever is needed. The improvements are for the better. They do not always make the style more flowing. But the changes give greater force, greater clarity, a fuller feeling of verisimilitude. It was this ideal truth at which Conrad aimed: he held that beauty and goodness are dependent upon it.

It must be admitted that this search for the right word has not commended itself to all great writers, either before Flaubert or since. Shakespeare never blotted out a line, Ben Jonson told Drummond, adding, "Would he had blotted out a thousand!" Fielding wrote with great rapidity. Scott would do a Waverly novel in six weeks. Cervantes did not revise Don Quixote, but let the story ramble on wherever the old don's fancy led him. And after Pater introduced the doctrine of "the right word" in England, there were voices raised against it. Francis Thompson, for instance, observed:

Theoretically, of course, one ought always to try for the best word. But practically, the habit of excessive care in word-selection frequently results in the loss of spontaneity; and still worse, the habit of taking the most ornate word, the word most removed from ordinary speech. (Essay on Shelley.)

There is much to be said for this view. Moreover, it may be doubted whether there is a single 'right' word in a given case, except by a subjective test. It will not do to agonize too long over one word.

Probably the happiest middle course is to write the first draft with a running pen, then do as Conrad did: strive for the best words and phrases in the process of revision. This makes every man his own critic; but it holds the more finicky, scrupulous habit of mind in abeyance while the actual composition is in progress.

In any event, the hunt for the right word is an offset to over-ready verbalism. The quest requires an extensive stock of words among which the choice is to be made. They must be, if not at instant command, not too far back in the recesses of memory. It is no use looking for the best word in a poverty-stricken, second-hand stock. The need for precision in the active vocabulary calls inevitably for a greater range.

SURENESS

Gains in vocabulary should come, however, step by step with increasing sureness in the use of words. In certain kinds of communication, precision is a vital necessity. In the chemical laboratory, directions must be written and carried out exactly: otherwise an explosion may occur. For military orders, the words must have only one possible meaning. So with laws. Ideally they should be drafted to be water-tight, though in fact acres of paper have been laid waste in wrangling over the exact intent of words used by legislators. In telegraphic messages or cables, where condensation is required, the utmost care must be taken that the meaning is still clear. It is an added merit if the words can be taken in only one way whether punctuation is used or not.

What holds for these practical necessities of communication, remains in force for the more leisurely and artistic modes of writing. Words should fit exactly into place, so that we would wish no other phrasing to be used than the writer has employed. There should be no vague and woolly fringes of meaning. To attain such sureness, however, requires more than ordinary feeling for rightness of diction.

How is this knowledge of diction to be acquired? Strong disgusts, said Pater, are the beginnings of good taste. The first step toward sureness in the command of words is to know what to reject.

6) Underline the mistakes in word usage and put the right word or words in the blank.

1. He gave me an invite to the party. (   )
2. Animals do not worry about their sins; humans do. (   )
3. They decided to go irregardless. (   )
4. She was all enthused over her new party dress. (   )
5. The story of *Beau Geste* intrigued me. (   )
6. There was a lot of apparatus in the laboratory. (   )
7. She was a nice girl, and had a grand and elegant turn-out. (   )
8. The police found him hiding in back of the woodpile. (   )
9. He came in previous to me. (   )
10. Haven't you had no raising? (   )

7) You have seen the speed sentences devised for typewriter practice, which include all the letters of the alphabet, e.g., "The quick brown fox jumps over the lazy dog." The passage which follows is built on a similar plan. It contains, that is, most of the very common errors in word-usage which are made in talk and writing. Point out these errors. (See STYLE RULE VI., in Appendix.) Recast the passage in correct American prose. Has it lost anything?

In the event even that he don't come, they would still wanta go on the party. I'm alooking for rough weather, but that big flat-bottomed row boat with the Evinrude attachment will stand up to most anything in the way of a storm which this here Lake can produce. Just between you and I, they hadn't-ought to be so hopped up about going. I doubt if anything will bust loose anyhow, and the longer they linger, they will get only into a worse stew over the possible danger. I wish I could of stiffened up their nerve with a little artificial first aid, but there ain't enough bootleggers in this dry zone to keep one respectable hi-jacker in cigarettes, due to the prissy Methodist folks hereabouts. Those kind of people are always the same: Anyway, after one more try, this is where I quit. It looks like a washout, this trip, and I ain't agona set around and hold the sack. I've laid around two weeks as it is, and can't hardly afford to eat off of my old man no longer. I see where these parties spotted a swell fishing-hole, and hopes to fish the same plumb to the last sucker. No one but I would do for 'em; they stuck out for me guiding 'em to the spot. They'll wish they wouldn't of come. But they can't seem to see it.

There has been, however, a great deal of prissiness and Nice Nellie finickiness as to fine points of diction. It is a melancholy thought, for those who believe in "schoolmarm" niceties, that perhaps the common people have the right instinct as to the historical trend of the English language, when they say *ain't, he don't,* and the like. The tendency in English is toward the decay of inflection. *Ain't* represents an attempt to establish an invariant form of the verb *to be.* One can say, *I ain't, you ain't, he ain't, we ain't,* or *they ain't,* without worrying over which person of the verb to use. For a while, in the eighteenth century, *ain't* appeared to be coming into respectable and universal use. So with *you was.* Horace Walpole, a fastidious dandy of language if ever there was one, wrote *you was* without a qualm. But the formal grammarians triumphed, and arrested the process by which our language was ridding itself of inflections. Since English depends largely on word-order to convey meaning, it might just as well have thrown overboard the remnants of inflection. Since it did not, what Dr. Johnson called a "decent respect for the opinions of mankind" still makes it obligatory upon us to observe the niceties of usage—or at least to refrain from barbarisms and illiteracies. Nevertheless, the argument above proves one thing. We should consider the common errors not as reflecting a social stigma upon their users, but rather as interesting evidence of language-processes.

Once we know the driving forces in language which lead to these mistakes, we are not so apt to make them. Add to this knowledge a comic association with errors, and the risk of falling into them is greatly lessened.

There is also a much trickier problem than the common error. Which words are in good use? On this point, the dictates of the schoolbooks are not final authority. Is there any doubt in anyone's mind as to which of the following forms represents living speech? A second grade boy in a Bowery school was asked to put this passage from a primer into his own words:

See the cow. Isn't the cow pretty? Can the cow run as fast as the horse? No, the cow cannot run as fast as the horse.

He said,

Pipe de caow. Ain't she a beaut? Can she hoof it wid de horse? Nit, she ain't in it wid de horse.

The first is clearly manufactured primer English. No one ever talked, wrote, or thought in such language. The Bowery version is racy, spoken in a spicy accent, and thoroughly in character. It is not correct, but it is alive.

This contrast shows one thing quite clearly. In dealing with slang, colloquialisms, jargon, vulgarisms,—and their counterpart, genteelisms,—it is better to view them with an eye to their natural and social history. Like the common errors, they reveal to a nice nose a great deal about the processes of language. It will not do to dismiss them with mere tut-tutting. To the student of linguistic science, these dubious words are no less interesting than the politest phrases of the King's English—or should we say, of White House American? Indeed, it is sometimes hard to tell where to draw the line, in the interest of vigorous idiom, between slang and colloquialism, between colloquialism and propriety in language.

8) Which of these words are colloquialisms? Which slang? Which are in good use? (Slang is "a peculiar kind of vagabond language, always hanging on the outskirts of legitimate speech, but continually straying or forcing its way into the most respectable company."—Greenough and Kittredge, *Words and Their Ways*, p. 55. The Macmillan Company, Publishers. —e.g., *scram* is slang.) (A colloquialism is a word usable in informal talk, but not in formal prose discourse. e.g., *phone*.)

1. banter 2. prof 3. out loud 4. blues 5. sham 6. bamboozle 7. bombast 8. jingo 9. nincompoop 10. high-kicker 11. ante up 12. crestfallen 13. woozy 14. wienerwurst 15. wag 16. slush 17. squiffy 18. phiz 19. quiz.

9) Which words are genteelisms? Which vulgarisms? Which are obsolete in prose? Which are in good use? (Genteelisms are over-polite words where common words would be better, e.g., *saleslady*.) (Vulgarisms are words that have come down in the world, e.g., *swell, lousy*.)

1. perchance 2. anent 3. well-nigh 4. erstwhile 5. howbeit 6. ere 7. the clite 8. expectorate 9. inebriated 10. mortician 11. genius 12. ingenuous 13. wretch 14. fetlock 15. fakir 16. lackadaisical 17. guild 18. syrup 19. pedagogy 20. ineffable 21. sunk 22. hoity-toity 23. awful 24. hoist 25. weird 26. hot (for ardent) 27. love-nest.

10) Which of the following words are jargon? (Jargon comprises technical words inappropriate in prose addressed to the general reader, e.g., *libido*.)

1. decision 2. insignia 3. id 4. maritime 5. sublimation 6. narcissism 7. dialectic 8. epitome 9. propaideutic 10. heterodox 11. archaic 12. hysteresis 13. dimorphism 14. kaleidoscope 15. cinematic 16. periscope 17. close-up 18. diurnal 19. deliquescence 20. finesse.

But we have dealt with cautions long enough. Prohibition laws do not work any too well in the sphere of words. Most of the borderline phrases which are tabu in formal prose may find a place in dialect stories or in off-hand talk. It is no doubt better to italicize slang with your voice, if you use it. But it has been wittily said,

"The place of slang is in everyday life." There we will leave it, for later systematic treatment, adding that no one ever spoke or wrote well who was too much afraid of violating the nicer points of usage.

Positive doctrine on diction is much more important than any prohibition. To choose from the common stock words which will best convey an idea, principles are needed which will apply over a wide field. How are words to be tested with a view to their fitness for the position which they are to fill?

There is a body of traditional lore on this subject, which one defies at his own risk. This lore has been summed up by the Fowlers, the wittiest lexicographers of our day. In the opening chord of their book, *The King's English*, they say that if one wants to cultivate a style which will be plain, lucid, simple, brief, and exact,

Prefer the familiar word to the far-fetched
Prefer the concrete word to the abstract
Prefer the single word to the circumlocution
Prefer the short word to the long
Prefer the Saxon word to the Romance

But the last injunction is to be taken with caution. It holds good only a little more than half the time. For the word of Latin origin may be simpler, or shorter, or commoner; and it may suit the texture of the writing far better. But if these five razors are applied one after the other, in trimming down the diction, the end result will usually be a much better piece of prose. To be sure, these five rules, like all others, have to be supplemented by the rule of reason. But they work quite well in practice.

11) Apply the five principles above, first noting carefully what are the sour notes, verbally speaking, in the following passage from a radio magazine. Can it possibly be rewritten in plain English?

"Probably one of the greatest reasons for his phenomenal microphone success was his early discovery that the microphone is a sensitive betrayer of sham and insincerity, revealing the truth with unmerciful accuracy. Despite accusations to the contrary, he never has been deliberately affectatious. He always has tried to reflect the warmth of life in his broadcasts. This, in toto, is the prime reason for the amazing bond of affection and understanding existing between this master showman and his listener public.

"When Roxy first entered the broadcasting scene in 1922, the industry was stranded high and dry in the mires of similitude. The infant art was in a highly nebulous state of formation. The melody of music and speech was buried under a galloping cacophony of static, and of dreary reiteration."

12) Is the general or specific word preferable?

1. Jefferson began with the ——————— (wish, proposition), that all men are created equal.
2. He told the Boy Scouts from the East that these trees were ——————— (evergreens, non-deciduous).
3. Having no ——————— (affairs, scandals) of their own, they interest themselves in other people's business.
4. Bring me my ——————— (bow, weapon) of burning gold.
5. On the shield, was a ——————— (griffin, heraldic device).
6. He was full of ——————— (unbelievable, breath-bereaving) insolence.
7. After the long siege, Paris was short not only of ——————— (cake, luxuries), but of ——————— (bread, necessities).
8. Jonson's comedy *Volpone*, showed ——————— (retaliation, the biter bit).
9. To produce stage thunder, they used in the loft overhead, ——————— (rusty cannon balls, the proper mechanical equipment).
10. Cellini was both ——————— (goldsmith, artist) and bravo.

13) Is the abstract or the concrete word preferable?

1. The two boys were ——————— (akin, cousins).
2. Stevenson played sedulous ——————— (mimic, ape) to other writers.
3. The farmer loaned his neighbor a ——————— (peck, quantity) of seed potatoes.
4. The sentence showed marked ——————— (bagginess, incoherence).
5. The old heavyweight had his ——————— (plenitude, bellyful) of fighting for once.
6. Jacksonian and Jeffersonian catchwords have always been ——————— (components, part and parcel) of Democratic doctrine.
7. The Universe is all in ——————— (apple-pie, uniform) order: a penny for him who finds the pea.
8. I was born in the spring, so that those who wished to send ——————— (flowers, tribute) might do so.
9. The gradual ——————— (cessation, halt) of this upthrust of the earth's crust dated back to the New Stone Age.
10. The current had a high ——————— (power, voltage).

What applies to words, holds also with phrases and sentences. The familiar, pithy phrase is better than an elaborate artificial coinage. A lively image is preferable to a dry commonplace. Idioms, even an occasional stock proverb, will carry more force than word-groupings which convey the impression of heavy artillery—especially if, as so often happens, the big guns of language are moved up to mow down a molehill. Such a cannonade of verbiage simply deafens the ears. Far preferable is that sinewy, idiomatic style which has a drive toward feeling or action.

The closer, in fact, a man's words fit his natural habit, the more organic they are to his make-up, the surer his touch in handling the language. It is toward this ideal that effort should be directed, in expanding the vocabulary. What is wanted is a stock of words that shall be varied and ample, ready of access, but always under sure control. With these principles firmly established, and with a rough-and-ready notion of your own present attainments in the field of words, it is now possible to proceed, first, to an examination of the traditional methods of vocabulary-building, and then to a statement of the novel devices which this work offers for the command of words.

The supplementary vocabulary tests which follow are not taken from a measured "reservoir," so it is not possible to state what these tests show as to your actual range of vocabulary. It is highly probable, however, that anyone who knew all these words would have a very wide range indeed. Many of the traditional tests of vocabulary were made up largely of such words as are found in these very difficult tests. These tests belong to a somewhat antiquated "literary" method of word study,—but how delightful a pastime it was,—and still should be!

14) Here is a list of one hundred words from among those treated by Archbishop Trench in his famous lectures on *The Study of Words,* first given in 1859. How many of these would you know if you encountered them in your reading?

aborigines, animosity, antistrophic, apocryphal, artesian, assentation, atavism, banter, barnacle, basilisk, blackleg, bohemian, bonhomie, boor, boycott, buccaneer, burke, cadaver, camelia, canonical, catchpole, chalcedony, chimerical, ciborium, cicerone, cockatrice, copperhead, cosmopolite, crypt, curfew, damask, damson, dedal, delator, desultory, dissimilation, distemper, eleemosynary, esemplastic, extradition, faïence, hansom, haversack, herculean, hidalgo, kickshaws, landau, leonine, libertine, long pig, lucubration, martinet, matriarch, maudlin, mausoleum, megrim, mentor, mercurial, miscreant, monody, morganatic, mosaic, neologist, orgies, ottoman, pantaloons, paramour, pasquinade, pedant, quadrivium, rationalist, regeneration, rodomontade, rubric, sansculotte, sarcenet, saturnine, secularization, simony, tawdry, theocracy, thrasonical, tontine, transliteration, transubstantiation, tribulation, turquoise, vaticide, virtuoso, voltaic, voluble, wench, worsted.

The following list of fifty words was chosen from *Words and Their Ways in English Speech* by Greenough and Kittredge.[1] How many of these do you know?

abalienate, alembic, amanuensis, ampersand, animadversion, argol, armiger, arras, bathos, bilboes, cabbala, calèche, camber, catchpoll, dotterel, effluvium,

---

[1] By permission of the Macmillan Company, publishers.

escheator, flexure, gar-pike, gasconade, gingiver, harveyize, holystones, jehu, jeremiad, junta, lanyard, latakia, lazaret, leal, liard, macassar, macrocosm, mammet, mellifluous, microcosm, mortmain, motoneer, ohm, orrery, piscatorial, purblind, putative, quiddity, sortilege, suborn, stellify, torsion, vaticination, vulpine.

These might be called "high-ceiling" tests. If you know all of these words at sight, you are probably a learned jurist or an expert linguist. You can safely offer to buy a dinner for any of your friends who can define all of these words correctly at sight. These lists, indeed, show that the learned authorities who have written on words have been fascinated by the strange, romantic, and esoteric words in which the English language is very rich.

15) The list which follows is a decided contrast to those above. It contains one hundred words chosen from among those recently added in *Webster's Dictionary* and in the *Standard Dictionary*. How many of these words are you sure you know? (The criticism is often made of the Thorndike ten million word count, on the basis of which you determined your reading vocabulary, that he did not use sufficiently recent books, magazines, and newspapers in his reckoning.)

ambivalence, audition, autogyro, ballyhoo, Cheka, empathy, gigolo, intelligentsia, kibitzer, racketeer, robot, television, reflation, fade-out, black-out, close-up, fuselage, amalgam, audiometer, automat, algolagnia, boot-legger, bingle, chiropractic, demarche, Fascisti, footage, hokum, jazz-band, milline, mortician, photostat, pogo, proton, tear-bomb, vitamin, acidosis, allocable, wisecrack, jay-walker, atmospherics, automotive, avigation, batik, Gestalt, blurb, botulism, catalyst, catwalk, cellophane, cinema, columnist, correctitude, curricular, broadcast, plywood, podiotry, propagandize, sal, gel, decelerate, selectivity, egocentric, surprint, extravert, walkaway, gene, crooner, fundamentalism, phony, tonsillectomy, moniker, post-operative, irredenta, introvert, insulin, strafe, neutron, deuton, rotogravure, imagist, aquaplane, heterodyne, allergy, dyarchy, dysgenic, endocrine, fabrikoid, kilocycle, Kultur, multiverse, negativism, preconscious, scenario, rucksack, soviet, stratosphere, whoopee, proton, kaoliang.

16) The words which follow occur in the text of the chapter which you have just read. They are all above the 8000 level as shown by Thorndike's list. The figures after each word refer to the thousand in which it is found. From encountering these words in context, can you give a definition of each? There is no more amusing exercise for vocabulary-building than the manufacture of a confusion test such as the first exercise in the chapter. Construct such a test, using these fifty words as examples, and try it out on your friends.

intricate (9	consecutive (10	cudgel (11	fastidious (13
chastity (9	reputable (10	sobriety (12	continuity (13
lucid (10	predicament (10	specifications (12	rote (13
revision (10	compile (11	barbarisms (12	psychological (13

preponderance (14

quadruple (14

antonym (14

amplify (14

behooves (15

nomenclature (15

abeyance (15

tentative (15

coalesce (16

anatomical (16

pithy (14

versatile (17

illiteracies (17

polysyllable (19

euphony (19

humanists (19

verbiage (20

idiomatic (20

subjective (20

invariant*

verisimilitude*

lexicographer (20

circumlocution (20

clarity (20

denominator (20

consensus*

euphoria*

acclimate*

italicized*

verbalism*

plethora*

linguistic*

obligatory*

nuances*

* Words which are above the 20,000 level frequency.

CHAPTER II

The traditional method for the enlargement of vocabulary is a resort to extensive and varied reading. The mind of a great writer is a rare instrument for the enlargement, clarification, and enrichment of experience. To take in his full meaning, the significance of each word must be clear. Hence there is, in reading such a writer, the strongest motive for deciphering words which are new to the reader. In the pages of a great novelist, Cervantes, Balzac, Tolstoy, or Conrad, the drive behind the words is so strong that the drift of the whole passage is usually clear, whether or not every word is familiar. Hence the new words fall into place in the whole pattern, and the reader insensibly acquires a knowledge of their meaning. There may be individual words which seem to call for a glossary, because they have to do with things which are foreign, or remote in time. But even on these, when they have been encountered several times, a good guess is possible.

In a sense, this guessing at new words is a kind of translation within our own language. It is by this process that everyone, from early childhood on, gradually increases his stock of words. Since this is a customary method of acquisition, it is only natural to continue it when the systematic enlargement of vocabulary is in question, even though guessing is a risky and inexact method.

What authors are best, to increase one's range of word-knowledge? Preferably those who have been accustomed to talk as well as write. For their written words have a ring of actuality, a sense of the will to act. Famous preachers, Swift, Newman, and Dean Inge, while they may not agree on doctrine, have this in common; all write with a nervous strength, a direct, forward-moving vigor, and a kind of lift which comes from deep and sincere conviction. Each of these has in addition certain qualities of his own: Swift, a kind of biting, incisive power of trenchant phrase; Newman a subtle and winding grace of expression; and Dean Inge a spare and hard force in argument. All are masters of a clear central English diction. Consider,

31

too, the essays of Emerson, and the nature-narratives of Thoreau. While Emerson's sentences are a little atomic, and the joints between them not always perfectly fitted, his economical use of words is a joy to see. Thoreau writes in a limpid prose which accomplishes his aim, the removal of all barriers between his own mind and the reader's. His long familiarity with the great Greeks gives his diction a classical simplicity and rightness. Then, to come nearer our time, the essays and lectures of Thomas Henry Huxley are marked by a clarity and lucidity of diction rarely equalled. H. L. Mencken thinks Huxley the best stylist among English prose writers. Certainly a reader of Huxley's address at the founding of Johns Hopkins in 1876, "A Liberal Education," might be pardoned for agreeing with Mencken. After sixty years, the speech still has a modernity of application and a freshness of ring such as modern occasional speakers might envy. It has not aged, nor is the style in any sense out of date. Curiously enough, this mastery over words seems to run in the Huxley family. Thomas Henry Huxley's two grandsons, Aldous and Julian Huxley, are writers whom the student of words can read with profit. Aldous, in particular, will introduce the reader to many new words, for he has a turn that way. He is, in some degree, a follower of Norman Douglas, whose *South Wind, Old Calabria,* and *Siren Land* can also be commended heartily to those interested in studying words as an old master alone can use them. Finally, the prefaces and pamphlets of George Bernard Shaw are rich mines of material. For all his claim that he is the last eighteenth century Irish gentleman, and that he has only revived the methods of classical comedy, Shaw is daring and provocative no less in his choice of words than in his ideas. Writing as he does at top speed, in his peculiar Pitman shorthand, he says what he has to say "with the most exasperating levity" at his command. His *Dramatic Essays and Opinions, The Sanity of Art,* or any of the prefaces to his plays will serve as a rich quarry for the student of words. And these are only a few of the authors who will so serve.

In addition to extensive reading, there are, for increasing the vocabulary, time-honored methods which are more deliberate. One of the best is the intensive study of words in a short passage, selected because it shows apt and effective diction. Analysis will give a glimpse, at least, of the cunning in the use of words which lends the passage its force and power. Take, for example, the following from T. H. Huxley,—he is speaking of the Bible:

Consider the great historical fact that, for three centuries, this book has been woven into the life of all that is best and noblest in English history; that it has become the national epic of Britain, and is as familiar to noble and simple, from John-o'-Groat's House to Land's End, as Dante and Tasso once were to Italians; that it is written in the noblest and purest English, and abounds in exquisite beauties of pure literary form; and finally, that it forbids the veriest hind who has never left his village to be ignorant of the existence of other countries and other civilizations, and of a great past stretching back to the furthest limits of the oldest civilizations of the world.

The opening chord is both simple and eloquent: *Consider the great historical fact.* The three key words, *consider, historical,* and *fact,* are of Greek or Latin origin, only *the* and *great* coming from the native Germanic strain. The arresting lift given by these longer words at the start, is a fine contrast to the long string of monosyllables which follows, broken only by *centuries,* which ties in with the very last clause in the whole sentence; and by the short Anglo-Saxon word *woven.* The break at *woven* draws attention to the daring image: a *book* is interlaced with *life* as web with woof in a piece of cloth. Just before the first semicolon, the words lengthen out, to give a rising tone to the voice. And Huxley is not daunted by the fact that he has already used *historical:* instead of casting about for a weak synonym, he boldly closes this period with *history.* In the next clause, he does not say, "from one end of Great Britain to the other," but *from John-o'-Groat's House to Land's End,* recalling the story of the Dutchman, John Groot, who built an octagonal house on the notheast tip of Scotland,—octagonal so that his eight relatives, who quarreled over precedence, could each enter by one of the eight doors, and take an equal place at an eight-sided table; and by the other allusion summoning to our minds the picture of that southwesterly tip of Cornwall, the land of dolmens and cromlechs, the last bit of England that the traveler sees as he sails out on the Atlantic from the southwestern ports. The slightly archaic flavor in the phrase, *noble und simple,* suits Huxley's theme. It is almost the only piece of old-fashioned phrasing which he permits himself, although he is dealing with the Authorized Version of 1611. And where he might have written "as Homer to the Greeks," he chose rather the makers of a modern vernacular, both, as it happens, religious poets: Dante and Tasso. Notice the sharp contrast between *veriest* and *hind,* the first from the Latin *verus,* 'true,' through the old French, and the second an Old English word meaning 'domestic,' 'serf,' one tied to the soil or the household of a lord. And the contrast is continued, in the sharp juxtaposition of the clause *who has never left his village* with the long rolling conclusion, in which Huxley gives us a true feeling of the great reaches of historic time. In this conclusion, he achieves great eloquence without once resorting to over-elaborate words. We feel from "how high a watchtower he looks out upon history" without ever having any sense that he is making a display of his vision. Note, too, the proportion of words which suggest action, change, or assertion: *consider, woven, become, written, abounds, forbids, left, stretching.* Instead of merely describing the Bible, he makes six statements as to what it has *done.* The one epithet which he applies to it, *national epic,* is freighted with historical and literary meaning; this epithet is reinforced by the reference to Dante and Tasso. For compression and expressiveness alike, Huxley's phrasing would be hard to equal. There is not one word which we would wish otherwise. Nor could one safely insert a word. Just put in the word 'native' before 'village,' and see how it spoils the tune, and causes a sag in the style. This consonance of words with thought, so that we would wish nothing added and nothing taken away, is the secret of that perfect rightness of diction toward which all study of words should aim.

17) Make a similar analysis of the diction in the following passages:

It is often said that unlettered people have a rough common sense and native shrewdness which education is apt to lose amid its books and papers; it is a view difficult of proof, but probably there is something in it. Yet having started on a course of general schooling which may soon be prolonged and expanded, there is nothing for us but to proceed on that course and back our hopes with our endeavors. The truly educated man is he who can look beneath a phrase, puts up an opposition to clamorous suggestion, is slogan*-proof, owns a sense of evidence, and refuses to build general theories on isolated facts or random assertions. Can that sort of prudence so essential to the good citizen be manufactured in the classroom? Certainly there can be no guarantee. All we can hope is that better education will lay better foundations.—Ivor Brown, in the *Manchester Guardian Weekly,* 15 Mar. 1935, p. 216.

Morning breaks as I write, along these Coniston fells, and the river mists, motionless and grey beneath the rose of the moorlands, fill the lower woods and the sleeping village and the long lawns by the lakeshore. Oh, that someone had but told me in my youth, when all my heart seemed to be set on these colours and clouds, that appear for a little while and then vanish

* Note, for example, *Slogan:* a war-cry, from Gaelic *sluagh-gairm* (sluagh = host, gairm = cry). Another form of the word is *slughorn.*

away, how little my love of them would serve me when the silence of lawn and wood in the dews of morning should be completed; and all my thoughts should be of those whom, by neither, I was to meet more.—Ruskin, *Praeterita*.

So strongly do I feel on this subject that if I had my way I would have a speculation master attached to every school. The boys would be encouraged to read the *Money Market Review*, the *Railway News*, and all the best financial papers, and should establish a stock exchange amongst themselves in which pence should stand as pounds. Then let them see how this making haste to get rich moneys out in actual practice. There might be a prize awarded by the head-master to the most prudent dealer, and the boys who lost their money time after time should be dismissed. Of course if any boy proved to have a genius for speculation and made money—well and good, let him speculate by all means.

If Universities were not the worst teachers in the world I should like to see professorships of speculation established at Oxford and Cambridge. When I reflect, however, that the only things worth doing which Oxford and Cambridge can do well are cooking, cricket, rowing and games, of which there is no professorship, I fear that the establishment of a professorial chair would end in teaching young men neither how to speculate, but would simply turn them out as bad speculators.—Samuel Butler, *Way of All Flesh*, Modern Library Edition, p. 348.

In making an intensive examination of the diction in a given passage, the primary concern is really with the meaning of words in context. Literally, *context* means 'weaving together.' It is concerned with the meaning which a word acquires in relation to what has gone before it and what comes after. As a naturalist studies plants *in situ*—in their natural environment—so the student of meanings must examine words in place; he must, like the naturalist, relate them to their surroundings, see how they derive support from neighboring words, and note how they take on the color of their context. The whole significance of a key word may not come home to the reader until the end of a passage in which it occurs.

In this contextual aspect, words are a part of the living tissue of thought. They have a fuller meaning than they could have when abstracted from context and set down in dictionary columns. Only as the word is seen in use, at different periods, and in the hands of different authors, can all its shades of meaning, all its possible figurative extensions of meaning, be fully felt.

By choosing among the various possible meanings of a word, we arrive at its precise, limited significance in a given context. This is its *denotation*: the exact idea, image, quality, act, or state for which the word is a symbol. If the context in plain prose has been

so molded as to narrow the meaning properly, the word should have
the same *denotation* for all competent readers or hearers.

18) What is the denotation of the italicized word or words in the following?

1. No man but a *blockhead* ever wrote except for money.
2. Nothing is so galling to a people, not broken in from birth, as a paternal
   or, in other words, a *meddling* government, a government which tells them
   what to read and say and eat and drink and wear.
3. There is some word, some phrase, some *idiom* that expresses a particular
   idea better than any other, but he cannot for the life of him *recollect* it:
   let him *wait* till he does. Is it strange that among twenty thousand
   words in the English language, the one of all others that he most needs
   should have *escaped* him? There are more things in *nature* than there are
   words in the English language, and he must not expect to lay *rash* hands
   on them all at once.—Hazlitt.

The *connotation* of a word is a different matter. Many words,
especially those having to do with the feelings or with the will, have
an aura of emotion which lingers around them. They have, in addition to their denotations, overtones, associations, additional shades
of meaning which they *connote*. They are, so to speak, common
words which have acquired suggestive or allusive power comparable
to that possessed by Biblical or classical allusions. When Landor
has Pericles write to Aspasia, as he lies dying of the plague, "The
happy never say, and never hear said, Farewell," the last word falls
on our ears like the toll of a bell; it marks the end, not only of a
great life, and a great love, but of a great age in human history.
In that sense, *farewell* is rich in connotations. Or, with quite a
different effect, when Irving Babbitt practices the "art of ruinous
quotation," the connotations of the word *ruinous* suggest that
"measured malignity of slander" in which Junius excelled. Or we
think of the proverbial phrase, "to damn a man out of his own
mouth." Again, when Norman Douglas writes, "The funeral was a
roaring success," it is certainly not the literal meaning of *roaring*
which is conveyed; nor, in context, is the remark heartless and in-
decorous. So much for prose instances.

In poetry, the connotations of words are vitally important. The
poet is dealing chiefly with emotion, or with sensory experience or
intellectual exploration as colored by feeling. A word may make
or break a line. And in the peculiar and unalterable collocations of
phrase which make a great poetic line—the best words in the best

order—there must be no jarring note; or if there is, as in the lines of Donne, Eliot, and Hopkins, it must be there by deliberate intent. But if poetry depends for its idea, or, as Dryden says, its wit, on the choice of the right words, how much does the feeling-tone hang upon the connotations of the words.

19) What are the connotations of the italicized word or words in the following?

1. Drest in a little brief authority,
   Most ignorant of what he's most assured,
   His *glassy* essence, like an angry ape,
   Plays such *fantastic* tricks before high heaven
   As make the angels weep.
2. 'Tis now the very *witching* time of night,
   When churchyards yawn and hell itself breathes out
   Contagion to this world.
3. The *shadow* of a dream.
4. They lard their *lean* books with the *fat* of others' works.
5. The *brazen throat* of war.
6. I have not the Chancellor's *encyclopedic* mind. He is indeed a kind of *semi-Solomon*. He half knows everything, from the *cedar* to the *hyssop*. —Macaulay.
   I wish I were as sure of anything as Macaulay is of *everything*.—Wm. Windham.
7. We *boil* at different *degrees*.

In prose, however, which is our main business, the connotations of words are no less important. At a primary level, the question of etiquette enters. What words are to be used for certain occasions? What are the verbal tabus of the group for whom we are writing? What is the usual company in which certain words are found? How are we, therefore, to avoid a mixed style? Behind good manners, in diction as in life, lies the need for considering the feelings and sensibilities of others. Hence, if we want to convey our own feeling-tone, our own actual attitude, we must attend to the selection of words which have the right overtones for our audience.

20) In the following passages which of the italicized words have the right connotations? Which have wrong connotations?

1. Someone needs to do for morals what that old *Pecksniff* Bacon got the *credit* of doing for science.—Samuel Butler.
2. Mrs. Lowe was knitting a stocking, first among that *deluge* of *amateur* work which was done so eagerly by women who longed to help and who

knew nothing else, and who toiled away at it to *appease* this longing, even when they felt sure of the *result's futility*.
3. Rules are only *props* to keep children from falling.
4. Roxy was born with the *smell of poverty* in his nostrils, in Stillwater, Minnesota, July 9, 1882.

In addition to extensive reading in good authors, the intensive study of words in selected passages, and the careful attention to the denotation and connotation of words in context, there are certain other time-honored methods for the improvement of vocabulary. The use of the dictionary is one,—more often honored in the breach than in the observance. The study of word-stems and roots is another. A third way is the investigation of the history of word-meanings, a fascinating pursuit in English, with its wealth of words having multiple meanings. Then there is the study of synonyms, and the development of discrimination in their use,—a faculty no less essential for a writer than a feeling for nice color gradations to a painter. Allied to this is a method much used in French schools. The student is asked to give an exact antonym for the word under observation. The theory is that if he knows the word of precisely opposite meaning, he must have a firm grasp on the original word. This seems a plausible way to sharpen one's sense of the significance of terms which express qualities and states.

All these modes of attack on the problem of vocabulary are traditional,—well-grounded procedures which have been used by great teachers since the Renaissance. They are methods which have the prescriptive force of authority. The rule of reason recommends them. The literati, whether in Oxford, Harvard, or Peking, have mastered words by following such traditional paths. These are roads in which all must walk who would learn the ways of words. In the pages which follow, these fime-honored methods will be fully explored.

Is it possible, however, to go beyond tradition in this field? Can there be found, if not easy short-cuts, at least new road-guides through the multitudinous country of words? It is possible. The work of Thorndike, already referred to, makes it feasible to indicate which words occur more frequently in our reading. Greater emphasis should be laid on these important words. That is why, in the word-lists which follow, in connection with the study of stems, synonyms, and the like, each word which is singled out for special study is followed by its frequency number in parentheses, if it comes within Thorndike's range of the twenty thousand words in most common use. These numbers will serve as danger signals, so to speak. We should stop and study carefully words with a frequency number higher than those in our usual vocabulary range. When we encounter these words again, they should stir in us a sense of familiarity, not of puzzlement. This procedure should make possible the building of an orderly and significant vocabulary structure. The older unsystematic way of vocabulary-building resembled somewhat the gradual agglomeration of a coral-reef, polyp by polyp, each word being added in random fashion. (Still the element of chance had a certain charm!)

When it comes to examining the Greek and Latin stems which afford the basis for a great part of our English stock, it is feasible, again, to discover which of these stems have fathered a really large number of words in general use. By concentrating on a relatively small number of roots, it is possible to acquire new words by the handful.

By taking advantage of the investigations of C. K. Ogden and his colleagues of the Orthological Institute in London, who spent ten years of arduous work in determining the *indispensable ideas* for which terms are required, it is practicable to group synonyms around those *key-words* which are found in Basic English, the simplified form of our language invented by this group for international use. To be sure, the aim of Basic English is exactly opposite to the pursuit upon which we are engaged. Ogden is trying to *shrink* vocabulary down to a basic minimum of words absolutely necessary for purposes of communication in business, science, and everyday intercourse. The Basic English vocabulary contains only 850 words. But in this process of shrinking, Ogden has determined the most important ideas,—operations, qualities, and things, he calls them,—and these fundamental notions will serve for grouping words in standard English, in such a way that they constitute idea-clusters. Words will no longer seem like particles loose in the void; they will group themselves into coherent and orderly patterns. It is perhaps paradoxical to take advantage of the shrinkage of vocabulary brought about in Basic English, in order to expand our word-stock in orthodox literary English; but after all, this is a legitimate by-product of the rigorous study of indispensable ideas, which is just as important for our purposes as it is for Basic. The great mass of existing English words (800,000, says Vizetelly; 600,000 in the 1934

Webster's New International) resembles, at first glimpse, an interminable forest with plentiful undergrowth and a tangle of luxuriant creepers. How are we to hack our way through? The first thing is to get a notion of the lie of the land. The Basic English words are great landmark trunks, the tops of which will serve as look-out points from which we can see our way through the forest. Having taken our bearings from such places of vantage, we can descend and blaze a trail through the trees, steering our way from one great trunk to another. We are no longer lost in the maze of words, but have brought under the reign of law what seemed at first an impenetrable jungle.

To bring *frequency numbers* to the aid of words, and to group words in accord with the *key-idea* to which they are related, should, then, serve to give more point and meaning to the traditional methods of building vocabulary.

Another step in advance is possible in the field of special and technical vocabularies. These are usually calmly dismissed as 'jargon.' So they are, in formal prose as written by the 'literati.' But the modern reader needs to know many 'jargon' words, as he reads of radio, television, automotive engineering, and aerodynamics (the theoretical science on which "streamlining" is based). Jargon is in like case with slang. Many jargon words eventually make their way into the standard literary idiom. Here the important point is once more, which jargon words does the general reader need to know? For their number is legion. Again, it is the minimum list of indispensable terms which is wanted. These must be sorted out,— and they will be, later in this work.

Finally, words should be studied not only in the light of their frequency, and their relationship to fundamental *ideas,* but they should be presented in such a way that they may be learned as part of a *pattern.* It is not enough to acquire, on the run, a vague notion of the dictionary meaning. The word should be pronounced, written, used in a variety of contexts, and made a familiar part of the mind of its user. It should become a part of the substance of his thought, not stopping on the tongue, or in the pen, but entering the very pattern of experience, inward and outward. The specific modes of building vocabulary, to which we now proceed, are only tools for the acquisition of words as symbols of ideas, as parts of the tissue of living thought and vital expression. Has this ideal ever been better summed up than in the following passage from Plato's *Dialogues?*

SOCRATES. I mean an intelligent word graven in the soul of the learner, which can defend itself, and knows when to speak and when to be silent.

PHAEDRUS. You mean the living word of knowledge which has a soul, and of which the written word is properly no more than an image?

SOCRATES. Yes, of course that is what I mean.

CHAPTER III

THE USE OF THE DICTIONARY

The most important single tool for the study of words is a good dictionary. Most of us are in the habit of consulting it casually, when we are in doubt as to the spelling or pronunciation of some particular word. Otherwise we are apt to take the dictionary rather for granted, as a dusty but familiar object. Yet it is one of the most entertaining and rewarding of books. Approach it with a fresh eye, as if it were a novelty encountered for the first time, and it will yield endless diversion. It is a guide to the country of words, containing, in small compass yet in rich variety, a great store of history, science, and art, a wealth of information made living and significant —to those who have a trained eye with which to read the compressed record. It was no accident that Norman Douglas, the most learned novelist of our time, advised his young friend Muriel Draper to read a page of the dictionary every day,—and learn all the words on it which amused her.

To read a dictionary with fully awakened interest, however, one must know the technique of condensation or system of shorthand employed. To use it with the least effort, one must know how to make cross-references, and how to fit the new words into a systematic pattern with those which are already known. New words should not be left cold and isolated as odds-and-ends in the mind.

In using a dictionary, it is first necessary to master the system of *accentuation* and *diacritical markings*. The guides to both are given in the introductory pages, and the key to the markings is repeated at the foot of the page in most lexicons. Once the accented syllable has been noted, and the sounds of the letters inferred from the diacritical markings, the pronunciation of the word should be clear. *Webster's Collegiate Dictionary* indicates the pronunciation of the word *inquiry* as follows: *in-quir'y* (ĭn-kwīr'ĭ). If you are not in the habit of accenting it on the first syllable, and pronouncing the second 'i' as short, you are one person in a thousand.

42

21) The following words are very commonly mispronounced. Mark them as you pronounce them. Verify the pronunciation in the dictionary.

acclimate	calliope	domicile	irreparable
adept	cerebral	exponent	irrevocable
adobe	chameleon	exquisite	lineament
aeroplane	clandestine	fungi	mauve
aggrandize	cognomen	genealogy	mischievous
alias	condolence	gondola	oleomargarine
alpaca	conduit	gratis	peony
amenable	conjugal	grimace	plagiarism
anchovy	contumely	harass	precedence
apotheosis	crematory	heinous	quay
apparatus	culinary	herculean	robust
aerial	cupola	holocaust	romance
arbiter	data	impious	sacrilegious
arctic	decorum	impotent	salmon
aspirant	defalcate	inchoate	satiety
barbarous	deficit	inclement	sinecure
bestial	despicable	incomparable	status
biography	desultory	indissoluble	vagary
blackguard	detonate	inveigle	vaudeville
blatant	diocesan	irremediable	xylophone
bouquet	dissoluble		

If one has occasion to divide words at the end of a line of print or typescript, it is well to note the device which the dictionary uses for indicating the syllabic divisions; and for distinguishing, too, instances of syllabic division points where one may not properly divide a word. It would be proper to divide *inquiry,* for instance after the *in,* if it were necessary to make a line of print come out right. But one could not divide it after the 'r,' thus leaving the 'y' alone on the next line. Webster shows this fact by omitting the light hyphen at that point. The rule is never to divide in such a way as to leave a single letter alone, even with the hyphen; and preferably not to divide even on two letters. There are also certain terminations which are never divided. The dictionary shows all these facts by its style of printing the word. (See also section IX of the STYLE RULE in the Appendix, on this matter of hyphenation.)

Besides pronunciation and hyphenation, the dictionary shows by symbols and abbreviations certain very important facts about any given word. What part of speech is it? What are its inflected forms? Is it slang, a colloquialism, a provincialism, a dialect word? Has it recently disappeared from use, i.e., is it *obsolete?* or *archaic,* found only in our older authors, from Chaucer to Milton? Is it in good use only in the United States? (This is usually indicated by the abbreviation U. S. at the end of the entry.) Is it a word in good use only in certain technical connections, as shown by such abbreviations as *Geog.* (Geography), *Math.* (Mathematics), *Archæol.* (Archæology), *Mil.* (Military), or the like? These abbreviations are in effect warnings that one uses the jargon word at his peril in prose addressed to the general reader. If *none* of these qualifying notes is added to a word-entry, it is presumed that the word is in good use throughout the English-speaking world; and that it belongs to the stock of *common* or *general* words which are in current use by good writers everywhere, alike in books, magazines, and newspapers. From this account, it is clear that it is a matter of vital importance to familiarize oneself with the *particular* set of symbols and abbreviations used by a given dictionary.

In the brackets preceding the definition or definitions of a given word, the *derivation* is given. This will afford a key to the fundamental or *root* meaning of the word. In many cases this derivation gives some notion of the original idea behind the word. The various figurative extensions of meaning can usually, though not always, be deduced from this *primary* meaning. So *fossil,* from a Latin word meaning *to dig,* meant originally anything *dug out* of the earth; then, a part of a plant or animal turned to stone, and *dug up* out of a stratum of rock; finally, a person of antiquated opinions, *dug up* out of the remote past. This last meaning is a true figurative extension. As another illustration of what is meant by *figurative extension* of meaning, take the opening sentences in Chamberlin's *Russia's Iron Age.* (By permission of Little, Brown and Company.)

The last few years in Russia have been an Iron Age, both in a literal and in a figurative sense. The drive for the industrialization of the country has been to a large extent a drive for more iron and steel. And the methods by which this industrialization and its twin process, the forcible collectivization of peasant agriculture, have been carried out have been iron in their ruthless crushing of resistance.

It is in the figurative sense that Bismarck was called the Iron Chancellor; recalling Swinburne's lines, "Not with dreams, but with blood and with iron, shall a nation be moulded at last."

This matter of figurative extension of meaning is of great interest in following down the various senses which a word has acquired. English is not only rich in synonyms, but it has also an embarrassingly large number of words with multiple meanings. The word *character*, as it appears in *Webster's Collegiate Dictionary*, is credited with ten different senses. These meanings appear in an order ranging from the literal, or primary sense of the word, through the successively more figurative extensions of meaning, to the final, most connotative significance of the word, "individuality, especially as distinguished by moral excellence." To choose the right meaning of the word *character* as it appears in a given context, a careful reader will look through the various meanings given. But the primary meaning, based on the derivation, will tell us that even this last figurative meaning is related to the fundamental idea in the Greek word from which our English word is transliterated.—*Character* is the stamp of a man, the brand or imprint left upon his nature by that sovereign *instrument for marking,* life itself.

It is interesting to observe that the great *Oxford English Dictionary* notes *nineteen* distinct shades of meaning for *character;* and even then, it is doubtful if any of the definitions given by that court of last resort will fully connote the meaning of the word as it is used in discussions of the drama and novel, in the phrase, *the development of character.* For in this sense, since Goethe and Coleridge first called the attention of readers to the extraordinary importance of 'character' in the modern scheme of things, the word has taken on great richness of significance. Character, in this sense, connotes more than the stamp of a man. It includes what he has been, and what he is apt to become in the future. It hints at the judgment which other persons form of his make-up. It includes his motives and his probable future acts. And *character* in this sense varies with time and with the observer. How many readings there have been of the "character" of Hamlet!

This figurative extension shows how hard it is to keep pace with the march of word-meanings. Words take on rich encrustations of meaning, acquiring a kind of patina like bronze long buried. But the dictionary entries are quite enough to start us thinking of what Plato called the "soul of a word"; a meaning not to be found in any precise definition, but which comes home to us as we encounter a word used with supreme aptness by some author who is a past grand master of diction.

22) The magician Houdini trained his assistants by taking them past jeweler's show-windows, allowing them to inspect the display for a minute or two, then asking them to turn away and itemize the contents of the exhibit.

Kipling has Kim trained by a similar device, when he is starting out on secret service work in India.—You have been looking at the pages of a dictionary, including the sample pages illustrating this chapter. In what order, in the particular dictionary you have been using, are the following items placed under each main word entry?

a) derivation
b) synonyms
c) pronunciation
d) part of speech
e) special and technical senses
f) inflections
g) status of the word
h) definitions

23) Are you sure of the meaning of the following dictionary abbreviations?

1. a., adj.	13. Hist.
2. Agric.	14. L.
3. Anat.	15. l. c.
4. AS	16. Mech.
5. Bib.	17. Med.
6. cap.	18. Mus.
7. colloq.	19. n., sb.,
8. ety.	20. Obs.
9. fem.	21. Phot.
10. ff.	22. Polit.
11. Gr.	23. Sp.
12. Gram.	24. subj.

24) Which meaning of the word *character,* under the entry in *Webster's Collegiate Dictionary,* did the author have in mind in the following instance? "Here is the whole set. A character dead at every word."

25) Which sense of the word *character* is employed in the following? "Micawber was a character, if ever there was one."

26) Could you substitute for *charge,* in "The Charge of the Light Brigade," any of the synonyms for it found in the dictionary, without a loss of rightness?

27) What kind of words lend themselves to definition merely by the use of synonyms? In the page from *Winston's Simplified Dictionary,* point out the words so defined.

28) What kinds of words require formal definitions? In these cases, you will note that the dictionary first names the class to which the thing, quality, or act belongs; then it gives the distinguishing characteristic which marks off this particular item from the other members of that class. Formulate such definitions for *botany, geology, teaching, architecture, bomb,* and *bohemianism.* Check your definitions by the dictionary.

29) What type of word calls for a picture or diagram, before it can be explained clearly? Point out such words in your desk dictionary.

30) What are the antonyms for the following words: *bitter, villain, right, enslaved, stingy, urban, antipathetic?*

31) There are many occasions when one desires not so much an exact logical definition of a word, as the feeling for its meaning in the particular context where it is found. How does the descriptive approximation of the word *fancy* in *Thorndike's Century Junior Dictionary* fit in with its use in the following:

> "Tell me, where is fancy bred,
> Or in the heart, or in the head?"

32) Which meaning of *graft* (See the specimen page of the *Concise Oxford Dictionary* in this chapter) is the right one in the following context:

"He managed to graft himself on to the main stem of the Republican party, though he had been a Whig and a Free-Soiler."

33) Divide into syllables and accent the following words: Use / / / for syllabic divisions, and ' for the accent, thus: hy'/phen/ate

1. aborigines	9. criterion	17. hemorrhage
2. accelerate	10. cupboard	18. jeopardy
3. aluminum	11. disappear	19. moccasin
4. antiquity	12. dubious	20. occupation
5. asparagus	13. erroneous	21. parliament
6. bookkeeping	14. extraordinary	22. perpendicular
7. cemetery	15. facsimile	23. quarantine
8. chocolate	16. fictitious	24. reciprocal

The greatest venture in the history of lexicography is the *Oxford English Dictionary,* sometimes called the *New English Dictionary,* and again *Murray's Dictionary,* from its first editor. Begun in 1858, and completed only in 1932, this work treats words on historical principles. For each entry, instances of the use of the word were gathered, these examples dating, in case of the older words, as early as 700 A.D., and coming down to very recent times. Five million quotations in all were collected, of which two million were finally used in the thirteen great folio volumes. So for each of the 215,000 main words, and the 200,000 subordinate word- and phrase-entries,

gradely 500 **grain**

to easy gradients; (Cattle-breeding) cross with better breed (*g. up*, improve thus); (Philol., in pass.) be changed by ablaut. [vb f. n., F, f. L *gradus* step]

gră·dely (-dll), a. (dial.). Excellent, thorough; handsome, comely; real, true, proper. [ME·*greidhlig* f. ON *greidhlig-r* (*greidh-r* = OE *geráede* READY, -LY¹)]

gră·dient, n. Amount of slope, inclination to the horizontal, in road, railway, &c.; proportional rise or fall of thermometer or barometer in passing from one region to another. [perh. formed on GRADE after *quotient*]

gră·din(e) (*also* -ade·n), n. One of series of low steps or tier of seats; ledge at back of altar. [f. F *gradin* f. It. *gradino* (*grado* GRADE)]

gră·dual¹, n. Antiphon sung between Epistle & Gospel. [so called as sung at steps of altar or while deacon mounted ambo; f. med. L *graduale* neut. adj. as n., see foll.]

gra·dual², a. Taking place by degrees, slowly progressive, not rapid, steep, or abrupt; *g. psalm,* = *song of* DEGREES. Hence **gra·duaLLY²** adv., **gra·dualNESS** n. [f. med. L *gradualis* (L *gradus -ūs* step, -AL)]

gră·duate¹ (-at), n. One who holds academic degree; chemist's graduated measuring-glass. [f. med. L *graduatus* (foll., -ATE²)]

gra·duăte², v.i. & t. Take, admit to (chiefly U.S.), academic degree, (transf.) qualify or perfect oneself *as*; mark out in degrees or portions; arrange in gradations, apportion incidence of (tax) according to a scale; pass *away* by degrees, change (intr.) gradually *into*; concentrate (solution) by evaporation. Hence **gradua·TION**, **gra·duator²**(1, 2), nn. [f. med. L *graduare* (*gradus -ūs* step), -ATE³]

gră·dus, n. Dictionary of Latin prosody used in schools to help in writing Latin verse. [for *g. ad Parnassum* step to Parnassus]

Gr(a)e·cism, n. A Greek idiom, esp. as imitated in another language; Greek spirit, style, mode of expression, &c., imitation of these. [f. F *grécisme* f. med. L *graecismus* (*Graecus* GREEK, -ISM)]

Gr(a)e·cize, v.t. & i. Give a Greek cast, character, or form, to; favour, imitate, the Greeks. [f. L *graecizare* (prec., -IZE)]

Gr(a)e·co-, comb. form of L *Graecus* GREEK, as -*Roman*. Hence **Gr(a)eco-MA·NIA**(C) nn., **Gr(a)e·coPHIL** a. & n.

graffi·to (-fē-), n. (pl. -*ti* pr. -tē). Drawing or writing scratched on wall &c., esp. on ancient wall as at Pompeii; decoration by scratches through plaster showing different-coloured under-surface. [It.]

graft¹, n., & v.t. Shoot or scion inserted in slit of another stock, from which it receives sap; (Surg.) piece of trans-

planted living tissue; process of grafting; place where g. is inserted. (Vb) insert (scion) as g. (*in, into, on, upon, together*), (fig.) insert or fix *in* or *upon* so as to produce vital or indissoluble union; insert graft(s); insert graft(s) upon (stock); (Surg.) transplant (living tissue); (Naut.) cover (ring-bolt &c.) with weaving of small cord; *grafting-clay*, -*wax*, composition for covering united parts of g. & stock. [for earlier *graff* n. & v. f. OF *grafe* f. LL f. Gk *graphion* stylus (*graphō* write), named f. similarity of shape; -*t* perh. due to use of g. as p.p. of *graff*, cf. HOIST, BASTE³]

graft², n. Depth of earth that may be thrown up at once with spade; crescent-bladed spade. [cogn. w. GRAVE²]

graft³, n., & v.i., (U.S. colloq.). Illicit spoils in connexion with politics or municipal business, practices intended to secure these; (vb) seek, make, g., whence **gra·fteR¹** n. [?]

grail¹, n. = GRADUAL¹. [f. OF *grael* f. eccl. L *gradale* var. of *graduale*]

grail², n. (Also *holy* or *saint g.*, or *sangreal*) platter used by Christ at Last Supper, & in which Joseph of Arimathea received his blood at the Cross. [f. OF *graal* f. med. L *gradalis* cup or platter, etym. dub.; *sangreal* was = *blood real* or *royal* (F *sang*) is erron. division]

grail³, n. Comb-maker's file. [f. F *grêle* (*grêler* make thin f. *grêle* adj. f. L *gracilis*)]

grain, n., & v.t. & i. A fruit or corn of a cereal; (collect. sing.) wheat or the allied food-grasses or their fruit, corn, a particular species of corn; (pl.; also *gg. of Paradise* or *Guinea gg.*) capsules of W.-Afr. plant used as spice & drug; (pl.) refuse malt after brewing or distilling; small hard particle of sand, gold, SALT, gunpowder (*large, small, -g. powder*), incense, &c.; smallest unit of weight, 1/5760 of lb. Troy, 1/7000 of lb. av., smallest possible quantity (*without a g. of vanity, love*, &c.); (Hist.) kermes, cochineal, or dye made from either of these (*dye in g.*, dye in kermes, dye in any fast colour, dye in the fibre or thoroughly; *in g.*, thorough, genuine, by nature, downright, indelible); (Poet.) dye, colour; granular texture, roughness of surface, mottling; texture, arrangement & size of constituent particles, in flesh, skin, wood, stone, &c.; lines of fibre in wood giving a pattern, lamination or planes of cleavage in coal, stone, &c., (fig.) nature, temper, tendency, (*against the g.*, contrary to inclination); *g.-leather*, dressed with the *g.-side* (on which the hair was) out; *g.-sick* n., cattle-disease, distension of rumen; hence **grai·nLESS**, **grai·nY²**, (-)**grainED²**, aa. (Vb) form (t. & i.) into gg.; dye in g.; give granular surface to; remove hair from (hides); paint in imitation of g. of wood or marble;

From the *Concise Oxford Dictionary*, publ. by the Oxford University Press. This is an abridgement of the great *Oxford English Dictionary*.

not only are definitions given which show all the meanings that the word has had, but examples of the use in each sense are given. The OED (as it is commonly abbreviated by scholars) is therefore a great treasury of passages from English literature, beginning with the eighth century, and coming down, in the last volume, to 1932. These illustrations, which give the word in *context*, are the most revealing method of displaying the actual significance which the word has had at different periods. By these means, the natural history of the word is unfolded. We learn also a great deal of the social history that lies embedded in the record of words. To trace the successive meanings of the word *humor*, or of the word *wit*, is an exercise which will uncover, incidentally, much of the history of the English mind and of English social thought during successive peri-

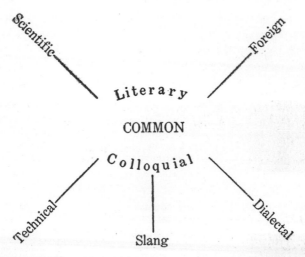

"The center is occupied by the common words, in which literary and colloquial words meet. 'Scientific' and 'foreign' words enter the common language mainly through literature; 'slang' words ascend through colloquial use; the 'technical' terms of crafts and processes, and the 'dialect' words, blend with the common language both in speech and literature. Slang also touches on one side the technical terminology of trades and occupations, as in 'nautical slang,' 'Public School slang,' 'the slang of the Stock Exchange,' and on another passes into true dialect. Dialects, similarly, pass into foreign languages. Scientific terminology passes on one side into purely foreign words, on another it blends with the technical vocabulary of art and manufactures. It is not possible to fix the point at which the 'English Language' stops, along any of these diverging lines."—OED, I, xxvii, note. (Quoted by permission of the Oxford University Press.)

ods. It is the massive collection of illustrative examples which makes this dictionary a great achievement in the science of language.

One of the most salient features of the OED, for our purposes, is the introductory article on the vocabulary of the English language. The article is unsigned, but one suspects it is by Sir James Murray, the first editor. There is one revelatory passage that brings into place with a sudden click the scattered bits of that huge kaleidoscopic assortment of words which a dictionary offers, so that we see, in a flash, an ordered, coherent picture of the English vocabulary, marked by strong and sure design. The passage just above, with the graphic diagram showing the relation of the parts of the vocabulary to each other, merits careful study.

Given this clear and orderly framework, it should be much easier to fit the detailed additions to vocabulary into the picture. The tolerance, the wide-ranging vision, the view of the development of the verbal resources of the language as a long social process with interactions between the various parts,—all these implications of the statement quicken and strengthen our interest in the study of the dictionary.

34) Group the following words according to the divisions of the English vocabulary shown in the diagram just above. Five of these words are *common,* five *literary,* five *colloquial,* etc. When you have the words arranged in the rimless wheel (rimless, because, as Murray (?) says, there are no fixed points at which the English language stops), check to see if the words in each 'spoke' bear the relationship to the adjoining group or groups which the legend beneath the diagram predicts that they should.

1. brachycephalic	14. counter	27. recondite
2. cavatina	15. palamino	28. obloquy
3. lasso	16. wanderlust	29. nipper
4. eviscerate	17. mortise	30. bamboozle
5. earth	18. phylum	31. jolly-doggism
6. higgledy-piggledy	19. exacerbate	32. bohunk
7. amplifier	20. feature	33. jointer
8. ineffable	21. won't	34. filum
9. fire	22. jaloppe	35. non sequitur
10. em	23. tenon	36. escape
11. colloid	24. foraminifera	37. pone
12. éclat	25. weltschmerz	38. skullduggery
13. picayune	26. prohi	39. bunk
		40. jigger

Does not such a discovery as this, in the OED, prove that Norman Douglas was right in maintaining that the dictionary offers much that is beguiling to the mind? And the large American dictionaries,

Webster's and the *Standard,* while they do not give any such range of quotations as the OED, and are indeed confined to the more usual limits of lexicography, have a richness of material which makes them second only to the OED; and for American readers they are in some ways more useful. In the most recent edition of *Webster's New International,* for example, there is found the following definition of *journalistic:*

"Characteristic of journalism or journalists; hence, of style, characterized by evidences of haste, superficiality of thought, inaccuracies of detail, colloquialism, and sensationalism; journalese."

And when we make the cross reference to *journalese,* there is "worse and more of it!"

"English of a style featured by use of colloquialisms, superficiality of thought and reasoning, clever or sensational presentation of material, and evidences of haste in composition, considered characteristic of newspaper writing."

Who is the author of these rich specimens of the higher mischief? One suspects William Allan Neilson, the general editor, though there is no way of proving it. As the first great mud-slinging journalist, Pietro Aretino, the Scourge of Princes and the Prince of Scourges, remarked, "If you want to annoy your neighbors, tell the truth about them." Will this edition of Webster's perhaps be known to history as the 'journalese' dictionary?—Again, the Funk and Wagnall's *Standard Dictionary* is immensely hospitable to new words and coinages. We may expect to see in the next edition such neologisms as 'boon-doggles,' 'gertrudesteining,' and 'Ogden-Nashery.' The pages of this dictionary are kept in type, so that changes can be made as fast as they occur. The *Standard* is thus a kind of recording instrument which keeps track of the new movements in language, English and American alike. Many persons regard it as the ideal readers' dictionary.

For ready desk use, there are five dictionaries which can be recommended, each having its merits for some particular purpose. There is the *Concise Oxford,* boiled down from the OED. It is full of the quiet and sardonic wit of the Fowler Brothers, who made it. *Webster's Collegiate* contains many supplementary features: pronouncing dictionary appendixes of geographical and biographical names; a vocabulary of rhymes; a list of quotations and phrases from foreign languages; a glossary of Scotticisms; a full style book for the odd; fantastic; as, a fanciful decoration. 3. imaginary; unreal; as, a fanciful story of the life of a penny. *adj. 12.*

fan cy (fan'si). All the meanings of fancy have something to do with the imagination or play of the mind. 1. picture to oneself; imagine. Can you fancy yourself in fairyland? 2. power to imagine; something imagined. Is it a fancy, or do I hear a sound? 3. like. I fancy the idea of having a picnic. 4. liking. He has a fancy for bright ties. 5. arranged especially to please, as, fancy dress, fancy dancing, fancy-work. 6. costing extra to please the mind, as, fancy fruits, a fancy price. *v.t., v.i., fancied, fancying, n., pl. fancies, adj., fancier, fanciest. 2.*

fane (fān), temple; church. *n. (used now only in poetry). 12.*

fan fare (fan'fär), 1. a short tune played on trumpets, bugles, or the like. 2. a showy parade. *n.*

fang (fang), 1. a long pointed tooth of a dog or wolf or snake. 2. something like it. *n. 9.*

fan tas tic (fan-tas'tik), odd; due to fancy; unreal; strange and wild in shape or manner. Many dreams are fantastic. *adj. 6.*

fan tas ti cal (fan-tas'ti-kạl), fantastic. *adj. 14.*

fan ta sy (fan'tạ-si), 1. imagination; play of the mind. 2. a picture in the mind. 3. a wild strange fancy. *n., pl. fantasies. 9.* Sometimes spelled **phantasy.**

far (fär), 1. a long way; a long way off. 2. more distant. He lives on the far side of the hill. 3. much. It is far better to go by train. This dress is the prettier by far. 4. **How far?** often means how much, what distance, or to what place? 5. **So far** often means to this place; to that place. 6. **A far cry** means a long way. 7. **Far and away** means very much. *adj., adv., farther, farthest. 1.*

far-a way (fär'ạ-wā'), 1. distant; far away. 2. dreamy. She had a far-away look in her eyes. *adj. 14.*

farce (färs), 1. a play full of ridiculous or absurd happenings, meant to be very funny. 2. a show of doing something so easily seen through that it is absurd or ridiculous. *n. 7.*

fare (fãr), 1. go, as, to fare forth on a journey. 2. do; get on. He is faring well in school. 3. **Fare well** or **ill** means have good or have poor food. **Good fare** means good food. 4. the money that one pays to ride in a train, car, bus, etc. 5. passenger. *v.i., n. 2.*

fare well (fãr'wel'), 1. good luck; good-by. 2. good wishes at parting. 3. parting, as, a farewell kiss. *interj., n., adj. 2.*

far-fetched (fär'fecht'), not closely related to the topic; forced; strained. *adj.*

farm (färm), 1. the land which a person uses to raise crops or animals. 2. raise crops or animals either to eat or to sell. 3. cultivate or till (land). 4. let for hire. Mr. Bond farms out the right to pick berries on his land. *n., v.i., v.t. 1.*

farm er (fär'mẽr), man who owns or works a farm. *n. 1.*

farm-house (färm'hous), the dwelling-house on a farm. *n. 8.*

farm stead (färm'sted), farm with its buildings. *n. 16.*

farm yard (färm'yärd), the yard connected with the farm-buildings or inclosed by them. *n. 7.*

far-off (fär'ôf'), distant; far away. *adj. 6.*

far-reach ing (fär'rē'ching), having a wide influence or effect. *adj. 14.*

far ri er (far'i-ẽr), 1. blacksmith who shoes horses. 2. veterinary; horse-doctor. *n. 12.*

far row (far'ō), 1. litter of pigs. 2. give birth to pigs. *n., v.i., v.t. 20.*

far-sight ed (fär'sī'ted), 1. seeing distant things more clearly than near ones. 2. seeing to a great distance. 3. looking ahead; shrewd; prudent. *adj.*

far-sight ed ness (fär'sī'ted-nes), 1. the ability to see distant objects more clearly than near ones. 2. the ability to see at a great distance. 3. the power of looking ahead; shrewdness. *n. 20.*

far ther (fär'ᴛнẽr), 1. more far. Three miles is farther than two. We walked farther than we meant to. 2. more; to a greater degree. Do you need farther help? 3. also; in addition. *adj., adv. 2.*

far ther most (fär'ᴛнẽr-mōst), most distant; farthest. *adj.*

far thest (fär'ᴛнest), 1. most far; most distant. 2. to the greatest degree; most. *adj., adv. 5.*

author, printer, and publisher. The *College Standard* carries similar material in the one alphabetical list, mixed in with the main word entries. Then there is the *Winston's Simplified Dictionary*, in which the definitions are put in plain and easy language, without loss of rigor or fullness. It contains also a number of appendixes most helpful to the student, including a list of all known alphabets and symbolic languages. The last three of these dictionaries are all rich in illustrations. Lastly there is *Thorndike's Century Junior Dictionary*, which is prepared especially for children, but which adults will use with great profit. For while it contains only the 25,000 words most commonly used, it gives after each word its frequency number, as we have already noted; and it is therefore a great help in the analysis of vocabulary. Thorndike has simplified the definitions, in many cases giving a description or image rather than the usual logical definition with *genus* and *differentia*. Also, he has taken great pains to define each word in terms less difficult than the word itself. He is in a position to do this with authority,—at least, if we grant that the commoner words are also the less difficult. (It may be remarked that the hardest task that the lexicographer confronts is the problem of defining the commonest words in the language.)—All in all, we are fortunate in having five portable dictionaries at once so interesting and useful. With such a wealth from which to choose, no one can call himself literate who does not own and employ one or more of these works. And everyone should have available for reference one of the large dictionaries. Even the great OED is now only one-fifth its original price.

Besides the common, garden variety of dictionary, there are many other special kinds. There are thesauri, word-treasuries, in which the words are classified under the heading of key-ideas. Of these *Roget's Thesaurus* is the most famous. It is an old work, but it has been subjected to many revisions. Dr. Sylvester Mawson has reworked it for modern use, publishing it with a complete alphabetical index, and with a useful addendum of foreign words and phrases. He has also put out an edition for school use, with the obsolete and unusual words eliminated under each subject-entry. This *Roget's Treasury of Words* (Thomas Y. Crowell Company) is a very compact volume. It should be pointed out, however, that a thesaurus will not take the place of a regular dictionary: it is only a supplemental tool. In this capacity, it is most useful.

116 INTELLECT **450 — 451**

CLASS IV

WORDS RELATING TO THE INTELLECTUAL FACULTIES

I. FORMATION OF IDEAS

450. INTELLECT. — *N.* **intellect,** mind, understanding, reason; rationality; intellectual faculties (*or* powers); senses, consciousness, observation, intellectuality, mentality, intelligence; conception, judgment, wits, brains, parts, capacity, genius; wit; ability; wisdom; ideality, idealism.

ego, soul, spirit; heart, breast, bosom; subconscious self, subliminal consciousness.

seat of thought, brain; head, headpiece; skull, cranium.

[Science of mind] psychology, psychanalysis *or* psycho-analysis; psychophysics; metaphysics; philosophy.

psychical research; telepathy, thought transference, thought reading; clairaudience; clairvoyance, mediumship; spiritualism etc. 992a.

V. **reason,** understand, think, reflect, cogitate, conceive, judge, contemplate, meditate; ruminate etc. (*think*) 451.

note, notice, mark; take notice of; be aware of, realize; appreciate.

Adj. **intellectual,** mental, rational; psychological; conscious, percipient, brainy [*colloq.*].

hyperphysical, subconscious, subliminal; telepathic, clairvoyant; psychic *or* psychical, spiritual, metaphysical, transcendental.

*** " my mind is my kingdom " [Campbell]; " stern men with empires in their brains " [Lowell]; " the mental condition of the modern world . . . the condition in which all natural explanations have broken down and no supernatural explanation has been established " [Chesterton]; " Friends, fellow mortals, bearers of the ghost That burns, and breaks its lamp, but is not lost " [Masefield].

450a. ABSENCE OF INTELLECT. — *N.* **want of intellect** (*or* mind, understanding); unintellectuality; imbecility etc. 490.

Adj. **unendowed with** (*or* void of) reason; unintelligent etc. (*imbecile*) 499.

451. THOUGHT. — *N.* **thought;** reflection, cogitation, consideration, meditation, study, speculation, deliberation, brainwork, cerebration; close study, application.

mature thought; afterthought, reconsideration, second thoughts; retrospection, examination.

abstraction, abstract thought, contemplation, musing; reverie etc. 458; depth of thought.

V. **think,** reflect, cogitate, consider, reason, deliberate; contemplate, meditate, ponder, muse, dream, ruminate, speculate; brood over, con over, study; bend (*or* apply) the mind; digest, discuss, hammer at, hammer out; weigh, realize, appreciate; fancy.

harbor, cherish, entertain, nurture (*as an idea*), imagine; bear in mind; reconsider.

suggest itself, present itself, occur to; come into one's head; strike one, come uppermost; enter (*or* cross, flash across, occupy) the mind.

Adj. **thoughtful,** pensive, meditative, reflective, cogitative, con-

35) Look up in the index to Roget's *Thesaurus* the word *intellect*, and turn to the entry in the body of the book, under that head. What are the closest synonyms for *intellect?* Why, do you suppose, did Roget not choose *mind*, as the more general word? (See index, again.) What is the adjective which corresponds to each of these synonyms for *intellect?* Are the synonyms for *intellect* interchangeable? What is the distinction which you would make between them? Consult a large dictionary to see how far you have guessed rightly. Why is Roget's *Thesaurus* not a substitute for a dictionary?

36) Suppose you want colloquial or jargon words for *captain, prison, scope, disobey,* the *authorities, butler, girl,* or *suitcase.* Look up these entries in Roget, and pick out the less formal equivalent for each.

37) What is the plan of classification which Roget uses for grouping words? (See the table of contents.) What are his main sub-divisions under Abstract Relations? How does he further sub-divide under Time? What are his main headings under Motion? What are the more usual modern words for Volition and Affections? Do these groupings suit your own needs in arranging your vocabulary by Ideas?

38) Recall some idea which you found difficulty in expressing. Look up a word connected with this idea in the index of Roget. Do you find the exact word or words which you wanted?

39) Which of the following words will fit the description of a controversy between diplomats at Geneva, and which will better apply to a bare-knuckle fight between two Irish boys? *discord, split, disruption, cross-purposes, altercation, fracas, imbroglio, brawl, hubbub, riot, Donnybrook Fair, schism, jar, bicker, at sixes and sevens, racket, bone of contention, scrimmage, knock-out blows, odds, dissidence, rumpus, Kilkenny Cats, unpacified, polemic.*

Besides Roget, there are many dictionaries of synonyms and antonyms which give full discussion of the distinctions in meaning between words nearly equivalent, with examples of their use. Fernald's *English Synonyms, Antonyms, and Prepositions* is one of the best known, and Allen's *Synonyms* is a usable book. Crabbe's *English Synonyms* is more than a century old, but it is still the longest treatment of the subject. It leans too heavily on etymological distinctions.

For allusions and references to well-known lines or phrases in our literature, there is *Bartlett's Familiar Quotations,* now available in an inexpensive edition, and Burton Stevenson's new *Home Book of Quotations,* rich in modern instances. There are glossaries and concordances for the Bible, for Shakespeare, Milton, Wordsworth, Tennyson, and many other famous English writers. There are dialect and slang dictionaries. Of the latter, Eric Partridge's *Slang*, a recent London publication, has appendixes listing British, American, and Australian slang, separately. The author gives with each entry the date of the first instance of the slang word which he has been able to find. He includes the slangy uses of reputable words. He notes also the changes in the meaning of slang terms. Supplementing his work on American slang, there is the comprehensive *Dictionary of American Slang* by Maurice E. Weseen (Thomas Y. Crowell Company, 1934). This work classifies the various types of slang under the headings:

I. Crooks' and Criminals' Slang
II. Hoboes' and Tramps' Slang
III. Railroaders' Slang
IV. Loggers' and Miners' Slang
V. Oil Drillers' Slang
VI. Cowboys' and Westerners' Slang
VII. Sailors' Slang
VIII. Soldiers' Slang
IX. Aviators' Slang
X. Theater Slang
XI. Circus and Carnival Slang
XII. Radio Slang
XIII. College Slang
XIV. Baseball Slang
XV. Football Slang
XVI. Boxing and Prize-fighting Slang
XVII. Sports Slang
XVIII. Drinking Slang
XIX. Eating Slang
XX. Money Slang
XXI. General Slang

Then there is Skeat's *Etymological Dictionary of the English Language,* in which he gives, for each important word in English, and for many an odd or curious word besides, an account of its root. Then he traces the route by which the word came into English. Often it has passed through three or four languages on its travels. Lastly, he adds entries which give some notion of how, from the literal root significance, it took on the figurative extensions of meaning which its modern use may show.

Skeat has a number of appendixes of great interest for our study. There are lists of prefixes and suffixes in English. There is a list of primary Indo-European roots occurring in English: only 461 are given. It is cheering to a student who is trying to find short-cuts for building up his vocabulary to learn how small is the number of basic root-ideas which English shares with the other members of the language-family to which it belongs. The total number of word-entries in a large Webster is now more than a thousand times 461. Evidently there is a short way through this labyrinth, and it must be possible to learn words by handfuls, by utilizing the lore of the expert. To be sure, one must look into a supplemental type of dictionary, to become clearly aware of the fact. But that is only because, as we have noted, the ordinary dictionary draws on Skeat's information on etymology, and reduces it to a shorthand entry.

There is still another appendix in Skeat which is of great interest. This is a distribution of English words according to their linguistic origin. We have all heard the advice to use plain old Anglo-Saxon words, and dubious advice it is. Skeat, however, gives us a list of such words, which go back to the literature of the Anglo-Saxon and Middle English periods. He follows this with lists from the other Germanic and Celtic branches of the Indo-European family. Then come long lists of words directly from the Latin; from the Latin via the French; from the Greek through the Latin and then the French; from the Greek direct; and so on. For our purposes, it is significant that of the (approximately) 13,300 words in Skeat's lists, about 33 per cent are of Germanic origin; 56 per cent are of Graeco-Latin origin, either directly or through the French; 2 per cent are from Celtic sources; 3 per cent are hybrids; and the remaining 6 per cent represent the contributions of Oriental, African, and Amerindian languages. If only the 12,000 words of Germanic and classical origin are considered, 37 per cent are from the first source, 63 per cent from the second. This agrees very closely with the figures given by Roland G. Kent, in his book *Language and Philology*. According to him, the classical words in the language make up about 60 per cent of the whole. Shakespeare's vocabulary shows about 65 per cent of classical derivatives. For every hundred *different* words used, sixty-five are from Greek and Latin, directly or through the French. But if a passage is taken at random, and the number of classical words in every hundred is counted, the figure runs about 21 per cent; for the often-repeated small change of the language, *the, of, to,* etc., is of Anglo-Saxon origin. As we have seen, fifty of these common words repeated make up half the total number of running words in the English of any period. Once these connectives and particles are ruled out of the estimates, the classical element predominates in the remaining words; and if each word used is counted only *once,* Graeco-Roman words often outnumber the Germanic element by two to one. In scientific and technical writing, the proportion is sometimes still higher. The conclusion which must be drawn from these figures, for our study, is that a knowledge of salient Greek and Latin stems is of enormous importance in building an English vocabulary. This is doubly true, for it is probable that most present-day words of the native Germanic strain are known to us at sight. But the classical or learned element will call for systematic attack.

As a result of this extended view, many rich vistas open up within the dictionary: the history of words, their comedy and romance; the changes in word meaning, often an epitome of social history; the study of slang, vulgarisms, argots, and jargons; the differences between American and British English. To these we shall later turn. But of all the short-cuts to word-mastery, it is clear that a study of basic roots will be the most rewarding. The most salient fact we have noted in examining dictionaries of various kinds is Skeat's list of 461 fundamental Indo-European roots employed in English. For if with this number of basic root concepts most of our words are built up, it is clear that we have here a short way to learn. To be sure, we shall take these roots in the modified Latin or Greek form in which they have entered into English word-building. It is the immediate ancestors of our English words that concern us most; and it may be well first to see how they came into our language.

DICTIONARY RECREATIONS

40) In the game of anagrams, it is essential to have a dictionary at hand to verify words which the players may claim to be actual words.

  a) Form six words from the letters NNDJI
  b) Form at least ten words from the letters SSEEELY
  c) Form at least seventeen words from the letters TTTRROE
  d) Form at least eight words from the letters MMMAAL
  e) Form at least thirteen words from the letters PLRAI

41) How many of the guide words at the top of the columns in a desk dictionary do you know sufficiently well to give approximate definitions for them? In *Webster's Collegiate Dictionary*, for instance, there are 2220 columns, and a like number of guide words in heavy black type. Since these guide words are determined by the exigencies of printing, they represent a random selection, or something pretty close to it. This is something like one word in 44 in this particular collection, the number of actual vocabulary entries in the main portion of the dictionary being given as 97,000; although the supplementary list of new words, etc., brings the total up to 107,000. (These figures are for the fourth edition, 1933; first published in 1931.) If you play this game of definitions with a partner, each taking turns in calling out the words, you should accept as correct any definition which is a good approximation of the meaning; for if you can come close enough to the meaning so that it is clear that you would understand the word *in context*, that is sufficient. To obtain your total vocabulary, as estimated by this means, (and it will take several evenings to go through a list of 2220 words) multiply your score of correct meanings by 44.

42) A variant of this dictionary game is as follows. You have probably heard of the method of the Vergilian lots. You open the book at random, shut your eyes, and put your finger on a particular verse. This verse is supposed to tell your fortune. The same method has been used with the Bible as an oracle. Try this, using the dictionary. Only instead of a cryptic response, at the meaning of which you must guess, you will be able to verify your knowledge or ignorance immediately. As soon as you have glanced at the main word nearest to the point where your finger lights (the more meticulous use a pin), look quickly away, and see whether or not you can define the word. If several play this game, the word-finder calls out the word, and the player whose turn it is attempts the definition.

43) For new words which interest you particularly, and which you want to make a part of your active vocabulary, make a card or slip (preferably 4"x6") on which you copy the dictionary account of the word, perhaps abbreviating the definitions, but giving the essential information about the term. If you have access to the OED, look up the word again, and copy on the card, below the word, a sentence or two illustrating its *recent* use. Draw a line across the slip, and add below it a few short sentences of your own, using the new word correctly. Keep these cards filed in alphabetical order, and run over them from time to time. Note, on the card, page references to books or magazine articles in which you find the word again.

44) The most entertaining of all dictionaries is H. W. Fowler's *Dictionary of Modern English Usage* (Oxford University Press). Try reading the articles on Anti-Saxonism, Back-formation, Barbarisms, Battered ornaments, Cast-iron idiom, Elegant variation, Facetious formations, Foreign danger, Gallicisms, Genteclism, Hackneyed phrases, Illiteracies, Literary critics' words, Long variants, Love of the long word, Malaprops, Mannerisms, Needless variants, Novelese, Novelty-hunting, Pedantic humour, Pedantry, Pomposities, Popularized technicalities, Saxonism, Sturdy indefensibles, Swapping horses, Trailers, Vulgarization, Wardour Street, Worn-out humour; though almost any page in this work is amusing as well as instructive.

45) If you have a copy of *Thorndike's Century Junior Dictionary*, which gives the frequency number after each word, a very amusing gambling game is possible. Let each contestant guess the frequency of a given word, and the one coming closest to the right thousand takes the pot. With a penny ante, or even at a tenth of a cent a word, this game is an agreeable substitute for poker, bridge, anagrams, or cross-word puzzles. It should be a most useful game for radio broadcasters, gag writers, and writers for the pulp magazines, who are concerned about the commonness and range of intelligibility of their vocabulary.

CHAPTER IV

WORD-FAMILIES AND WORD-BUILDING

English is a language of many layers. Successive deposits of words have been left by the various peoples who have conquered England. Since Queen Elizabeth's time, the language has also borrowed freely from foreign sources, not only from Latin, French, and Greek, but from nearly all the civilized languages of earth, and from primitive and barbaric tongues as well. To find the "native woodnotes wild," or "Dan Chaucer's well of pure English undefiled," one would have to go pretty far back, into the fens and bogs of the Picts, Scots, and other Celtic Britons, whose language survives today in Welsh.

From the original Celtic there are a few words in present-day English, such as *down,* which in Celtic meant 'hill.' Our preposition *down* is from this stem, being a shortened form of *adown,* coming through Anglo-Saxon. Paradoxically we now say 'down in a valley,'—literally, 'hill in a valley.' *Avon* and *Esk,* both meaning 'water' in Celtic, are found in the names of English rivers and the towns beside them; many other place names are Celtic. The first thin layer of Latin words comes through these Celts: *street* from *(via) strata,* 'paved road'; *mile,* from *milia (passuum),* 'thousands (of paces)'; *Chester* from *castra,* 'a camp,' this stem appearing in Lan*caster;* and -*coln,* in *Lincoln,* from *colonia,* a 'settlement.' *Wall,* from *vallum,* also belongs to this first Latin layer. Considering that the Britons were under Roman rule from 80 A.D. until 410 A.D., when the Emperor Honorius withdrew the legions, this is not a very large deposit of words. Most of these, even, come, like *down,* through the Anglo-Saxon.—There seems to be something about the English climate which affects the Celtic temperament and makes it hostile to the tongues of Roman and of Saxon: witness the revival of ancient Irish in our day, the persistence of Gaelic, and in completer fashion, of Welsh; there are a good many sardonic wits who would claim that James Joyce is trying quite effectually to escape from the bounds of English in *Ulysses,* still more in *Work in Progress.* Seriously speaking, the Celts, like all peoples, were, and are, deeply attached to their native tongue.—But to return to our geological task, of digging out the earlier strata of the English language.

In 449 A.D. the first Teutonic freebooters under Hengist and Horsa landed in England, to take over the rôle of governing class which the Romans had given up. This is no place to recount the struggle among the various dialects of the Angles, Saxons, and Jutes for literary supremacy. When in the last half of the ninth century the Anglo-Saxon civilization was at its height under Alfred, King of Wessex, who became king also of all Southern England, Alfred's language, West Saxon, was brought by his efforts as translator into the ascendancy. It maintains this primacy with modern students because more of its literature survives.—The last page of the *Anglo-Saxon Chronicle* was written in 1154, a century after the Norman Conquest. But the emergence of Modern English from an Anglian dialect, Mercian, comes a century later.

This Germanic dialect, Anglo-Saxon, forms the groundwork of English, its most important early layer. It gave us such grammar as we have; the inflections of words, of which only vestiges remain; and most of the names for common things and actions. Our terms for the plants and animals native to England are largely Anglo-Saxon. The names for the outward parts of the body, and for the inward anatomy visible upon dissection; the names of common household articles and simple tools; the qualities of objects easily apparent to the senses; the commoner phases of emotion and thought; the self-evident platitudes about character: all these we owe to the Anglo-Saxon element in English. Embedded in this great stratum, there are two other thin layers, which thread their striations in and out of the main Anglo-Saxon deposit.

One of these streaks may be called the second layer of Latin. It began when St. Augustine arrived in 597 A.D., to Christianize Britain. Since Anglo-Saxon had no words to express the ideas and trappings of Christianity, Latin words were adopted, some of them originally from the Greek or Hebrew. From the Greek through Latin through Anglo-Saxon, we have *church, devil, minster, school, clerk, deacon, synod, stole, anthem, organ, pope, priest;* and from the Latin through Anglo-Saxon, *alb, cope, nun, shrine, mass, font,* and *shrove.*

It takes close inspection to isolate the other intrusive element in the Anglo-Saxon stratum. The words at first glimpse do not differ from the rest of the Saxon group. But to an expert linguist, *scalp, score, skill, sky, gate, give, get, guest, ken, keel, kid, kilt,* and *kink,* reveal themselves as of Scandinavian origin. The Danes, who ravaged England in Alfred's time, and ruled it for a century after him, brought these words into the Anglo-Saxon vocabulary. Their language was first cousin to Anglo-Saxon, so it is not strange that the Scandinavian words are hard to pick out.

The next great layer of words came as a result of the Norman Conquest of England in 1066. But the Anglo-Saxon and the Norman-French languages existed side by side for more than a century, without much interpenetration. Contrary to the older view on the subject, William the Conqueror and his successors did not try to blot out the Anglo-Saxon tongue. William even made a futile effort to learn it. But the language of the court, of the law courts, and of polite literature was Norman; and Anglo-Saxon died out as a literary language. Hence it ceased to expand to meet the needs of a growing culture. Yet it maintained a rude vitality as a spoken language, and eventually conquered its conquerors.

But the blending of the two languages did not occur at once. It is a mistake to think that any great number of French words came into English before 1200; even after that, the process of amalgamation was a slow and gradual one. After 1154, the line of Norman kings gave way to the Angevins, who spoke "French of Paris," as Chaucer calls it. Both Norman French and Parisian French words were assimilated with Anglo-Saxon. *Catch,* for instance, comes from Norman French, and *chase* from Parisian; but both go back to the same Low Latin original, *caciare,* supposedly from the Latin *captare,* to capture. Two words of this type from the same root are called *doublets.* Often they have acquired quite different meanings in English. The commonest type of doublet occurs where we have borrowed a Latin word twice, once through the French, and a second time directly; so we find *frail* and *fragile, poor* (through French) and *pauper* (direct), *treat* and *tract.*

In 1362 the English language was first required in the courts of law; and Henry IV, born in Chaucer's lifetime, was the first Angevin king who spoke English as his mother tongue. Chaucer was the first important author to write the new blend of Anglo-Saxon and French which, partly by his use of it, established itself once and for all as the true English language.

This French stratum, which became so important in the fused language, was really just bad Latin, a late descendant of the soldier's

Latin spoken in Gaul in the centuries after the Roman occupation. A good case can be made out for calling this new stratum the third Latin layer. Embedded in this stratum were a few Celtic words which came in through the French: *baggage, bar, basin, barrel, button, carry, pottage, truant, varlet,* and *vassal,* etc.

In 1485, with the reign of Henry VII, came the beginning of a great influx of learned Latin words into English,—the fourth Latin layer. This is the period of the Renaissance, which in England coincides pretty closely with the reigns of the Tudors: Henry VII, Henry VIII, and Queen Elizabeth. Humanism, "the study of human nature in the great books of the ancients and in the life of man in our own age," gave many English scholars such complete familiarity with the great works of Latin antiquity that when they came to write familiarly in English they imported directly many Latin words in practically unchanged form.

This importation of Latin words into English went on until about the time of William and Mary, in 1689. After this date the language crystallized sufficiently so that the literary vocabulary ceased to expand by this means. Many of these learned Latin words did not finally make their place in the language, being used only by such erudite Latinists as Burton and Browne. The story runs that Burton wrote *The Anatomy of Melancholy* originally in Latin, but failing to find a printer, he translated it two-thirds into English. Certainly it still reads like a macaronic mixture of Latin and English. The later Renaissance also saw a great influx of Greek words into English, largely through the Latin.

This infiltration of Greek and Latin words is in fact still going on, in the scientific, though not so much in the literary, vocabulary. The inventions since the Industrial Revolution and the great advances in science have necessitated the adoption of new words for technical and scientific purposes. The ordinary words in the language are not suitable, because they are already attached to common objects or ideas. What is wanted, for scientific purposes, is a learned word which, untarnished by general use, can have only one meaning. This is why we say *television* instead of *far-seeing,* *telephone* instead of *far-speaker,* which is the literal rendering of the German word for telephone, *Fernsprecher.* This fifth layer of classical derivatives marks the end of the great *strata* which have piled up to form the English language.

Besides these main layers, there are many odd words embedded like strange pebbles in the composite structure of English. These are the words from nearly all the main languages of the globe, on which tribute has been levied by English soldiers, sailors, merchants, colonists, travellers, and translators. The following lists are typical:

From the Hebrew: amen, cabal, cherub, jubilee, manna, sabbath, squirrel, etc.
From the Italian: balcony, citadel, concert, motto, opera, pistol, etc.
From the Spanish: bravado, buffalo, cargo, cigar, cork, sherry, tornado, etc.
From the Portuguese: caste, commodore, lasso, palaver, and tank.
From the Dutch: aloof, bluff, boor, brandy, elopes, skates, wagon, yacht, etc.
From the German: feldspar, loafer, meerschaum, nickel, plunder, poodle, etc.
From the Slavonic: calash, czar, knout, polka, sable, slave, and steppe.
From the Persian: bazaar, caravan, checkers, chess, ghoul, hazard, horde, etc.
From the Hindu: calico, chintz, jungle, pagoda, shampoo, sugar, and toddy.
From the Turkish: bey, janissary, ottoman, and tulip.
From the Malay: bamboo, bantam, gong, gutta-percha, mango, rattan, and sago.
From the Polynesian: boomerang, kangaroo, taboo, and tattoo.
From the Chinese: china, junk, nankeen, serge, silk, tea, and typhoon.
From the Arabic: alcohol, algebra, alkali, candy, chemistry, cipher, etc.
From the N. A. Indian: hominy, moose, raccoon, skunk, squaw, and wigwam.
From the West Indian: buccaneer, cannibal, canoe, hammock, maize, and tobacco.

We still have not taken into account the additions made by American, Australian, and South African usage. Some wag has maintained that these are the living forms of English.

Finally, it should be added that the comparison of the layers of the English language to geological strata is not wholly exact. For the two main layers, the Anglo-Saxon and the Romance (French and Latin), were finally fused by 1375—fused much as if they had been affected by high volcanic heat. Chaucer's works show how far the process had gone. This fusion was given wide popular currency by Tyndal's version of the Bible, later by the Authorized Version (1611), and the Book of Common Prayer. The language remained in a more or less fluid state, as has been noted, until about 1689, when its literary vocabulary settled into a fairly stable form. Defoe or Swift could be printed in a modern newspaper; and except that their prose would stand out as notably better written than most of the adjacent journalistic material, it would pass muster as contemporary.

To take in, however, the whole picture of the gradual process by which English has been built up, it may be well to exhibit our language as an archaeologist might imagine it, with its early and later layers.

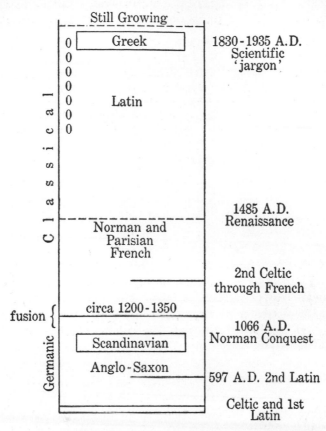

THE STRATA OF ENGLISH
(00 - Borrowed Words
from Various Languages.)

An interesting fact emerges from an inspection of this historic record. The Romance element in English (Latin, French, Greek) represents in a sense the superstructure. It towers up above the Anglo-Saxon, though it depends on the Germanic foundations furnished by that language. Since the terms used in law, politics, the more difficult arts and sciences, and in abstract thought, are largely from the Latin and the French, it is evident that the main effort in the extension of reading vocabulary must be directed toward a mastery of words of Romance origin. The stems, or roots *(root, in philology, means the simplest primitive form which words* once had; but in common usage the term *root* serves also to label *the later stem forms from which new words are made)* will be found to occur in English not only in their original Greek or Latin form, but in the variant modifications of these classical stems which French developed and passed into English. After this long historical preamble, we can now pass to the question of how to make these roots serve us in the rapid extension of vocabulary.

Classical Word-Families

To sharpen our attack, consider this line of argument. Words are intermediaries between thought and things. They are the signs of things, names arbitrarily associated with them, and with their images; and they are also symbols of thought, of ideas which are relational and which have grown up through connections within the mind. As has been noted, words which are the signs of things must be learned largely by sheer main strength, through contact with the things themselves, or pictures of them. No word-finder or thesaurus will take the place of a wide-ranging contact with the external world. There is no royal road through the country of concrete words. Learning the words which stand for concrete objects is much like learning proper names: each must be acquired by itself. It takes a politician's memory and habit of mind to retain them. Luckily, as the historical sketch showed, the bulk of English words which cover the realm of abstract thought, and which can be mastered by systematic attack, are derived from the Greek and Latin. Since at least three-fifths of our English vocabulary is of classical origin, it is evident that a study of the important stems and roots from the ancient languages will effect a great shortening of our work in learning the words which are symbols of thought.

Which of these root-words in Greek and Latin are basic to the largest number of English words? Take, first, ten Latin verbs:

facio, do or make	*pono,* place
duco, lead	*teneo,* hold, have
tendo, stretch	*fero,* bear
plico, fold	*mitto,* send
specio, see, observe	*capio,* take, seize

Add two Greek words: *logos,* speech, word, reason, study, thought, science—it has all these meanings and more; and *grapho,* write. These twelve words, ten Latin and two Greek, enter in some form or other into the composition of 2500 English words.[1] Though no rigorous and exhaustive count has been made, there are at least 156 English words in the formation of which *logos* plays a part. Some of them follow. How many can you define?

analogy, angelology, anthology, anthropology, apologue, apology, archeology, astrology, bacteriology, biology, catalogue, chronology, conchology, cosmology, criminology, decalogue, demonology, dialogue, doxology, eclogue, entomology, epilogue, eschatology, ethnology, etymology, eulogy, genealogy, geology, histology, illogical, logarithms, logic, logistics, logogram, logotype, logograph, metereology, mineralogy, monologue, morphology, mythology, neologism, ornithology, osteology, pathology, philology, phraseology, phrenology, physiology, psychology, prologue, tautology, technology, terminology, tetralogy, theology, travelogue, trilogy, zoölogy.

Many terms in the preceding list are needed only in reading learned works. But once the roots are known, such words will offer little difficulty. The important point is that in most of the words above, the one stem, *logos,* means either 'study (of),' 'science (of),' 'account (of),' or '(mode of) reasoning'; the word in the original Greek having these meanings, all deriving by figurative extension from the primary sense of 'speech' or 'word.' Indeed, if we were here interested in tracing the stem still further back, we could find in Skeat that *logos* derives from the Greek verb *legein,*—to collect, select, tell, speak; and that verb in turn from the original Indo-European root LAG (or RAG), to collect, put together, hence to read,—by putting together meanings.

Similarly, if we take the stem *graph,* from *graphein,* to write, we can observe a great family of English words from this source:

autograph, bibliography, biographer, calligraphy, cerograph, chirography, cinematograph, cosmography, dictograph, digraph, geography, graphic, holograph, lexicographer, lithograph, logograph, monograph, multigraph, orthography, paragraph, photographer, pyrography, seismograph, stenographer, stylograph, telegraph, typography.

Closely allied is the stem *gram-,* from *gramma,* a letter.

In Latin, the word meaning 'to write,' *scribere,* which comes from the same Indo-European root as *graphein,*—SKARBH, meaning 'to

---

[1] I. Colodny. *Words.* Los Angeles, 1934.

cut into,' or 'engrave,' from the primitive mode of writing,—is the ancestor of many English words:

ascribe, circumscribe, conscript, description, indescribable, inscription, manuscript, nondescript, postscript, prescribe, proscribe, rescript, scribble, scribe, script, scripture, subscriber, superscription, transcribe.

In the case of many of the words in this list, we note that a prefix has been joined to the stem *scrib-*, to give a certain shade of meaning, fixing thus a special sense of writing. Where in Saxon English, we must say 'write him down as one who is to be killed,' the Romans said 'proscribere,' to *proscribe;* the method being usually to 'write forth,' or 'publish' his name in a list of those to be executed. To prescribe is 'to give advance directions,' 'to write beforehand (prae-)'. To *circumscribe* is 'to write around,' hence 'to limit.' Some of these Latin prefixes came into English already joined with the stems with which they are found today. But English writers since the Renaissance have gone on using certain of these prefixes in compounding new words whenever they felt the need for them. So the word *co-director* has been manufactured, and its meaning is evident to everyone.

So strong has been the influence of these Latin,—and in lesser measure, Greek,—prefixes, that they have largely displaced the Anglo-Saxon prefixes, when it comes to the manufacture of new words. To be sure, the old Teutonic habit of stringing nouns together to form what are virtually new compounds is still in evidence, as when a headline writer presents us with "Life Insurance Directors Meet Postponed." Such simple pairs as *king-emperor, restroom,* and *tree surgeon* are easily made. But word-compounding by a different method is also possible, one involving the use of prefixes and suffixes, of which the most important ones are Latin and Greek, as in the case of the many words from the stems *scrib-*, and *graph-*, noted above. Once these *affixes,* as prefixes and suffixes together are called, are familiar, it is possible to break down words of classical origin into their component parts; and, if one is interested, to build up from a given stem a large number of English words. Before the important stems and their derivatives are taken up, it may be well to consider these common prefixes and suffixes, adding for good measure at the end of the chapter, a complete reference table of the classical and Anglo-Saxon affixes. When we come to analyze words from Greek and Latin into their component parts, we shall find these apparently unimportant affixes of great significance, in shortening our work in deciphering meanings.

Many of these classical affixes are still in active use in English. Using *ante-*, the Latin prefix meaning 'before, in front of,' we make new words quite freely, writing *ante-chamber, antediluvian, ante-date,* without any worry over the fact that these words did not exist in classical Latin. Similarly, we use *post,* 'after,' when we speak of *post-war* legislation, just as we use the antonym of *post, prae,* in *pre-war.* *Co-,* a combining form of *cum* 'with,' provides us with *co-respondent,* 'one jointly answerable with another,' now specialized to refer to the 'other man' or 'other woman' named in a divorce suit. We have *co-ed,* a colloquial abbreviation from *co-education.* Since girls did not formerly go to college, it is they who are 'educated *with*' boys; though that is not quite the connotation of *co-ed,* which is more nearly conveyed by the maxim, "Co-education is the thief of time."

The prefix *re,* meaning 'back' or 'again,' we feel free to use in countless ways. We even add it to a Latin word which arrived in our language already equipped with it, and say *re-refer;* or if the word already exists with the prefix *re,* we write the *re* with a hyphen when we employ the word in a new or literal sense, as in the case of *release,* 'to let go,' when it is used in a more literal signification, as *re-lease,* 'to lease again.'

As a reference to the table at the end of the chapter will show, many of these Latin prefixes alter their form when they are combined with stems beginning with consonants other than the terminal consonant of the prefix. So the final consonant of *sub* for the sake of euphony often changes to correspond to the initial letter of the stem, as in *success, suffer, supplant;* or it softens to an 's,' as in *sustain.* Most of these changes had occurred in Latin itself; but when we make new words with *sub,* this Latin practice is still followed, if euphony requires. If *sub* precedes a stem beginning with a consonant which follows easily, without slurring, after the final 'b,' there is no change. So *submarginal,* which was first used in 1829 (OED), keeps the 'b' unchanged. *Super,* 'above,' usually requires no change. It is still a very active prefix, as the new words *super-heterodyne* and *superpower* show.

Of the Latin suffixes, *-tor,* meaning 'one who' or 'that which,' is still in current use in forming English words. Witness the recent coinages, *realtor,* and *aviator;* there is a feminine suffix *-trix,* correspond-

ing to the masculine *-tor*, which we see in *aviatrix*. Then there are
the very common Latin suffixes, *-tion*, *-ity*, *-ment*, all of which help
to form a whole host of long-tailed words that express abstract qualities, states, or processes based on the meaning of the stem: *diversity*,
'the quality of being diverse'; *conglomeration*, 'the state or process
of becoming conglomerate (literally, 'rolled into a ball')'; *presentiment*, 'the state of feeling something in advance (pre).'

Sometimes the suffix *-ty*, denoting 'quality of, state of being,' is
attached even to Anglo-Saxon stems, as in *oddity*. This stem seems
to have a special drawing power for classical suffixes, since *oddment*
also occurs; although the native suffix is found in *oddness*. The
three words of course express, rather arbitrarily, different shades of
meaning. *Oddness* is always the state of being odd, in general;
whereas, while oddity may be the state of being odd, an *oddity* may
also be any queer article or person; while an *oddment* is any left-
over or odd fragment, such as, in printing, any pages that do not
appear in the regular numbered sequence of the main text,—title
page, or contents, or the like.

Another common Latin suffix still active in English, is *-able*, 'able
to be, fit to be, causing,' found in innumerable words. So with *-acy*,
-ancy, *-ence*, 'state of being, or act of,' occurring in *profligacy*, *bril-
liancy*, *excellence*, and in slightly different form, *excellency*. Still
in use is *-mony*, 'state of,' 'that derived from,' as in *matrimony*,
patrimony, and *acrimony*. There is *-il*, *-ile*, 'belonging to,' as in
servile,—'belonging to a slave,—and hence submissive, cringing.' A
very common one is *-ive*, 'relating to,' or 'involving,' as in the instances *fugitive*, 'relating to flight,' *cursive*, 'involving running,' as a
'*cursive* hand,' referring to the difference between a running and a
disjoined or printed script. There are many other Latin suffixes,
but it is easy, for the most part, to keep their meaning in mind by
summoning up a known word containing the suffix, and then infer-
ring the sense of the suffix from this instance.

The Greek suffixes and prefixes are fewer in number, and are
usually used in a fixed and invariant sense. The prefix *anti*, meaning 'against,' is one of the most common. A man may be an *anti-
prohibitionist*, an *anti-suffragist*, an *anti-royalist*, an *anti-Town-
sendite*, or, like the cartoon character in *Life*, *Old Anti-Everything*.
Or such a person may be, colloquially speaking, just a plain 'anti.'
The Greek prefixes *apo*, 'from'; *cata* or *kata*, 'down'; *dia*, 'through';
ec, 'out of,' 'from'; *hyper*, 'over'; *hypo*, 'under'; *meta*, 'beyond,

after'; *peri,* 'around'; and *syn,* 'with,' are still actively employed in compounding words that the Greeks knew not of. Recently coined are *catalyst,* a chemical that 'breaks down' others, remaining itself unchanged; *diathermy,* 'a heating through,' by deep heat which warms the tissues beneath the skin, without necessarily heating up the surface.

The only tricky Greek prefix is the so-called 'alpha privative,' *a* or *an* (before vowels), meaning 'not,' or 'apart from.' It is easily confused with Latin *'a,'* a shortened form of either *ab,* 'from,' or *ad,* 'to.' It may also be confounded with the Anglo-Saxon *a,* meaning 'at,' 'in,' 'on.' But the alpha privative is a convenient prefix in some cases where there already exists a compound made with the Latin prefix *in (im),* also meaning 'not,' and where we want to distinguish a different shade of meaning. So Americans and George Bernard Shaw say *amoral,* when they mean 'unconcerned with morality,' 'apart from morals.' This is quite different from 'immoral,' which implies 'something downright opposed to morality.' Starchier lexicographers in England maintain that there is no need for the word *amoral,* which involves coupling a Latin stem, *mori-,* 'custom, right,' with a Greek prefix. They say that the word *unmoral* already exists to express the meaning "unconcerned with morality." But *unmoral* involves blending an Anglo-Saxon prefix, *un,* also meaning 'not,' with a Latin stem. Also, *unmoral* carries to some persons a connotation of wickedness. So where is the difference in purity? Apparently it is a matter of time, which sanctifies a hybrid. The OED gives *unmoral* as in use from 1841, common from 1860. *Amoral,* first used by Stevenson in 1882, is marked as a nonce-word in the original entry; but in the supplement, half-a-dozen English and American examples are given. Apparently *amoral* is gradually making its way.

When it comes to Greek suffixes, there are only eight in use in English, but they are hard-worked. *-Ism* is found in countless words, so much so that we speak of 'isms,' when we mean doctrines that are much discussed,—such as Communism, Bolshevism, Fascism, Nudism, and New Humanism. By changing the ending slightly, we get the suffix *-ist,* which denotes an adherent of any of these 'isms.' *-Sis* or *-sy* denotes an action or state with reference to some concrete stem, as *analy-sis,* 'act of breaking up'; *synthe-sis,* 'act of putting together.'

Then there is the Greek verbal suffix, *-ize,* meaning 'render, make like, combine with, etc.' It forms such compounds as *systematize*, to make systematic'; *automatize*, 'to render automatic,' often used to refer to the reduction of a person to an automaton through hypnosis, or to the process of making a complicated learning-pattern an almost unconscious habit. With Latin stems, the same Greek suffix gives us *civilize, terrorize, actualize*. We also hitch this suffix freely onto proper names: *Hooverize*, for 'using food substitutes, as during Hoover's food administration,'—or 'starving during the last year of his presidency'; *Fletcherize*, for 'chewing food long and minutely, as advocated by the well-known food-faddist'; *Hitlerized* for 'reduced to a pitiable state of subjection by a sadistic and insolent tyranny, full of vaunting, vulgar, and kicking ignorance.' Similarly, we speak of *Hitlerism*, for the ideology accompanying this appalling and brutal tyranny; but we call a follower of this system a *Hitlerite*, using the Latin suffix for euphony.

Besides these regular Greek suffixes, parts of Greek words are sometimes split off, and used to compound new words, by analogy. *Walkathon*, made by analogy with *marathon*, is a case in point. Here folk linguistics is at work with a vengeance. *Walk* is a good Anglo-Saxon word, and to see it provided with an appendage which is part of a Greek word, but in no proper sense a suffix, is curious indeed. And now, made by analogy with *walkathon, talkathon*, for a long-winded talking contest, or a Senatorial filibuster, is creeping into the newspapers. This shows that the language-making processes have little respect for formal rule, and still less regard for the sensibilities of learned purists, who wince at these vulgar words. Worse folk-coinages than *walkathon* and *talkathon* have made their way into the literary language.

These odd words are in the nature of 'sports,' for usually Greek affixes are attached to Greek stems, or at worst, to Latin stems. But it is only right, in embarking on this study of meanings, as tied in with the derivation of words, to note these exceptions. True, the Latin affixes are usually attached to the Latin stems, and Anglo-Saxon affixes to Anglo-Saxon primitives. But the hybrid nature of English is nowhere more clearly illustrated than in the absent-minded habit of hanging Anglo-Saxon suffixes on Latin stems:

painter, pointer, mariner; sackful, bookful; tutoring, signing, painting; scarceness, immenseness, plenteousness; priestcraft, statecraft, dukedom, martyrdom; falsehood, parenthood; membership, scholarship, clerkship; Johnny, Bessie; flowery, palmy, savory; feverish, brutish, tigerish; useless, artless, countless; courtly (adj.); useful, artful, merciful; quarrelsome, cumbersome, venturesome; barbed, colored, turreted, armed; churchward, cityward; millionth, billionth; roundly, rudely, savagely, (adv.); crosswise. (What does each suffix mean? See table at end of chapter.)

None of these seems strange to our ears. Just so the hybrid cross, *automobile*, from the Greek *auto*, 'self,' and the Latin *mobile*, 'moving,' although it may pain purists, is yet sound American English, made so by custom and time-honored prescription. For the most part, however, this difficulty will not arise, in the analysis of words actually before us. Greek suffixes, particularly *-ize*, or *ist*, are often added to Latin stems; but the Romans themselves did this freely, so why should we refrain? As a general rule, however, as we have noted, the Latin stems take Latin affixes, and it is fairly safe to count on this.

By using the complete table of affixes, at the end of the chapter, it is easy to see how many words are made from one stem. Take, for instance, the stem *tend*, also found in the form *tens-* or *tent-*. The primary sense of the root is 'stretch,' hence 'to strive' or 'try.' Prefix to the stem *tend* the prefixes *ad, con, dis, ex, in, por, pre, pro, sub*, and *super*, and the result is a group of common English words: *attend, contend, distend, extend, intend, portend, pretend, subtend, superintend*, and the rare word *protend*,—'to stretch forth, prolong in time.' Soften, in the stem *tend*, the final 'd' to a 't,' or 's,' for most of these words, and add the suffix *-ion* to each in turn, and the outcome is the abstract words which name the acts or states of *attention, contention, distention, extension*, and so on. By experimenting with the second form of the stem, *tent*, we get *extent, intent, portent*, which express a different kind of abstract meaning from their cousins with the *-ion* suffix. One well-known work on word-building also gives *content* from this stem; but it is not directly from it. It comes from the Latin *contentus*, 'satisfied,' the past participle of *continere*, 'to contain,' or 'hold back'; the feeling is that of our word 'self-contained,' used of one who is held within himself, or satisfied. Originally *tenere*, to hold (tight), came from the same root as *tend*, to stretch. But there is a shade of difference. A man is *content* only after he has stretched. This possibility of confusing stems illustrates another danger of the etymological method; but it is a danger well worth the risk. Nothing ventured, nothing gained.

The groundwork for word-analysis once laid, it is easy to see rich possibilities of adding large *blocs* of words to the vocabulary by mastering a single Latin or Greek stem.

The list which follows comprises those classical stems, in their various forms, which have contributed most largely to the vocabulary of English. The Frenchified form of the Latin stem is often given, too. Each stem is followed by a list of derivatives. Numbers in parentheses refer to the frequency of the word, as shown by Thorndike's count. These numbers will indicate which words you should expect to be beyond your ordinary vocabulary range. How does the meaning of the Latin stem afford a clue to the present meaning or meanings of the English word? The sentences which follow the list under each group contain blanks to be filled in with the appropriate word. Before attempting the sentences, study the words in detail.

Take, for example, the word *malediction,* given as coming from the stem DIC, DICT, 'to say' or 'speak.' Break up the word into *male-,* and *-diction.* Note, in the table of Latin prefixes (at the end of the chapter), that *male-* means 'bad' or 'evil.' *Diction* splits up further into *dict,* and the suffix *-ion,* which according to the table of suffixes means 'act of.' We now have

male	DICT	-ion
evil	speaking	act of

So *malediction* means the 'act of speaking evil.' Or, by transference of meaning (see p. 119) it may refer to the evil saying once it has been uttered. It is then a 'curse' or 'evil utterance.'

Or, take as an instance the word *agoraphobia.* It comes from two Greek words, *agora,* 'the marketplace,' and *phobia,* 'fear.' 'Fear of the marketplace' is the literal meaning of the term used in psychiatry to characterize a pathological and abnormal fear of open spaces. The opposite sort of fear is *claustrophobia,* the 'fear of being shut in,' 'the fear of closed places.' *Claustro-* means a closed, hidden, or secret place. We get also the word *cloister* from this stem.

The general procedure to be followed should be clear from these examples.

First, single out the *primary stem* of the word given in the list, (as is done for *trans* act *ion* in the first list below, under AG.)

Second, break the word up into its component parts.

Third, look up the meaning of the prefix or suffix, or both.

Fourth, look up the meaning of any other stem which is used, besides the main stem included. (See list of additional Greek and Latin root-words following Exercises 45 and 46.)

Fifth, from these elements, give the literal meaning of the complete compound.

Sixth, is this its usual present meaning, in actual usage? If not, how has the figurative meaning been achieved? (The processes by which changes in meaning occur will be fully treated in the next chapter, q.v.)

(Study the stems, and the words derived from them, at the rate of five stems a day; or, at the outside, not more than ten. There are several thousand words in these lists. Try to associate the derivative with the right stem, and fix the meaning of that root firmly in your mind. Take plenty of time to look up in the dictionary all the words of which you have the least doubt. Work on these lists, a mastery of which should come close to doubling your vocabulary; but spread out the work over several weeks, while you are continuing with the rest of the book and the accompanying shorter exercises.)

Note: There are in each list more words than there are blanks to be filled in the sentences. There is no connection between the Thorndike frequency numbers in parentheses, and the numbers in the blanks of the sentences. The latter refer to the answers in the key at the end of the text.

LATIN STEMS

46) AG, ACT (ig, g, actu), from *agere, actus:* to do, move, urge on, put in motion, drive.
act (1); ex act (2); man ag e (2); ag ency (4); act or (5); ag ent (5); man ag(e) ment (5); man ag er (6); agitat ion (7); en act (7); prod ig al (8); trans act ion (9); mit ig ate (9); nav ig ate (10); syn ag ogue * (10); ped ag ogue * (11); amb ig (u)ous (12); vari eg ated (12); actu ate (14); co g ent (14); ex ig ency (14); lit igat ion (14); cast ig ate (19); co gitat e (19); man ag(e) able (20); ag enda.
* Strictly, from the Greek through the Latin.

The Communist _____1_____ was crushed. The estate was in _____2_____. The secretary drew up an _____3_____ for the meeting. The Governor was asked to _____4_____ this punishment on the grounds that it was too severe. Tapestries of _____5_____ pattern hung in the great hall.

APT (att, ept), from *aptus:* fit or fitted, the p. p. of obsolete verb *apere,* to fasten, join together.
apt (5); attitude (5); adapt (8); adaptation (8); aptitude (14); adaptability (19); adaptable; inapt; inept.

Can a man's _____1_____ to certain work be measured by _____2_____ tests? He was an _____3_____ bungler. Uttering platitudes in stained glass _____4_____s.

ART (artis, ert), from *ars, artis:* skill, art, method.
art (1); artist (3); artificial (5); artistic (5); artillery (7); artful (8);

inert (8); artifice (9); artisan (9); artless (11); artificer (14); inertia (15); inertly; artifact.

Bromine is an _____1_____ element. The anthropologist dated the _____2_____ by observing the rock stratum in which it was found. No mere man could tell at a glance whether the girl was being _____3_____, _____4_____, or _____5_____, so great was her command of _____6_____ .. (With apologies to Gertrude Stein.)

AUD, AUDIT (audi, edi, ey, eis), from *audire, auditus:* to hear.
obey (2); audience (4); obedience (4); obedient (5); disobey (5); audible (8); auditor (10); disobedience (10); obeisance (11); auditory (12); auditorium (13); inaudible (13); audit.

An _____1_____ speaker cannot hope to hold the attention of his _____2_____. Outward _____3_____ in deed is often accompanied by inward _____4_____ in thought. The _____5_____ at the State College showed that the funds had been juggled.

CAN, CANT (cent, chant), from *canere, cantus:* to sing.
accent (4); chant (5); enchant (5); enchantment (7); cant (11); accentuate (13); canto (14); recantation (14); recant (15); canticle (16).

The _____1_____ of the morning was _____2_____ by the heavy dew glistening on every fern frond. A _____3_____ of a poem is like a chapter of a story. Galileo was forced to _____4_____. In march rhythm the first beat in each measure should be _____5_____.

CAP, CAPT, CAPTUS (cip, ceiv, cept, ceipt, ceit), from *capere, captus:* to take, seize, hold.
except (1); accept (2); occupy (2); deceive (2); principal (2); perceive (3); capable (3); conceive (3); capture (3); occupation (3); capacity (4); captive (4); exception (4); reception (5); captivity (5); conceit (5); deceit (5); capacious (6); exceptional (6); precept (6); participate (7); anticipation (8); incapable (8); principality (8); susceptible (8); acceptable (9); deception (9); emancipation (9); municipal (10); capability (11); recipient (12); participle (15); incipient (16); participant (16).

_____1_____ is greater than realization. Her _____2_____ apron pockets caused her to be the _____3_____ of varied articles of importance to the very young, for 'safe-keeping.' So _____4_____ was he to feminine charm that he was utterly _____5_____ of refusing to grant the slightest wish of any of his lady parishioners.

CAPIT (cipit, cipic, capt, chatt, catt), from *caput, capitis:* the head.
captain (1); cattle (2); capital (2); chapter (4); precipitate (7); capitalist (9); precipitous (10); chattel (11); precipitation (11); capitulation (15); recapitulation (20); precipitant; occipital.

His ____1____ of the salient points in the report interested all. The dislodging of a single stone may ____2____ an avalanche; particularly where the slope is ____3____. Any ____4____ action at this time may bring our creditors down about our ears. The sudden ____5____ of the enemy was a surprise to all of us.

CED, CESS (ceed, ceas), from *cedere, cessus:* to go, yield, give up. proceed (2); success (2); succeed (2); proceed (2); exceed (3); process (3); successful (3); recess (3); ancestor (4); procession (4); access (5); decease (5); precede (6); predecessor (7); concede (9); intercession; procedure (9); accessory (10); cede; recede (10); accessible (11); antecedent (11); cessation (11); precedent (11); accession (14); abscess (10).

His ____1____ in my behalf saved me from being expelled. The ____2____ of my ____3____ made possible my ____4____ to the position which I now hold. It was not the dress itself, but the ____5____s she wore with it, which made it an unusual costume. The extension of our public highways has made ____6____ even the most remote parts of the Rocky Mountains.

CERN, CRET (cre), from *cernere, cretus:* to see, to sift, to distinguish, to separate. certain (1); secret (2); concern (2); secretary (3); decree (4); discern (4); certainly (5); certificate (5); discreet (6); discretion (7); secrecy (8); secretion (8); certify (10); excretion (11); indiscreet (11); discernment (12); discernible (18); secretive.

____1____ is the better part of valor. It was easily ____2____ from his manner that he desired the utmost ____3____ in regard to his movements on July 27. People of ____4____ natures are inclined to be ____5____ in their conduct.

CLAM, CLAMAT (claim), from *clamare, clamatus:* to call, to cry out. claim (2); exclaim (3); proclaim (3); clamor (4); exclamation (7); proclamation (7); reclaim (7); clamorous (8); acclaim (13); reclamation (13); claimant (15); declamation (15); declaim (20); exclamatory (20).

The ____1____ was received with great ____2____ by the townspeople. ____3____ remarks often punctuate the sentences of excitable people. The first ____4____ of the reward was entitled to it. John's ____5____ won first prize in the oratory contest.

CLAUS (clos), (clud, clus, in compounds), from *claudere, clausus:* to shut. close (1); include (2); conclude (3); closet (3); exclusive (4); inclose (4); clause (5); conclusion (5); exclude (7); cloister (9); exclusion (9); seclude (11); seclusion (13); preclude (14); recluse (14); closure (17); inclusion (20).

One's life as a ____1____ necessarily ____2____s extensive contact with the outside world. One is forced to ____3____ from your remarks that you are unalterably opposed to the ____4____ of a new course in the curriculum. It is proper to ____5____ the words of a title in quotation marks.

COR, CORD, CORDI (cour), from *cor, cordis:* the heart.

according (2); record (2); courage (2); encourage (3); accordingly (3); cordial (3); accord (4); discourage (4); courageous (6); discord (6); concord (7); core (7); encouragement (8); recorder (13); concordance (16).

The ____1____ onslaught you made on the head of the institution expresses views which are in complete ____2____ with those held by the majority of our group. The resultant ____3____ is most unpleasant, but if the eventual result is one of ____4____, we extend to you our most ____5____ thanks.

CRED, CREDIT (cre), from *credere, creditus:* to believe, trust to.

credit (3); creditor (6); credulity (7); creed (8); credulous (8); incredulous (9); discredit (10); creditable (12); incredulity (12); credential (13); miscreant (13); credible (14); accredit (15); credence (15); incredible (7).

You have given a ____1____ account of yourself. The ____2____ adventures of Popeye the Sailor are fascinating alike to old and young. His ____3____ placed him at the mercy of all sorts of speculators and promoters. Never, my son, in word or deed, do anything to the ____4____ of our family name. He lived by a simple ____5____.

CUR, CURAT (ur), from *curare, curatus:* to take care of, care for, heal.

sure (1); secure (2); cure (2); procure (4); assurance (5); insurance (5); security (5); accurate (7); surety (7); accuracy (8); reassure (8); curate (11); curator (16); inaccurate (16); insecurity (19).

What ____1____ have I to believe that you can ____2____ proper ____3____ for this note? A ____4____ is an assistant to the clergyman, while a ____5____ refers to the person in charge, as of a museum. The ____6____ of detail in this report ____7____s me as to your ability to fill the position.

CURR, CURS (curri, corri, cur, cor, couri, cours), from *currire, cursus:* to run, more quickly.

course (1); current (2); occur (2); incur (5); excursion (6); corridor (7); occurrence (7); succor (7); recur (9); courier (11); courser (12); concur (13); cursory (16); discursive (16); precursor (17).

A few days of rainy, windy weather is often the ____1____ of spring. A ____2____ glance sufficed to furnish the reason for the ____3____ of this phenomenon. It is to be hoped the judges will ____4____ in their opinions. This long, ____5____ treatise served to weaken, rather than to strengthen, his cause.

DAT, from *dare, datus:* to give, do, plan, yield, put.
add (1); date (1); addition (2); render (2); surrender (4); tradition (4); edition (6); editor (8); editorial (8); perdition (9); rendezvous (11); traditional (12); edit (13); datum, data (14); antedate (15); extradition (16); dative (13); abscond (20); editorship (20); extradite (20).

Common use of a new word in the language usually ____1____ its appearance in the dictionary. All the ____2____ in regard to the qualifications of the different candidates for the ____3____ is now ready for examination. ____4____ papers are being made out to effect the return of the bank cashier who ____5____ed with the funds.

DIC, DICT, from *dicere, dictus:* to speak, say.
interdict (12); diction (14); predicate (14); abdication (15); addict (16); contradict (16); malediction (17); dictum (17); dictatorial; ditto; adjudicate; dictaphone; dictograph; valedictory; valediction.

The flawless ____1____ of this self-educated man amazes all who are acquainted with his humble origin. These facts ____2____ my original contention. The old crone's evil countenance served all the more to emphasize the force of her ____3____. Facts which ____4____ each other are useless as criteria for judgment.

DIGN (digni, deign, daint, dain), from *dignus:* worthy.
dignity (4); dainty (4); disdain (4); indignation (4); dignify (5); indignant (6); disdainful (9); indignity (10); dignitary (13); daintiness; condign.

No ____1____ should ever be forced to endure the ____2____ of inadequate recognition. With ill-concealed ____3____ Mary Ann shrugged her shoulders. His ____4____ at this affront was equally ill-concealed.

DUC, DUCT (duk, duch, duit), from *ducere, ductus:* to lead, to bring forth.
produce (2); conduct (2); product (2); education (3); introduce (3); reduce (3); duke (3); induce (4); conductor (5); production (5); educate (6); introduction (6); seduce (6); duchess (7); reproduce (7); reproduction (7); productive (8); conduit (9); dukedom (9); conduce (11); deduce (11); deduct (11); aqueduct (12); conducive (12); deduction (13); viaduct (13); ducal (14); seductive (14); ducat (15); adduce (16); ductible (16); educe (16); traduce (16); duchy (16); abduct (19); induction (19); abduction; conducible; deducible; induct; seduction.

His manners and ____1____ were not conducive to his ____2____ the ____3____ to ____4____ an ____5____ to the ____6____. ____7____d by a large sum in ____8____s, the prince ____9____ed the princess, ____10____ed her guards to ____11____ her to the border, and returned to the ____12____, where he publicly ____13____ed her to her people.

EQU (equi), from *aequus:* equal, just.

equal (1); equality (6); equity (6); unequal (6); equator (6); equivalent (7); adequate (8); equation (8); inadequate (9); equatorial (10); inequality (11); equable (12); equitable (13); equivocal (13); equinox (14); equinoctial (15); equanimity (16); coequal; equivalence.

The actor's performance was said by the critics to have been ____1____; which is ____2____ to saying that it was third-rate. During the ____3____ gales, the ship was just crossing the ____4____ when it was lost with all hands.

FAC, FACT, FACTUR (fic, fair, feat, feas, fash, featur, futur), from *facere, factus:* to do, to move.

fact (1); perfect (1); difficult (2); effect (2); fashion (2); affair (2); benefit (2); feature (2); manufacture (2); sacrifice (2); affect (3); factory (3); official (3); sufficient (3); affection (3); defeat (3); difficulty (3); perfection (4); artificial (5); defect (5); faculty (5); feat (5); forfeit (5); imperfect (5); certificate (5); edifice (5); faction (6); fashionable (6); deficiency (7); defective (7); effective (7); facility (7); factor (7); beneficial (8); counterfeit (8); efficacy (8); efficient (8); infection (8); affectation (9); artifice (9); benefactor (9); efficiency (9); facile (10); facilitate (10); forfeiture (10); surfeit (10); unaffected (10); imperfection (11); proficient (11); feasible (12); inefficiency (12); sufficiency (12); confection (13); affected (14); disaffection (14); manufactory (14); unification (14); beneficiary (15); defection (15); edification (15); efficacious (15); malefactor (15); pontifical (16); putrefaction (16); refection (16); versification (16); exemplification; comfit (19); facsimile.

Samson ____1____ed the Philistines single-handed with the jaw-bone of an ass: a ____2____ of great ____3____, which earned him the title of ____4____ to mankind. King John of England died of a ____5____ of lampreys. This is an historical ____6____. He neglected the wound, which had become ____7____ by poison, until putrefaction set in, costing him the ____8____ of his arm. This ____9____ was overcome by an ____10____ limb. He became very ____11____ in manipulating this, and after receiving a ____12____ from business college, he was able to prove himself a thoroughly ____13____ secretary. Later on he received an ____14____ position in a large ____15____ of buttons, both because of his ____16____ and the kindness of a ____17____. Here, however, he found his colleagues split up into ____18____s. He found himself disliked from the start, which did not _____19_____ his advancement. Finally he was obliged to _____20_____ his position; after which he went to the bad, had his head turned by _____21_____ society, and when last heard of was having trouble with the police for passing _____22_____ money. Probably he will contrive a _____23_____ plan of escape, or at least present _____24_____ reasons for his nefarious deeds.

FER LAT (lay), from *ferre, latus:* to bear, carry.

difference (1); different (1); offer (1); suffer (1); delay (2); elate (2); prefer (2); differ (3); refer (3); relate (3); relation (3); relative (3); confer (4); conference (4); fertile (4); transfer (4); translate (4); ferry (5); reference (5); fertilize (6); preference (7); prelate (7); sufferance (7); circumference (8); defer (8); fertility (8); infer (8); proffer (8); translation (8); inference (9); deference (11); referendum (11); superlative (11); coniferous (14); referee (17); vociferous (17); correlation (19); pestiferous (20); transference (20); ablative; floriferous; fructiferous; illative; oblate; prolate.

The _____1_____ at the football game _____2_____ several _____3_____ reasons for the _____4_____. The _____5_____ _____6_____d in church that there was no _____7_____ between the _____8_____ of animals and their _____9_____ size. This statement was received with _____10_____ applause by all his _____11_____s who were present. A _____12_____ plant bears flowers; a _____13_____ tree bears fruit; a _____14_____ tree is _____15_____ from these because it produces cones. Johnson was allowed into the _____16_____ chamber only on _____17_____. The _____18_____-boat was _____19_____ed for several hours in the vicinity of a circular swamp of large _____20_____, which emitted a _____21_____ odor.

FORM, from *forma:* figure, shape, appearance.

form (1); inform (2); information (3); uniform (3); reform (4); transform (5); conform (5); deform (6); formal (6); formation (6); formula (8); informal (8); reformation (8); transformation (8); deformity (9); formality (9); formulate (9); reformer (11); uniformity (12); conformation (15); formulation (15); informer (15); conformable (16); formulary (17); reformatory (17); formalism (20); informality.

After a _____1_____ had been removed by a surgical operation, a _____2_____ had been worked in her appearance. The temperance _____3_____ could not _____4_____ to the _____5_____ies of the stag party. On entering the reformatory he was requested to fill out a _____6_____, giving all _____7_____ about himself. Then he was dressed in the official _____8_____, which was considered to be more _____9_____ to his new status in life.

FRANG, FRACT, FRACTUR, from *frangere, fractus:* to break.

frail (3); fraction (5); fragment (5); frailty (6); suffrage (7); fragile (8); fracture (9); infringe (10); refractory (14); infraction (16); refraction (18); frangible; inrefrangible, infringement, irrefragable, refrangible.

A _____1_____ from a newspaper dated during the woman _____2_____ riots demonstrates that even _____3_____ women were capable of violent _____4_____s of the King's peace, many receiving complicated _____5_____s in the cause. This tends to detract from the legend of the _____6_____ of the gentler sex; though, of course, the suffragettes represented only a _____7_____ of the entire female population of England.

GER, GEST, GESTUR (gist, gistr, jest), from *gerere, gestus:* to bear, or carry on, perform.

register (2); suggest (3); jest (4); gesture (6); suggestion (6); digest (7); digestion (7); digestive (8); indigestible (9); indigestion (9); registration (9); congestion (10); belligerent (12); congest (12); jester (12); gesticulation (15); gerund (19); congeries; vicegerent.

The Latin professor always became _____1_____ on the subject of _____2_____s. A _____3_____ in the class _____4_____ed that this was attributable not so much to enthusiasm as to _____5_____. His face would become _____6_____ed, his _____7_____s wild, until finally, just after _____8_____ week at the university, the _____9_____ official, acting in the absence of the President, was obliged to remove him from office.

GRAT (gratu, grati, grai, gre), from *gratus:* pleasing, deserving thanks, thankful; *gratis,* by favor, without reward.

grace (1); agree (2); agreeable (3); disgrace (3); gracious (3); grateful (3); gratitude (4); disagreeable (6); congratulation (7); gratify (7); disagree (9); gratification (9); graceless (11); disagreement (12); ingrate (18); gratuity (19); ingratitude (20).

This _____1_____ caused much _____2_____ among his colleagues. They _____3_____d among themselves that his fall from _____4_____ was a subject for mutual _____5_____. Others, however, _____6_____d with this opinion, and, in _____7_____ for his past services, chipped in with contributions and presented him with a large _____8_____.

HAB, HABIT (ab, habitu, hibit), from *habere, habitus:* to have, hold.

able (1); debt (2); habit (3); ability (4); enable (4); exhibit (4); inhabit (4); inhabitant (5); prohibit (5); exhibition (6); habitation (6); debtor (7); prohibition (7); habitual (8); disable (9); habitable (10); inhibit (14); habitat (15); inhibition (15); debility (16); habiliment (17); rehabilitation (17); prohibitive (18).

However, a natural _____1_____ in his moral fibre, encouraged by the release of _____2_____s attendant upon his removal from the college atmosphere, drove him at last into bad _____3_____s. When the gratuity was spent, he got deeply into _____4_____, neglected to pay the rent of his modest _____5_____, and was finally reduced to pawning his

___6___s to ___7___ him to purchase the bare necessities of life. An automobile accident finally ___8___d him completely, and he is now to be found making an ___9___ of himself at street corners with a hurdy-gurdy and a monkey.

JECT (jet, jut), from *jacere, jactus:* to lay, throw, cast.
object (1); subject (1); reject (4); jet (5); objection (5); project (5); jut (6); abject (7); adjacent (7); adjective (8); conjecture (8); inject (8); projection (8); subjection (8); eject (10); dejection (11); injection (10); rejection (13); objective (14); projectile (14); ejaculation (15); interjection (15); jetty (15); trajectory (20); subjective (20); conjectural; ejection; jetsam.

When a young author gets his first ___1___ slip it casts him into a state of deep ___2___. His misery is so ___3___, that he feels like flinging himself into the sea from the nearest ___4___. In most cases, however, the mood passes after some ___5___ of unsuitable language. The door of the saloon burst open, and a wretched piece of human ___6___ was ___7___ed with violence. His condition was so bad that he was taken to an ___8___ hospital and given an ___9___. His chances of recovery were said to be ___10___.

JUNG, JUNCT, JUNCTUR (join, joint, jointur), from *jungere, junctur:* to bind, connect, unite.
join (1); joint (3); adjoin (5); enjoin (6); conjunction (8); injunction (8); conjugation (9); junction (9); adjunct (10); conjugate (10); rejoin (11); subjunctive (11); conjugal (15); joiner (15); juncture (15); subjugate (15); disjoin (16); conjoin (18); conjunctive (20); jointly; disjunction; jointer; jointure; conjuncture.

Having completed several ___1___s, the ___2___ went to his house, which he shared ___3___ with his wife, with whom he lived in ___4___ harmony. Later in life he attempted completely to ___5___ his wife to his will, but she obtained an ___6___ against him in the courthouse which ___7___ed their small property.

LEG, LECT, LECTUR (lig, less), from *legere, lectus:* to read, gather, choose.
lesson (1); collect (2); elect (2); neglect (2); collection (3); election (3); lecture (4); legion (4); coil (5); legend (5); selection (5); dialect (7); recollect (7); colleague (8); cull (8); intellect (8); legacy (8); collector (9); intelligible (11); elegance (12); eligible (13); legible (14); predilection (15); dialectics; illegible.

The bill- ___1___'s ___2___ would not make him ___3___ for ___4___ for the command of the Foreign ___5___. Were it not for the fact that he had recently received a large ___6___, enabling him to live with some degree of ___7___, he would have been quite ___8___ed by the best people at the fashionable ___9___ on ___10___. I ___11___ that he always had had a passion for out-of-the-way ___12___s, and odd folk- ___13___s. His handwriting was ___14___, in spite of his large ___15___ of antique pens.

MAN (manu, main), from *manus:* the hand.
manner (1); maintain (2); manage (2); manifest (4); manure (6); manuscript (7); manual (8); emancipation (9); manifestation (10); manoeuvre (11); manipulate (14); manufactory (14); manacle (15); manicure (15); manifesto (16); amanuensis (18); manumission (20); bimanous; quadrumanous.

He ___1___d with difficulty to get agreement on the ___2___, after which he was obliged to send for his ___3___ to copy the ___4___. The ___5___ of the slaves struck the ___6___s from the limbs of thousands of negroes. The ___7___ in which the ___8___ ___9___ed the ___10___ was a good advertisement for the ___11___ of instructions in the ___12___ which he had read before taking the job.

MITT, MISS (mit, mis), from *mittere, missu:* to send, cast, throw, let go.
promise (1); admit (2); permit (2); commission (3); commit (3); committee (3); submit (3); omit (4); mission (5); remit (5); compromise (7); surmise (8); emit (9); intermittent (9); remittance (9); submissive (9); transmit (9); admittance (10); emissary (12); intermit (14); missile (14); missive (14); remiss (15); demise; commissary; manumit.

He ___1___d faithfully not to ___2___ the ___3___of justice into the house. Will you ___4___ me to ___5___ to you a small ___6___? As my car was out of ___7___, I was obliged to ___8___ to much indignity while walking through the tenement district. One man actually hurled a heavy ___9___ in my direction.

MOD (modi), from *modus:* measure, manner, fashion.
model (2); modern (2); mode (3); modest (3); moderate (3); accommodation (6); commodity (7); modify (9); commodious (10); modification (12); moderator (16); modulation (10); modish (17); commode (19); modicum (19); modal.

Having expensive tastes, she would have liked to live in a more ___1___ style than her ___2___ income permitted. Her entertainments were limited by the size of her house, which was not sufficiently ___3___, nor, as it had been in the family for many generations, was it ___4___ enough. In his Symphony in D Minor, the composer Cesar Franck has introduced many interesting ___5___s from key to key.

MOV, MOT (mo), from *movere, motus:* to move.
moment (1); move (1); automobile (2); motion (2); remove (2); mo-

tive (3); movement (3); motor (4); remote (4); emotion (5); locomotive (5); mob (5); movable (6); promotion (6); commotion (7); removal (8); immovable (9); momentous (12); momentum (15); motif (15); movie (15); mobilize (18).

My stomach was upset by the irregular ____1____ of the ____2____, which, although it was a V-8, swayed more and more as its ____3____ increased. The agitator created such a ____4____ in the ____5____-house, where he was endeavoring to harangue the ____6____, that militia had to be ____7____d to effect his ____8____.

NOT, from *noscere, notus,* or *gnoscere, gnotus:* to know.
note (1); notice (1); noble (2); ignorant (3); notion (3); ignorance (4); notable (5); notify (5); ignoble (6); denote (7); notorious (7); recognition (8); notary (9); notation (13); cognizance (15); cognition (18); incognito (19); annotation (20); connote; connotation; denotation.

____1____-men frequently travel ____2____ in order to keep the masses ____3____ of their identity. He received a short legal ____4____ from his ____5____, ____6____ing him of the court's ____7____ of the justice of his claim. When the book was returned to the library it was found to be filled with marginal ____8____s in pencil. The previous borrower professed complete ____9____ of this violation of the rules. The ____10____ crimes of the ____11____ gangster ____12____d his base nature.

PAND, PANS, PASS (pac), from *pandere, pansus* or *passus:* to spread, step.
pass (1); pace (2); compass (2); passage (3); passenger (3); surpass (5); expand (6); trespass (6); expansion (7); encompass (9); expanse (9); expansive (13); passable (16).

During the ____1____ of the ship from Accra to Seccondee, several of the first-class ____2____s ____3____ed upon the privacy of the bridge to look at the ____4____. A forward ____5____ placed the ball in Jimson's hands, and he began to rush up the field at a terrific ____6____. The windows looked out upon a wide ____7____ of moorland.

PAR,* PARAT (ver, pair), from *parare, paratus:* to see, to get ready, or make ready.
prepare (1); several (1); repair (2); preparation (3); separation (5); sever (5); apparatus (7); preparatory (9); reparation (13); dissever (15); irreparable (15); separable.

When the ____1____ exploded during the experiment, the damage done was ____2____ because of the lack of materials for ____3____.

* Do not confuse with *par,* equal.

In decapitation, death results from the ____4____ing of the spinal cord. When all ____5____s had been made for the picnic, it was found necessary to ____6____ ____7____ extra baskets of food.

PART (port, parti, par, pars), from *pars, partis:* a piece, portion, share. part (1); party (1); apart (2); depart (2); particular (2); portion (2); department (3); parcel (3); partner (3); proportion (3); impart (4); apartment (5); departure (5); partial (5); particle (6); impartial (7); partition (7); compartment (10); counterpart (11); apportion (15); parse; partitive.

At the birthday ____1____ he found that his dancing ____2____ was ____3____ to cocktails. Mabel never came out of a ____4____ store without leaving her ____5____s behind her. He was ravenously hungry, but there was not a ____6____ of food left in the larder so he ____7____ed from his two-room ____8____ and went to a restaurant, where he was very ____9____ in his instructions to the waiter to bring him double ____10____s of everything. The two sleeping ____11____s were separated only by a flimsy wooden ____12____. To ____13____ a sentence is to split it up into its component ____14____s.

PET, PETIT (petu, peat), from *petere, petitus:* to ask, to seek, to rush at, to fly to. repeat (2); appetite (3); petition (5); competition (6); repetition (7); compete (8); competitor (8); impetuous (8); competent (9); impetus (11); incompetent (14); petulant (15); centripetal.

When his ____1____s for more money from home remained unanswered, he lost his temper and became ____2____. A watch-maker who is too ____3____ at his work will do an ____4____ job. A locomotive moves by the ____5____ given to it by compressed steam. His ____6____ was so enormous that he had no ____7____ ____8____s at the pie-eating contest.

PLAC, PLACIT (pleas, plais, plead, plea), from *placere, placitus:* to please. please (1); pleasant (1); pleasure (1); plead (3); plea (6); placid (7); pleasing (7); complacent (10); implacable (10); pleasantry (12); complaisance (16); placate.

If you insist on doing what you ____1____, you will not be very ____2____ company. Old age is an ____3____ enemy of ____4____. After receiving a legacy of $1,000,000 he contemplated the future with a ____5____ mind.

PLIC, PLICAT, PLICIT (ple, pli, ply, ploy, play, plex), from *plicare, plicatus:* to fold, bend, turn. reply (1); simple (1); apply (2); employ (2); application (3); display

(3); multiply (3); employee (4); simplicity (4); comply (5); ply (5); multiplication (6); complex (7); employer (7); imply (8); supplication (8); plait (9); simplify (9); supple (9); complication (10); pliant (12); implication (14); implicit (14); explicit (15); multiplicity (15); pliable (16); duplicity (17); duplex (18); replica (19); plexus (20); complicity; misapply; deploy.

He received no ____1____ to his ____2____ for ____3____. Grade-school work is too ____4____ for college graduates to do accurately. When you ____5____ for a job, always ____6____ with the suggestions of your prospective ____7____. The automobile industry ____8____s many workers. Rabbits ____9____ with great rapidity. Her hair was ____10____ed with great ____11____ in a single ____12____. In spite of his efforts to ____13____ his life, it became increasingly full of ____14____s. On the mantel-shelf stood a ____15____ in marble of the Statue of Liberty. Athletes keep their muscles ____16____ by exercise. However, severe blows in the solar ____17____ will generally cause them some inconvenience.

PON, POSIT, POSTUR (pound, post), from *ponere, positus:* to place. post (1); opposite (2); deposit (3); position (3); composition (4); postage (4); compound (5); disposition (5) opposition (5); positive (5); postal (5); proposition (5); opponent (7); exposition (8); posture (8); impostor (9); postpone (9); component (10); imposition (10); preposition (10); supposition (10); deposition (12); composite (13); decomposition (13); exponent (13); depository (15); interposition (15); compost (16); juxtaposition (16); impost (17); apposite (18); expositor (19); propound; positivist; transposition.

The promoter claimed to have discovered large ____1____s of gold in Southern Oregon, but investors, when he disappeared with their savings, believed him to have been an ____2____. Thinkers who ____3____ the theory that man has no free-will are called ____4____s. It is an ____5____ on the good nature of one's fellows to expect to live without working. The two ____6____s in a boxing match try to knock each other out. The Japanese are great ____7____s of the art of jiu-jitsu. A ____8____ apartment is composed of two apartments in ____9____.

PORT, PORTAT, from *portare, portatus:* to carry, convey, bear along. important (1); report (1); port (2); sport (2); support (2); import (3); transport (3); porter (4); transportation (4); export (5); deportment (8); portable (3); purport (9); importation (10); exportation (13); deportation (15); disport (15); comport (15); deport (19).

An alien who becomes a public charge is liable to ____1____ from the nearest ____2____. The great summer ____3____ in England is cricket, a game which has been ____4____ed into America. In case of fire it is highly ____5____ to ____6____ immediately to the fire department. A husband is expected to ____7____ his wife. A hill-billy cannot be expected to ____8____ himself in a drawing-room with any degree of ease.

PREHEND, PREHENS (prign, prent, pris, priz), from *prehendere, prehensus:* to seize, lay hold of.
apprehend (6); apprehension (7); apprentice (9); apprise (15); apprisal; comprehend (9); comprehension (11); comprise (7); enterprise (5); impregnable (12); prehensile; prison (2); prize (2); reprehend (14); reprehension; reprisal (14); surprise (1); surprisal.

The inventor's young ____1____ ____2____d his employer by his wide ____3____ of the subject. As a reward for his great ____4____ in experimental work, he was awarded a ____5____. The monkey seizes the branches of the trees with his ____6____ tail. The ____7____ at Alcatraz Island is believed to be ____8____.

QUER, QUISIT (quir, quest), from *quaerere, quaesitus:* to seek, search for, ask, inquire.
acquire (3); acquisition (8); acquisitive (20); conquer (2); conqueror (4); conquest (3); disquisition (16); exquisite (5); inquest (16); inquire (3); inquisitive (8); inquisition (9); perquisite (17); question (1); request (2); quest (5); require (1); requirement (7); requisition (14); requisite (7).

The Norman ____1____ of England by William the ____2____ took place in 1066. An extremely ____3____ man, he would always ask most inconvenient ____4____s. The student's adviser gave him a long ____5____ on scholastic ____6____s. A waiter would not be able to live were it not for ____7____s in the form of tips. When the research was finished Andrew sent in a ____8____ for the money. The latest ____9____ of the local museum is a hat worn by Dillinger.

RAP, RAPT, RAPTUR (rav, rept), from *rapere, raptus:* to seize, snatch, hurry away.
rapid (1); rapids (1); rapine (7); rapacious (14); rapt (6); rapturous (4); ravage (8); raven (3); ravenous (9); ravine (11); ravishing; surrepititious.

His ____1____ gaze was fixed on his friend in the canoe, who was about to shoot the ____2____s. Although she was a woman of ____3____ beauty, she possessed a ____4____ appetite, which, for the sake of decorum, she could only satisfy ____5____ly in a locked room. The German army ____6____d Flanders with murder and ____7____.

REG, RECT (roy, rig, regi, ress, recti), from *regere, rectus:* to rule, direct, arrange.

address (2); correct (2); corrective (20); dress (1); dressing (1); dressy (1); direct (1); direction (2); director (4); directory (13); erect (2); erection (10); incorrigible (14); insurgent (12); insurrection (7); irregular (4); real (1); realty (5); realist (12); reality (5); rectify (10); rectitude (12); rector (9); redress (6); regal (5); regimen (13); regiment (6); regnant; reign (2); regular (2); resource (6); resurrection (9); ruler (3); source (3).

Convalescents from infantile paralysis are much benefited by a rigid _____1_____ of _____2_____ exercise. During the _____3_____ of King John, who was a bad _____4_____, there were many _____5_____s. Edgar Allen Poe, though he was a great poet, was an _____6_____ drunkard. The _____7_____ of the parish, who was _____8_____ in black, spoke in church concerning the _____9_____ of a new parish hall.

RUPT, RUPTUR (rout, rut), from *rumpere, ruptus:* to break, destroy, burst.

abrupt (7); bankrupt (8); corrupt (4); corruption (6); disrupt (20); eruption (9); incorruptible (13); interrupt (3); irruption (15); rout (6); route (3); routine (8); rupture (13); rut (13).

The sight of a volcano in _____1_____ is calculated to _____2_____ the regular _____3_____ of life. When it came to taking bribes, the banker was quite _____4_____. Some people claim that this is why he went _____5_____. The U. S. immigration officials tightened up on issuing visas to aliens owing to the great _____6_____ of cheap labor and criminals from Europe and the Orient.

SAL, SALT (sali, sili, sail, sult, sault), from *salire, saltus:* to leap, rush, issue suddenly forth.

assail (5); assault (4); desultory (11); exult (7); exultant (13); exultation (8); resilient; result (2); resultant (15); salacious (5); salient (13); salmon (6); saltation.

The thug _____1_____ his victim with a blackjack. The fisherman was not a talkative man; he confined his conversation to a few _____2_____ remarks about _____3_____ canning. His illogical arguments left open many _____4_____ points. Seized by divine frenzy, the congregation raised their voices in a hymn of _____5_____.

SCRIB, SCRIPT, SCRIPTUR (scriv, scrip), from *scribere, scriptus:* to write.

ascribe (7); ascription (20); circumscribe (12); circumscription; conscription (18); describe (2); description (3); inscription (7); manuscript (7); nondescript (16); post-script (6); prescribe (4); prescription (9); proscribe (14); rescript (16); scribble (9); scribe (9); script (14); scripture (5); subscribe (7); superscription (14); transcribe (12).

His activities as a football player were somewhat ____1____d by the fact that he had only one leg. The plays of Shakespeare are frequently ____2____d to Bacon. At the end of the ____3____, which was written with pencil, there was a ____4____ containing a quotation from the ____5____s.

SED, SESS (see, sidu, siz, sid), from *sedere, sessus:* to sit.
assess (11); assiduous (10); assize (15); insidious (11); possess (2); prepossess (16); preside (5); president (2); reside (4); residue (10); resident (5); residuary.

Be ____1____ in your studies, my boy, and you will grow to be ____2____. The ____3____ influence of power made itself felt as soon as the tyrant ____4____ed the insignia of office. ____5____s of sulphur were found in the vat.

SENT, SENS (senti, sensu), from *sentire, sensus:* to feel, think, perceive.
assent (7); consent (2); dissent (9); nonsense (5); nonsensical; presentiment (13); resent (7); resentful (17); scent (16); sense (2); senseless (7); sensible (4); sensibility (9); sensual (9); sensuous (14); sentence (3); sententious (13); sentiment (5).

No ____1____ man could ____2____ to this ____3____ proposal. Why should you express your petty ____4____s in such ____5____ words? I ____6____ your using this cheap ____7____, Mary. Although he had a ____8____ that the ____9____ would be severe, now that it was pronounced at last, he felt ____10____ of the judge's ____11____ cruelty.

SEQU, SECUT (sec, sequi, su, sect, suit), from *sequi, secutus:* to follow.
consecution; consecutive (10); consequence (3); consequently; ensue (5); execution (5); executive (5); executor (8); obsequies (12); obsequious (10); persecute (5); persecution (6); prosecute (9); prosecution (9); prosecutor (18); pursue (2); pursuance (16); pursuit (4); second (1); secondary (7); sect (6); sectary (15); sectarian (18); sue (6); suit (1); suitable (4); suite (9); suitor (7).

Tormented by ideas of ____1____, he lived in constant fear of being ____2____d by the ____3____s of his wife's estate. In ____4____ of his friend's desire, he made ____5____ arrangements for the most elaborate ____6____ the town has ever seen. At last the great ____7____, wearing a shabby ____8____, appeared at the door of his ____9____, surrounded by ____10____ underlings.

SERV,* SERVAT, from *servare, servatus:* to save, protect, give heed to.
conserve (8); conservation (7); conservative (7); conservatory (11);

* Do not confuse with 'to serve' from *servio, servire.*

observe (2); observer (8); observance (7); observation (4); preservation (8); observation (4); preserve (2); preserver (10); preservative (12); reservation (7); reserve (3); reservedness; reservoir (8); unobserved (9); unreserved (15).

A member of the ____1____ party slipped, ____2____, into the ____3____, where radicals, having no fear of ____4____s, aired their views without the slightest ____5____. An ____6____ obedience to the law will ____7____ you from grievance. This large ____8____ is full of creosote, which, as you know, is a good ____9____.

SIGN, from *signum:* a sign.
assign (3); assignment (9); assignation; consign (7); countersign (18); consignment (18); design (3); designer (10); designation (13); insignificance; resign (3); resigned; resignation (8); sign (1); signal (4); signet (8); signature (5); signify (5); significance (7); signification (19); undesigned; undersigned.

She did not come to the ____1____ and he had to ____2____ himself to a dull evening. The whole affair is really of no ____3____, I merely lost my ____4____ ring. At a ____5____ from the manager, the famous ____6____ himself came to wait on the important customers. The crating is so rotten, I doubt that this ____7____ of goods will reach its destination.

SPEC, SPIC, SPECT (spici. speci, spy, spi), from *specere (spicere), spictus:* to look at
aspect (5); auspices (13); auspicious (11); circumspect (13); circumspection (15); despicable (15); especial (2); espial; espionage (18); expect (1); expectant (8); expectation (5); inauspicious (16); inspect (7); inspection (7); introspective; perspective (9); perspicacity; perspicuity (19); prospect (3); prospective (9); respect (2); respectable (7); respective (5); retrospect (14); retrospection (19); special (2); specification (12); specify (12); specimen (6); specious (11); spectacle (4); spectacles; spectator; speculation (8); spice (3); spy (2); suspicion (5).

The ____1____ was staged under the ____2____ of the Association of Maiden Ladies; the ____3____s were held spellbound, and many a ____4____-glass was trained on this or that trim ankle. We had every reason to ____5____ the ____6____ general. The ____7____ did not please us much, especially, as he had the knack of appearing at the most ____8____ moments. Her ____9____ husband, a magnificent ____10____ of manhood, comes from a very ____11____, if somewhat dull family. In his conversation he impresses one as a man of great ____12____; his writing, unfortunately, lacks ____13____.

STA, STAT, SIST (st, stet), from *stare, status:* to stand; intensive, *sisto, sistere,* to (cause to) stand.

arrest (4); armistice (14); assist (4); assistance (4); consist (8); circumstance (3); circumstantial (13); consistency (9); constable (6); constant (2); constitute (5); constituent (9); constitution (3); contrast (4); desist (10); destitute (7); distance (1); distant (2); equidistant (17); establish (2); estate (3); exist (4); existence (4); extant (10); inconsistency (12); insist (3); instance (3); instant (2); instate; institution (12); irresistible (8); obstetrics; obstacle (5); persist (6); prostitution (15); reinstate (15); resist (4); resistance (7); restate; rest (1); restitution (11); solstice (15); restive; stable (2); stanchion (15); stanza (9); state (1); stately (4); station (1); stationary (7); stationery (9); statuary (10); statue (3); statute (6); subsist (8); substance (3); substantial (4); substantive (11); substitution (16); superstition (5); transubstantiation (17).

Although there was no ____1____ proof of his guilt, the ____2____ decided to ____3____ him on ____4____ evidence. Because of a peculiar concatenation of ____5____s I lost my ____6____ and was left completely ____7____. Thanks to the timely ____8____ of my friends I managed to eke out a precarious ____9____, made endurable only by the ____10____ hope of ____11____ in some not too ____12____ future. This ____13____ edifice that looks like a railway ____14____ is an ____15____ for youthful delinquents. Shortage of ____16____ forced the young poet to curtail the last ____17____ of his poem. When in a ____18____ mood, my friend is frequently seized with an ____19____ desire to break glassware. At such times, it is useless to beg him to ____20____, he will ____21____ on having his fun.

STRING, STRICT, STRICTURE (strain, straint, strait, stren), from *stringere, strictus:* to bind, draw tight, filter.
astringent (16); constrain (6); constraint (11); constrict (18); constrictor; distrain; distress (3); distressing; district (2); restrain (3); restraint (5); restrict (10); strain (3); strainer (11); strait (3); straiten (11); strict (4); strictness (19); stricture (16).

It must be most ____1____ing to be ____2____ed in one's movements by a ____3____-jacket. Don't forget to put in the ____4____, or you will clog the drain. The boa shows admirable ____5____; it ____6____s its victim before swallowing it. In the European concessions in China, the natives are ____7____ed to walk in the gutter.

TANG, TACT (ting, tag, tigu, tain, teg, tegr, tactu, tast), from *tangere, tactus:* to touch, to reach, to handle.
attain (3); attainment (12); contact (7); contactual; contain (1); contagion (10); contagious (8); contiguous (13); contingent (14); intact (11); integrity (7); integer (19); integral (14); integration (18); tact (8); tactful (20); tactile; tactual; tangent (16); tangible (13); taste (1); tasteless (19).

A fresh _____1_____ of troops arrived yesterday bringing with them a _____2_____ disease. The _____3_____ spread so rapidly, that the authorities had to use all their _____4_____ to avert an open rebellion of the natives. An asymptote is the limiting position of the _____5_____ whose point of _____6_____ moves off to an infinite distance from the origin. I had reasons to doubt his _____7_____, but his mathematical ability, and particularly the ingenuity with which he performed _____8_____, filled me with admiration for his _____9_____s.

TEN, TENT (tin, tinu, tain), from *tenere, tentus:* to hold.
abstain (7); abstinence (11); appertain (10); content (7); contentment (8); continual (3); continue (1); continent (3); countenance (4); detain (4); discontent (4); entertain (3); impertinent (10); incontinent (10); lieutenant (4); maintain (2); obtain (2); pertain (6); retain (3); retinue (10); sustain (4); sustenance (10); tenable (17); tenacious (13); tenant (5); tenement (7); tenure (12); untenable.

In spite of his _____1_____ with everything, he _____2_____d to _____3_____ a _____4_____ grip on life. The young lieutenant was court-martialed for being _____5_____ to a general in the royal _____6_____. The _____7_____ difficulty we encountered in providing ourselves with even the most essential means of _____8_____, forced us to _____9_____ from all luxuries.

TEND, TENS, TENT, from *tendere, tensus, or tentus:* to stretch, strive, try.
attend (1); attendant (3); attention (2); contend (9); contention (6); distend (11); distension; extend (1); extension (5); extensive (5); extent (4); intend (2); intendant (17); intensive (16); intent (3); intention (4); ostensible (11); ostentation (12); portend (10); portent (11); pretend (3); pretender (15); pretense (5); subtend; superintend (9); superintendent (5); tend (3); tendency (6); tendon (10); tense (11); tension (12); tensile; tent (2).

In an equilateral triangle, equal sides _____1_____ equal angles. The _____2_____ to the throne and his _____3_____s were dressed with great _____4_____. Comets are regarded by many as _____5_____s of evil. Under the _____6_____ of suppressing a radical _____7_____, the _____8_____ fired several workers.

TRAH, TRACT, (trac, trail, train, tray, trait), from *trahere, tractus:* to draw.
abstract (8); abstraction (10); attract (4); contract (3); contractor (10); contractile (12); distraught; detract (18); distract (5); entreat (5); extract (5); portray (9); portrait (9); protract (11); protractor (10); retract (13); retraction; subtract (6); subtrahend (19); tract (4); tractile; traction (14); trace (2); trail (3); train (1); trainer; trait (14).

The quantity to be subtracted is called a ____1____. Dostoëvsky was wont to ____2____ men and women ____3____ with passions. In order not to ____4____ attention to our hiding place, we decided to destroy every ____5____ of our passage along the winding ____6____.

UT, US, USUR (usu), from *uti, usus:* to use.
abuse (3); abusive (16); perusal (14); disuse (10); misuse (8); peruse (7); usage (8); use (1); useful (2); useless (3); usual (1); usury (10); utensil (7); utility (7); utilitarian (13).

This kitchen ____1____ has lost its ____2____ because of continual ____3____. After a thorough ____4____ of the book, he found it ____5____ and began to ____6____ the author.

VEN, VENT, VENTU (veni, venu, ventu), from *venire, ventus:* to come.
contravene; adventure (3); avenue (2); circumvent (15); covenant (6); advent (9); convene (9); convenient (3); convent (5); convention (4); conventual; event (2); eventually; intervene (8); invent (3); inventive (15); inventory (11); prevent (2); revenue (5); supervene (20); venture (3); venue.

The ____1____ of the ____2____ was a glorious ____3____ for inhabitants of Ninth ____4____. In that ____5____ we must ____6____ to ____7____ the ____8____. An ____9____ of goods was taken to determine the amount of ____10____.

VID, VIS (vey, vic, view), from *videre, visus:* to see.
advice (2); evidence (4); advise (2); evident (3); providence (4); provident (15); provision (3); prudent (5); purvey (15); review (2); revise (7); revisit (16); supervise (11); supervision (9); surveillance (14); survey (4); surveying; view (1); visage (7); visit (1); visitant (14).

It soon became ____1____ that the existing ____2____ was insufficient, and acting on the ____3____ of our geologists, we decided to ____4____ the country, to ____5____, if possible, the data of the previous ____6____. Nothing escaped the ____7____ of this mysterious ____8____.

VOC (voice, vou), from *vox, vocis:* voice.
advocate (7); avocation; convocation (9); convoke (18); invoke (9); equivocation (15); irrevocable (14); provocation (7); provoke (3); revoke (9); univocal; vocal (6); vocable; vocation (10); vociferous (17); voice (1); vouch (9); vowel (7).

After much ____1____, the ____2____ persuaded the court to ____3____ his client's sentence. The decision was met with ____4____ applause. Medicine was Eric's ____5____, painting his ____6____

The ____7____ refused to ____8____ for the integrity of one of its members.

GREEK STEMS

47) ARCH (arche, archi), from *arché*, beginning, rule, chief.
archangel, anarchy, archives, archetype, archduke, architect, archipelago, architrave, hierarchy, monarchy, oligarchy, patriarch.

The lowest division of an entablature is called ____1____. The system of government in which the power is vested in a few is called ____2____; the sovereignty of one is ____3____; complete absence of government is ____4____. ____5____s rank above seraphim and cherubim in the ____6____ of angels.

AGON, a contest.
protagonist, agonizing, agony, antagonist.

The ____1____ of this novel goes through an ____2____ conflict with his ____3____.

ALLOS, another.
allotrope, allomorph, allopathy, allophane, allegory.

Diamond is an ____1____ of carbon. Any one of Æsop's fables may serve as an example of ____2____.

ASTER or **ASTRON,** a star.
aster, asterisk, astral, astrolabe, disaster, asteroid, astrology, astronomy.

An ____1____ is an instrument used for determining the altitude of heavenly bodies. ____2____ treats of ____3____ influences on human affairs.

BIBLOS or **BIBLION,** a book.
bibliophile, bibliography, Biblical, bibliomancy, Bible, bibliomania.

Divination by books, e.g., by passages in the ____1____, is called ____2____. The students were asked to construct a ____3____ of ____4____ criticism.

DEMOS, the people.
democracy, epidemic, demos, demotic, democrat, demagogue.

Woe to ____1____ when power falls into the hands of a ____2____. An ____3____ of Plague devastated Europe in the 14th century.

DRAO, I do, act.
dramaturgy, dramatics, melodramatic, dramatize, drama.

After a few lessons in ____1____ we decided to ____2____ a ____3____ sea story.

DUNAMIS, power.
dynamics, dynamite, hydrodynamics, aerodynamics, dynamometer, dynamo, dyne.

____1____ is that part of mechanics which treats of forces and of motion. If it deals with liquids, it is called ____2____; if with air— ____3____.

EIDOS, form.
kaleidoscope, spheroid, geode, cycloid, anthropoid.

A gorilla is an ____1____—man-like—ape. ____2____ is the figure of the earth; it approximates to a ____3____ of revolution.

ERGON, work.
energy, metallurgy, allergy, erg, ergometer.

An ____1____ is a device for measuring ____2____, usually in terms of ____3____s. The art of extracting metals from ores is called ____4____.

GE, the earth.
geography, geology, geometry, geomorphology, geodesy, geodetic, geoid, geode, geocentric.

That branch of physical ____1____ which treats of various topographic forms is called ____2____. ____3____ surveying is based on the laws of ____4____ and trigonometry.

GRAPHO, I write.
biography, telegraph, autograph, geography, graph, graphic, graphite, historiographer, lithograph, photograph, stenography, topography, typographer.

The ____1____ gave a very ____2____ description of the World War. This ____3____ed copy of the great man's ____4____, illustrated with many ____5____s, is a masterpiece of the ____6____'s art.

HUDOR, water.
hydraulic, hydrogen, hydrophobia, hydro, hydrostatic, hydrant, dehydrate.

The dog would not come within sight of a ____1____. He was suffering from ____2____. A curious paradox—after a night of drinking, one feels ____3____d.

HOMOS, the same.
homograph, homologue, homonym, homomorphy, homologous, homogeneous.

The words pair and pare are _____1_____s, the words fair (market) and fair (beautiful) are _____2_____s.

IDIOS, one's own, peculiar.
idiom, idiosyncrasy, idiot, idiocy, idiomorphic, idiocracy, idiomatic.

The _____1_____ of his _____2_____ borders on _____3_____. Freddie is not a moron; he is a downright _____4_____.

ISOS, equal.
isochronous, isosceles, isotherm, isostacy, isogonal, isocline, isobar, isotope.

Lines joining points of equal temperature on a map are called _____1_____s; those joining points of equal pressure are _____2_____s. The angles at the base of an _____3_____ triangle are equal.

KOSMOS, the world, order.
cosmogony, cosmography, macrocosm, microcosm, cosmos, cosmic, cosmopolitan.

Man is a _____1_____ within _____2_____. One of the purposes of stratospheric ascensions was to determine the nature of _____3_____ rays. _____4_____ attempts to solve the problem of the origin of the universe or _____5_____; _____6_____, treats of the universe without bothering about its origin.

LOGOS, a word, speech.
(See p. 67 above)

METRON, a measure.
anemometer, barometer, diameter, gasometer, geometry, hexameter, hydrometer, meter, pentameter, perimeter, symmetry, thermometer, trigonometry.

In stately _____1_____s the poet sang the beauties of _____2_____, and praised the _____3_____ of circles and triangles. Desirous of making some meteorological observations, we took with us an _____4_____ to measure the force and speed of wind, a _____5_____ to give us data on atmospheric pressure, and a _____6_____ to discover the variations in temperature from day to day.

MONOS, alone.
monarch, monastery, monosyllable, monogamy, monolith, monomania, monograph, monogram, monocle, monotony.

The _____1_____, who was a bit of a fop, wore a _____2_____ in his eye. Bored by the _____3_____ of _____4_____, Michael decided to become a Mohammedan. Mary's fondness for _____5_____s on her lingerie amounted to a _____6_____.

NEOS, new.

neology, neophyte, Neocene, neon, neolithic, neologism, neoplasm.

In matters of love he was a mere ___1___. A large ___2___ sign announced an exhibit of ___3___ implements.

NOMOS, a law.

gastronomy, economy, astronomy, autonomy, Deuteronomy.

Being an abstemious epicure, I permitted myself to indulge in a little ___1___, but only with the greatest ___2___.

PHOBOS, fear.

Anglophobia, hydrophobia, claustrophobia, phobia, agoraphobia.

A victim of ___1___, Guy had fits of trembling rage when left alone in a small, dark room. Among many morbid fears or ___2___s, the fear of water, or ___3___ is the most dangerous.

PHOS, light.

phosphorus, photograph, photometer, phosphate, photosynthesis, photostat.

Most fertilizers contain ___1___. The process by which plants in the presence of sunlight convert water and carbon dioxide into sugar and starch, is called ___2___.

PHILOS, loving, fond of.

philology, philosophy, philanthrophy, philharmonic.

Our professor of ___1___ was frequently to be seen at the concerts in the ___2___ auditorium. A man of means, he was able, upon his retirement, to devote his time and money to ___3___.

PHONE, a sound.

antiphon, euphony, euphonious, phonetics, phonic, phonograph, polyphonic, phonology, symphony.

The sounds of the ___1___ might have been more ___2___ if it had not been for the dilapidated state of our ___3___. ___4___ is the science of speech sounds.

PHUSIS, nature.

physiognomy, physiography, physic, physicist, metaphysics, physician, physiology.

I'd rather die than take this nauseating ___1___ which my ___2___ prescribed for me. Many a ___3___ forsakes his science to dabble in ___4___. ___5___ is that branch of geology which treats of the features, or shall we say, the ___6___ of the earth.

POIEO, I make.
onomatopoeia, poesy, poetry, prosopopoeia.

"___1___ we will call Musical Thought!" Tennyson's lines: "The moan of doves in immemorial elms, the murmuring of innumerable bees . . .", are a classical example of ___2___.

PROTOS, first.
protonotary, protocol, protomartyr, protoplasm, proton, prototype.

Let us address our prayers to the ___1___ Stephen! ___2___ is the essential substance of cell-bodies and the only form of matter in which life is manifested.

PSUCHE, soul, mind.
psychiatry, psychoanalysis, metempsychosis, psychosis, psychotherapy.

___1___ is a method of ___2___ developed by Dr. Freud of Vienna.

SKOPEO, I see.
bishop, episcopal, kaleidoscope, microscope, sceptic, telescope, stereoscope, stethoscope.

The ___1___, the instrument used in auscultation of the chest, was invented in 1819 by Laënnec. The ___2___ who presided at the Ecclesiastical Congress was resplendent in his purple ___3___ robes.

TECHNE, an art.
pyrotechnics, technique, technics, architect, technology.

The ___1___'s lack of originality was somewhat disguised by his excellent ___2___ in drawing. The Fourth of July is usually celebrated with a noisy ___3___ display.

THESIS, a placing.
synthesis, synthetic, epithet, anathema, antithesis, hypothesis, thesis.

Failing to confirm his ___1___ with experimental data, the physicist had a fit of rage, and showered ___2___s and ___3___s on the heads of his innocent assistants. Taking things apart is analysis, putting them together is ___4___.

TOPOS, a place.
topic, topography, toponym, topical, toparchy.

The possibility of founding a small independent state or ___1___ was the ___2___ of conversation between the two adventurers. The rugged ___3___ of the region was obviously the result of deforestation.

ZOON, an animal.

zoölogy, zoöphyte, zodiac, epizoötic, protozoan, Azoic, azote, zoön, zoötomy.

The ___1___ has twelve constellations or signs. A ___2___ is a unicellular organism. The science of biology is divided into botany and ___3___.

LATIN ROOT WORDS

48) The Latin root-words which follow, while they have not given rise to so many derivatives, are yet very important as a source of English words. This list will be of great use in deciphering the meaning of many Latin compound words which appeared in the preceding lists. Several derivatives are given for each root-word. In each case, can you add two or three more?

acer (acris), *sharp:* acerbity, acrid, acrimony.

ædes, *a building:* edifice, edify.

æquus, *equal:* equality, equator, equinox, equivalent.

æther, *the sky:* ether, ethereal.

ager (agri), *a field:* agrarian, agriculture, agronomy.

alo, *I nourish:* aliment, alimony.

alter, *another, the other:* alteration, alternate.

altus, *high:* altitude, alto, exalt.

amo, *I love:* amiable, amorous.

angulus, *a corner:* angle, angular, triangle.

anima, *breath, life:* animal, animate.

animus, *mind:* equanimity, magnanimous, unanimous.

annus, *a year:* annual, anniversary, biennial.

antiquus, *ancient:* antique, antiquity.

aperio (apertum), *I open:* aperient, aperture.

appello, *I call:* appeal, appellation.

aqua, *water:* aquatic, aquarium, aqueduct.

arbor, *a tree:* arboreal, arbori-culture.

arcus, *a bow:* arc, arcade, archer, [F.].

ardeo, *I burn:* ardent, ardor, arson [F.].

arma, *arms:* armada, armor, arms.

augeo (auctum), *I increase:* augment, auction.

barba, *beard:* barb, barber.

beatus, *blessed:* beatify, beatitude.

bellum, *war:* bellicose, belligerent.

bis, *twice:* biscuit, bisect, bissextile.

brevis, *short:* abbreviate, brevity.

cado, *I fall:* cadence, accident, decadence.

cædo (cæsum), *I cut; kill:* decide, precise (*lit.,* to cut off in front).

canis, *dog:* canine.

caro (carnis), *flesh:* carnal, carnivorous.

causa, *cause:* causal, excuse [F.].

cavus, *hollow:* cave, cavity, excavate.

celer, *swift:* celerity, accelerate.

centum, *a hundred:* cent, century, centurion.

cingo (cinctum), *I gird:* cincture, precinct.

cito, *I call, summon:* cite, citation, recite.

civis, *a citizen:* civic, civil, civilize.

clarus, *clear:* clarify, clarion, declare.

clino, *I bend:* decline, incline, recline.

cœlum, *heaven:* celestial.

colo (cultum), *I till:* cultivate, culture.

copia, *plenty:* copious, cornucopia.

corona, *a crown:* coronation, coronet.

corpus (corporis), *the body:* corps, corpse, corporation.

creo, *I create:* create, creation, creature.

cresco, *I grow:* crescent, decrease, increase.

crux (crucis), *a cross:* crucifix, crucify, cruciform.

cubo, *I lie down:* incubate, recumbent.

culpa, *a fault:* culpable, culprit, inculpate.

curtus, *short:* curt, curtail.

curvus, *bent, crooked:* curve, curvature.

decem, *ten:* decimal, decimate, December (the *tenth* month among the early Romans).

dens (dentis), *a tooth:* dental, dentist, indent.

densus, *thick:* dense, density, condense.

deus, *God, a god:* deify, deity, deist.

dexter, *right-handed:* dexterous, dexterity.

dies, *a day:* diary, diurnal.

doceo (doctum), *I teach:* docile, doctrine.

dominus, *a lord, master:* domination, domineer.

domus, *a house:* domestic, domicile.

dormio, *I sleep:* dormant, dormitory, dormouse.

duo, *two:* dual, duel, duet, duplex, duplicate.

durus, *hard, lasting:* durable, duration, endure.

edo, *I eat:* edible, inedible.

ego, *I:* egoism, egoist, egotism, egotist, egotistic.

emo (emptum), *I buy:* exemption, preëmption, redeem.

eo (itum), *I go:* exit, transit, circuit.

erro, *I wander:* err, errant, error, aberration.

esse, *to be:* essence, essential.

facies, *a face:* facial, face, facet [F.].

facilis, *easy:* facile, facilitate, facility.

fames, *hunger:* famine, famish.

felix, *happy:* felicity, felicitous.

femina, *a woman:* feminine, effeminate.

fido, *I trust:* confide, diffident, fidelity.

filius, *a son:* filial, filiate.

filum, *a thread:* file, fillet, profile.

finis, *the end:* finish, finite, infinite.

flecto (flexum), *I bend:* inflect, inflection, flexible.

flos (floris), *a flower:* flora, floral, florist.

fluo (fluxum), *I flow:* fluent, fluid, flux.

folium, *a leaf:* foliage, portfolio.

fortis, *strong:* fortify, fortitude, fortress.

frater, *a brother:* fraternal, fraternity, friar [F.].

frico, *I rub:* friction, dentifrice.

frigeo, *I am cold:* frigid, frigidity.

frons (frontis), *the forehead:* front, frontal, frontier.

fugio, *I flee:* fugitive, refugee.

fumus, *smoke:* fume, fumigate.

fundo (fusum), *I pour:* foundry, refund, funnel, fuse, fusible.

fundus, *the bottom:* foundation, founder, profound [F.].

gelu, *frost:* gelid, congeal, gelatin, jelly (formerly *gelly*).

gens (gentis), *a race, people:* gender, gentile.

gradus, *a step:* grade, gradient, degrade.

gravis, *heavy:* grave, gravity, grieve.

grex, *a herd, flock:* aggregate, congregate, gregarious.

hæreo (hæsum), *I stick:* adhere, cohere, cohesive.

halo, *I breathe:* inhale, exhale.

homo, *a man:* homicide, homage [F.], human.

hora, *an hour:* horologe, horoscope.

hospes, *a guest:* hospice, hospitable, hospital.

hostis, *an enemy:* hostile, hostility.

humidus, *moist:* humid, humidity.

humus, *earth, ground:* exhume, humble.

ignis, *fire:* igneous, ignite, ignition.

impero, *I command:* imperial, imperative, empire.

initium, *a beginning:* initial, initiate.

insula, *an island:* insular, peninsula.

ira, *anger, wrath:* ire, irate.

judex (judicis), *a judge:* judicial, judge.

juro, *I swear:* abjure, juror, jury, perjure.

jus (juris), *right, law:* just, justice, jurisdiction.

juvenis, *a youth:* juvenile, rejuvenate.

labor (lapsus), *I glide:* lapse, collapse, relapse.

lac, *milk:* lacteal, lactic.

lapis (lapidis), *a stone:* dilapidated, lapidary.

latus, *wide:* latitude, latitudinal.

latus, *a side:* lateral, bilateral.

laus (laudis), *praise:* laud, laudable, laudation.

lavo, *I wash:* lave, lavatory.

laxus, *loose:* relax, lax, laxity.

lego (legatum), *I send:* legate, delegate.

levis, *light:* levity, alleviate.

levo, *I lift up:* elevate, lever.

lex (legis), *a law:* legal, legislate, legitimate.

liber, *free:* liberal, liberty, liberate.

liber, *a book:* librarian, library.

libra, *a balance:* equilibrium, librate.

licet, *it is lawful:* illicit, licit.

lignum, *wood:* ligneous, lignify, lignose.

ligo, *I bind:* ligament, religion, liable.

linquo (lictum), *I leave:* relinquish, relict, relics.

liqueo, *I melt:* liquid, liquefy.

litera, *a letter:* literal, literary, literature.

locus, *a place:* local, locate, dislocate.

longus, *long:* longitude, long.

loquor (locutus), *I speak:* elocution, loquacious.

ludo (lusum), *I play:* delude, elude, interlude.

lumen, *light:* illuminate, luminary, luminous.

luna, *the moon:* lunar, lunacy.

luo (lutum), *I wash:* ablution, dilute.

lux (lucis), *light:* lucid, elucidate.

macula, *a spot:* immaculate, macule, maculate.

magnus, *great:* magnify, magnificent, magnitude.

malus, *bad:* malady, malevolent.

mando, *I bid, order:* mandate, mandatory.

maneo (mansum), *I remain:* manse, mansion, permanent.

mare, *the sea:* marine, mariner, maritime.

Mars, *the god of war:* martial, Martian.

mater, *a mother:* maternal, matricide, matron.

maturus, *ripe:* mature, immature, premature.

medius, *the middle:* medium, mediate, immediate.

melior, *better:* ameliorate, meliorate.

memor, *mindful:* memory, memorize, memorial.

mens (mentis), *the mind:* mental, mentality, demented.

mergo (mersum), *I dip:* emerge, emergency, immersion.

merx (mercis), *wares:* merchant, merchandise, commerce.

miles (militis), *a soldier:* military, militant, militia.

minuo, *I lessen:* diminish, minute.

miror, *I admire:* admirable, miracle.

moneo (monitum), *I warn:* monition, monitor.

mons (montis), *a mountain:* cismontane, ultramontane, promontory.

mordeo, *I bite:* mordant, remorse.

mors (mortis), *death:* mortal, mortify, immortal.

multus, *many:* multiple, multiply, multitude.

munus (muneris), *a gift:* munificent, remunerate.

murus, *a wall:* mural, immure.

muto, *I change:* mutable, transmute.

narro, *I relate:* narration, narrative.

nascor (natus), *to be born:* nascent, natal, native.

navis, *a ship:* naval, nave, navigate, navy.

necto (nexus), *I tie:* connect, connection, annex.

nego (negatum), *I deny:* negative, negation.

nihil, *nothing:* annihilate, nihilist.

nocco, *I injure:* innocent, innocuous, noxious.

nomen, *a name:* nominal, nominate, cognomen.

norma, *a rule:* normal, enormous.

novus, *new:* novel, novelty, novice, renovate.

nox (noctis), *night:* equinox, nocturnal.

nudus, *naked:* nude, denude.

numerus, *a number:* numeration, enumerate.

nuntio, *I declare:* announce, denounce.

octo, *eight:* octagon, octave, October.

oculus, *the eye:* ocular, oculist.

odi, *I hate:* odious, odium.

odor, *smell:* odor, odoriferous.

omnis, *all:* omnibus, omnipotent, omniscience.

onus, *a burden:* onus, onerous, exonerate.

opus (operis), *work:* opera, operate, coöperate.

ordo (ordinis), *order:* ordinal, ordinary, ordinance.

orno, *I adorn:* ornament, adorn.

oro, *I speak:* oration, orator.

ovum, *an egg:* oval, ovate.

pareo, *I appear:* apparent, apparition, appearance.

paro (paratum), *I prepare:* apparatus, preparation, repair [F.].

pasco (pastum), *I feed:* pastor, pasture, repast.

pater, *a father:* paternal, parricide [F.], patrimony.

patior (passus), *I suffer:* passion, passive, patient.

pax (pacis), *peace:* pacific, pacify.

pecco, *I sin:* peccant, peccable, impeccable.

pecunia, *money:* pecuniary, impecunious.

pello (pulsum), *I drive:* compel, expel, repel, impulsive.

pendeo (pensum), *I hang:* pendant, suspend, suspense.

pes (pedis), *a foot:* pedal, pedestrian, biped.

planus, *level:* plain, plane, plan [F.], explain.

plaudo (plausum), *I clap the hands:* applaud, applause, explode.

pleo (pletum), *I fill:* complete, complement, supplement.

plus (pluris), *more:* plural, plurality, plus.

pœna, *punishment:* penal, penalty, penance.

pons (pontis), *a bridge:* pontiff, pontifical, transpontine.

populus, *the people:* population, depopulate.

possum (potens), *I am able:* potent, impotent, possible.

primus, *first:* primary, primer, primitive, primrose.

probo, *I try, prove:* probe, probation, approve.

proprius, *one's own:* proper, property, appropriate.

pungo (punctum), *I prick:* punctual, pungent, expunge.

puto (putatum), *I reckon, think,* also *cut, prune:* compute, repute, amputate, count [F.].

quartus, *fourth:* quart, quarter, quartet.

radix (radicis), *a root:* eradicate, radical, radish [F.].

ramus, *a branch:* ramify, ramose.

rex (regis), *a king:* regal, regicide.

rideo (risum), *I laugh:* deride, ridicule, ridiculous, risible.

rodo, *I gnaw:* corrode, rodent.

rogo (rogatum), *I ask:* derogatory, interrogation, rogation.

rota, *a wheel:* rotary, rotate, rotund, round.

rus, *the country:* rustic, rusticate.

sacer, *sacred:* sacerdotal, sacrament, sacrilege.

sal, *salt:* saline, salinity.

sanctus, *holy:* sanctify, sanctuary, saint [F.].

sanguis, *blood:* sanguinary, sanguineous.

sanus, *sound:* sane, insane.

sapio, *I taste:* sapid, insipid.

scando (scansum), *I climb:* ascend, descend, scan, scansion.

scio, *I know:* science, scientific, omniscience.

seco (sectum), *I cut:* bisect, dissect, section.

senex (senis), *old:* senate, senator, senile, senior.

septem, *seven:* septennial, September.

sidus, *a star:* sidereal.

similis, *like:* similar, similitude, resemble [F.].

sisto, *I stop:* desist, resist.

socius, *a companion:* social, socialist, society.

sol, *the sun:* solar, parasol.

solus, *alone:* solitary, solitude, sole.

solvo (solutum), *I loose:* absolve, dissolve, resolve.

spero, *I hope:* desperate, despair [F.].

spiro, *I breathe:* aspire, inspire, spirited.

struo (structum), *I pile up, build:* construct, construe, structure.

studeo, *I attend to, study:* student, studious.

suadeo, *I advise:* dissuade, persuade.

sumo (sumptum), *I take:* assume, assumption, consume.

surgo, *I rise:* insurgent, surge.

tacitus, *silent:* tacit, taciturn.

tego (tectum), *I cover:* integument, detect.

tempus (temporis), *time:* temporal, contemporary, extempore.

terminus, *an end, boundary:* terminate, term.

terra, *the earth:* subterranean, Mediterranean.

terreo, *I frighten:* terrify, terror.

testis, *a witness:* testify, testimony, protest.

texo (textum), *I weave:* text, textile, texture.

timeo, *I fear:* timid, timidity, timorous.

tono, *I sound:* intone, monotone, tone.

torqueo (tortum), *I twist:* torment, torture, retort.

tremo, *I shake:* tremor, tremulous.

tres (tria), *three:* triad, trinity, trident, trefoil.

tribuo, *I give:* tributary, tribute, contribute.

umbra, *a shadow:* umbra, umbrage, umbrella.

unda, *a wave:* undulate, undulous, undine.

unguo (unctum), *I anoint:* unguent, unction.

unus, *one:* uniform, union, unit, unite.

urbs, *a city:* urban, urbane, suburb.

valeo, *I am strong:* valor, valiant, invalid.

vanus, *empty:* vanish, vanity, vain [F.].

veho (vectum), *I convey:* vehicle, conveyance [F.].

verbum, *a word:* adverb, proverb, verb, verbal.

verto (versum), *I turn:* convert, divert, versatile.

verus, *true:* verify, verity, aver.

vestis, *a garment:* vest, vesture, invest.

via, *a way:* deviate, previous, voyage [F.].

video (visum), *I see:* evident, provide, visit, vision.

vinco (victum), *I conquer:* convince, victor, victory.

vita, *life:* vital, vitalize, vitamine.

vitium, *a fault:* vice [F.], vitiate.

vivo (victum), *I live:* revive, survive, vivid.

volo, *I will, wish:* benevolence, volition, voluntary.

volvo (volutum), *I roll:* involve, revolve, volume.

voveo (votum), *I vow:* devote, vote, vow [F.].

vox (vocis), *the voice:* vocal, vocalist.

vulgus, *the common people:* vulgar, Vulgate, divulge.

vulnus, *a wound:* invulnerable, vulnerable.

GREEK ROOT WORDS

49) The number of words directly derived from Greek is small, though important. A great many of our scientific words come from this source. Can you add one or two, in each case, to the examples given?

aer, *the air:* aëronaut, aëroplane, aërostat.

agora, *marketplace:* agoraphobia.

angelos, *a messenger:* angel, evangelist.

anthos, *a flower:* anthology, anthologist.

anthropos, *a man:* misanthrope, philanthropy.

arctos, *a bear:* arctic, antarctic.

aristos, *best:* aristocracy, aristocrat.

arithmos, *number:* arithmetic.

atmos, *vapor:* atmosphere.

autos, *self:* autocrat, autograph.

ballo, *I throw:* hyperbole, symbol.

bapto, *I dip:* baptise, baptism.

baros, *weight:* baritone, barometer.

bios, *life:* biography, biology.

cheir, *the hand:* chirography, chiropodist.

chole, *bile:* choler, choleric, melancholy.

chrio, *I anoint:* chrism, Christ.

chronos, *time:* chronic, chronicle, chronology.

chroma, *color:* chrome, chromolithograph.

daktulos, *a finger:* dactyl, date (fruit).

deka, *ten:* decade, decalogue.

dendron, *a tree:* dendrology, rhododendron.

doxa, *opinion, praise:* doxology, orthodoxy, heterodoxy.

eikon, *an image:* iconoclast, icon.

elektron, *amber:* electricity, electrotype.

gamos, *marriage:* polygamy, monogamy.

gaster, *stomach:* gastric, gastronomy.

glossa (glotta), *the tongue:* glossary, glottis.

gramma, *a letter:* grammar, monogram.

gune, *woman:* gynecology, misogyny.

haima, *blood:* hemorrhage, hemorrhoids.

hekaton, *a hundred:* hecatomb, hectogram.

helios, *the sun:* heliograph, heliotrope.

hepta, *seven:* heptagon, heptarchy, Heptateuch.

hieros, *sacred:* hierarchy, hieroglyphic.

hippos, *a horse:* hippodrome, hippopotamus.

hodos, *a way:* exodus, method.

ichthus, *a fish:* ichthyology, ichthyic.

kakos, *bad:* cacophony, cacography.

kalos, *beautiful:* kaleidoscope.

kardia, *the heart:* cardiac, pericardium.

klaustros, *hidden, secret:* claustrophobia, cloister.

krino, *I judge:* criterion, critic, hypocrite.

kuklos, *a circle:* cycle, cycloid, cyclone.

kuon (kunos), *a dog:* cynic, cynicism.

lithos, *a stone:* lithograph, aërolite.

lusis, *a loosening:* analysis, paralysis.

mania, *madness:* mania, monomania.

meter, *a mother:* metropolis, metropolitan.

mikros, *small:* microcosm, microscope.

misos, *hatred:* misanthrope, misogynist.

morphe, *shape:* morphology, metamorphosis.

muthos, *a fable:* myth, mythology.

naus, *a ship:* nausea, nautical, argonaut.

nekros, *a dead body, dead:* necromancy, necropolis.

neuron, *a nerve:* neuralgia, neuritis.

nosos, *a disease:* nosology, nosography.

ode, *a song:* ode, palinode, prosody.

oikos, *a house:* economical, economy.

onoma, *a name:* anonymous, patronymic, synonym.

orthos, *right:* orthodoxy, orthography.

paideia, *education:* cyclopedia, encyclopedia.

pais (paidos), *a boy:* pedagogue (lit., a boy-leader), pediatrics.

pathos, *feeling:* pathetic, sympathy.

pente, *five:* pentagon, Pentateuch.

petra, *a rock:* petrify, petrography, Peter.

phaino, *I show:* phantom, phenomenon, fancy.

polis, *a city:* police, politics, metropolis.

polus, *many:* polygon, polygamy, polytheism.

pous (podos), *a foot:* antipodes, tripod.

potamos, *a river:* hippopotamus, Mesopotamia.

pseudes, *lying, false:* pseudonym, pseudo-apostle.

pur, *fire:* pyrotechnic, pyre, pyrography.

rheo, *I flow:* rhetoric, rheumatic, rhythm.

sophia, *wisdom:* philosophy, Sophist.

sphaira, *a ball, sphere:* hemisphere, planisphere.

stello, *I send:* apostle, epistle.

stichos, *a line, row:* distich, hemistich.

stratos, *an army:* stratagem, strategy.

strepho, *I turn:* apostrophe, catastrophe.

tele, *far, far off:* telegraph, telephone, telescope.

theos, *God, a god:* theist, atheist, theology.

therme, *heat:* thermal, thermometer.

treis (tria), *three:* triangle, trinity, tripod.

trepo, *I turn:* trophy, heliotrope.

tupos, *the mark of a blow, impression:* type, stereotype.

LATIN PREFIXES

ab (a, abs)—from, away from.

*ad (a, ac, af, ag, al, am, an, ap, ar, as, at)—to, against.

ambi (amb, am, an)—around, on all sides.

ante (an)—before.

bene—well.

bi (bin, bis)—two, twice.

circum (circu)—about.

contra (contro, counter)—against.

cum (co, col, com, con, cor, coun)—with, together, or adds force.

de—away, down, from, or adds force.

dis (de, des, di, dif)—apart, not, opposite act.

du (duo)—two.

ex (a, e, ec, ef, es, (e)s)—out of, from.

extra—beyond, without.

in (en, i, il, im, ir)—not.

in (am, an, em, en, il, im, ir)—in into, on, upon.

inter (enter, intel)—among, between.

intro—within.

juxta—near to.

male (mal)—badly, evil or ill.

ne, nec (—*ne+que,* neg)—not.

non (*ne+unum*)—not, not one.

ob (o, oc, of, op, os, o(b)s)—against, upon.

pen (poene)—almost.

per (par, pel, pil)—through.

post—after.

pre—before.

preter—past, beyond.

pro (prod, prof, pol, por, put, pru)—for, forth, forwards.

re (red)—again, back, against, or opposite act.

retro—backward.

se (sed)—away, from.

semi—half.

sine—without.

sub (sou, suc, suf, sug, sum, sup, sur, sus)—under, from below.

subter—under.

super (sur)—over, above, beyond.

trans (tran, tra, tres)—beyond, across, through.

tri (tre)—three, thrice.

ultra—beyond.

vice (vis)—in place of.

*For the sake of euphony the last letter of the prefix is often changed to the first letter of the root, or is dropped. See the words compounded from the stem *scribe* on page (68).

LATIN SUFFIXES

(The part of speech formed by the aid of the suffix is indicated by the letter placed after the definition: *n*, noun; *a*, adj.; *v*, verb; *ad*, adverb.)

able (abil, abl, ble, bl); **ible (ibil, ibl, bil, bl)**—able to be, fit to be, causing. (a)

aceous, acious—having the quality of, full of. (a)

acy—state or quality of being. (n)

ad—See *at*. (n)

age—state of being; act of; that which; a collection of. (n)

al, el (1)—pertaining to; the act of. (a n)

an, ain, ane, ean, ian—pertaining to; one who. (a n)

ance, ancy (anc)—state of being; act of. (n)

and, end—L. fut. part. ending. (n) =about to be, ought to be.

ant—See *ent*.

ar—pertaining to. (a)

ary (ari) ar—belonging to; one who; place where. (a n)

at, it—p. part. ending; ending of L. n. stem also. (n v)

ate (at)—having; one who; to make. (a n v)

ble—See *able*.

bulum, bule (bul) ble—place, that which or by which. (n)

culum, cule (cul), cle, cher—place/ that which or by which. (n)

ce—See *acy*.

cle, cel, cule (cul)—little (diminutives) (n)

cy—See *acy*.

ee—one to whom. (n)

eer—See second *er*, below. (v)

el, eel—See *al*.

ence (enc), ency—state of being. (n)

ens—of, belonging to. (n)

ent—one who; that which; being or *ing*.

er, (r), eer, ier—one who. (n)

ern—of, belonging to. (a)

ery, ry, er—place where; state of being; collection; art of. (n)

esc—to grow to or become. (v)

ess—denotes female agent. (n)

esque—somewhat, like. (a)

est—of, belonging to. (a)

estr—of, belonging to. (a)

ette, et—little (diminutive). (n)

ey—See *y*.

ible—See *able*.

ic, ical—pertaining to; made of; one who. (a n)

ice—state or quality of being; thing that. (n)

id—quality, pertaining to. (a)

ier—See *eer*.

ile (il)—able to be; relating to. (a)

ine (in)—belonging to; (n) ending also. (a)

ion—act of; state of being; that which. (n)

ique—belonging to. (a)

ish—See *esc*.

ite—one who; being. (n a)

ity (ty)—state or quality of being. (n)

ive (iv)—one who; that which having power or quality. (n a)

ix—denotes a female. (n)

ix—that which. (n)

ize (iz), ise (is)—to make, to give. (v)

le (l)—frequentative. (v)

le (l)—See *al, el*.

lence—abundance of. (n)

lent—abounding in. (a)

men—that acted upon. (n)

ment—state of being; act of; that which. (n)

mony (moni)—state of being; that which; that derived from. (n)

ocr—pertaining to. (a n)
on, oon, ion—one who. (n)
on—See *ion*.
or—one who; that which. (n)
or, our—state or quality of being; place where. (n)
ory (ori)—relating to; place where; thing which. (a n)
ose (os), ous—full of, having. (a)
ot—one who. (n)
r—er or or—one who. (n)
rix—denotes female agent.
ry—See *ery*.

sion, son—See *ion*.
time—belonging to. (a)
tion—See *ion*.
tude (tud, ude)—state of being. (n)
ty—See *ity*.
ul—prone to. (a)
ule, ul—little (diminutives). (n)
ure (ur)—state or act of; that which. (n)
urn—belonging to. (a)
y (i)—state of being; that which. (n)

GREEK PREFIXES

amphi—on both sides.
an (a)—not.
ana—again, back, through.
anti (ant)—against.
apo (ap)—from.
cata (cat)—down.
di (dis)—twice, two.
dia (di)—through.
dys—bad, ill.
ec (ex)—from, out of.
en (em)—in, on.
epi (ep)—upon.

eu (ev)—well.
hemi—half.
hyper—over.
hypo (hyp)—under.
meta (met)—beyond, after, change.
mono (mon)—alone, one.
para (par)—beside.
peri—around.
poly—many.
pro—before.
pseudo—false.
syn (syn, sum, sys, sy)—with.

GREEK SUFFIXES

ac—pertaining to. (a)
et—one who. (n)
ic, ical—pertaining to; made of; one who. (a)
ic, ics—science of. (n)

ise, ize—to make; to give. (v)
ism—state of being; doctrine. (n)
ist—one who. (n)
y—state of being. (n)

ANGLO-SAXON, OR ENGLISH, PREFIXES

a—at, in, on, or adds force.
after—behind.
all (al)—wholly.
be—to make, cause, by.
for—against, not, or adds force.
forth—forward.
full—completely.
gain—against.
in (im)—in, into, within; sometimes, intensive.

mis—wrong, wrongly.
never—not ever.
off—from.
out—beyond.
over—above, in excess.
to—at, the, this.
un—not, opposite act in verbs.
under—beneath.
well (wel)—rightly.
with—against, from, back.

ANGLO-SAXON, OR ENGLISH, SUFFIXES

ar—one who. (n)
ard—one who. (n)
dom—state of being; domain of. (n)
ed, d, t—past tense and p. participle ending. (v)
en—made of; to make; past par. little (diminutive). (a v n)
er—one who; that which. (n)
er—more (comparative degree). (a)
er—(frequentative or causative.) (v)
er—(adjective ending.)
est—most (superlative degree). (a)
ful—full of, causing. (a)
head, hood—state or quality of being. (n)
ie, y—little (diminutives). (n)
ing—the act; continuing. (n v a)
ish—somewhat; like; to make. (a v)
kin—little (diminutive). (n)
le—denotes frequent action. (v)
le—that which. (n)

less—without. (a)
let—little (diminutive). (n)
ling—little (diminutive). (n)
ly (li, y)—like, manner. (a ad)
ness—state or quality of being. (n)
ock—little (diminutive). (n)
or—one who, that which. (n)
ow—to make. (v)
s or es—the plu. ending of nouns and the ending of 3d per. sing. of verbs. (n v)
's or '—denotes possessive case. (n)
ship—state of, office of. (n)
some—full of, causing. (a)
st—state of being. (n)
ster—one who. (n)
th, t—state of being. (n)
ward, wards—direction of. (ad)
wise—manner. (ad)
y—See ie. (n)
y—full of, having. (a)
y—See ly. (a ad)

50) To find out how far you have increased your vocabulary range, see how many of the following words you can define correctly. Take advantage of your new knowledge of Latin and Greek roots. Suppose, for example, you wanted to find the meaning of 'omnipotent.' Recall the stem *omni-*, 'all' and the stem *potens, potentis*, 'powerful'; 'omnipotent' therefore means 'all-powerful.' Check your definitions by the dictionary. From the Thorndike frequency numbers in parentheses, it should be clear that this is a much harder test than the earlier one in Chapter I.

abatement (15)
commendation (8)
dogmatic (15)
phlegmatic (13)
ægis (16)
delectable (12)
heterogeneous (10)
fatuous (20)
cataclysm (16)
blatant (13)
analogous (13)
litigious (18)
perfidious (12)

obtrude (14)
meed (10)
irascible (17)
beatific (15)
opprobrium (20)
evanescent (15)
dialectic (18)
immutable (12)
factious (13)
adamant (10)
chimerical (15)
lugubrious (19)
usurious (20)

misanthrope (20)
propinquity (18)
synchronous (20)
tocsin (16)
zany (17)
alpha (20)
bourgeois (12)
malnutrition (20)
galvanize (13)
portentous (10)
congruent (20)
juxtaposition (16)
mundane (15)

quiescent (16)
recumbent (13)
poignant (14)
temerity (17)
stentorian (19)
verbiage (20)
tyro (18)
bight (15)
omniscient (16)
luminary (15)
requital (15)
spontaneity (15)
cadaverous (20)
rescind (16)
stalactite (18)
posthumous (15)
tractable (14)
verbose (18)
antithesis (16)
cygnet (17)

bate (15)
assiduous (10)
generic (20)
expatiate (14)
dulcet (15)
éclat (20)
heinous (10)
controversial (16)
imputation (14)
incorporation (16)
incognito (19)
parlance (16)
nefarious (18)
olfactory (11)
mendicant (14)
perspicuity (19)
necromancer (16)
scurrilous (16)
extempore (16)
fracas (20)
hibernate (13)

iconoclast (19)
ebullition (16)
halcyon (16)
encomium (15)
permeate (12)
lachrymal (19)
scion (11)
prefatory (20)
contrition (15)
habiliment (17)
appellation (13)
parvenu (20)
constrain (6)
postulate (14)
satellite (12)
culpable (15)
prolix (16)
cupidity (20)
conglomerate (19)
furtive (10)

CHAPTER V

Etymology has great merit as a basic attack on the problem of the meaning of a word; and it serves to link many words to a single stem. The study of the root sense is primary. But etymology is not enough to account for the current meaning—or meanings—of a given word. There have been many forces at work to change word-meanings.

Foreigners trying to acquire our language complain bitterly that an English word may have a dozen meanings. Filipinos and Asiatics, who have been taught chiefly from the older classics of our literature, often use a word in a bookish or archaic sense, so that their talk or writing has a strange ring. We label it 'babu English,' a kind of over-educated literary Pidgin (see page 177), in which the words, while they convey the sense readily enough, are used in the wrong company. These verbal sour notes ruin the harmony of phrase. Once more it is brought home to us that words have over-tones which limit the chordal combinations in which they may be used.—Lately over the radio, with the deluge of Tennessee and Kentucky mountaineer ballads, there has come many a phrase which in both pronunciation and meaning harks back to early eighteenth century English, brought over the Cumberland Gap in the first great westward movement. These phrases have been preserved by oral tradition among the 'hill-billies' of the Appalachians, though they have passed out of use in England and the rest of America.—Evidently English words do not stay put, but change their meanings as they travel in space and time.

Occasionally, in reading eccentric writers such as Carlyle, Mencken, and Joyce, one feels that Humpty-Dumpty was right, when he told Alice in Wonderland, "When I use a word, it means just what I choose it to mean." There is more than a half truth in this defiant assertion. For there is no necessary connection between the sound and sense of a word. An exception must be made in the case of a few onomatopoetic words such as 'hum,' 'whirr,' 'buzz,' and 'whistle'; or in such exclamations of feeling as 'woe,' 'hurray,' and

112

the like.   Here the 'bow-wow' or 'ding-dong' theories of the origin of
language seem persuasive.

Normally, however, a word takes on a certain sense by the force
of custom and convention.   As Greenough and Kittredge put it,
"Words are conventional signs.   They mean what they are intended
to mean by the speaker and understood to mean by the hearer."
(*Words and Their Ways*, p. 220.)   As more and more speakers and
hearers come to attach a fixed meaning to a term, it gradually acquires a 'common' sense in which everyone understands it.   This
significance may change, from age to age, because of alterations in
fashion.   An old word may be adapted to new uses; or there may be
a change in that general reading of human nature politely called
psychology, which shifts the meaning of terms having to do with the
feelings, the instincts, the mind, and the will.   But the social spread
or diffusion of the word in a changed sense always depends on convention, or general acceptance and use.   A word acquires a common
denominator of meaning only in this way.

Each particular definition in the fullest lexicon represents, after all, not
so much a single meaning as a little group of connected ideas, unconsciously
agreed upon in a vague way by the consensus of those who use the language.
(Greenough and Kittredge.   *Words and Their Ways*, p. 263.   By permission
of The Macmillan Company, Publishers.)

There are certain known ways, however, in which words change
their meanings.   Before engaging in detective work on the disguises
of meaning which words may assume, it is well to learn the possible
tricks and shifts by which the sense is changed.   The history of
words is the most fascinating branch of the history of language.
Words may not have a magic potency, as the ancients thought.   The
term 'word' has no such mystery around it as 'rune,' or 'spell,' or
'oracle.'   Except perhaps in poetry, words no longer have the power
to cast spells,—unless 'spell-binder' is to be interpreted literally.
Words will not open treasure caves, or summon up demons or angels.
But they are still powerful instruments in the hands of an able
speaker or writer, so it behooves us to command the lore of words,
—or perhaps it is better to say, the science of word-meanings, for
which the modern learned jargon is 'semantics.'   (Greek *semantiké*,
'pertaining to meaning.')   This lore of words is worth while for its
own sake.

Of the various processes by which words change sense, there are two so closely allied that they must be considered together. These are the processes of *extension* and *restriction* of meaning, or, as they are often called, *generalization* and *specialization* of meaning. These twin processes work back and forth, like a shuttle which now pulls the threads taut and thin, and now flairs them out wide and loose on the spindle. When the threads are all in a taut line, the meaning is specific; when they are spread out spindle-wise, the word covers a large area of meaning, so becoming generalized.

The word *gear*, for instance, was used by the Elizabethans much in the way we use *thing* or *affair*. They said, "Here is a fine gear," meaning "Here is a pretty state of affairs." *Gear* had a wide, loose, generalized sense. But in our day *gear* has become restricted in meaning to "a wheel having teeth that fit into teeth of another wheel," or, at its most general, to "an arrangement of parts for some purpose, such as harness, tools, machinery, clothing, or household goods." We should not dream of using *gear* in the sense of 'affair' or 'thing.' This is the shuttle working in one way: toward a restriction or narrowing of meaning.

The opposite shift, toward a generalization of meaning, is easily illustrated from a word the meaning of which is now in process of extension. *Contact*, as a verb, is properly used in electrical engineering to signify the establishment of a juncture between two poles of an electrical circuit. It is also used in an allied sense in military discussion, where the scouting forces of opposed armies come in 'contact' with one another. To 'contact' the enemy is a natural extension of meaning, aided by the ready shift from noun to verb in English where the noun is the name of an act or state. But there is now going on a gradual extension of 'contact' to include the whole range of meanings covered by the phrasal verb combination, 'to get in touch with,' which has long been sound American for 'communicated with,' even when no actual tactile connection, but only a figurative 'touch,' is implied. So we read, in business and educational journals, and in works devoted to personnel administration, "We *contacted* certain parties, with entirely satisfactory results," or, by an adjectival extension, of "a *contact* man." These both sound barbarous to literary ears, and it is a speculative question whether or not the verb will ever be accepted as in good use, in this extended and generalized sense. Still, 'contact' is one word, whereas 'get in touch with' is four. The law of parsimony usually has its way in English idiom.

The words *angle, line,* and *proposition* are now also feeling the thrust toward generalization, and are going the way that *thing, business, concern, regard, account, circumstance, fact, matter, condition,* and *state* have all gone in the past, until they have become the "counters and markers of the game of speech." Journalists write of "the financial *angle* of a *proposition,*" which to a logician doesn't make sense; and "along those lines" is a common barbarism. But there is no saying how soon these expressions may be sanctioned by good usage.

As a rule, the process of generalization results in the 'fading' of a word. From having a rich, concrete, specific sense, it becomes worn and characterless, yet well suited to furnish connective tissue or commonplace stuff in the ordinary run of prose. Such a word blends well in any company. But the word does not always remain thus colorless and general. As in the case of *gear,* the process is often reversed at a later period, and a word long general and diffuse in sense acquires once more a limited and special meaning. *Croon* is a case in point. A 'crooner' is no longer merely any singer of lullabies. The word is now both specialized and debased in meaning.

Probably in the early stages of language development most words start out with a special, limited, concrete significance, and some of them never lose it. But even such a definitely qualitative word as *blue* or *red* may take on figurative senses. So 'blues,' shortened from 'blue devils,' comes to mean 'melancholy'; while 'a Red,' as used to refer to a left-wing radical, has become something close to a profane epithet in the mouths of reactionaries. Perhaps the similarity in sound between 'red' and *radical* helped to give currency to 'Red' as a handy abbreviation. Whether the word has lost its color in this case may be doubtful, but it has certainly acquired a figurative extension of meaning. In this case, it is rather a particularization of sense. But the meaning of 'red' had also to be stretched to cover more ground than the literal color word. No doubt there was an intermediate stage here. 'The Red Flag' and the 'Red Square' finally fixed the color of radicalism, although the red stocking-caps of the Jacobins of 1789 had foreshadowed the association. Since traditionally the anarchists of the '80's and '90's had red as their color, it was natural enough for both friends and enemies of the radicals to agree on this color as a distinguishing earmark. Finally the word as used by reactionary newspapers came to have the stigma of abusive hatred and contempt attached to it. Thus the case of

one harmless color-word illustrates figurative extension, particularization, and degradation, of meaning.

Specialization of meaning is constantly taking place. We are not
conscious of the process when it happened centuries,—or even decades—before our time. So *myth*, which in Greek, and at first in
English usage, meant any kind of 'story,' now means a particular
kind, usually referring to a god or superhuman being in one of the
'mythologies' of the world. There is also a further specialized sense
of the word, used by students of comparative religion, to mean the
'story' which is a central feature of a particular cult,—as the 'myth'
of Osiris, or the 'myth' of Balder. It is to be noted that as the word
is used in this highly specialized sense, there is no intent to pass on
the historic truth of the story. So orthodox historians of dogma will
speak of the central 'myth' of Christianity. Sometimes 'myth' in
this last sense is written 'mythos,' using the full Greek spelling.
The word *fable* similarly used to mean any 'tale.' As Dryden used
it, he intended it to cover the ground which we include under 'fiction'; it also had the narrower sense of 'plot.' But the word, while
it still has its generalized sense, as in the phrase 'fact or fable,' is
more apt to suggest to us now its *specialized* sense, of "a narration
enforcing some useful truth, especially one in which animals speak
and act like human beings." *Æsop's Fables* have no doubt helped
to give the word this special turn.

Another instance of limitation of sense is the word *silly*. When
the Elizabethan poet wrote a cradle song beginning, "Come little
babe, come silly soul," he meant nothing more by 'silly' than 'innocent,' or 'blessed.' But the range of innocence has been narrowed
until 'silly' now means 'foolish': someone who was not only born
innocent, but who has remained in an infantile and vacuous state.

Sometimes the presence in the older language of a homonym
which has gone out of use leads to a curious confusion in the mind
of the modern reader. So when Shakespeare writes, in the "Owl
Song" in *Love's Labours Lost*, "While greasy Joan doth keel the
pot," many casual readers take it to mean that she clumsily made
the pot 'keel over.' But 'keel' to Shakespeare meant 'cool,' usually
by stirring the pot to keep it from boiling over. 'Keel over' is a
figurative use of a nautical phrase, from the 'keel' of a ship, a sense
still current, as 'keel' meaning 'cool' is not. Evidently it is necessary
to be a bit wary in concluding that a word which has decidedly
changed its meaning is always identical with an archaic term that

had a different sense. There may have been homonyms of which only one has survived.

Another instance of specialization has come about in recent years in the case of 'run.' It is one of the words in the language which has a most broad and inclusive range of meaning. If, however, we make a noun of it and speak of 'a run,' most Americans will think of baseball, and most Englishmen of cricket. A sheepman would understand by 'a run,' 'a sheep-run,' a chicken rancher would think of a 'chicken run.' A salmon fisherman would think of 'a run' of fish upstream to spawn; a horse-racer perhaps of 'gave him a run for it,' meaning that the runner-up in a race pressed the winner hard; a roulette player would understand the term to refer to 'a long run on the red or the black.' It is thus that "every man is his own specializer."—Further discussion of this type of specialization, which depends on the professional interest of the person using a word, will be given in the chapter on special and technical vocabularies. (Chapter VIII.)

51) What was the original specialized (or limited) sense of each of the following general words? (Some of the concrete meanings you should be able to guess from the root, as in the case of *circumstances,* which originally meant 'things standing round about'; others will require a reference to the OED or to Greenough and Kittredge, *Words and Their Ways,* Chapter XVII.)

thing, affair, business, concern, regard, account, article, state, condition, position, situation, way, means, respect, matter, gadget, detail, tendency, substance

For some of these words just given, there is still a definite, specialized sense, in addition to the generalized meaning. Where this is the case, point it out, and use the word in a sentence in the specialized sense.

52) What general sense is sometimes given to each of the following words, which when they stand alone usually have a specialized meaning?

body, head, key, end, engine, machine, motor (British English), costume

Besides the shuttle-like reciprocal action of specialization and generalization, there is a third important process by which words extend their meaning. This is the method of 'radiation.' Take the word *action,* for example. Its primary or central meaning is 'doing.' It may refer (1) to actual and simple doing ('a prompt action'); (2) to a state of activity ('the regiment in action'); (3) to initiating court procedure ('starting an action to recover'); (4) to a religious ceremony ('the next action was elevating the host'); (5) to enterprise ('a man of action'); (6) to the succession of events in a play ('there must be unity of action'); (7) to attitude or position expressing a certain passion ('the action denoting extreme agony in Laokoön'); (8) to a military or naval battle ('the action at Jutland began during a fog'); (9) to the natural or intended motion of anything ('the action of the cardiac muscle'); and, finally, to (10) a mechanism acting ('the valve action of the motor'). Notice that in these many and varied senses of *action,* the primary notion of 'doing' remains in all of them. By the necessities of printing, the various meanings are given one below the other, as if they succeeded each other in time. But actually, as Greenough and Kittredge maintain, the meanings really radiate out from the central sense of 'doing,' like the spokes of a wheel; and if the conventions of lexicography permitted, they should be so arranged. Only so would it be clear how words of this type acquire extensions of meaning, *at the same time* retaining the primary meaning. This is what is meant by 'radiation.'

53) Other words the meaning of which has become extended by radiation are *power, force, head, foot, class, rank, order.* Look these words up in a dictionary, and arrange the various meanings as the 'spokes.' *Order* may require a large wheel, and several small wheels joined on at the end of spokes, where the particular sense has radiated again, developing a satellite wheel tangent to the main one. Make the radiation wheel large enough so that you can write a short sentence or phrase illustrating the use of the word in each radiated sense.

There is a fourth way in which words shift meaning. Ruskin complained about it, in the well-known passage on the pathetic fallacy. Quoting from *Alton Locke,*

> They rowed her in across the rolling foam—
> The cruel, crawling foam

he continues,

The foam is not cruel, neither does it crawl. The state of mind which attributes to it these characters of a living creature is one in which the reason is unhinged by grief. They produce in us a falseness in all our impressions of external things, which I would generally characterize as the "pathetic fallacy." *(Modern Painters,* vol. 3, chap. 12.)

Yet this projection of feeling upon inanimate objects or forces is as common as the illusion by which, when we touch the table with a pencil, we feel the contact at the far end of the pencil, though a moment's reflection will show that there can be no sentience in the pencil. But the pathetic fallacy and the projection of feeling to the end of the pencil are analogous to a general method of changing word-meanings, which comes about through *transference*. At its lowest level, this transfer of meaning occurs in 'a cold day.' It is we who are cold, not the day.

What is true of terms describing sensations, holds with the remaining range of words which deal with mental conceptions. Such words face either toward the person who entertains the notion, or toward the person or thing affected by it; or they may—and here arises the *transference*,—shift back and forth from one to the other.

The word *character* illustrates the point admirably. "He gave his servant a *character*," an Englishman writes, meaning that a testimonial letter was given the servant, telling what, in the opinion of the writer, the servant was like, and how far, in the light of his past performances, he could be depended upon. The *character* in this case is really a *reputation*, as we call the estimate which other persons form of a man's character. The term *character* was long employed in this objective sense. In the seventeenth century, it meant a generic portrait of a certain type of person. On the other hand, when we speak of the development of Hamlet's *character*, as reflected in his successive soliloquies, we think of something happening within him; the *character* of a man, as he himself conceives it, in any event, is subjective. The term really faces both ways, and is transferred from the subjective to the objective sense quite easily. In fact, this process accounts for a good deal of confusion in the discussion of problems of character; for it is not always clear, as we have noted, how far the locus of character is in the person, and how far in the mind of the beholder. The moral aspect of character, in particular, has often been disputed bitterly, because of uncertainty as to whether the moral qualities are in the man himself, or in the minds of his judges. The Greeks, of course, did not bother about this difference between subjective and objective. They used the word *ethos* to mean the character, considered as including both the inward and outward aspects. We prefer the word *personality* for the impression which a man makes on other people, but the Greeks, since they did not make the distinction, had no word for it.

Nor did the Romans, for they used *mores* ('manners,' 'habits,' hence 'character') to include both phases of character. What a man appeared to be, he was, and that was the end of it. But we distinguish between inward and outward aspects of experience. Hence the numerous terms in English which can be 'transferred' from subject to object, and vice versa.

A fifth method by which words shift their meaning is exemplified by such instances as *villain, churl,* and *boor,* fully discussed on p. 135 This is the process of *degeneration* or *degradation* of meaning, by which words once respectable and good in their connotations slide down in the world, until they acquire a derogatory sense. *Lady* is now becoming suspect, because of its misuse as a genteelism in such combinations as *saleslady,* and *washlady.* The word *genteel,* according to H. W. Fowler, is "now used, except by the ignorant, only in mockery." Many words have lost caste by this process, and there are some which are in process of losing it. *Outstanding* is on its way down, largely because it is overworked as an "omnibus" word by journalists. *Adequate* is now deteriorating, implying, when uttered in a slightly contemptuous tone, that the person or thing to which it is applied will barely pass muster. "The rest of the caste were *adequate*" is a critic's condescending sop to minor actors. So when one professor says of another, "He's a dear good fellow," he often implies also that the man is a literary jackanapes. *Respectable* now conveys the notion of a poor, proud, and shabby-genteel creature, rather than its literal sense, 'worthy of respect.' Charles Lamb started the word on its downward path when he said, "Th-thank G-God I have no respectable friends." It was the stuffiness of respectability which Lamb disliked.

Striking instances of the process of degradation may be noted in the case of certain words used by our older poets. In modern usage these words now have humorous or derogatory associations, though when the poet wrote this was not true. So Ralegh, in the verses made the night before he was beheaded, thinks how he will meet in Paradise with other pilgrims, and take them

> To slack their thirst
> And then to taste of Nectars suckettes
> At these clear wells
> Where sweetness dwells
> Drawn up by saints in heavenly buckets.

And when our bottle and all we
Are filled with immortality
Then those holy paths we'll travel
Strew'd with rubies thick as gravel. . . . (spelling modernized)

'Suckets,' and 'buckets,' are no longer poetic words, while to fill up yourself and your bottle with immortality is somehow faintly wrong. But to Ralegh's contemporaries there was nothing amiss about these words. Strictly speaking, the process involved here is also one of *restriction* of meaning, as well as *degradation*. 'Suckets' would be in keeping only in a humorous poem, such as "The Great Rock Candy Mountains"; and 'bucket' we have in "The Old Oaken Bucket." The words with us are familiar and homely, not suggesting proper furnishing for Paradise. It is not only in queering the pitch of the older poetry that this process is at work. It accounts also for a good deal of slang, which is to be discussed later.

The degradation of meaning leads to one amusing consequence: verbal soft-pedalling, commonly called euphemism. The word *servant* having acquired a derogatory connotation, middle westerners spoke of 'the hired girl,'—and she ate with the family. Or 'hired help' was the saving circumlocution. The radical speaks of himself as a 'wage slave,' defiantly reversing this euphemistic habit of phrase. He appears on the books as an 'employee,' but this seems to him too genteel a term for his status.

Euphemism is apparently felt, for the most part, as a mode of elevating the social status of any act, craft, or place. So an *undertaker* becomes a 'mortician,' a *barber-shop* is re-labeled a 'tonsorial parlor,' the proprietor of a beauty shop blossoms out as a 'beautician.' ('Mortician' and 'beautician' are formed by analogy with 'physician,' 'musician,' 'dietitian,' and the like.) It is somehow not thought delicate to stick to the usual trade-names for these professions. As a matter of fact, the simplest and plainest phrase to designate any calling is the best; and good speakers and writers will stick to it. The snobbery or inverted snobbery involved in genteel euphemisms is bad enough: the false delicacy is even worse. A euphemism is almost always a second thought. A moment's hesitation gives the speaker away. It is as if he were taking one of the free association tests which are now used in the psychological detection of guilt. If the victim takes twice as long to answer on a key word connected with the crime, the chances are he is guilty. So with a euphemism. Why say 'a difficulty in finances,' when you mean 'short of money'?

This is not to say that one should refuse to abide by the ordinary verbal tabus of the tribe. A radio speaker who absent-mindedly comes out with any of the words which are barred by twentieth century polite usage, is usually cut off untimely by the control room. But the chances are that the fake-genteel variety of euphemism will not be in this class.

The affected use of foreign words and phrases, to cover up a reference to things ordinarily tabued, always provokes ribald laughter from the back gallery. Putting a French fig-leaf on a naughty idea is only a way of accenting it.

The only safe principle in regard to the use of foreign words and phrases, is this: Employ the foreign word only when English has no word for it. And the chances are that in these few cases, the foreign word will not be a euphemism, but an indispensable idea. We have no single term in English for 'general philosophic outlook,' or 'world-view.' It is natural enough to use the German compound *Weltanschauung*. So for a very important concept in regard to language. Suppose you feel strongly that a certain turn of phrase, while technically accurate, is still not good idiomatic English. You say that the sentence runs counter to 'the feeling of the language.' The Germans have a word for this: *Sprachgefühl*, and we naturally use it, because we have no exactly equivalent expression. Neither of these foreign terms is a euphemism; and each fills a real need. But in general, it is preposterous to interlard good prose with foreign phrases.

At the opposite pole from euphemism is another process by which words decay in force: hyperbole. Instead of the timid cough of the soft-pedaller, we have, in this type of exaggeration, the search for heroically strong expressions which will convey the extremes of approval or denigration. Such words as *delightful, magnificent, splendid, superb, wonderful, overpowering, tremendous,* or *enchanting* are used as exclamatory superlatives; and, at the other extreme, to mark disapprobation, *outrageous, bestial, atrocious, horrible,* or *nauseating* will be attached as a label to some petty annoyance that hardly seems to call for such strong language. Words of both types are used as carelessly as profanity, and with as little sense of the strict meaning. *Awful* is a good instance of a strong word which has degenerated from its original high estate, until it now seems strange to encounter it in the prayer-book in its proper sense of 'awe-inspiring.' Each hyperbole of this kind soon loses, like discharged lightning, all its real potential; then another and still stronger expression is devised, which in turn degenerates. The word *egregious*, as used in the sixteenth century, had its literal sense, 'towering above the herd'; it has now become specialized to mean exclusively a bad eminence, as 'an *egregious* mistake,' or 'an *egregious* scoundrel.' The most recent blanket expression for all kinds of excellence is *outstanding*, though curiously enough the 1934 *Webster* does not give it a figurative extension. But to the journalist anything or anybody that gets into headlines is *outstanding*. Already the word is acquiring a comic connotation for serious writers; and it is probably on its way down. It may eventually acquire a pejorative sense, like *egregious*. All these over-enthusiastic methods of employing words are pretty good evidence that the Greeks were right when they held that the irony of under-statement is a better way of securing emphasis. The deadly quiet style wears better and carries more weight in the long run.

So much for the five chief processes by which words change meaning: generalization, specialization, radiation, transference, and degeneration. All five are of great utility in tracing the case-histories of individual words.

Word Histories

Detective work on words is one of the most amusing of all pursuits. It has its humors, its puzzling problems, and its serious moments. The history of words is in part at least the key to the history of ideas, and especially of social ideas. In tracing the travels of a word across space and through historic time, there is many an adventure by the way.

Some words have been altered strangely, both as to form and meaning, by folk etymology, with its desire to make words look like something familiar and intelligible in the light of ordinary experience with the language. The folk have little respect for learned etymology. When the word *cutlass* was taken over from the French *cotelas*, fighting sailors changed it to *cutlash*, which seemed to whistle through the air better. Tommy Atkins turned Ypres into 'Wipers,' as the eighteenth century sailors had transformed the *Bellerophon* into the 'Belly-ruffian.' *Asparagus* was altered to 'sparrow-grass,' which was in good use during the eighteenth century. *Rake* is from an old English word *rakel,* 'reckless,' perhaps from the Norse *reikall,* 'a vagrant.' Folk etymology changed *rakel* to *rakehell,* and by the clipping habit of slang, this was shortened to *rake.*

Only less amusing than folk etymology are the errors of the learned. Scientific men with small Latin and less Greek have manufactured some fearful and wonderful compounds. Uplifting etymologies have been devised by Carlyle, Ruskin, and their followers. So *God* is derived from *good,* with which it has etymologically no connection. Writers on pedagogy regard it as providential that (as they think) *education* comes from *edūco,* 'to lead or draw out' (the powers of the student); actually it comes from *edŭco,* 'to train.' *Religion* is claimed to be from *religo,* 'to bind' (the human with the divine). Actually it comes from *relego,* 'to take notice of' (with especial reference to the omens or auguries which signified the will of the gods).

Then there are the amusing mistakes of lexicographers. The classic example is *curmudgeon.* Dr. Johnson entered it in his dictionary as "a vitious manner of pronouncing *coeur mechant, Fr.* an unknown correspondent." He meant *Fr.* as an abbreviation of *from,* since the note regarding the derivation was received from an unknown correspondent. John Ash, in his dictionary of 1775, reading *Fr.* as 'French,' gave the derivation of curmudgeon as "from the French *coeur,* unknown, and *mechant,* a correspondent."

Even more comical are the words which are no words, ghost-words, as Weekley calls them. These, often faithfully copied from one dictionary to the next, are mistakes arising from a misprint or a misreading. At the end of the OED there is a long and amusing section devoted to laying these ghost-words.

Folk etymology and the mistakes of the learned alike serve as caution to the student of word-histories. He must work with care.

There are many types of words which have interesting histories. Especially will words repay our study which have to do with the feelings, the will, the instincts, or the mind—in short, all terms which relate to human nature and its interpretation, whether individual or social psychology is concerned. For while the old saying of the humanists, that human nature is always the same, may be partly true, so soon as one raises the question, wherein does the sameness consist, a great variety of answers will be offered. And there is no simpler way to study the many readings of human nature than by tracing the changes of meaning in a single psychological term. We have already noted this fact, in examining the word *character*. But there are terms which yield just as much.

The word *humor*, for example, means literally, in Latin, 'liquid.' It early came to be specialized in English to the four bodily *humors*, which according to Aristotle and Galen and ancient physiologists generally, determined, by their balance, the temperament of a man. If the blood was dominant, a man had a *sanguine* temperament; if the choler was in excess, he was *choleric*; if the bile ruled over his body, he was *melancholy*; and if the phlegm was in the ascendancy, he was *phlegmatic*. These terms remain in the language, though the science from which they come is outmoded. By an easy transfer, the word *humor* was also applied to the mood or emotional set resulting from a predominance of one humor over the others. Again, as Ben Jonson puts it, speaking of the use of the term to which he was to give a wide currency,

> It may, by metaphor, apply itself
> Unto the general disposition;
> As when some one peculiar quality
> Doth so possess a man, that it doth draw
> All his affects, his spirits, or his powers
> In his confluctions, all to run one way,
> This may be truly said to be a humor.
>
> BEN JONSON—Induction to *Every Man Out of His Humour*.

Humor in this sense meant more than a quirk or queer vagary: it implied a single dominant passion or preoccupation; and Shadwell in the late seventeenth, and Dickens in the early nineteenth, century employed this conception of a humor as the basis for character construction, just as Ben Jonson had done. Uriah Heep is an animated *humor* walking around, a bundle of sneaking, crafty submission. From the fact that *humors* characters were employed on the stage as comic creatures, the word *humor* acquired the further extension of meaning which it now has. It came finally to mean a gay, good-tempered variety of the comic; in *humor* proper in the modern sense, one is inclined to laugh both with and at the person, or in some cases, only with him. *Humor* still retains its association with the emotions, although they are only lightly involved; and it is distinguished by this emotional content from *wit*, which is thought to be largely intellectual, though there is perhaps a sudden shrinkage of feeling even in the case of wit.

54) With the help of the OED, or Weekley's *Etymological Dictionary of Modern English,* trace the history of each of the following terms relating to human nature (or psychology, if you like the systematic science better than the older term):

complexion	passion	tropism
wit	quintessence	animism
instinct	influence	tabu
affect (noun)	aspect	apathy
pathos	mesmerism	personality
temper	spirit	epicure

Common nouns which derive from proper names furnish much amusement for the antiquary of words. A *sandwich* gets its name from the eighteenth century Earl of Sandwich, who saved time at the gambling table by putting in layers the bread and meat which his servant brought him. The short coat known as a *spencer* takes its name from the Earl of Spencer, who laid a bet that he could make fashionable a top-coat which would show his tail-coat hanging down below it. Hence the traditional doggerel:

> Two noble earls, whom if I quote
> Some folks might call me sinner;
> The one invented half a coat,
> The other, half a dinner.
>
> WEEKLEY—*Romance of Words,* p. 36.

The cheerful *grog* comes from a nickname which the sailors applied to Admiral Vernon, who from his *grogram* or coarse cloth breeches, was dubbed "Old Grog"; when he gave orders that henceforth the regular tot of rum was to be diluted with water, the sailors gave his nickname to the mixture. The familiar adjective *quixotic* is of course from Cervantes' hero; and it is a concept which could hardly be translated into Latin. So with the name *Hamlet,* used to characterize an indecisive person, sicklied o'er with the pale cast of thought. Until Goethe and Coleridge had familiarized us with this reading of Hamlet's character, the term would have had no such meaning. In the case of names from literature or history which are used in this general allusive fashion, we feel that the words have almost the force of common nouns. These characters have added stock patterns to our reading of human nature.

55) Students of prehistoric man often argue as to the period when a certain tool or device came into use. As an exercise in cultural history based on word-study, look up the origin of the following terms, and fix the approximate date at which each contrivance or concept came into use:

mackintosh	ohm	brougham
shrapnel	ampere	victoria
maxim	volt	derrick
derringer	watt	macadam
bowie knife	wellingtons	listerine
bovril	mafficking	orrery

56) In each case, what kind of character do you give a person by applying to him the following name? And what is the source of each allusion?

Shylock	Babbitt	Circe
Micawber	Lothario	Adonis
Bobadil	Mrs. Grundy	Xantippe
Job	Munchausen	Magdalen
Maecenas	Jehu	Frankenstein
Benedick	Nimrod	Tartar
Don Juan	Juno	Diogenes
Goliath	Apollo	Lycurgus
Narcissus	Diana	Jeremiah
Tulliver	Bacchus	Beau Brummel
Bowdler	Catiline	Wat Tyler
Comstock	Bayard	Nestor
Mohock	Apache	Thersites
Tartuffe	Peter Pan	Dogberry
Bumble	Jezebel	Belshazzar

The title *Chancellor* has a curious history. It comes ultimately from *cancer,* 'a crab.' This had a plural diminutive *cancelli,* which meant 'a grating,' from the resemblance of cross-hatched bars or lattice-work to a crab's tentacles. *Cancelli* was thus the name given to the gratings which separated from the rest of the chamber the part of a large hall used as a court. The usher of the court, who stood just inside the gratings, was *ad cancellos,* 'at the cross-bars'; he was called *cancellarius,* which became 'chancellor' in Law French. As his office grew in dignity, the title came to be one of great honor; and it is now applied to a high legal official or the head of a great educational system. The original connection with crabs and gratings is usually quite forgotten.

Of all the proper names which have become common nouns, perhaps the richest in historical associations is the word *bedlam,* now used to mean a tumultuous confusion, or mad jumble of noises. Late in the era of the Crusades, there was a religious house in the

Holy Land dedicated to St. Mary of Bethlehem, that is, the Virgin. A branch of this in London was at first a hostel for visiting members of the order traveling in England. Eventually this London branch devoted itself to caring for a certain type of afflicted, namely lunatics. When Henry VIII disestablished the monasteries, this hospice was turned over to the City of London, which continued it as an insane asylum, under the name of *Bethlehem Hospital,* or *Bedlam,* as it was called for short, with that turn for telescoping proper names so marked in England,—as witness the pronunciation 'Chumley' for *Cholmondeley,* and 'Marchbanks' for *Marjoribanks.* *Bedlam* came next to be applied to any insane asylum. From the continual din heard in *bedlams,* it was not long until the word became a general term for any noisy confusion.

It is interesting to observe that in the history of this word we have involved the founding of the Christian religion, the passing of the Holy Land into the control of the Saracens, the Crusades, which restored it to Christianity, the continued relations between the Latin Orient and Western Europe, the whole theory and practice of monastic institutions and fraternities, with their labors in behalf of the poor and sick, the Reformation in general, and, in particular, the Reformation in England under Henry VIII, with its confusion of religious and secular motives.—GREENOUGH and KITTREDGE. *Words and Their Ways in English Speech,* p. 389. (Used by permission of The Macmillan Company, publishers.)

In addition to these striking instances, there are many ordinary words in the language which have peculiar case-histories. *Kickshaws,* petty triffles or gewgaws, is a corruption of the French *quelques choses,* 'some things,' often used to mean 'odds-and-ends.' *Jingo* is a word which first appears, says Weekley, in conjuror's jargon of the seventeenth century. It has been conjectured to be from the Basque *jinko,* 'God.' In 1878, when England was on the verge of war with Russia, a music-hall singer, McDermott, sang to large audiences

"We don't want to fight, but by *Jingo* if we do,
We've got the men, we've got the ships, we've got the money too."

Horatio Bottomly claimed that he first wrote the word as a common noun, at the dictation of his uncle. Certain it is that the journalists put it into use, from the song, as an epithet for a shouting, imperialistic patriot; and it has held the field ever since. *Tennis* is from the French *tenez,* 'hold,' which early French players of the indoor game called out when they struck the ball. *Cabal*, for a political intrigue or a group of conspirators, comes from the Hebrew word for a hidden or mysterious interpretation of the Scriptures: *kabbala*, which we have borrowed in this more proper form, to refer to the mystical writings of medieval Jewish schoolmen. But *cabal* was reinforced in its present sense by the accident that Charles II had a clever and intriguing cabinet council for foreign affairs whose initials spelled CABAL: *C*lifford, *A*rlington, *B*uckingham, *A*shley, and *L*auderdale. And so it goes. There are countless words whose record is interwoven with the movements and events of history.

57) Look into the OED, or Greenough and Kittredge's *Words and Their Ways in English Speech*, Weekley's *Romance of Words* or his *Etymological Dictionary of Modern English* to trace the history of the following words:

tawdry	magnet	ambergris
pub	buccaneer	electricity
zoo	hick	blackguard
blurb	hoodlum	van (luggage)
mammet	larrikin	van (advance guard)
snickersnee	hock	rack
patter	bureau	belfrey (not from *bell*)
palaver	whiskey	maverick
jest	canter	demijohn
jaywalker	antimacassar	mandrake
shilly-shally	antic	touchy (not from *touch*)
brummagem	cordovan	Old Nick
bowdlerize	buncombe (bunkum)	gramarye
coxcomb	bench	viking (not from *king*)
cashmere	abracadabra	bacteria
yard	kris	

The study of word-histories, and of the fashions which have prevailed in the use of words, is in fact one of the most rewarding of occupations for the speaker or writer who wants to acquire a nice sense of diction. When this study is pursued in the light of the general processes by which words shift their meaning, it leads up naturally to the study of synonyms. For when it is a matter of choosing which one of several words is to be employed in a given context, the history of the terms in question will furnish something of a guide to an understanding of the full connotations of the word finally chosen. The full flavor of a word cannot be felt without knowing its history. The incredible aptness in word-choice of such masters as Bernard Shaw and Havelock Ellis is in no small degree due to their full feeling for the history of words. The amateur of words cannot hope to reach readiness and precision in diction without studying the history of the words which go to make up a group of synonyms. After the history, comes the matter of the current use of the word, as it is now employed by the liveliest writers. It is to this study of synonyms in current use that we now proceed. But it is well to bear in mind the light which semantics and word-histories will throw upon synonyms and their various shades of meaning.

58) a)   Select from your current reading twenty words which strike you as curious or peculiar, and look up their histories.

b)   Trace the history of each striking word in the passages from our older writers quoted in the chapter on The Art of Conversation toward the end of the book.

CHAPTER VI

No one except Gertrude Stein aspires to write monotonously and repetitiously. She can talk to herself and get everybody else to listen; but those who have not yet got the world by the ear must pay some attention to variety in diction. Variety calls for a study of synonyms. To be sure, it may be well to take a leaf out of Miss Stein's book. She knows what she is doing, even if most of her newspaper critics do not. She is not out of her mind, just outside of everybody else's. And she brings home to us a necessary caution in regard to the over-free use of synonyms: a caution so obvious that it takes Miss Stein to notice it. If the meaning calls for a repetition of the word itself, we should not use a synonym, but have the courage to repeat the word, and let euphony go hang. Not many of us can worry an idea as long as Miss Stein, nor does the idea come home to us with the poetic vividness which forces her to repeat the same words over and over, like a refrain. Allowing, therefore, for the difference between her purposes and those of the ordinary prose writer, the study of synonyms is still essential if we are to avoid tedious and unnecessary iteration.

There is another valid reason for the investigation of synonyms. Mark Twain pointed it out by the horrible example which he made of Fenimore Cooper. Cooper was addicted to the habit of using vague, general words which did not exactly convey his meaning, but just hit somewhere near it. This, said Mark Twain, was one reason Cooper never rose above the second-rate. A writer who will not bother to distinguish between fine shades of meaning, will never become a master of his craft.

The demand for variety, and the need for precision in diction call, then, for an extensive inquiry into synonyms. Such an inquiry is one of the best ways to bring the vocabulary into exact focus, so that the words selected give clear, sharp, and definite edge to the meaning. There will be no woolly fringes, no fuzzy and ill-defined borders, if the right synonym is chosen to express the shade of meaning in the

131

writer's mind. Indeed, the effort to choose the right phrasing, in a list of nearly equivalent terms, will in itself help to clarify the thought.

Rather than begin with a long and confusing list, however, it seems more natural to embark on the study of synonyms by considering the dilemma which confronts a writer or speaker when he hesitates between two words, so closely equivalent in meaning that there is little to choose between them on any grounds but those of taste and usage.

Because of the composite nature of the English language, which was traced historically in the chapter on "Word-Families," there are for many of the commonest *meanings* in the language two words, one of Anglo-Saxon, one of Latin origin. Usually the Anglo-Saxon word is the commoner, and for ordinary purposes it is to be preferred. No one would speak of a *lupine* appetite, when he meant *wolfish;* or describe a wrestler as having a *taurine* instead of a *bull-like* neck. A politician is *foxy,* not *vulpine;* and a *horsy* face means more than an *equine* countenance.

But there are many cases where the word of Latin origin has become more familiar than the native Saxon. *Doctor* or *physician* is more usual than *leech,* which is now archaic. *Contradict* has displaced *gainsay, baleful* has given way to *destructive,* though *harmful* has maintained its ground on a par with *injurious.* In formal writing, the word of classical origin is sometimes stronger than the Saxon term.

59) In the following pairs, the Saxon word is given first, the classical second. In which cases is the word of Latin origin more forceful than the native term?

steep, precipitous	sleepy, somnolent
fall, collapse	talkative, loquacious
skin, flay	blush, erubescence
stir, commotion	house, domicile
work, labor	spit, expectorate
thin, emaciated	meal, repast
twisted, contorted	lewd, libidinous
sparkle, scintillate	widow, relict
strike, collide	fast, rapid
hate, abominate	walker, pedestrian
learned, erudite	dead, defunct

60) Give the synonym of classical origin for each of the following native words (e.g., clothing—raiment):

chew, drink, dwindle, draft, earnest, find, gainsay, give, mad, mound, mislead, outside, burdensome, healing, manly, glee, lore, lighten, shorten.

There are usually wide differences in connotation between the Saxon word and its classical synonym. It is hard to lay down any general rule, taste and usage having operated in this sphere. We speak naturally of an *ardent* interest, but of *hot* soup; of *navigating* an ocean liner, but of *sailing* a small boat; of the *inculcation* of doctrine, but of *teaching* the ABC's. The cashier of a bank *embezzles*, while a common yegg *steals*. The astronomer makes an *error* in his calculations, the schoolboy either an *error* or *mistake*. We talk of the *Serpent* in the Garden of Eden, hardly of the *snake;* of the *abatement* of a nuisance, but of a *lessening* of the tension on a cable; of the *intelligence* of a scholar, but of the animal *cunning* of an athlete in a tight place; of the Amsterdam synagogue pronouncing its solemn *anathema* on Spinoza, but of General Hugh Johnson giving a good round *cursing* to refractory capitalists; of a *benefaction* to a great cathedral, and a little *help* for the unemployed.—If, upon inspecting these examples, a rule were to be ventured, it would run something like this. In general, the classical derivative is used in formal and dignified circumstances. It is used where a figurative rather than a plain and literal meaning is intended. If the occasion is a speech from the lecturer's rostrum, the classical word is often to be expected. If it is just a plain talking match, where everyone may join in, the Saxon word is more apt to fit. Nothing will so quickly queer the pitch of ordinary lively talk as interlarding it with pretentious Latinized words. But these words have their place, too, and English prose cannot get on without them. In many cases, the words from the learned languages have naturalized themselves, and have clipped or foreshortened their form, until it is hard to tell them from Saxon words,—as was noted in another connection.

61) Which of the following are "good old Anglo-Saxon words"?

age, art, case, cent, cost, fact, form, ink, line, mile, pain, pair, part, pen, piece, price, rule, sound, ton, tone, and vail; apt, clear, cross, crude, firm, grand, large, mere, nice, pale, plain, poor, pure, rare, real, rich, round, safe, scarce, sure, vain, and vast; add, aid, aim, boil, close, cook, cure, fail, fix, fry, mix, move, pay, save, serve, try, turn, and use; bull, jilt, inch, pan, pin, pit, date.

Another source of the wealth of synonyms in English is the large stock of doublets, words that came from the same stem, but which entered at a different stage of the development of the language. We noted *catch* and *chase*, from Low Latin *caciare*, one coming through Norman, and the other through Central, French. The usual pair of doublets comprises one word from the Latin through the French, and one from the same Latin word direct. Sometimes they have diverged widely in meaning; but in other cases the general significance is the same, only the words are used for divergent occasions and with somewhat different connotations. We *abbreviate* a word, but we *abridge* a book. A *canal* is an artificial *channel*. An employer can be in a *devilish* bad humor without having *diabolical* intentions. A *crevice* in rock is not as dangerous as a *crevasse* in a glacier. Not all *debts* are *due*, in a time when moratoriums are common. A university may be *endowed* with money, without being *endued* with the virtues of learning. An *example* may or may not be a fair *sample* of a mass of data. A mushroom may be *edible* but not *eatable* after a bad cook has ruined it. The *warden* of a penitentiary may also be, like Thomas Mott Osborne, an admirable *guardian* of the interest of society in reforming the criminal. We *hurl* a boomerang, but after it is started, it *hurtles* through the air. *Palsy* now suggests the quivering which follows partial *paralysis*. All these doublets had originally much the same area of meaning, and even yet, in the instances chosen, there is a similarity of meaning, but not an identity. Perhaps *eatable* and *edible* are most nearly interchangeable. But try translating Wilde's epigrammatic description of the English country squire chasing the fox, "the *unspeakable* in full pursuit of the *uneatable*." Using the classical words, this becomes "the *ineffable* in full pursuit of the *inedible*." This is more than faintly wrong. Even Dr. Johnson would never have said this, at his most sesquipedalian.

62) Of the following doublets, which can be used interchangeably?

zero, cipher
pry, peer
reprieve, reprove
mode, mood
naked, nude
guarantee, warranty
entire, integer
enwrap, envelope
evil, ill
plum, prune

shuffle, scuffle
snivel, snuffle
tight, taut
squall, squeal
naive, native
fiddle, viol
complacent, complaisant
church, kirk
guile, vile
fancy, phantasy

Where you claim that the members of the pair can be used interchangeably, prove it by writing sentences where either doublet will serve. Write also sentences illustrating the use of the doublets which are not interchangeable.

There are also closely allied words from the same root, which, while not doublets, are particularly tricky. An *urban* person may or may not be *urbane*, though the original implications of the latter adjective held that a city man was automatically polished in his manner; while a *rural* dweller was bound to have a certain *rusticity*. The adjective *rustic* is now applied mostly to quaint pastoral scenery; the noun *rustic* has that flavor, at once derogatory and condescending, which all words associated with the farm and farm life seem finally to acquire in literary language determined by the cityfied. The word *villain*, originally a serf (*villanus*) attached to a country estate (*villa*) came to mean, in the Middle Ages, anyone not of noble birth, hence unacquainted with courtesy and chivalric manners; so *villain* was applied to a baseborn or low person, and finally *villainy* came to mean any low conduct. Eventually it took on its present notion of scoundrelism. The words *churl* and *boor* have come down in the world in much the same way; while the word *farmer* is not the proud title that it once was. In some parts of the West, it is safer to call a man a *rancher*. In such cases as these, it is surely well to keep the synonyms straight. (The Westerner has quite a choice list of retaliating synonyms for 'dudes' and 'city slickers.')

Interesting as the approach to synonyms through etymology may be, it is not a direct frontal mode of attack for the writer who is worried over the right word. He cudgels his wits for a synonym when he has to refer several times, in the same sentence or successive sentences, to a term or an idea. Pronouns of reference will go only so far to meet this need. Here is where plenty of practice is required, in conjuring up, on short notice, synonyms for the most common words,—and ideas.

63) It is easy to summon up synonyms for some common words. *Balance,* for instance, at once suggests *equilibrium, question* calls up *interrogation, teaching* implies *instruction.* But not all common words are so easily matched.

Supply one or more close synonyms for each of the following. Formulate in your mind, or write, a sentence using the original word, and see if the synonym you propose can be substituted without a loss, or even decided change in meaning. (The numbers in parentheses after the words refer to the Thorndike frequency.)

1. account (1)
2. act (1)
3. adjustment (8)
4. amount (1)
5. amusement (5)
6. approval (7)
7. argument (3)
8. attention (2)
9. attraction (5)
10. balance (2)
11. base (2)
12. birth (2)
13. breath (2)
14. burn (1)
15. burst (2)
16. cause (1)
17. chance (1)
18. change (1)
19. comfort (2)
20. company (1)
21. control (2)
22. cover (1)
23. current (2)
24. damage (3)
25. death (1)
26. degree (2)
27. earth (1)
28. edge (1)
29. effect (2)
30. error (2)
31. exchange (2)
32. feeling (2)
33. fiction (6)

34. government (1)
35. harmony (3)
36. hate (2)
37. history (2)
38. humor (3)
39. increase (1)
40. insurance (5)
41. interest (1)
42. join (1)
43. learn(ing) (1)
44. level (2)
45. limit (2)
46. liquid (3)
47. loss (1)
48. mass (2)
49. measure (1)
50. middle (1)
51. move (1)
52. music (1)
53. nation (1)
54. need (1)
55. offer (1)
56. opinion (2)
57. order (1)
58. pain (1)
59. pleasure (1)
60. point (1)
61. power (1)
62. price (1)
63. produce (2)
64. profit (2)
65. protest (4)
66. punishment (3)
67. push (2)

68. question (1)
69. range (2)
70. rate (2)
71. reaction (9)
72. reward (3)
73. rule (1)
74. scale (2)
75. self (1)
76. sense (2)
77. sex (4)
78. shade (1)
79. shock (2)
80. side (1)
81. size (1)
82. sleep (1)
83. slope (2)
84. sort (1)
85. statement (4)
86. stretch (2)
87. suggestion (6)
88. support (2)
89. surprise (1)
90. system (2)
91. thing (1)
92. time (1)
93. trade (1)
94. trouble (1)
95. twist (3)
96. way (1)
97. writ(ing) (1)
98. word (1)
99. work (1)
100. wound (2)

It is of interest to note that these 100 words are all from the Basic English list of 400 names of "general things," which the Orthological Institute headed by C. K. Ogden regards as the most essential ideas —for which terms must be maintained in the severely constricted vocabulary of Basic, numbering only 850 words in all. Presumably, therefore, these ideas will recur again and again in all kinds of ordinary discourse; hence it is particularly necessary to build up a stock of synonyms for these words.

Basic English also furnishes a great simplification in the task of dealing with synonyms in the field of verbs. Because of a peculiarity of our language which permits the formation of phrasal verbs by adding to a simple verb a preposition indicating direction, it has been possible for the makers of this supplemental form of English to cover 4000 common verbs by 16 simple verb forms and the prepositions, etc. Instead of *detour* they say 'go round.'—These sixteen verbs, plus the prepositions, will replace most of the words which render actions or states, and will express the same range of meaning.

To be sure, Basic English is not without names for actions; about two hundred of the names which it retains for 'things' are nouns designating actions or states. Many of these nouns are also verbs in standard English. In Basic, for instance, one writes, using one of the sixteen remaining verbs (they are called operators in Basic), not 'change,' but 'make a change'; not 'walk' but 'take a walk' or 'go for a walk.'

In the main, however, it is possible to use the phrasal verbs, formed from the sixteen in the Basic list by the addition of various prepositions, to express the immense number of actions for which English normally needs at least 4000 verbs, mostly of classical origin. For our purposes, in the study of synonyms in orthodox English, this fact is of great significance. By starting with the sixteen Basic verbs, which are the most general expressions of action, we can build up a whole synonymy for this important part of the vocabulary. Take the Basic verb, *go*. To 'go about' is to *travel;* to 'go round' is to *circle,* to *detour,* or to *skirt;* to 'go down' is to *descend;* to 'go in' is to *enter;* to 'go up' is to *ascend,* or to *climb;* to 'go with' is to *accompany;* to 'go away,' to 'go out,' is to *depart* or *leave;* to 'go through' is to *traverse;* to 'go against' is to *oppose;* to 'go off' is to *explode* or to *diverge* (from a course or track); to 'go before' is to *procede;* to 'go after' is to *follow,* to 'go under' is to *submerge;* while in a slang sense, 'go for' is slowly making its way in the sense of 'to be enthusiastic over.' When the statement is made that English has no exact synonyms, these two modes of expressing a given action have been forgotten. They are so closely equivalent in meaning that it would be no misnomer to put a sign of equality between them, in each case.

64) Using the prepositions commonly employed in forming phrasal verbs, *about, round, down, in, with, from, to, through, for, against, out, over, off, up,* etc., write out the possible phrasal verb forms to be made from the following eleven Basic verbs, and place opposite each of these combinations the single verb, usually of classical derivation, which is equivalent in meaning (as was done for 'go,' above):

come, get, give, keep, make, put, take, do, say, see, send.

The next step in expanding this list of synonyms for verbs is to subdivide each one into the various modes or methods of *coming, getting, giving, keeping,* and so on. When Shakespeare wrote, "Stand not upon the order of your going" (Macbeth III iv), the advice was good for his character, but not apt for the reader who is curious about synonyms. For the order of going is important. The various orders, or better, the ways, of *going* are: *to walk, to run, to ride, to fly, to crawl, to swim, to jump.* Each of these main ways of *going* has in turn a good many synonyms, to distinguish still further the various manners of walking, running, riding, flying, and crawling:

WALK, plod, trudge, hobble, limp, stalk, strut, tramp, march, shuffle, toddle, waddle, mince, stroll, saunter, ramble, amble, careen, slouch along, lumber, promenade, pace, tread, prowl, meander, loiter, linger, lag, stride. (Cf. the slang, 'mosey along.') (Cf. 'barge,' as 'barge in to a room.')

RUN, scamper, scurry, scuttle, scud, scour, pace, gallop, trot, lope, sprint, sweep.

RIDE, gallop, trot, lope, canter, jog, amble, motor, cycle.

FLY, flit, hover, wing, glide, soar, dart, float.

CRAWL, creep, 'inch along,' grovel, drag.

SWIM, dive.

JUMP, dive, hop, leap, skip, vault, hurdle.

65) For each of the other Basic verbs, complete a similar list showing the main modes of *getting, giving, keeping, making, putting, taking, doing, saying, seeing,* and *sending.* For each of the subordinate words, provide a full list of synonyms, resorting to the dictionary, or dictionaries of synonyms, only when you have exhausted your own stock. To aid you in making them, a partial "breakdown" list of synonyms for each of the main Basic verbs is given herewith. Can you add to them?

COME, (The modes of coming are essentially comprised under *going,* above) approach, arrive, befall, occur, attend.

GET, acquire, obtain, attain, gain, win, earn, procure, receive.

GIVE, bestow, grant, furnish, supply, confer, impart, present.

KEEP, hold, detain, retain, preserve, save, observe, fulfil.

LET, permit, allow.

MAKE, create, frame, fashion, prepare, construct, form, fabricate, mold, forge, invent, establish, manufacture.

PUT, place, locate, establish, fix.

SEEM, appear, look.

TAKE, seize, confiscate, grasp, grab, gain, acquire, accept.

DO, accomplish, achieve, effect, perform, execute, act, make.

HAVE, possess, own, hold.

SAY, utter, pronounce, state, declare, affirm, aver, asseverate, allege, assert, avouch, avow, maintain, claim, depose, predicate, swear, suggest, insinuate, testify.

Speak, discourse, expatiate, descant, comment, argue, persuade, plead, lecture, preach, harangue, rant, roar, spout, thunder, declaim, harp.

Talk (noun in Basic), chat, chatter, prate, prattle, babble, gabble, jabber, tattle, twaddle, blab, gossip, palaver, parley, converse, mumble, mutter, stammer, stutter, confer.

Tell, narrate, reveal, blab, set forth, recount, inform, disclose, recite (and in a different sense, order, indicate, etc.).

SEE, perceive, descry, distinguish, espy, discern, note, notice, watch, observe, witness, behold, view.

Cf. *Look* (noun in Basic), glance, gaze, stare, peer, scan, scrutinize, gloat, glare, glower, lower, peek, peep, gape, con, pore, ogle, leer, view, survey, inspect, regard, watch, contemplate.

SEND, dispatch, transfer.

MAY, equals 'be permitted to,' 'be allowed to.'

WILL, the closest equivalent is *wish,* but this is not very close. There is really no possible exact substitute for these two Basic words.

CAN, be able.

The admirable feature of verb-synonyms built up in this systematic fashion is that it is easy, without a great amount of memory work, to retrace one's steps through the whole 4000 English verbs, by using the sixteen Basic "operators" as keys which unlock the complete hoard. One need remember only the essential verb expressing the notion in most generalized form, quickly reconstruct the chief sub-divisions under it, and the needed synonym to express the precise variety of action is quickly on the tongue or pen.

The case is altered, when nouns and adjectives are in question. Here there is no such short-cut. But the Basic English list will also permit a lightening of the task, once certain barriers are cleared out of the way.

The English vocabulary is blessed,—or cursed,—with a wealth of "omnibus" words, upon which a writer may load a great many meanings, without being sure which meaning, if any, will get off, when the omnibus word stops in front of a reader. Such words, in our time, are *case, thing, line, experience, object;* or those more recently worked to death in the newspapers, *angle, slant, proposition.* There are also adjectives, which, as used in an exclamatory sense, have had all specific meaning stretched out of them: *awful, fine, grand, ideal, lovely, outstanding,* and *weird.* These words, when employed rhapsodically, are almost as empty of content as trite profanity. They mark the return of language to the bow-wow theory of its origins; for while such words may vaguely express an emotional attitude, they show that the speaker or writer did not bother to define, even to himself, his exact meaning. Such words say nothing in particular and say it very ill. What is worse, they are all words which have a proper use, and it is sad to contemplate their ruin. If language were mechanical, and we wanted words to be interchangeable, like the spare parts for a given make of car, omnibus words would be admirable. But words in context should be alive, not mechanized.

An exception must be made for that kind of logical or scientific writing which aims at the widest generality, and which employs, therefore, abstract or generalized symbols, such as "a," "x," or "y," C for carbon, N for nitrogen, π for the ratio of the circumference of a circle to its diameter, etc.,—arbitrary sign language emptied of all concrete content. These are really convenient hieroglyphics, not words at all in the humanistic sense. Such a procedure is quite different from working real words to death. In most writing, what is wanted is words which shall be uniquely expressive, and which shall convey the exact shade of meaning which the writer intends. Nothing else will do.

A word apt for all occasions is really fit for none. To say of a drawing that it is *interesting,* or that one *appreciates* it; to remark of a dress that it is *cute,* or of a movie that it is *thrilling,* is to exalt one's own feeling without telling anything about the drawing, the dress, or the movie. Omnibus words are usually found in such gush as this. They smack, indeed, of girls' boarding school dialogue, or of literary and artistic chatter at the corresponding level. Omnibus

words also sprawl lazily over the pages of a writer who is too careless, lazy, hasty, or ignorant to bother about finding words which
will render his meaning in concrete and specific fashion. Such a
writer lives always in a world of fog and shadows. As Goethe remarked, all theory is grey; and greyness is a quality little desirable
in lively talk or spirited writing, however admirable it may be in
scientific discourse.

There is the less excuse for using omnibus words because the English vocabulary has a greater wealth of synonyms than any other
known language, ancient or modern. It compensates for assigning
many senses to one word, by having a variety of words to express
different shades of the same meaning. There is no better way to
enlarge, and at the same time sharpen, the vocabulary, than by an
investigation of the use of these words of similar but by no means
identical meaning. As soon as we embark on this study, we realize
at once that omnibus words derive from the lazy man's habit of
taking advantage of a general law of language. This is a tendency,
already described at length, to changes of word-meaning in the direction of greater generality. (The shuttle also works the other way,
general words acquiring more specialized meanings, as we also
noted.) But an investigation of words of generalized meaning will
soon obliterate the habit of using omnibus words. Such general
terms are not omnibus words in the bad sense.

Any systematic examination of synonyms in large groups must
begin, indeed, with an inquiry as to what words cut the widest swath
of meaning, or include the most comprehensive and general notions.
For if we are to group synonyms, we want at the head of the list the
word which includes the maximum area of meaning; the lesser words
will include only a part of the larger area, though perhaps adding
a further zone of meaning not found in the main word.

Take, for example, *comparison:* the act of examining two or more
things or persons to find in what respects they are like, and in what
respects unlike. An examination disclosing their general unlikeness
is referred to as *contrast,* which thus takes in only part of the area
of meaning included under *comparison.* A refinement of *contrast* is
achieved by *differentiation,* when we trace the dissimilarities item
by item; while the classification of objects according to their differences is *discrimination.* The last word often connotes an ability to
distinguish subtle differences. When two parallel clauses of con-
trasting meaning are set sharply against one another, we call this
special form of contrast *antithesis.* Returning to the primary word,

comparison, we find that a particular kind of comparison, involved in placing two variant versions of a manuscript or text side by side, in order to determine the right reading, is known as *collation*. Again, if a passage from North's *Plutarch* is placed side by side with a passage in Shakespeare's *Julius Cæsar*, and we note close *correspondences* in the phrasing, we speak of this kind of comparison as the establishment of a *parallelism*,—unless we import modern literary morality, and call it plagiarism. Figures of speech involving comparison are *similes*, when the connective *like* or *as* is used to introduce the image; while if an *identification* is boldly asserted between the original thing and the image, we speak of *metaphor*. Notice that while *comparison* includes all these meanings, none of them will serve as a complete equivalent for *comparison*. The process is not reversible. This is the best test to establish the maximum generality of the first term chosen. Its synonyms must express shades of its meaning, and usually it should be possible to substitute for one of the synonyms the primary word; but not vice versa.

This process may be represented diagrammatically:

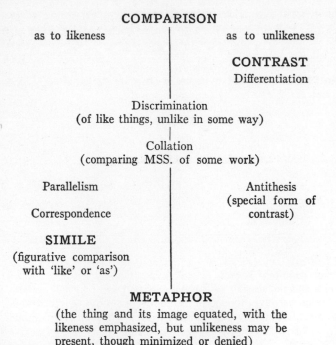

COMPARISON

as to likeness   as to unlikeness

CONTRAST
Differentiation

Discrimination
(of like things, unlike in some way)

Collation
(comparing MSS. of some work)

Parallelism   Antithesis
(special form of
Correspondence   contrast)

SIMILE
(figurative comparison
with 'like' or 'as')

METAPHOR
(the thing and its image equated, with the
likeness emphasized, but unlikeness may be
present, though minimized or denied)

It is not hard to construct diagrams of this type, which show in schematic form the *differentiation* in the use of words closely synonymous. Here are some characteristic tables, which show how synonyms have become specialized in function. They are worthy of close inspection.

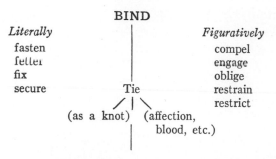

BIND

Literally		*Figuratively*
fasten		compel
fetter		engage
fix		oblige
secure	Tie	restrain
	╱ │ ╲	restrict
(as a knot)	(affection,	
	blood, etc.)	

(Literally): We *bind* objects together with rope, string, or rubber bands. A rip in one's clothing is temporarily *fastened* together with pins. A policeman *fetters* the wrists of his prisoner with handcuffs.

(Figuratively): The necessity of obtaining food and shelter *compels* men to work. If the work is pleasant, we *engage* ourselves to perform it without distaste. A maniac must be *restrained* forcibly from murdering his grandmother. If one speaks only one language, one's reading is *restricted* to books written in that language. To join the two ends of a piece of string we must *tie* them into a knot. Many more people would travel were it not for family *ties*.

TOLERATE

Allow		*Endure*
permit		abide
brook		bear
concede		suffer
admit		sustain
grant		undergo
sanction		
yield		

On Christmas day, we *allow* our children to annoy us with loud noises. We do not definitely *permit*, or authorize, them to do this; but, realizing their youth and the amount of happiness given them by such innocent activities, we resign ourselves to *endure* the annoyance. If a friend, who is stupid, but well-meaning, does us an unintentional injury, we *tolerate* the inconvenience. One of two wrestlers is obliged to *yield* to the superior strength of his opponent. The match could not, however, be won by foul fighting, since this is not *sanctioned* by the rules of the game. In all sports and games, the participants are expected to *abide* by the rules. After *sustaining* a severe fracture of the hip, the patient must *undergo* a surgical operation.

HARMONY

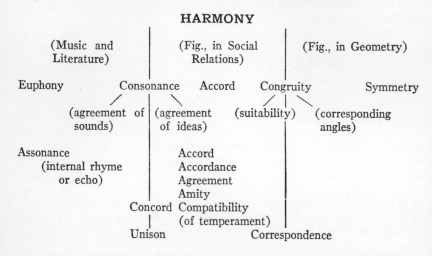

| (Music and Literature) | (Fig., in Social Relations) | (Fig., in Geometry) |

Euphony   Consonance   Accord   Congruity   Symmetry

(agreement of sounds)   (agreement of ideas)   (suitability)   (corresponding angles)

Assonance (internal rhyme or echo)

Accord
Accordance
Agreement
Amity
Concord Compatibility
| (of temperament)
Unison   Correspondence

Sit at the piano and strike two notes simultaneously: if these happen to be, for instance middle C and the seventh note above middle C, or B, the sound produced will be disagreeable to the ear. If, however, middle C and E are struck together, the ear is satisfied by two sounds in *harmony*. By extension, any combination of sounds, musical or verbal, or of thoughts or ideas, which gives to the senses a feeling of satisfaction and finality, is a *harmonious* combination. For instance, when a man and his wife are able to live in perfect *agreement* of ideas over a long period of time, we say that they have achieved domestic *harmony*. When the quality of a sound gives to the ear an impression of sweetness, that sound is *euphonious*. *Euphony* is well illustrated in some of the head-notes produced by radio crooners, or in the Vox Humana stop of the organ. In poetry, two words which agree in sound are in *rhyme:* moon and spoon. Words whose last accented vowels are in *rhyme,* but whose final consonants differ, have *assonance:* baby and lady. *Consonance* is a synonym of *harmony,* but it is also used figuratively to express complete *agreement.* Literally, it means two sounds uttered simultaneously, whether these are in *harmony,* or in *unison:* as, two singers both singing middle C. *Unison,* then, is *consonance* of pitch. *Harmony* in human relationships. Besides the example of domestic *harmony* given above, we may speak of two men living together in *amity,* or in perfect *accord* as to their domestic habits and general tastes. *Congruity* as used in geometry, applies to a state of *correspondence* between two plane figures, such that one could be exactly superimposed on the other, all parts matching.

RECORD

One's Known Actions	Of Events
character (what one is)	history
	chronicle
reputation (what one is	annals
thought to be)	archives
	register
	memoirs
	biography
	account

A *record* in general is a written *account* of events or facts. *History* is a systematic *account* of events, *chronicles* are also *records* of events; but while an historian selects and emphasizes this or that event, a chronicler merely *records* them in their succession in time. An *annal* is a yearly *record*. *Histories* are frequently based on *archives*, or public *records*. A *biography* is an *account* of a man's life by somebody else, *memoirs* are autobiographical, that is, they are written by a man about himself and his experiences. A written *record* of *character* is given to a servant when he applies for a new position. One's *reputation* is how one's *character* appears to others, judged by one's speech and actions.

MISFORTUNE

(reparable)	(irreparable)
misadventure	calamity
mishap	disaster
mischance	cataclysm (Never of a single person; it implies a disaster on a grand scale, usually one caused by irresistible natural forces.)
	casualty

Misfortune, mishap and *misadventure* all signify ill luck or bad fortune, but *misfortune* is the strongest of the three words, and implies serious consequences. To lose all one's money and be left destitute is a *misfortune;* to lose a few coins from one's pocket is a *mishap;* to miss an appointment is a *misadventure. Calamity* is an overwhelming *misfortune,* involving many persons, a nation, or a race. The Black Death which visited Europe in the Middle Ages was a *calamity.* An earthquake is a *cataclysm,* and if it results in human suffering, it becomes a *disaster.* A fire at sea is not a *cataclysm* but a *disaster.* The magnitude of a *disaster* is measured by the number of *casualties.* The word *casualty* means an unfortunate occurrence, but it is most frequently used to designate *mischances* involving loss of life or serious injury.

IMAGE

(Actual image or imitation)	(Verbal or mental image)	(Image representing something else)
Mold — connotes shape of image	Apprehension — understanding	Emblem — representation
Facsimile ⎱ ..a duplicate Replica ⎰	Conception — (one's ideas of)	Sign
Copy—(often in another medium)	Impression — (on the mind, which is like wax)	Symbol
Design — suggests pattern of image	Conceit—(a far-fetched figure of speech)	Token — (a charm or memento)
	Fancy—	
	Imagination — (power of imaging and of fusing images)	

(Names of specific images
or figures of speech:

simile
metaphor
et cetera)

A *copy* is a reproduction of something, not necessarily exact; a *facsimile* is an exact reproduction; a *replica* is an exact reproduction, especially of a work of art, by the creator of the original. No *facsimile* of the papyrus being available, I made a rough *copy* of it. This floral *design* gives me the *impression* of having been done by an artist who lacked *imagination.* The word *impression* may also be used to designate the total number of copies of a book. Both *fancy* and *imagination* combine and modify mental *images,* but *fancy* is light, whimsical, while *imagination* is deep and serious. A great poet possesses both—Shakespeare was gifted with dramatic *imagination* but he frequently gave free play to *fancy* and ornamented his writings with *conceits. Fancy* being non-essential, a scientist has little use for it; *imagination,* on the other hand, is the very fountain-head of scientific discovery. *Apprehension* denotes understanding, but it also signifies anticipation of evil. In the first case it is synonymous with comprehension, in the second—with presentiment. A mathematician has an *apprehension* of the significance of algebraic *symbols.* The inhabitants of the besieged city lived in a state of nervous *apprehension.* To form a true *conception* of a subject, it is necessary to *apprehend* it. An *emblem* is an object suggesting another by association or actual resemblance; a *symbol* may be entirely arbitrary. A laurel wreath is an *emblem* of victory; H — is a chemical *symbol* or *sign* of hydrogen. A *token* is a *symbol* which serves as a guarantee or a memento. A wedding ring is a *token* of undying love; it is also an *emblem* of eternity.

BLUFF

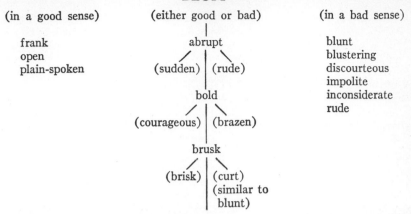

(in a good sense)	(either good or bad)	(in a bad sense)
frank	abrupt	blunt
open	/ \	blustering
plain-spoken	(sudden) (rude)	discourteous
		impolite
	bold	inconsiderate
	/ \	rude
	(courageous) (brazen)	
	brusk	
	/ \	
	(brisk) (curt)	
	(similar to blunt)	

Bluff is an epithet that can be applied in two senses. One speaks of a *bluff* old English squire, meaning *frank, open, plain-spoken*. Then, in a bad sense, a man may habitually 'speak his own mind' with the emphasis on disagreeable home-truths. Such a man is *blunt, impolite*, even *rude*. One who neglects common politenesses of everyday behavior is *discourteous;* and when his behavior manifests a blindness to the feelings of others, he is *inconsiderate*. Synonyms of *bluff* which may be applied either in a good or a bad sense are: *abrupt*, which may refer merely to habits of speech; *bold*, which contains the implications either of bravery or of deliberate rudeness; or *brusk*, which is hardly distinguishable from *abrupt*, or *curt*. A man who refuses to remove his hat in the presence of ladies is *discourteous*. His *inconsiderate* behavior manifested itself in complete disregard for the feelings of his family. After a few drinks, the old farmer became very *bluff* and hearty. A very *blunt* man, he lost many friends through his habit of speaking his mind.

AIM

(the act of aiming). > (by transference) . . . > (that at which one aims)

Determination (strong decision)
  purpose
  intent
  intention
  endeavor (action toward end)
  design (use of means toward an end)

    object
    end
    mark

Aspiration (noble aim)
  inclination (a leaning)
  tendency (lit., a stretching toward)

    goal
    objective
    (education jargon, borrowed from gunnery)

Aim may mean both the object aimed at, and the act of aiming. In gunnery to *aim* the weapon is to train it on an objective. To have an *aim* in life is to be motivated towards some definite *goal* of achievement: as a physicist whose entire life is spent in an *endeavor* to split the atom. *Purpose, intent, intention,* are the mental efforts which lead to the attainment of the *aim,* whether this be good or bad. An *aspiration,* however, implies nobility of *purpose. Inclination* and *tendency* are weaker forms of *purpose* and *intention.* One may have an *intent* to write a great novel, but be too lazy to do it. One may have the *intention* to do something without taking any action in the matter. When action is taken as a result of the *intention,* we endeavor to reach our *goal,* or *aim.* Many poets fail financially because their *aspirations* are too noble. The hunter missed the deer because his *aim* was bad. He had no other *aim* in life but making money. Mary promised to stay at home, but she had no real *intention* of doing so.

EXAMPLE

(As a Thing or Object)	(According to Class or Types)	(In the Ideal Sense)
ensample	type	precedent
model	archetype	ideal
pattern	prototype	standard
sample		exemplar
specimen		exemplification

(As a *thing*): Death by poisoning is an *example* of one way in which a man may die. To illustrate the function of his invention, he made a small *model* of it. The dress did not fit when it was finished, because the paper *pattern* used was full of errors. Before the editor would employ a reporter he insisted on seeing several *specimens* of his work.

(According to *class* or *types*): Cro-Magnon man is the *archetype* of modern civilized white man. Stevens' "Rocket" is the *prototype* of the modern locomotive.

(In the *ideal* sense): An athlete who makes a record sets a *precedent* for all others who attempt the same feat. Christ's ethical teachings are the *ideal* of behavior towards which all Christians strive. A Bohemian, in the figurative sense, is a person whose *standards* of living are opposed to the accepted conventions. In *exemplification* of his physical prowess, the strong man would snap a poker with his naked hands.

To become really expert in choosing the right synonym from a number of words which occur to the mind, it is essential to practice extensively, in situations where the synonymy is supplied, but the exercise of discrimination is left to the writer's judgment. The study of lists of synonyms in which the distinctions are supplied, is not enough.

66) The nouns and adjectives which head the following lists of synonyms are chosen from the Basic English vocabulary. They are chiefly the words of a highly general meaning, which supply *indispensable ideas* without which communication cannot be carried on in any civilized language. They call, in ordinary English prose, in which repetition is far from euphonious, for an ample and varied stock of synonyms. Also, in writing that pretends to subtlety and grace, mere communication is not enough; the nuances or fine shades of feeling and sense are required. Hence each of the *key* words is followed by a list of synonyms, usually equated to the widest and commonest sense of the main word. No discriminations are given. But the lists are followed by sentences, each blank in which can be properly and adequately filled only by *one* of the synonyms (including in many cases, however, the main word as one alternative). Proceed by trial and error to find, by gradual elimination, which synonym will make sense in a given blank. The cues are purposely left somewhat vague in a good many cases, to put you on your mettle; and there is, in solving these verbal enigmas, a good deal of the same kind of interest that attaches to the solution of crossword puzzles. There is this difference, however: you should check your solutions, not only by the Key, but by a reference to the dictionary, both to track down any error which you may have made, and to fix once and for all your feeling for the various shades of meaning in a list of synonyms.

N.B. Notice that in most cases, some of the commonest synonyms for a word are omitted. These omissions are mostly very common words, according to Thorndike's tables of word-frequency. Can you supply the additional common synonyms for the key-words? Numbers in parentheses refer to Thorndike frequencies; they have nothing to do with the numbered blanks in the sentences.

ABLE (1), proficient (11), competent (9), qualified (8), dexterous (11), cogent (14), potent (6), adroit (11), apt (5), adequate (8), adept (16).

Ann has many attributes: she is ____1____ in the culinary art, and she is a ____2____ seamstress as well. In truth, she is ____3____ in every way for her domestic life as John's wife. She is an ____4____ conversationalist, and a ____5____ knitter, and quite ____6____ to the task of carrying on both activities simultaneously; while John, reading aloud from the day's news makes comments which he fancies are ____7____ and ____8____.

ADDITION (2), augmentation (16), accretion (12), accumulation (11), annexation (11), addendum, adjunct (10), appendage (9), reenforcement (20), increment (17), supplement (9), agglomeration.

The English possessions in South Africa were enlarged by the ____1____ of the Orange Free State. A coral reef is formed by the process of ____2____. The ____3____ of a great fortune is an arduous task. ____4____ is a well-known word-building process. The taking of interest was opposed by the Medieval church on the grounds that gold and silver have no such natural _____5_____, as do flocks and herds. A _____6_____ annexed to a report is sometimes called an _____7_____. A monkey's caudal _____8_____ helps him in swinging from one tree to another. The new radio station proved a most useful _____9_____ to the extension division. Blücher's army proved exactly the needed _____10_____ for Wellington. He noticed an _____11_____ of volcanic rocks.

ANGRY (2), indignant (6), wrathful (9), exasperated (10), irritable (9), maddened (10), infuriated (13), wroth (6), acrimonious (18), virulent (15), irascible (17).

The _____1_____ nonagenarian _____2_____ his heirs by his seeming immunity to all _____3_____ diseases. His _____4_____ comments and _____5_____ disposition were of necessity borne with, for _____6_____ as those around him might become, and _____7_____ as they were, almost beyond the point of endurance, yet, the immense wealth which he controlled was sufficient to suppress any _____8_____ retorts they might be tempted to make.

ATTENTION (2), alertness (19), observance (7), circumspection (15), scrutiny (12), inspection (7), cognizance (15), heedfulness (17), vigilance (9), solicitude (10), surveillance (14).

The _____1_____ of national holidays has come to mean relief from routine affairs rather than the commemoration of historic events. The _____2_____ of opposing politicians has manifested itself in a close _____3_____ of the private lives of the candidates: their most insignificant acts are under constant _____4_____ and only the greatest _____5_____ will serve to avoid calumny. It is well to approach any new idea with _____6_____, for a full _____7_____ of all factors involved is necessary to intelligent action. The _____8_____ with which the internationally famous detective made his _____9_____ of the room where the crime was committed, impressed the local officers. Your _____10_____ in his behalf is commendable.

AUTHORITY (2), ascendancy (15), predominance (15), corroboration (16), credential (13), prestige (12), supremacy (9), voucher (9), dispensation (9), jurisdiction (9), prerogative (8).

What is your _____1_____ for the contention that the _____2_____ of the white race since the 17th century according to Orientals may be ascribed to the possession of superior weapons and machinery? I am looking for _____3_____ of the report that Communism is in the _____4_____ among the trade-unionists. His _____5_____ was assured by the _____6_____ letter we received from the Governor of his native state. The Dean of the School had _____7_____ over all members of his department and exercised this _____8_____ to the fullest extent. The _____9_____ of the white race in all respects has never been questioned by the white race. The ____10____ for the pay checks has long been over-due.

AUTOMATIC (7), involuntary (7), instinctive (7), mechanical (7), unwitting (13), impulsive (14), unthinking (14), spontaneous (8), unintentional (16), unintelligent, self-acting.

Gerry was not an ____1____ girl, but she blundered through life with an ____2____ rudeness of demeanor which appalled new acquaintances, and vexed old ones, even those who rightly attributed her *gaucheries* to the ____3____ acts of an ____4____ head-strong tomboy. Often she was so absent-minded that she ate her meals in a ____5____ fashion, committing any number of ____6____ errors in table etiquette, and occasionally entering the conversation with a ____7____ outburst of approval or disapproval of some stray comment which penetrated her consciousness. She had an ____8____ dislike for punctiliously polite people and her inevitable reaction to them, although an ____9____ one, was to become ruder than ever.

BAD (1), noxious (11), pernicious (8), malignant (9), deteriorated (13), unsatisfactory (10), deplorable (13), detestable (11), depraved (13), detrimental (15), onerous (15).

The Devlin boys were a ____1____ influence on other boys in the neighborhood. It was not that they were hopelessly ____2____, but rather that they found the ordinary boyhood chores ____3____ to a high degree, and took a ____4____ glee in awakening others to the idea that such tasks were ____5____. Consequently, most of the mothers in the vicinity felt that the continued presence of the Devlin family was ____6____ to the best interests of the community.
When they arrived in Nepal, they found the climate ____7____, the living quarters most ____8____, and conditions among the natives ____9____.

BEHAVIOR (7), bearing (8), breeding (17), demeanor (7), deportment (8), comportment (16), guise (8).

His proud ____1____ and polite ____2____ bespoke good ____3____. Under the guise of a Russian nobleman, he became famous for his courtly ____4____.

BELIEF (3), dogma (11), tenet (14), precept (6), conviction (9), credence (15), reliance (10), assurance (5), vagary (11), supposition (10), predilection (15).

His critical faculty was warped by religious ____1____s. Success filled him with ____2____ of his position in society. He had a ____3____ for blondes. Many people are led astray by the ____4____s of their own temperaments. Never place any ____5____ in the prognostications of palmists. If they tell you: "You are a rich man," they are not informing you; if they tell you: "You will be rich next year," it is a mere ___6___.

BROKEN (1), shattered (4), sundered (7), ruptured (13), severed (5), collapsed (8), violated (4), disconnected (13).

Stumbling over a ___1___ gas pipe, he ___2___, ___3___ an artery, ___4___ a tendon, and ___5___ a window.

BUSINESS (1), employment (5), profession (5), function (5), craft (5), mission (5), pursuit (4), career (4), chore (13), vocation (10).

One of the new ___1___s of preparatory schools is to aid the student, through a "guidance" program, to select the ___2___ or ___3___ for which he is best fitted. It is now the fashion for women to busy themselves at home by the ___4___ of their spare time in ___5___ of the old ___6___s and arts, such as knitting, weaving, and crocheting. The ___7___ of a good press agent is to further the ___8___ of his employer by favorable publicity.

CARE (1), adversity (7), discretion (7), prudence (6), anxiety (8), precaution (8), vigilance (9), solicitude (10), circumspection (15), forethought (17), heedfulness, scruple, alertness (19), watchfulness.

NB: Some of these words appear as synonyms for **ATTENTION**, but meanings overlap so much in English words that this is unavoidable.

Prosperity makes friends, ___1___ tries them. No one could question the diplomat's ___2___ in affairs of state, but many people criticized his lack of ___3___ in money matters. He evidenced always the greatest ___4___ for her physical comfort, but gave no thought whatever to her ___5___ of mind. Every ___6___ was taken to assure the safety of the settlers; none ventured outside the fortress without the utmost ___7___; and especial ___8___ was required of the guards on duty. His bald statement of opinion showed very little ___9___.

CERTAIN (1), positive (5), inevitable (5), reliable (6), definite (6), infallible (9), unmistakable (11), unquestionable (12), undeniable (13), indisputable (16), indubitable (16), established (2), secure (2), incontestable.

The ___1___ conclusion to be drawn from such ___2___ facts, is that even governors are not ___3___. The results of the election were ___4___; there was a ___5___ majority of 500,000 votes for our candidate. ___6___ reports from ___7___ and ___8___ sources have given the Democratic candidate a black eye not easily overlooked. Now that Jeremy's position is ___9___ in the community he feels that his future is ___10___.

CHIEF (1), essential (5), vital (5), cardinal (6), significant (8), paramount (10), weighty (11), momentous (12), influential (12), salient (13), consequential (20).

He summarized briefly and forcefully the _____1_____ features of the plan. The creed of the modern educator may be summed up in what he calls the Seven _____2_____ Principles of Education. _____3_____ to the life of the community are such _____4_____ conveniences as water, streets, light, and sewers. It is a _____5_____ fact that decisions of _____6_____ importance in city affairs never operate to the disadvantage of the _____7_____ and _____8_____ members of the community. The dedication of the new street-lighting system was beginning to assume the proportions of a _____9_____ and _____10_____ event.

COMMON (1), normal (5), customary (6), prevalent (7), habitual (8), conventional (9), accustomed (9), hackneyed (10), widespread (10), rife (11), trite (16).

The use of _____1_____ and _____2_____ phrases is _____3_____ to some authors. The _____4_____ ravages of the dread disease made it impossible for us to go about the _____5_____ business of everyday life with our _____6_____ ease and dispatch. The ranks of the younger generation are _____7_____ with rebellion against _____8_____ creeds and codes. With the arrogance of one _____9_____ to speak with authority he dismissed the _____10_____ theories of the day with a terse "Nonsense!"

COMPARISON (4), ratio (7), relationship (8), similarity (12), simile (8), similitude (10), metaphor (10), allegory (12), identification (12), parallelism (16), parable (9).

The _____1_____s 2 to 7, 4 to 14, and 20 to 70 are the same. The _____2_____ of the loaves and the fishes is familiar to most of us. The _____3_____ by the reader of himself with the character in the book is a common occurrence. "The bloody sun at noon" is a _____4_____; while "No bigger than the moon" is a _____5_____. It is a nice _____6_____. Spenser's *Faerie Queen* is one of the best-known _____7_____s in literature. Their _____8_____ lay in the _____9_____ of sentence structure. The _____10_____ of men and animals has changed with the ages. No longer fearing them, man with superior cunning now domesticates his former foes.

COMPETITION (6), contention (6), controversy (6), emulation (8), rivalry (9), disputation (10), tournament (10), antagonism (15), opposition (5), contest (3), strife (3).

A keen spirit of _____1_____ existed among the older men of the mining camp and as the day of the horseshoe _____2_____ drew nearer, each evidenced his _____3_____ for the other contestants by derisively spitting at the nearest knothole whenever anyone's name but his own was mentioned as a possible winner. Any discussion of the approaching _____4_____ always resulted in _____5_____ and _____6_____ which fell little short of physical combat. Intense _____7_____ to chain stores has developed where once was a spirit of friendly _____8_____.

COMPLETE (1), achieved (4), fulfilled (4), dispatched (7), accomplished (7), consummated (8), intact (11), exhaustive (14), integral (14), undivided (14).

His initial goal once _____1_____, he should not feel that his life is _____2_____. She _____3_____ every prediction which had been made about her. The chairman _____4_____ the business at hand with incredible rapidity, putting through the disputed measure _____5_____.

COMPLEX (7), involved (4), entangled (6), tangled (8), complicated (8), intricate (9), mazy (14), labyrinthine (15).

The _____1_____ second-floor plans of most fraternity houses are confusing to college freshmen. The _____2_____ mop of hair which she sported as her crowning glory was a source of constant wonder, for it was piled into a superstructure both _____3_____ and _____4_____. He became _____5_____ in every local political intrigue with the zest with which small boys become _____6_____ in barbed-wire fences.

CONDITION (1), state (1), plight (5), reservation (7), proviso (10), predicament (10), category (13), stipulation (13), postulate (14).

I have but one _____1_____ to make in regard to your conduct; please endeavor to get into no _____2_____ from which you are unable to extricate yourself unaided. He was in a sorry _____3_____; the _____4_____ of his clothing was one of unbelievable filth; in fact his appearance readily placed him in the _____5_____ of "the great unwashed."

CONNECTION (3), alliance (7), relationship (8), junction (9), kinship (14), consanguinity (15), cohesion (16), affiliation (18), adherence (18), ligature (19), fastening (20).

_____1_____ refers solely to blood _____2_____; while _____3_____ may refer as well to _____4_____ by marriage or tribal relations. At the _____5_____ of the two roads was a great clump of English hawthorn. His _____6_____ with the Republican party was surprising to those who knew his political history. The _____7_____ of what three great European powers was known as the Triple Entente? Strict _____8_____ to the rules may be admirable, but it is not much fun.

CONSCIOUS (4), perceiving (3), realizing (3), comprehending (4), discerning (4), intelligent (5), apprehending (6), mental (7), rational (9), observant (12), cognizant (20).

A _____1_____ reply to an _____2_____ question indicates that both the questioner and the questioned are _____3_____ of the main factors involved. Without _____4_____ it the newcomer slowly gained a reputation for a sharp and _____5_____ wit.

DECISION (4), conclusion (5), determination (7), ascertainment (7), verdict (8), estimation (8), arbitrament (11), deduction (13), valuation (13), corollary (16).

At the _____1_____ of the trial the jury's _____2_____ was "not guilty." Both teams accepted the _____3_____ as final. In my _____4_____ his powers of _____5_____ are second only to the _____6_____ with which he carries out a _____7_____ once arrived at.

DELICATE (3), exquisite (5), fragile (8), effeminate (8), scrupulous (7), discriminatory (9), unsubstantial (18), frail (3).

One may speak of fine china as being _____1_____; of its _____2_____ translucency, and of its _____3_____ character if used in an all-night coffee stand. _____4_____ is an adjective more politely applied to a woman's health than to her morals; while the word _____5_____ is descriptive of the shadow tracery in a leaf pattern on the wall. One who is _____6_____ in his conduct is usually _____7_____ in his choice of companions.

DEPENDENT (7), subjugated (15), enthralled (14), enslaved (10), subordinate (9), contingent (14).

I may hold my hearers _____1_____; but this condition may be only _____2_____ upon my power of oratory.

DESTRUCTION (3), abolition (8), obliteration (10), annihilation (15), eradication (9), extermination (11), cataclysm (16), demolition (16), devastation (14), disruption (18), disorganization (12), sabotage.

Which of the above words does each of the words below call forth?

(1) _____ of slavery, (2) _____—chaos, (3) _____ of rats, (4) _____ of ink spots, (5) _____—Battle of Thermopylae, (6) _____—dynamiting a building, (7) _____ of footprints, (8) _____—labor disturbances, (9) _____—dust storms of the Middle West, (10) _____—World War.

DEVELOPMENT (4), construction (4), unfoldment (5), extension (5), formation (6), expansion (7), evolution (9), evolvement (14), increment (17), outgrowth (18).

(1) _____ of Boulder Dam. (2) _____ of rock strata. (3) _____ of time. (4) _____ of a bud. (5) _____ of species. (6) _____ of steam.

DIFFERENT (1), diverse (8), divergent (9), distinctive (9), heterogeneous (10), variegated (12), incongruous (14), diversified (15), dissimilar (16), contradictory (16), antithetical (16).

Ellis Island, when an immigrant ship comes in, presents a ____1____ collection of nationalities. The Biblical character Joseph wore a coat of ____2____ colors. To wear a tuxedo with pajama trousers is considered an ____3____ combination by tailors. Species of the beetle family are infinitely ____4____.

DIRECTION (2), I. In the sense of *trend*, (9), bearings (8), tendency (6). II. In the sense of *guidance* (9), leadership (7), management (5), regulation (6), supervision (9), auspices (13), tutelage (20), superintendence (17).

I. A drunken sailor has a ____1____ to lose his ____2____.

II. The ____3____s laid down by the ____4____, under the ____5____ of the administration, involved personal ____6____ of each department. After five years under the ____7____ of a prosy schoolmaster, the boy's mind was somewhat confused.

DISTANCE (1), remoteness (4), aloofness (5), span (5), extension (5), separation (5), interval (5).

Her ____1____ was such that he did not like to accost her. In Portland there is an ____2____ of the University of Oregon. Because of its ____3____, Mars would be very difficult to reach by aeroplane. The ____4____ of life is too short for long ____5____ from one's fellow human beings to be tolerable.

DISTRIBUTION (5), appropriation (8), dispensation (9), broadcast (10), diffusion (11), dissipation (12), dispersion (13), allotment (14), apportionment (14), radiation (16), dissemination (18).

Some university work is financed by ____1____. An ____2____ of arable land to every unemployed man might solve the unemployment problem. Heat from the fire reaches the skin by ____3____. Dandelions are propagated by the ____4____ of their seeds by the wind. Radio ____5____s are often spoiled by static.

EDUCATION (3), attainment (12), cultivation (7), culture (6), scholarship (12), inculcation (14), training (7), guidance (9), breeding (17).

Under the ____1____ of efficient tutors, Annabel, aided by her personal ____2____s, prepared herself by intensive ____3____ for the ____4____ of learning into the reluctant heads of high school students. In spite of this pedant's ____5____, he is noted for his good ____6____.

ELASTIC (5), springy, resilient, buoyant (8), recoiling (6), flexible (7), bouncing (7), expanding (6), expansive (13), rebounding (12).

In the game of squash, the ball is kept ____1____ from a wall. For varicose veins, ____2____ stockings are sometimes worn. A balloon is, fundamentally, an ____3____ envelope filled with a gas lighter than air. Rubber, unlike iron, is naturally ____4____.

EQUAL (1), selfsame (5), identical (7), equivalent (7), symmetrical (9), coincident (13), equitable (13), synonymous (16), indistinguishable (17), convertible (18), tantamount (19).

To call a man a pig, in France, is ____1____ to an insult. Twins are persons whose birthdays were ____2____. When two words approximate to the same meaning, they are said to be ____3____. America is a nation dedicated to the proposition that all men are created ____4____.

EXISTENCE (4), reality (5), essence (6), vitality (9), verity (14), entity (14), subsistence (15), actuality, substantiality.

The poor lose much ____1____ by working for a mere ____2____. Under the influence of stimulants, men get out of touch with ____3____. An ____4____ may be either a thing in itself, or an ideal construct. In scholastic terminology, ____5____ is distinguished from substance.

EXPANSION (7), extension (5), enlargement (12), amplification (16), augmentation (16), dilation (19), inflation (18), aggrandizement (20), dilatation, exaggeration (11).

The ____1____ of a tire is brought about by a pump. Ivan was so pleased with the snapshot that he had an ____2____ made of it. Fat men suffer from a ____3____ of the stomach due to overeating. Nowadays, even the dullest lectures can be heard all over the hall by a system of ____4____. Self-____5____ has been the cause of much disillusionment.

EXPERIENCE (2), cognizance (15), cognition (18), insight (10), sophistication (15), enlightenment (7), comprehension (11), recognition (8), familiarity (10).

He could not take ____1____ of his surroundings. Few people have real ____2____ into life. ____3____ is a way of living, rather than a style of speech and dress. Hard study of the subject brought him no ____4____. Only after a long conference with the professor did he arrive at a full ____5____ of the subject. When he met his *fiancée* at the masked ball, ____6____ was instantaneous.

FALSE (2), imitation (8), counterfeit (8), pseudo- (19), fallacious (14), invalid (7), perjured (12), fabricated (14), forsworn (13), illusory (17), erroneous (8), fraudulent (12), specious (11), incorrect (9), deceptive (19), dishonest (9), casuistic (14), spurious (12), mendacious, perfidious (12).

After being taken by the police for uttering ____1____ money, Jim the Penman ____2____ed his way out of a long sentence. Brittania metal is a feeble ____3____ of silver. Phrenology is a ____4____ science. "It rains because the crops need it" is a ____5____ statement. After five years, a British passport becomes ____6____. ____7____ sense impressions are those of which we cannot be any too sure—e.g., 'pink elephants.' A name given by the French to England is "____8____ Albion."

FERTILE (4), productive (8), fecund (14), luxuriant (8), prolific (8), copious (7), generative (17), profitable (5), life-giving, originative (8).

After a ____1____ supply of the ____2____ fluid had been administered to him, the starving biologist was able once again to turn his attention to the ____3____ habits of newts. The late Edgar Wallace was considered an unusually ____4____ writer. Brown agreed that his dog was a little too ____5____ when the ninth litter greeted him one morning in the bath tub.

FOOLISH (2), silly (4), stupid (4), puerile (16), frivolous (8), fatuous (20), idiotic (19), asinine (19), driveling (16), injudicious (15), nonsensical (5), insensate (17), maudlin (16), misguided (15), imprudent (16), foolhardy (16).

____1____ by ____2____ companions, and spurred on by ____3____ potations, Jane would frequently be found in a ____4____ condition. Jacob was so ____5____, that at times his expression closely resembled that of the patient donkey. "This is ____6____, I know," murmured Thaddeus, as he sprang from the top of the Empire State Building, "but I'm in a hurry to get to the bottom."

FORCE (1), impulsion (18), extortion (12), compulsion (11), coercion (16), goad (9), intensity (7), vehemence (8), puissance (14), soldiery (13), regiment (6), necessitate (8).

When the donkey refused to budge, we had recourse to a sharp-pointed ____1____ as a means of ____2____. But after this had been applied with some ____3____, it almost ____4____d the services of a ____5____ of ____6____ to restrain the animal from leaving us altogether.

FREQUENT (2), reiterated (8), habitual (8), inveterate (12), incessant (7), prevalent (7).

The ____1____ use of alcohol ____2____ among college students bodes no good to the country. An ____3____ smoker, his ____4____ demands for cigarettes were ____5____.

GENERAL (1), customary (6), habitual (8), unspecified, panoramic (12), widespread (10), accustomed (9), encyclopedic (17), generic (20), catholic (4).

With persons of ____1____ taste, it is ____2____ to enjoy a ____3____ range of intellectual pleasures. The author of this book has an ____4____ mind. Visitors from eastern cities are not ____5____ to the ____6____ scenery of the West.

GROWTH (3), expansion (7), dilation (19), transition (7), maturation, development (4), vegetation (7), germination (11), herbage (11), luxuriance (16), flowerage, foliage (6), organism (7), evolution (9).

It became difficult to walk through the field because of the ____1____ of the ____2____. Belladonna is used by oculists to produce ____3____ of the pupil. The doctors removed a small ____4____ from the brain. This was considered to have been the cause of the child's arrested ____5____.

HELP (1), assistance (4), coöperation (8), ministration (11), remuneration (13), avail (5), weal (9), succor (7), encouragement (8).

His pleas for monetary ____1____ were of no ____2____,—no one would come to his ____3____. A ____4____ is an association of persons working for common ____5____. Florence Nightingale's ____6____s to the wounded during the Crimean campaign won her an undying fame.

IDEA (2), conception (7), perception (8), abstraction (10), reflection (5), concept (15), apprehension (15), sentiment (5), impression (4), supposition (10).

On some days, ____1____s seem to flow easily from a writer's mind, on others, he is not able to formulate a single ____2____. After mature ____3____, Socrates began to formulate a system of philosophy on the ____4____ that he himself knew nothing. In the expression of this ____5____ alone, however, he gives a distinct ____6____ of wisdom.

IMPORTANT (1), momentous (12), significant (8), influential (12), notable (5), salient (13), eventful (10), vital (5), essential (5), trenchant (13), paramount (10).

The World War was one of the most ____1____ happenings of our ____2____ era. The art of jiu-jitsu consists in hitting your opponent in a ____3____ spot.

IMPULSE (7), impetus (11), momentum (15), propulsion (20), instigation (12), incitement (16), spurt (12).

Under the ____1____ given it by the ____2____s of the agitator, the mob rushed forward, and carried by its own ____3____ broke through the gates of the palace. Stimulated by the cheering of the crowd, the runner made a final ____4____ and broke the tape.

INDUSTRY (2), assiduity (15), constancy (8), diligence (7), exertion (8), persistence (10), sedulousness (15), perseverance (7).

Football cannot be played without much physical ____1____. Students rarely listen to their lectures with sufficient ____2____. His one aim in life was to own a car, and he worked to this end with unshakeable ____3____. His ____4____ to one brand of canned soup was remarkable. In spite of all opposition, Hercules' ____5____ finally overcame all obstacles. Most young writers play the ____6____ ape to their betters.

INSTRUMENT (3), factor (7), operator (8), performer (12), promoter (13), apparatus (7), appliance (9), implement (5), utensil (7), mechanism (8), weapon (3).

The trouble was that the ____1____ did not know how to use his ____2____s. Great care must be exercised in handling chemical ____3____.

KNOWLEDGE (2), erudition (13), intelligence (4), intuition (13), learning, lore (10), perception (8), recognition (8), scholarship (12), apprehension (15), comprehension (11).

His ____1____ being limited to a smattering of Oriental ____2____, he could not be called a man of ____3____. The candidate's ____4____ gave some ____5____ to his examiners.

LANGUAGE (2), barbarism (12), dialect (7), diction (14), expression (5), idiom (17), vernacular (14), vocabulary (7).

The ____1____ 'to suicide' is a ____2____. To have a large ____3____ is not enough, good ____4____ is necessary if you aspire to become a writer. Every ____5____ is characterized by its peculiar ____6____.

LIKE (1), analogous (13), equivalent (7), homogeneous (14), resembling (4), similar (3), uniform (3).

Obsidian is a ____1____ amorphous rock ____2____ in appearance to dark glass. Ice cream should be of a ____3____ texture throughout. Kwass is a Russian drink, made out of bread and mildly intoxicating,

_____4_____ to beer. The Dionne quintuplets are five babies _____5_____ one another closely.

PROCESS (3), procedure (9), transaction (9), routine (8), disposition (5), performance (5), transition (7), evolution (9).

When the _____1_____ of the day was over, they went to a local _____2_____ of the "Beggar's Opera." The _____3_____ of learning to milk cows is facilitated if the animal involved is of amiable _____4_____. _____5_____ represents man in a continuous state of _____6_____ from a lower to a higher type.

QUALITY (2), attribute (5), faculty (5), endowment (9), qualification (8), distinction (5), peculiarity (8), trait (14).

Such character _____1_____s as these persons possess are, however, rarely natural _____2_____s, but arise from misuse of the _____3_____s. The _____4_____ of mercy is frequently strained by the _____5_____s of politicians.

REGULAR (2), undiversified (20), invariable (7), equable (12), consistent (8), methodical (13), symmetrical (9), habitual (8), unbroken (8), systematic (10).

It was his _____1_____ rule to think in the morning, act at noon, eat in the afternoon and sleep at night. In this program he was strictly _____2_____, and it was _____3_____ from day to day. By such means he hoped to design a _____4_____ pattern of living, continuing over an _____5_____ chain of years.

RELATION (3), analogy (14), similarity (12), consanguinity (15), affinity (9), lineage (11), affiliation (18), alliance (7).

One's nearest _____1_____s are never necessarily one's closest _____2_____s. It might even be maintained that, in many instances, _____3_____ is the mother of contention. To form an _____4_____ with a person of ancient _____5_____ often illustrates both the perils of _____6_____ and the attraction of opposites.

RELIGION (3), devotion (5), righteousness (6), morality (8), theology (8), divinity (6), piety (6), sanctity (8), holiness (6), consecration (7), veneration (14), regeneration (12), conversion (8).

After Hank's _____1_____ to _____2_____, he exhibited a degree of _____3_____ hardly to be expected from such a man. Though he had been a playboy all his life, his _____4_____ was complete, his _____5_____ for the church unshakeable, his knowledge of _____6_____ profound.

REPRESENTATIVE (3), exponent (13), emissary (12), envoy (11), delegate (5), deputy (5), legate (10), expositor (19), trustee (8), nominee (17).

James was an ____1____ of the art of defrauding ____2____. A papal ____3____ is an ____4____ of the Pope, acting in the capacity of the Pope's ____5____. When all the ____6____s had cast their ballots, the ____7____ from California had the majority.

RESPONSIBLE (6), accountable (12), answerable (14), liable (6), conscientious (9), regardful, prudent (5), veracious (2), reputable (10).

The day of judgment has been pictured as that time when each man is held ____1____ for his deeds. He who is always ____2____ in his manner, ____3____ in his speech, ____4____ in the performance of his duty, and ____5____ of others, will, I fear, be lonely in that vast assemblage of those brought together for the pronouncement of the final decree.

SELECTION (6), preference (7), option (13), specification (12), designation (13).

In making a ____1____ between two desired objects, we have no ____2____ but to choose that which is fitted to the depth of our purse. This engineer failed in business because his ____3____ was always for ____4____s which involved him in exorbitant expenditures.

SEPARATE (1), disjoined (16), discontinuous, disjunctive, isolated (7), insular (16), asunder (6), bisected (13), divergent, alienate (11), estrange (10), dismember (16), disband (9), disintegrate (11), partition (7), rupture (13), bisect (13), halve (11), sunder (7).

Islanders are, by definition, temperamentally ____1____. These twain shall not be torn ____2____. To ____3____ is to cut into two equal pieces. The two rooms were separated by a filmsy ____4____. Millikan is interested in ____5____ing matter. The two wrestlers fought with such enthusiasm that one of them was completely ____6____ed. Their married life was idyllic, until a ____7____ occurred between them.

SOCIETY (2), humanity (5), mortality (7), civilization (7), confederation (9), federation (8), coalition (15), alliance (7), syndicate (13).

____1____ may be said to have been in existence ever since Cro-Magnon man etched his rude pictures on bits of bone. Many institutions, started in the name of ____2____, have fallen into the hands of capitalistic ____3____s. There are two kinds of ____4____: that into which we are born, the other into which we must buy our way.

TRUE (1), accurate (7), scrupulous (7), literal (7), unerring (10), genuine (5), candid (12), guileless (17), trustworthy (11), undeniable (13), infallible (9), demonstrable (20), incontrovertible (19), indisputable (16), indubitable (16), scientific (7), veritable (11), mathematical (11), sterling (8), unimpeachable, veracious.

Even ____1____ laws, unless ____2____, are not ____3____. ____4____ proof must be forthcoming before any scientific finding may be considered ____5____. No man should condemn dishonesty in others unless his own character is ____6____—and not even then.

UNIT (6), monad, ace (11), integer (19), module, solitary (4), companionless (19), isolated (7).

An ____1____ is a whole number. Until his meeting with Lena, Heyst lived ____2____ on an ____3____ island. The recalcitrant prisoner was within an ____4____ of being condemned to ____5____ confinement.

USE (1), addiction, prevalence (9), etiquette (11), recourse (9), expediency (16), appliance (9), disposal (6), consumption (6), manipulation (15), exploitation (17).

From motives of ____1____, he had ____2____ to the ____3____ of stocks. Although this involved the ____4____ of widows and orphans, he was too near bankruptcy to be deterred by mere questions of ____5____. Finally, thanks to the ____6____ of gullible people among his clients, he soon had vast sums of money at his ____7____.

VALUE (1), assessment (13), appreciation (8), estimation (8), measurement (5), quotation (7), appraisement, utilization (18), expenditure (8), emolument (14), productiveness (17), superiority (11).

After ____1____ of the property had been made, it was found to have decreased in ____2____. In the auditor's ____3____ this was due to a falling off in the ____4____ in the factories, and an increased ____5____ of foreign-manufactured goods. This may be attributed to the superiority of the latter, their cheapness, and the constantly increasing overhead ____6____ on this side.

VIEW (1), panorama (12), scrutiny (12), contemplation (6), survey (4), discernment (12), inspection (7), prospect (3).

A famous Chinese philosopher expounded a theory that a state of spiritual ease could be achieved through ____1____ of a certain portion of the anatomy. A ____2____ of the available materials convinced us that the ____3____s of completing the work at minimum cost was excellent. His immediate ____4____ of the salient points of the case was little short of miraculous. Behave with circumspection and avoid the ____5____ of the virtuous.

WASTE (1), prodigality (12), overplus (20), extravagance (11), profusion (13), squandering (10), exorbitance (16), lavishness (5), dissipation (12), superfluity (11), dross (9).

His substance was soon wasted away owing to his ___1___. When all the fish had been eaten, she did not know what to do with the ___2___. A habit of ___3___ money will soon result in bankruptcy. If all is not gold that glitters, there must be a preponderance of ___4___

WEIGHT (1), encumbrance (16), incubus (16), lading (10), cargo (4), ballast (9), preponderance (14), emphasis (7), predominance (15), ponderousness, authentication, corroboration (16), prominence (13), potency (11).

The ___1___ of the ___2___ involved the removal of considerable ___3___, owing to the ___4___ of fat men in the crew. The ___5___ that the speaker gave to his words lent additional ___6___ to an argument that was already succeeding by its ___7___.

WISE (1), sagacious (10), rational (9), sapient (17), astute (17), perspicacious, cognizant (20), erudite (19), authoritative (9), sophisticated (12), judicious (8), oracular (12), provident (15), prescient (19), enlightened (7).

It is a ___1___ animal that can choose between two masters. He was so ___2___ that he could almost see through a brick wall. A man who can discriminate between two vintages of wine is said to have a ___3___ palate. He was so ___4___ that he knew no words of one syllable. The ant, who makes provision for the winter, is more ___5___ than the grasshopper, who fiddles while the summer sun burns.

CHAPTER VII

Purists have long waged bitter war on slang. They rarely know much about it. The pedant who vilifies slang often makes, in discussing it, comical 'howlers' at which any schoolboy would snicker. It is sad to listen to some Nice Nellie quoting—inexactly and ineptly —slang which is six months past its vogue. There is only one thing sadder. That is a messy mixture of slang phrases of different periods,—say 'skidoo' in company with 'hot shot,' 'kiddo' in the same breath with 'some babe,' or 'Tarnation strike me' in the same sentence with 'the cat's pajamas.' These unhappy blends often occur when an English novelist attempts to wield American slang. Clearly, if the purist is to talk or write about slang, he should study it as the atheist studies scripture, and at least know what he is trying to confound. The chances are that with intensive study he will be converted, perhaps not to use slang himself, but to the conviction that it has its uses.

And what are the uses of slang? It now and then enriches the language. Who would say arbitrarily that 'razz' and 'scram' will not make their way into the common stock? They express vivid shades of meaning for which the language has had no short and forcible words. Does *bedevil* or even *heckle* equal 'razz,' or *depart hurriedly* take the place of 'scram'? And what term could replace the expressive and convenient 'blurb,' which Professor Weekley thinks has come to stay?

Again, slang is the life of humorous stories. It is vulgar and racy. It may even serve as a secret code. The motive of secrecy accounts for a great deal of that special kind of underworld slang which is one form of *cant*, many terms from which make their way into the general slang vocabulary. There is a story by O. Henry which illustrates this use of slang for keeping a secret. The American envoy in a banana republic wanted to tip off the American consul at the seaport that the President of the comic opera republic had skipped out of the capitol with the money in the treasury, and an opera

165

singer of whom he was enamored. Knowing that the Spanish telegraphers would translate any message sent, and apprise the escaping President, the envoy set his wits to work and concocted the following:

His Nibs has skedaddled with the spoof in the kitty and the bundle of dry-goods he's crazy about and is making for the briny.

Their English dictionaries were no help to the puzzled Spanish telegraphers. Yet this mélange of poker lingo, Bowery American, and English slang is intelligible enough to most American readers. To be sure, the lingo is that of 1905, 'His Nibs' even dating back to 1819 in England; and the tune is American, not English. But here is slang neatly used for secrecy and for humorous effect.

Above all, for the student of linguistics, slang shows the processes by which language has evolved. Slang is perhaps the only living language, in the sense that it is actually in process of formation right before our ears. Evidently worth studying for its own sake, it is instructive and amusing, if taken calmly and detachedly, with an eye to its natural history.

Incidentally, there is no better way to avoid falling into slang than to know all about it. The horror of the purist is largely due to ignorance. The slips of the vulgar (i.e., everybody except the purist), even when they mean to talk correctly, are due to the same cause. Anyone who is thoroughly conversant with the ways of slang, its nature and origins, and the laws of language which slang formations follow, will never use it absent-mindedly, but only when he chooses. He will italicize it with his voice, or put quotation marks around it when he writes it. But it is first necessary to be sure what is slang, and what is not.

Select a dozen persons who pride themselves on the purity of their language. Ask them the status of the phrase 'make yourself scarce.' To a man, they will label it American slang. It is not. It is given by the OED as a respectable English colloquialism, with examples from Scott and Thackeray,—used, to be sure, in familiar writing, not in full-dress formal discourse. There is a hint that the phrase may have come down from Scotland. In any event, it is not American slang, except that it sounds like it, and that anyone who used it in public discourse would get a black mark from the purist.

Slang is in like case with solecisms, those gaucheries of the half-educated which so worry the school grammarian. It is easy to mistake a racy colloquialism for slang or a solecism. So before anyone sets up as gratuitous adviser and self-appointed expert on other people's mistakes in usage, he should make sure that he knows whereof he speaks.

Professor Kittredge, the Fowlers, and the higher grammarians generally, have had more fun with pretenders to learning than with the supposed errors of the vulgar,—some of which the experts will defend. All higher grammarians approve 'go *slow,*' 'sleep *sound,*' 'buy *cheap* and sell *dear*' on the very simple ground that *slow, sound,* and *cheap* are true adverbs, even though for historical reasons they are minus the usual *-ly* termination. Similarly, Logan Pearsall Smith defends 'have got' on the ground that "the verb *have,* being used as an auxiliary, has lost whatever kinæsthetic associations it originally possessed, and since it now describes a static, or merely grammatical relation, 'got,' from the dynamic verb 'get' has been added to it, to give the vividness which comes from an idea of action, in however vague a form." (*English Idioms,* p. 49.) Similarly, he defends 'get on,' as in 'get on in the world.' He does not, however, underwrite the use of 'get' as an omnibus verb, quoting as a warning the following passage from Brewer's *Dictionary of Phrase and Fable:*

I got on horseback within ten minutes after I got your letter. When I got to Canterbury I got a chaise for town; but I got wet through, and have got such a cold that I shall not get rid of it in a hurry. I got to the Treasury about noon, but first of all got shaved and dressed. I soon got into the secret of getting a memorial before the Board, but I could not get an answer then; however, I got intelligence from a messenger that I should get one next morning. As soon as I got back to my inn, I got my supper, and then got to bed. When I got up next morning, I got my breakfast, and, having got dressed, I got out in time to get an answer to my memorial. As soon as I got it, I got into a chaise, and got back to Canterbury by three, and got home for tea. I have got nothing for you, and so adieu.—Smith, Logan Pearsall. *S. P. E. Tract No. XII English Idioms.* Ox. Univ. Press, Oxford, 1923, p. 49. (Try re-writing this, to test your command of synonyms.)

The admirable collection of idioms which Logan Pearsall Smith has brought together in this monograph should stand as a warning against damning too readily any vivid colloquial turn of speech which we never happen to have heard before. For as this author points out, English is peculiarly rich in idioms, "phrases which transgress either the laws of grammar or the laws of logic." Idiom is often slang which has established itself.

The only sure procedure, in passing on slang and jargon, is to consider the time and place in which these dubious words are used. Much depends on who uses them, when they are employed, what the purpose is, and who the hearers are. Always remember that a fraction of the slang of one century makes its way into the literary language of the next; while a word such as *broadcast* may be jargon in one decade (Oliver Elton wrote it with quotation marks in 1912) and in perfectly good use two decades later, both in the literal and the figurative sense.

Now all this is not meant as a blanket defense for dubious words. Certain it is that the most tolerant reader or listener will gag at slang and jargon on some occasions. On other occasions, he will probably use them himself. If they were wholly ruled out, the gayety of nations would be lessened. How could O. Henry have 'got on' without them? It is difficult to lay down hard and fast laws about the use of these words under suspicion. It is a matter of tact and taste,—and knowledge.

A professional wit once defined a gentleman as a man who never insults anyone unintentionally. This suggests a basis for dealing with these dubious words. If slang or jargon is used, it should be only with full awareness of the risk, after conscious calculation. To fall into slang unconsciously, or to use it habitually, is to show yourself lacking in a language sense. Slang ceases to be alive in the mouths of the weak-minded, who talk nothing else, and merely poll-parrot the slang clichés of the moment (1935), such abominations as 'O.K.,' 'sweetie,' 'all rightie,' 'dearie,' and 'cutie.' Such worn-out stereotypes defeat the very purpose of proper slang, which aims to be humorous, grotesque, and original. An occasional sprinkling of well-chosen slang is good spice,—but who wants to live on spice?

Not that a dash of slang necessarily means your social ruin. If you take care to use slang only in the hearing of a professional expert in the science of language, he will be too busy accounting for your phrase in the light of language tendencies, to bother about investigating your family upbringing or your social credentials. Slang addicts are also a safe audience. But not all listeners will be so resigned to slang. If you are yourself addicted to it, you should not swear off all at once. But you should choose your slang with discrimination.

The line between slang and idom is often hard to draw, unless you are sure exactly what is English—or, in some cases, American, idiom. "I would not grow hot in a cold cause," wrote Robert Burton in 1626, and showed how closely sinewy idiomatic English can skirt upon slang, without falling into it. Yet slang is an artful creature, and can assume a variety of forms. Its tricks are many and crafty. They call for a good hard look.

Old and respectable words are brought low in the world, becoming vulgarisms. This is the fate which has lately overtaken *swell, hot, tight,* and *lit ;* as for *lousy,* it was used in its present vulgar sense as early as 1386 (OED), and has often been employed by the best authors. The OED defines *lousy* in this sense as

dirty, filthy, obscene. Also as a general term of abuse: Mean, scurvy, sorry, vile, contemptible.

This seems pretty well to cover the present day slang sense. Then follows the annotation, "Now *rare.*" Not even the authority of the OED can persuade us of the truth of the annotation; though never, ironically enough, was there a better proof of the need for historical method in studying words. Some of the examples of this use of *lousy* sound singularly modern, though for once this is no flattery to our own age:

1663 DRYDEN *Wild Gallant* I 1 And to discredit me before strangers; for a lousy, paltry sum of money?

1708 *Brit. Apollo* No. 38 2/1 Wicked Rhimes. . . . sung to lowsey Tunes.

1893 STEVENSON *Catriona* 65 The lousiest, lowest, story to hand down to your namesake in the future.

All these examples from the best authors do not make *lousy* anything but a slang vulgarism in present day usage.

The most prolific source of slang, however, is the trick of labeling things or persons by another name which usually lessens their dignity, to put it mildly. A *pessimist* becomes a 'calamity howler' (—1920) ; a *thrifty escort* a 'cheap skate' (—1926) ; a *railroad detective* a 'cinder bull' or 'yard-dick' (—1920) ; a *human fossil* a 'dodo' (—1890) from the extinct bird; a *foreigner* a 'bohunk' (at first applied only to Bohemians) ; the *police patrol* a 'hurry buggy' (—1920), or more commonly, a 'Black Maria' (imported from England, where it occurs as early as 1874). This is slang as derogatory metaphor. It covers a large range. 'Dumb-bell' is a good inclusive epithet which applies to 'dimwits,' 'boneheads,' 'dumb bunnies' (with a further insult due to the diminutive), and all stupid and inept persons generally. A 'jawbreaker' is an army biscuit, or a hard candy. 'To build fences' if used in a political meeting, would now rarely be taken in the sense in which any rail-splitter of the '50's would have understood it. A politician out 'mending his fences' may be boorish, but he is not likely to have the frontier virtues, even though he may talk of 'rugged individualism,' which is almost a cant phrase itself. When somebody 'kicks like a mule,' we do not expect to find the 'kicker' in very 'starchy' company, so far as the adjoining words are concerned. (Yet the Latin derivative 'recalcitrant' means 'kicker.') Similarly 'high kicker,' if used of an actress, may or may not be complimentary. So with the epithet 'fast stepper.'—All these locutions are made up of words or phrases that have come down in the world. While we have to label them slang in the context in which they are found, it is the particular use which makes them so. These words, by themselves, and in ordinary surroundings, are mostly not slang at all. Someone who wants to call attention to himself or his ideas has bent them to his uses, and soon they are current among all the fashionables, who fall into using them as the cheapest and easiest way of concealing the absence of thought. Since there is inflated emphasis to begin with, this cheap currency finally loses all value, and passes into limbo. For a while, the word which was worsened may retain its derogatory connotations, so that it is barred from serious use. But the words employed, which were the 'gold backing,' so to speak, of the slang currency, are eventually returned to normal circulation, none the worse for their fling. After all, words cannot take out social insurance against fools who want to use them in a grotesque sense.

Slang as metaphor has, however, great value as entertainment. And it lends variety, for there is great inventive power displayed. Suppose we look for modern parallels to the Elizabethan locutions described in that amusing passage of Richard Carew's which he wrote in 1595:

. . . neither can any tongue . . . deliver a matter with more variety than ours, both plainly and by proverbs and metaphors; for example, when we would be rid of one, we use to say *be going, trudge, pack, be faring, hence, away, shift,* and by circumlocution, *rather your room than your company, let's see your back, come again when I bid you, when you are called for, sent for, intreated, willed, desired, invited, spare us your place, another in your stead, a ship of salt for you, save your credit, you are next the door, the door is open for you, there's nobody holding you, nobody tears your sleeve,* etc. (spelling modernized)

In American slang, to meet this need, we have had, successively, *absquatulate* (1833), *vamoose* (1848), *skedaddle* (1861), *scat* (1880), *cheese it* (1900), *git* (?), *skiddoo* (1907), *fade away* (1911), *take a sneak* (1911), *Rous* (1919), *scram* (1920), *beat it* (1926), and the end is not yet. These examples are dated, to emphasize the importance of fixing the time at which a slang word first came in, or at least when it first got into print. As to its final exit, that is a difficult matter to determine. A vaudeville actor would no doubt remark that slang words rather 'fade out,' than vanish in a 'blackout.'

Occasionally, as has been noted, a slang word makes its way into the language. So *banter,* which pained Swift, is now a word in good literary use; and about half of the terms which he inveighed against in his celebrated *Tatler* paper (No. 210, published in 1710) have now made a place for themselves, either as proper literary words, or as decent colloquialisms. Among the other words which Swift condemned, were 'mob,' a clipped form of *mobile vulgus,* 'the fickle crowd'; 'phiz,' bobtailed from *physiognomy;* 'sham,' supposedly a fashionable coffee-house mispronunciation of *shame;* 'bully,' a form of 'bully-rook,' from the Low Dutch *buller-brook,* a noisy, rough fellow; and 'palming,' in our sense of 'deceiving' by 'palming-off.' All these words except 'phiz' are now in good literary use, though they would not be if Swift had had his way in establishing an official English Academy to regulate the language.

Swift's examples show another way in which slang words are manufactured. This is by clipping or foreshortening existing words. Modern college students have whittled down respectable words into 'prof,' 'math,' 'ag,' or 'aggie' (again the contemptuous diminutive), —the last standing for a student of agriculture, or one at an agricultural college; students say 'barb,' for barbarian,—one outside the Greek fraternity pale, though the only Greek known in most of these 'tong-houses' is found on the front-door plate,—'exam,' and 'quiz' (for examine),—which is allowed by Webster's Dictionary as a word in good use in the United States. In its other sense, this word *quiz* was slang in Swift's day, roughly equivalent in meaning to our present slang word 'kid.' *Quiz* then meant, and for that matter still does, if anyone cares to make his meaning obscure by using it, 'to chaff or mock with pretended seriousness.' It is a nice question, how many college escorts would divine this meaning, if a girl said, 'Oh, you're quizzing me.' 'Why give me the bird?' is closer to the current idiom. 'To ride' or 'to rib' someone is an alternative phrase; while a 'Bronx cheer' is the term for stronger derision.

Another mode of manufacturing slang is the distortion of words which lend themselves to it. 'Picture-askew,' for *picturesque,* and 'fattygued' for *fatigued* are examples. This is closely allied to the method of manufacturing slangy comic compounds by telescoping two or more words. So the Yankee dialect made 'slantindicular' from *slantin'* and *perpendicular.* There are 'portmanteau' words— as they are often called—, for instance 'brunch' (c. 1900), a telescoping of *breakfast* and *lunch.* Lewis Carroll gave a great impetus to the fashion for portmanteau words, and Joyce, in our day has carried this method of making verbal potpies to its final fantastic conclusion. What he began as a comic trick in *Ulysses,* he has adopted as a serious method in his *Work in Progress.* Some of his coinages are highly diverting, some far-fetched, fantastic, and intelligible only to erudite philologians—most of whom are not among Joyce's readers. Here, for the curious, is one of Joyce's most famous lists, the Foreign Friends of the Emerald Isle. Each name is a satiric comment on the nationality of its bearer.

67) Can you name the language and point out the pun in each case?

Commendatore Bacibaci Beninobenone, Monsieur Pierrepaul Petitépatant, the Grandjoker Vladinmire Pokethankertscheff, the Archjoker Leopold Rudolph von Schwanzenbad-Hodenthaler, Countess Marha Viraga Kisaszony Putrapesthi, Hiram Y. Bomboost, Count Athanatos Karamelopulis, Ali Baba Backsheesh Rahat Lokum Effendi, Señor Hidalgo Caballero Don Pecadillo y Palabras y Paternoster de la Malora de la Malaria, Hokopoko Harakiri, Hi Hung Chang, Olaf Kobberkeddelsen, Mynheer Trik van Trumps, Pan Poleaxe Paddyrisky, Nationalgymnasiummuseumsanatoriumandsuspensoriumsordinaryprivatdocentgeneralhistoryspecialprofessordoctor Kriegfried Ueberallgemein.

The great humorists have all been given to this trick of comic compounds. So Aristophanes has 'a lone-eatingest dog' and a slave who has been happy only four times in his life, but whose woes are as the 'sands-of-the-sea-in-number.' Rabelais writes of 'The for Godsake of Salvation,' 'vine-branch-like flourishes,' 'doddi-poljoltheads,' not to mention his punning proper-names fearfully and wonderfully compounded: Colonel Mawl-Chitterling, Lord Suckfist, and Judge Bridlegoose. Shakespeare, in *Love's Labours Lost* concocts 'Honorificabilitudinitatibus,' which the Baconians unscramble into *Hi ludi Fr. Bacono nati tuiti sibi*—"these plays fathered by Fr. Bacon are their own protection." Actually Holofernes spoke it as a piece of resounding learned gibberish.

English is quite rich in reduplicated and rhyming compound words, many of them perhaps not quite respectable in formal prose. They are readily used, however, in colloquial passages, and are found in the dialogue of our comic drama. It is easy to see that the invention of new words of this type is in accord with the genius of our language. The double word with internal rhyme is in fact one of the most amusing types in English. Such are

willy-nilly, hocus-pocus, helter-skelter, tag-rag, namby-pamby, pell-mell, hab-nab, hodge-podge, hugger-mugger, hurly-burly; shilly-shally, mingle-mangle, tittle-tattle, prittle-prattle, driffel-draffel, riff-raff, see-saw, slip-slop.

These Trench gives as still in use (i.e. in 1881); and he laments that the following have passed out of vogue:

kaury-maury, trolly-tolly *(Piers Plowman)*, tuzzie-muzzie *(Promptorium)*, hufty-tufty, kicksy-wicksy (Shakespeare); hibber-gibber, rusty-dusty, horrel-lorrel, slaump-paump (all in Gabriel Harvey), royster-doyster *(Old Play)*, hoddy-doddy (Ben Jonson); skimble-skamble, bibble-babble (Shakespeare), twittle-twattle, kim-kam (both in Holland), trim tram, trish-trash, swish-swash (all in Gabriel Harvey), whim-wham (Beaumont and Fletcher), mizz-mazz (Locke), snip-snap (Pope), flim-flam (Swift), tric-trac.—Trench. *English Past and Present.* New York, The Macmillan Company, 1881. pp. 214, 215.

As a matter of fact 'flim-flam' is quite common in American writing; the OED gives examples also of recent use. Trench's list does not exhaust the stock. *Tic-tac* is a common name for a spool device which children employ on Hallowe'en to produce a grinding whirr on a window. Such dialectal compounds as 'briggle-diggle,' or 'briggle-dick' meaning 'to procrastinate in trivial fashion,' are frequent in the Middle-West. It is curious that Trench does not mention 'higgledy-piggledy' or 'hitty-missy.' The latter is used by Galsworthy in *The Pigeon.*

These verbal high jinks are proof that there is a great deal of fun to be had in playing with words. It is not only the ordinary run of wordsmiths hammering out new slang who enjoy this form of play.

The turn for reciting malapropisms and verbal slips is widespread. The spoonerism, which takes its name from Canon Spooner of Oxford, is very popular in learned circles. The trick of transposing initial consonants, supposedly by accident, was one of which the Canon was not often guilty. But when he jumbled the words in the line of the hymn "Conquering kings their crowns shall keep," reading it out as "Kinkering conks," his famous accidental slip was enough to fasten his name to this particular kind of metathesis. The legendary stories which grew up about him are innumerable. He was at the Oxford station leaving for London; he kissed the guard (in U. S., 'the conductor') good-by, gave his wife a sixpence, and said, "Guard, wrap my bugs in the rag." Whether the next spoonerism has found its way into the numerous collections which are issued from time to time in England, I do not know. It is elaborate, but it is one of the best.

"Mardon me, padam, you are occupewing the wrong pie. May I sew you to a new sheet?" (A church usher speaking.)

"Cheautiful birch you have here." (The lady speaks, as she is being ushered to the new seat.)

"Many thinkle peep so, madam."

The implied awkwardness of the situation makes the mix-up somehow more plausible, and the exquisite English courtesy adds to the effect.

In contrast to these deliberate inventions of academic circles, are the malapropisms current among prize-fighters and their managers. These are closely allied to slang. Perhaps they are better labeled a variety of cant. Dan Parker, in the N. Y. *Daily Mirror* of the 7th and 21st January 1933 gives a list which is almost too good to be true:

Pacifist. 'To make a pass at someone with the fist.'
Larynx. 'An animal something like a wild cat found in Canada.'
Paragon. 'A country in South America.'
Superficial. 'One who puts on full evening dress.' (soup and fish!)
Ratify. 'To squeal on a pal.' (Rat!)
Blemish. 'A language spoken by Belgian fighters.' An unintentional blend
   of Belgian and Flemish!
Etymologist. 'One who studies the art of eating.'

Incinerator. 'One who makes nasty cracks about people.' (The word malapropized is 'insinuator.')
Circumference. 'What the boss is in when the insurance agent calls.' (All quoted in Partridge's *Slang*, 317-18.)

Even Mrs. Malaprop herself could not surpass the virtuosity of these choice specimens. Notice, however, the curious anomaly that each of these words is in itself in good use. It is only when the fight managers start in wrecking the language that these terms take on their curious extensions of meaning.

To return, however, to slang proper. There is a large range of it which is due to the desire to find an off-hand euphemism for serious situations, to enable the speaker and hearer to soften the tragedy, or pretend to take it casually. Consider the following slang synonyms for 'to die': check out (—1913), cash in one's checks (1870), cock one's toes, go to grass, hop the twig (1797), kick the bucket (—1785), lay down the knife and fork, be rubbed out (1848), snuff it (1885), turn up one's heels, wake on the other side, be gone to Kingdom Come, be gone to the Diet of Worms, be gone to Ratisbon (i.e. Rot-his-bone), shuffle off (this mortal coil), to turn one's toes to the daisies (1842). Many of these euphemisms hail from the underworld, or from soldier slang. But some of them have come into general use, at least in men's clubs and smoking-rooms, and in hard-boiled fiction where sentiment is not at a premium. Actually, this is a case of hardening the language in order to soften the concern which is felt at the fact of death.

Closely allied in motive to this hardening sort of euphemism, is the employment of slang to minimize the solemnity of conversation, or even of informal prose. So in the chaste pages of the *New Republic* and the *Nation*, critics recently (1935) have used 'phoney,' without any quotation marks; while 'haywire' and 'cock-eyed' (which is an old word) have been fast making their way in good newspapers. The figurative extension of 'chisel' which President Roosevelt brought into vogue is hardly slang. 'Wisecrack' has a respectable antecedent in 'witcrack,' which Shakespeare used (both as noun and verb) in the same sense. 'Crack' in this slangy sense is in fact quite old. 'Crack down,' curiously enough, had an older slang sense of, 'work hard,' getting into print in 1920; but General Hugh Johnson has applied it in a more apt way, and his idiosyncratic use of it appears likely to fix the generally accepted meaning. The phrasal verb is always available to the inventive manufacturer of slang; and such inventions are perhaps more often accepted into the language than any other type.

This discussion has been carried on without attempting a precise definition of slang. It is easier to describe and exemplify than to define. Professor McKnight has said that slang is to language what jazz is to music. The figure is an apt one. For slang, like jazz, uses the same elements and the same devices as normal language, but it uses them with comic intent, and, unfortunately also like jazz, often with tedious iteration. Slang is always a little off the beat, it slurs and clips and blurs legitimate words; like jazz, it often borrows classical phrases and weaves them into a grotesque pattern. It is given to odd intervals and a queer pitch. Like the 'blues,' the melancholic variety of jazz, slang is often used for serio-comic effects. And finally, like jazz, slang makes a good interlude but a bad steady diet. It seems to come from nowhere, but it easily falls into tiresome stereotypes—like the Tin Pan Alley product. At its most vital, slang consists, like jazz, of gutter idiom which is on its way up in the world. Society slang is usually feeble and artificial; college and university slang in strength and merit midway between the gutter and 'high-life' varieties.

The sources of slang have here been noted only incidentally. The most recent authority on its vagaries, Eric Partridge, lists and describes "the kinds of slang other than the standard" as coming from the following sources:

Cockney, Public House, Workmen, Tradesmen, Commerce, Publicity, Journalism, Literary Criticism, Publishing and Printing, The Law, Medicine, The Church, Parliament and Politics, Public Schools and Universities, Society, Art, The Theatre, Sports and Games, The Turf, Epsom's Attic Salt, Circus Life, Sailors, Soldiers, Yiddish, Cant, Miscellaneous.

This may be compared with the classification of American slang by Maurice E. Weseen which was noted earlier (p. 56). These varieties of slang suggest its point of merger with the other grand division of dubious words: Jargon.

Jargon is used in several senses. Its widest meaning is "talk that is considered both ugly-sounding and hard to understand." In American, it means loosely any kind of gibberish which the hearer does not understand or doesn't much like. Strictly, it is applied (1) to a macaronic mixture of two languages, as in the German-American dialect poem, "Hans Breitmann gaf a party"; or in the comic line from Folengo compounded out of Latin and Italian

Heu quantis noster orbis musolinis abundat

which may be rendered, "Worse luck, how the world is over-run with little musolinis." This was written in 1519, and the particular *musolinis* referred to were 'little muses,' mostly female kitchen mechanics who inspired the macaronic poets to dream of rivers of fat broth and mountains of cheese and jelly. This sort of macaronic language apparently has its uses, at least for quotation. It is seen at its best in the *Ingoldsby Legends* of Barham, with their quaint mixture of French and English. Closely allied to this form of jargon is that found in dog-Latin, and in the 'little languages' of children, comic-strip characters, lovers, and boarding house groups,—such as Balzac's characters in the Maison Vauquer *(Père Goriot)*, who, after they had attended the cyclorama, added -*rama* to all the words that would take the suffix.

Even closer to the macaronic type of jargon is Pidgin English. It grew up in China as a language medium, a lingua franca, for communication between Chinese and foreigners. The Chinese could see no sense in the elaborate constructions and roundabout phrases of ordinary English, so they simplified it, adapting the English vocabulary to Chinese phonetics and grammar; the latter having had longer to wear out, is a good deal more decayed than ours—a lucky condition! Pidgin is still used as a trade language pretty well throughout the Pacific from Hawaii to Hongkong, from Manila to Vladivostok. It is also widely used in the best social circles in the tropics. It is so much less effort. Instead of saying, "I regret that a previous engagement prevents my accepting your kind invitation," one simply says, "No can do." 'Catchum' does duty for nearly all the verbs. If you want to order a bottle of Johnny Walker, you ask the Chinese boy, "You catchum one piecee Johnny Walker?" "Can do," he says, and gets it. A Chinese gardener in Hawaii was told to let the children know when a litter of little pigs arrived. He came to the house, called for the children, and announced, "Him cow pig have kittens." The merits of this 'lingo' are obvious. It is commonly supposed that it suggested the possibility of Basic English.

Another sense of *jargon* (2) is that fixt by Quiller-Couch in his famous essay using the word as a title. By it Sir Arthur means the use of vague 'omnibus' words, roundabout official circumlocutions; what the Germans call *Kanzleistil*, the woolly ponderous generalities of official documents. He quotes a specimen:

There can be no doubt that the accident was caused through the dangerous nature of the spot, the hidden character of the by-road, and the utter
absence of any warning or danger signals.

"Mark," he says, "the foggy wording of it all! And yet the man
hit something and broke his neck." Q is particularly aggrieved because spots do not have a nature, and by-roads do not have a character.

Quiller-Couch's pet aversion is really a special case of the most
important type of jargon, which H. W. Fowler defines (3) as "the
sectional vocabulary of a science, art, class, sect, trade, or profession,
full of technical terms." When this jargon is used out of working
hours, it is often called 'shop talk.' If it is thieves' or gangsters' language, it is a kind of 'cant.' The purpose of maintaining secrecy is
not confined to thieves' jargon: the learned professions use it for
the same purpose.—Sir John Adams once remarked that "Education" has now become a profession, because it has ten dollar books
and a learned jargon!—

When a word from any of these technical lingoes wanders into
prose meant for the general reader, it may or may not be well received. The jargon of golf, bridge, or (in the United States) poker
may pass almost unnoticed, if it is not too technical or too freely
intruded. Much depends on what games are in fashion; and still
more on the audience addressed. Tennis jargon, for instance, was
dangerous in the days of Theodore Roosevelt; tennis was still an
aristocratic game, and slightly 'sissyfied' as well. But the game
having been democratized, its jargon has been vulgarized as well.
It would probably not go very well in a Marxian harangue, even
now. In general, it may be said that jargon, like slang, limits the
speaker's audience; and marks a writer as addressing a narrower
group than he could reach with standard English.

The professional literary man has all too long claimed special
exemption, calmly taking for granted that critical or artistic 'lingo'
is not jargon, but that all other technical language is beyond the
pale. The truth is that literary jargon is one of the worst kinds.
It makes a craft mystery of literature and philosophy, going contrary to the long and admirable Anglo-American tradition that it
is possible to discuss works of art, letters, and thought in plain and
simple language.

The only place for technical hieroglyphics of any kind is in technical writing, addressed to the inner circle of initiates in the particular mystery concerned. Even then the terms may well be confined to those required by the exigencies of technical expression. If a common word will not do, because it has other connotations, or if the object or relationship is a specialized one, the technical term is the only one to use. Otherwise a writer or speaker with a sense of humor will fight shy of it.

The inept use of jargon in prose addressed to the general reader is a fruitful source of diversion to those who have learned to keep an eye out for this particular occupational disease. Here are a few choice specimens. Can you detect the profession or trade of the offender, in each case?

68) 1. Around 8 o'clock this morning there was ordered dispatched to the Luckenbach dock several gangs of men who were not members of the I. L. A. by the officials on duty under federal supervision and one gang from the I. L. A.
Matt Meehan of the I. L. A. is alleged to have directed I. L. A. members to the Luckenbach docks and picket the same. As a result of this and other action, a large number did go to the Luckenbach docks and as they came out, took checkers and other employes of the dock with them. *(Portland Oregonian,* August 21, 1934.)

2. But for one who believes that poetry is not a glamorous phase of life, but a vital function of life coöperating with other functions and occupying a definite place in the whole round of man's activity, there is a hierarchy of values to which all good poetry is subject and by which some poems are esteemed great and others are thought to be of minor excellence. p. 91.

The achievement of the minor poet is Form—the macrocosmic organism that style, design, precision and all the other merits of minor poetry manifesting as *characteristics* of an essence that animates them. p. 92.

Behind the elaborate inconsequence of her stylistic behavior, the swiftness of her mental movements, so swift that connectives are dropped out, the complexity of her reconnoitres, the bewildering patches of her learning, there peers at moments simplicity, humble and timid, immature and shy, disliking sophistication and "complexity moreover, that has been committed to darkness, instead of granting itself to be the pestilence that it is." But to reach the elements that compose this simplicity, through what labyrinths one must work, what traps for the inattentive one must evade! GORHAM B. MUNSON, *Destinations.* p. 94. (Sears Publishing Company.)

3. True, the belief on A.'s part that he had a *bonâ fide* sayee in B., saves his speech quâ him, but it has been barren and left no fertile issue. BUTLER, SAMUEL, *Essays on Life, Art and Science.* (A. C. Fifield, 1908.) p. 183.

4. *Intellectual and Personality Problems of Education.*
This course deals with those functions of education relating to the development of intellectual powers, attitudes and social intelligence. These general functional objectives of education are studied and defined, as are also the relations of the special subject-matter fields, such as the social sciences, the natural sciences and the arts, to the general functional objectives. Methods of motivating the attainment of these objectives, methods of teaching adapted to their attainment, and methods of measuring their attainment are studied. Each student is required to carry the work through his special field of interest as an individual project.

5.   WAX CHARACTERS EAT
time and postage. False, jarring figures ruin a story. Create personalities. With _____'s classified TEMPERAMENT BOOK, $1, you will choose words that individualize your characters, their manners and personal habits. For powerful characterization use HUMANITOME always. Try Action Book, $1; Emotion and Its Expression, $1. Complete satisfaction or money back.

_____'s HUMANITOME
A Guide to Character Delineation and Human
Description

6. Thou speakest as one having tongues and who putteth the speed behind the ole rhombencephalon comprising the cerebellum and the medulla oblongata. . . .

The benisons of eventide to you, Barney. May your circulation proceed unchecked and particularly the dorsal carpal branch of the ulnar artery, in which connection, comrade, Prof. Dr. Col. Egbert Arrowsmith and I would fain trifle with another bottle of that renowned strawberry pop. SINCLAIR LEWIS, *Arrowsmith*, p. 61. (Harcourt, Brace and Company.)

7. Can you add further specimens from your own reading? Journalese is most frequently encountered.

CHAPTER VIII

SPECIAL AND TECHNICAL VOCABULARIES

There are times when shop talk is very much in place. A 'cut-back' or 'close-up' in a movie could hardly be briefly designated by any other term. Once conquer the novelty of these nouns made from phrasal verbs, in accordance with the traditional habit of our language, and no one will boggle at them, even when they are used in some other context. The reader who wants to range afield from conventional and traditional literature soon finds it necessary to pick up words from special and technical vocabularies, so rapid has been the spread of popularized scientific language. We accept without question words which have made their way into the literary language from astrology, theology, medicine, law, philosophy, and military science. Why should we bar terms from the movies, from radio, from automotive engineering, from aeronautics? Or why refuse to import an occasional word from recent medicine? Or shut out recently coined terms in the various fields of learning, if these new symbols fill a definite need in the language? It will do no good to bar them, in any event: many of them will make their way, as we noted in the list of terms recently admitted into the dictionary (end of Chapter I).

The real problem before the general reader is: Which of these terms in various special and technical vocabularies are a necessary part of his equipment, if he only now and then cruises into semi-scientific fields? What part of each specialized vocabulary most often percolates into general use? This shows a path to follow through what otherwise might appear to be a hopeless thicket; for with the growth of science and technology, the number of special terms is almost unlimited.

Moreover, no single reader will require a command even of the commoner terms in *all* technical fields. Everyone will want a bowing acquaintance with the jargon of the movies, radio, the airplane, and the automobile. The terms of psychology, and of its step-child, psychoanalysis, are widely and loosely used. Beyond these, there

181

lie a great many branches of learning which impinge more or less on the ordinary reader's experience. It will depend on one's taste and range of interest, in how many of these learned disciplines a knowledge of the commoner terminology will prove of service.

There is a certain interest attached to acquiring these new technical words. They often describe devices or theories which are on the frontiers of learning; they deal with novel ideas; and they reveal something of the habit of mind of the inventors and discoverers who are engaged in extending the boundaries of experience. "The five senses are our gateways of reality in this world," wrote Blake; but a diligent study of the terms of the sciences, while not comparable in interest to a study of the phenomena and relationships involved, will at least open up vistas into the imaginative reason which the great scientist shares with the great artist. The symbols of the scientist are not without a magic suggestiveness, even though he tries to use them to delimit meaning. Ideally, he prefers a word that fixes a single invariant object, or a definite and unique relationship. Science is the most characteristic mode of deciphering reality in our time; and no one who wants to be conversant with the living currents of thought in our age, can neglect the language of science and technology.

It has been noted in another connection (Chapter IV) how helpful the study of classical stems may prove to the student of the more abstract and scientific vocabulary of English; and the literal meaning of many of the terms which follow can be deciphered with the aid of the amateur etymologist. For their precise sense in a given learned discipline, the dictionary is the only resource; and in the case of more recent words, even it will sometimes fail. Then it is necessary to have recourse to a treatise on the subject; and it may be worth while here to repeat da Vinci's warning against mistaking words for things.

Certainly, there is nothing worse than the inaccurate use of scientific terms by half-baked pretenders to learning. This can be seen at its worst in such detective stories as those of S. S. Van Dine, whose pedantic and preposterous detective mouths a jargon made up of various scientific lingoes hastily 'gotten up' for the occasion by the author. The supposedly learned footnotes are the last straw. In the works of a truly erudite writer, also in the field of detective fiction, such as R. Austin Freeman, the learning is worn lightly, and the technical terms come in aptly and inevitably. Dr. Thorndyke, the medico-legal expert whom Freeman has created, is, like his creator, versed in medicine and law; but he uses scientific terms from these fields, and from psychiatry, only when ordinary language will not serve. He is a genuine scientific investigator, whose laboratory methods and modes of deduction were so convincing that the French *Service de la Sûrêté* actually took some hints from Freeman and installed many of Thorndyke's procedures in their bureaus of research. It is significant that Freeman usually explains, by careful indirection and unobtrusive description, the meaning of most terms which Thorndyke employs. This is a courtesy which the more civil sort of author will usually extend to the reader; the difficulty is to make an explanation which will not insult those readers who already know the meaning. The choice between condescension or obscurity is not a pleasant one; and this is why a shrewd writer limits his employment of technical terms to the minimum. But where they are essential to the sense, the bold writer does not hesitate; so the reader who is audacious enough to follow must learn the new language. Luckily this is not so hard as it seems.

69) Before you begin on the task of extending your technical and scientific vocabulary, try the following exercise, devised to test the knowledge of high school and college students who have had only a year's work in general science. If you have read *Popular Science* or *Popular Mechanics,* or have had ABC work in the sciences, you should score 95 out of a hundred. Notice that this is a further test of *roadiness* in the command of words, but in a specialized field. How many of the key words are in current *literary* use?

INSTRUCTIONS: Can you fit the right word into the right place and spell it correctly? Use the first letter and the suggestions in parentheses to help you find the ONE word you need. None of the words in parentheses is the one you want. When you have thought of the right word, spell it correctly and completely in the proper space on a sheet of paper numbered to correspond to the blanks in the test.

Example. We use the m—(pertaining to a system of measurement commonly used in the natural sciences) scale in physics.   1. metric.

1. We felt the v—(quick motion to and fro) of the engine.

2. The airplane has a greater v—(speed) than the automobile.

3. The t—(act of sending from one person or place to another) of sound without even the aid of a wire was a great discovery.

4. We have a t—(an instrument to measure heat) in the school room to aid us in keeping the room at an even temperature.

5. Brine is a s—(preparation made by dissolving a solid in a liquid) of salt and water.

6. The air was s—(full of) with the perfume of flowers.

7. The violin string is r—(able to return sound).

8. Wool and fur have a r—(quality of not yielding to force) against wind and cold.

9. The mirror causes a r—(change in the direction of rays of light).

10. We feel the r—(emission of rays of light or heat from a center) of heat from the stove.

11. That is a n—(medium) tint of blue.

12. The n—(unfinished photographic picture) was shown to us before we ordered the pictures finished.

13. A man comes to read the m—(an instrument to measure gas) each month.

14. The m—(power of attraction) of the lodestone draws many things to it.

15. They used a l—(a bar used to sustain a weight at one point of its length) to pry up the board.

16. I—(illustrating the distribution of heat) lines connect points on the earth's surface having the same annual temperature.

17. We shall i—(separate from other bodies by means of non-conductors) the electric wires.

18. Sand is i—(incapable of being dissolved).

19. We did not have i—(white or glowing with heat) lights in Benjamin Franklin's time.

20. Water is composed of h—(a chemical element) and one other gas.

21. A h—(pertaining to fluids in motion) pump was placed in the well.

22. Oregon has much h—(moisture) in the air.

23. They will f—(use a device for straining liquid) the water at the camp before drinking it.

24. The f—(that change of organic substances by which their starch, sugar, gluten, are broken up and recombined in new compounds) of the grape juice caused it to become wine.

25. Rust causes the e—(eating away) of iron.

26. One of the e—(an essential ingredient) of the air is argon.

27. There is much e—(peculiar condition of the molecules of a body or of the surrounding ether developed by friction, chemical action, heat, or magnetism) in the air tonight.

28. We saw the big d—(a machine that converts mechanical into electric energy by rotation of copper wire coils in a magnetic field) that furnishes us with electric power.

29. The d—(operation of extracting spirit from a substance) of whiskey from corn and other grains has been legalized.

30. The d—(compactness) of iron is greater than air.

31. We will wait for the leaf mold to d—(decay).

32. The c—(shrinking) of rails on the railroad is caused by the cold.

33. Air is held in a liquid state by c—(to bring within narrower limits of space).

34. An automobile has an internal c—(development of light and heat accompanying chemical combination) engine.

35. The b—(quality of floating) of the balloon enabled it to go a long way.

36. The b—(apparatus that is essential to ignition) in an automobile is a new one.

37. The b—(an instrument for determining the weight or pressure of the atmosphere) shows there is going to be a storm.

38. Along the coast of Florida, there are many a—(wells formed by boring into the earth till the instrument reaches water, which, from internal pressure flows spontaneously like a fountain) wells.

39. We find much a—(one of a class of caustic chemical bases, soda, potash, ammonia, and lithia) in Eastern Oregon.

40. Vinegar is an a—(chemical that is sour, sharp or biting to the taste) derived from apples.

41. Spring is the time for the g—(sprouting) of seeds.

42. The e—(undeveloped) plant is in the seed that is put in the ground.

43. Alfalfa is a p—(that which comes up year after year).

44. The c—(green coloring matter) is the thing that makes the leaves green.

45. B—(the science which treats of plants) should be interesting to a farmer.

46. We should s—(make pure) the jars before canning.

47. We found the s—(bony framework) of a bear in the woods.

48. The liver s—(to separate, elaborate, and emit by natural process) bile.

49. S—(liquid poured into the mouth) helps in the digestion of our food.

50. His r—(act of breathing) was natural.

51. We shall p—(sterilize by exposure to high temperature) the milk before using.

52. We need plenty of o—(colorless, tasteless gas) to breathe.

53. Some things we eat do not have much n—(food value) in them.

54. Do not i—(draw into the lungs) the poisonous gas.

55. The i—(that which poisons or corrupts) caused blood poisoning in his arm.

56. One of the vital organs of the body is the h—(organ that serves to keep up the movement of the blood).

57. There are many g—(tissue in animals or plants, producing some peculiar substances) in the body.

58. A bud is a g—(portion of organism capable of becoming a new one) of a fruit or a leaf.

59. The g—(fluid produced in the mucous membrane of the stomach) juice helps to digest food.

60. We shall f—(to expose to smoke or gas as in cleansing clothing) all our old clothes.

61. People e—(give off from the lungs) waste products in the form of gas.

62. We shall d—(cleanse from disease) the house.

63. The d—(breaking up and absorption of foods) is the work of the alimentary canal.

64. We have red and white c—(minute discs) in the blood stream.

65. He has poor c—(movement of blood through the body).

66. Each c—(a small closed cavity) in the body is a living organism.

67. The end of bone was covered with c—(a smooth, whitish, elastic sub stance).

68. When we breathe we take in air and throw off c—(a gas that contains impurities).

69. The water rose through the soil by c—(attraction by which liquid is drawn up) action.

70. The b—(microscopic rod-shaped vegetable organism) are found in decomposing liquids.

71. The a—(act of taking a substance through the tissues) by the plant is a wonderful process.

72. Wheat grown anywhere without attention to the selection of pure seed is likely to show many v—(deviations from a standard type).

73. The t—(a small mass of the roots of leguminous plants) on the roots of the clover are of the highest value to the farmer.

74. People now know that t—(cultivation of the soil is of greatest importance during times of drouth).

75. The farmer tries to enrich the s—(the bed of earth which lies immediately below the surface soil) when it is plowed.

76. G—(insertion of a small shoot of a tree into another tree) has improved our apples in the Northwest.

77. The farmer has a large s—(pit or airtight chamber for ensilage) near his barn.

78. Spring is the time for p—(lopping off, as superfluous branches of trees) of apple trees.

79. The p—(spreading or extension of anything) of plants from seeds is a form of agriculture.

80. The honey bee is a great help in the p—(conveyance of pollen to the pistil of the plant) of plants.

81. N—(an atmospheric gas) is necessary for plant life.

82. A mass of growing bread m—(woolly fungus growth formed on moist surfaces) is composed of many white threads.

83. We sometimes find m—(growth of minute fungi on plants) on the under side of grape leaves.

84. The youngberry is a h—(cross between two varieties of plants) between the loganberry and the blackberry.

85. Flowering plants are unable to flourish unless there is considerable h—(vegetable mold) in the soil.

86. H—(gardening) is a fundamental industry.

87. The fruit tree had fire b—(a kind of plant disease).

88. Plants that have food stored up in their roots during the first summer's growth and grow seeds in the second season are called b—(two year long).

89. Sugar cane is a s—(juicy) plant.

90. The mud was made by the s—(matter which subsides to the bottom) in the pond.

91. There is more n—(nourishing) value in cereals than in fruits.

92. We worked out the experiment in the l—(place for scientific experiments).

93. There is much e—(changing of water into vapor) on a warm day.

94. The c—(to cause to change into a curd-like state) of the food in the stomach is caused by the action of the juices on the food.

95. A part of the sugar is converted into c—(substance forming framework of plants).

96. C—(many heat-giving food stuffs—sugar, starch) form a large part of all plants.

97. Copper is a good c—(that which transmits) of electric current.

98. We can use this stone as a f—(point of support for a pry) when we pry open the man-hole.

99. Do you know of any s—(liquid in which a substance will dissolve) for rubber?

100. The p—(living substance, that of which all living things are made) of each living thing, from the daisy to the elephant, varies a trifle from any other in its chemical composition.

70) The lists which follow comprise the technical terms in most common use in various branches of learning. The lists are far from exhaustive; but it is believed that for the fields covered those terms are given which are most apt to be found in books and periodicals, which, catering to the general reader, still make some effort to keep up with the progress of the sciences. Readers of scientific fiction, that curious substitute for the romantic tale of the occult and magical, will find here most of the terms which occur in their craft mystery.—In accordance with the policy generally followed in this work, the terms from carpentry, metal-working, and other crafts, which have found their way into pretty general use, are not given; rather the emphasis is on terms from the pure sciences and from the newer branches of technics, where the terms, being of more learned origin, may be novel to the reader, and require more systematic study.

There are no lists for Education or Sociology. Most of the terms used in those jargons will be found under other heads, mainly under Psychology, Economics, Statistics, and Anthropology. There is no well-defined and commonly agreed upon professional jargon for Education or Sociology, apart from the terms borrowed from these other fields.

Except for the test on literary terms, no exhaustive list of rhetorical, grammatical, and critical terms is given; the curious will find these grouped and defined by Fowler, in the *Dictionary of Modern English Usage*, under "Technical Terms." This Alexandrian grammarian's lingo has rather gone out of fashion of late years; and it is no part of my intent to lend countenance to reviving it. The jargons of science are bad enough, without the cant of the rhetorician to reinforce them.

It is not expected that all readers will be equally interested in all the lists. But there is something here for every taste.

The passages following certain of the lists are designed to test the completeness of your mastery of each set of terms. The passages written particularly for this work usually employ in italics a great number of the words just above; and these instances are meant, in part at least, to illuminate the exact significance of the term in the science. After you have mastered the full meaning of all the terms in a given list, you should be able to read the illustrative passage with complete understanding. It is not too much to say that a thorough mastery of these terms in a given field will enable you to understand what an expert in this subject is aiming at; and there is probably no better way to test a layman's appreciation of a technical subject than by examining him on the terminology.

ANTHROPOLOGY

Alpine race, Amerindian, anthropoid, anthropometry, archeology, artifact, autochthonous, brachycephalic, Bronze Age, Caucasian race, cephalic index, couvade, cranium, Cro-Magnon, cultural epoch, diffusion, dolicocephalic, endogamy, Eoanthropus, epicanthic fold, ethnology, exogamy, Finno-Ugric, folkways, fossil man, frontal angle, half-breed, herd instinct, Homo sapiens, Indo-European, Iron Age, linguistic family, magic, marital, matriarchy, matrilinear descent, Mediterranean race, migration, Mongoloid, monogamy, Neanderthal, Neolithic, Negroid, Nordic, Paleolithic, patrilinear descent, petroglyph, pictograph, Pithecanthropus erectus, polyandry, polygamy, polygyny, prehistoric, prognathism, race, stock, taboo, totem.

As the *Paleozoic* era had been dominated by the grotesque *trilobite,* the *Mesozoic* by the ponderous *dinosaur,* so the *Psychozoic* era is essentially the age of another fanciful manifestation of the primordial slime—Man. The first manlike creature known to science is the *Pithecanthropus erectus* or the ape-man who walked erect. The remains of this *fossil man*—three teeth, *cranium* and the left *femur*—were discovered in the early *Pleistocene* beds of Java. *Anthropometric* measurements of these relics show that the creature had a low *cephalic index* (it was narrow-headed), *prognathous,* snout-like jaws, and the *cranial capacity* half as great again as that of an adult gorilla. Although more similar to man than to the *anthropoid* apes, the 'Java Man,' is not included among man's direct ancestors and is classed in a distinct *genus—Pithecanthropus.* The first truly human race of which many remains, both bones and *artifacts,* have been found is the *Neanderthal* race of the Lower *Paleolithic.* The *Neanderthal* man was short and stocky, had heavy *supraorbital ridges* and *prognathous* jaws, but his cranial capacity approached that of modern man, he made chipped stone *implements* not inferior to those of some living *primitive tribes,* knew fire, and buried his dead. The *Neanderthals* became extinct about 25,000 years ago and were succeeded in Europe by a very superior race—the *Cro-Magnons.* These men of magnificent physique are the first to be classified as *Homo sapiens* and are regarded as the ancestors of the White or *Caucasian race.* The *Cro-Magnons* made tools and weapons of stone and bone; they lived in caves and created an art of high excellence. Their figurines in stone and ivory and the naturalistic *polychrome* paintings are not inferior to the creations of some modern artists. With the *Cro-Magnons,* the *Paleolithic Age,* the age of chipped stone tools, came to an end. The *Neolithic* man discovered the art of making pottery, invented the bow, and ground and polished his flint and chert* implements. The *Neolithic* merges gradually into the *Age of Metals* and furnishes a link between *prehistory* and history.

All living *races* of man *(Homo sapiens)* are divided into three main groups or *stocks: Caucasian, Negroid* and *Mongoloid.* Three of the four *Caucasian races* live in Europe, they are: the *Nordic,* the *Alpine* and the *Mediterranean;* the fourth consists of *Hindus.* The *Nordic,* the *Mediterranean,* and the *Hindu races* are narrow-headed, or *dolicocephalic;* the *Alpine race* is broadheaded, or *brachycephalic.* The texture of the hair in *Caucasians* is wavy, the body *hirsute,* the color of the skin varies from very white in the *Nordics* to brown in the *Hindus.* The stature also varies from tall to medium, *prognathism* (protrusion of the jaw) is on the whole slight. The *Mongoloid races* inhabit Asia and America. They tend to be *brachycephalic,* straighthaired, glabrous, and brown-skinned. Some *Mongoloids,* notably the Mongolians and the Chinese, have oblique eyes produced by overdevelopment of

---

* Flint and chert are partly *crystalline,* partly *amorphous* varieties of *quartz.* Both are very hard and have *conchoidal fracture.*

the *epicanthic fold*. The *Negroids* are broad-headed, woolly-haired, glabrous, and 'black'-skinned. They are *indigenous* to Africa and Melanesia. Among many curious customs pertaining to *marital* institutions of mankind, that of the *couvade* is particularly interesting. According to this custom, when a couple has a child, the mother gets up immediately and goes about her work, while the father takes to bed to receive the congratulations of the neighbors. The *couvade* obtained among the Basques of the Pyrenees until a century ago and is still practised by the *cannibalistic* Indian tribes of Brazil.

ART AND ARCHITECTURE

acanthus, arabesque, arcade, arch, architecture, architrave, background, baluster, balustrade, baroque, bas-relief, battlement, blue-print, brocade, bungalow, buttress, canvas, capital, colonnade, caryatid, ceramics, chalet, chateau, cloisonné, column, console, Corinthian, cornice, dais, decorative, design, diagram, Doric, dormer, easel, eaves, enamel, engraving, entablature, etching, eye-level, façade, flamboyant, flutted, folio, foreground, foreshorten, freehand, fresco, frieze, gable, gargoyle, glaze, Gothic, graphic, grotesque, half-timbered, ink-wash, Ionic, landscape, lithography, mansard, minaret, molding, mortise, mullion, mount, mural, nuance, obelisk, oil, order, ornament, pagoda, pallette, pavilion, panel, pastel, patio, pedestal, pediment, perspective, pilaster, porcelain, portico, pottery, primitive, profile, projection, proportion, *puce*, rococo, retouching, scroll, sculpture, serif, sienna, silhouette, sketch, still-life, stained glass, tapestry, textile, technique, T-square, tenon, tracery, vault, volute, water color, woodcut.

The *architects* of ancient Greece used three distinct *orders*, or styles in building their temples. Each style was marked by the use of its peculiar form of *column*, and, accompanying this, was a series of *moldings* and *proportions*, found only in conjunction with that *column*. The noblest example of the earliest *order*, the *Doric*, is the Parthenon. The plan of this temple is rectangular. The inner chamber is surrounded by a *colonnade*. At each end of the temple there is a *portico* formed by eight outer and six inner *columns*. The *shafts* of the *columns* are *fluted*, have no *bases*, and are surmounted by very plain *capitals*. The *entablature*, i.e., that part of the structure which rests on the *capitals*, consists of three parts—the *architrave*, the *frieze* and the *cornice*. Above the *entablature* is the triangular space, or *pediment*, which forms the *gable* of the roof. The *pediment* of the Parthenon was decorated with *sculptures* which are now preserved in the British Museum and are known as The Elgin marbles. The *Ionic order* is more ornate than the *Doric*. The columns are more slender; they are placed on *molded bases* and have rather elaborate *capitals* with *Ionic spirals* at each of the four corners of the *cushion*. Sometimes the minor *porticoes* of an *Ionic* temple are supported by female figures or *caryatids* in the place of *columns*. The *frieze* is frequently decorated with *bas-reliefs*. The third *order*—the *Corinthian*—is characterized by highly ornate *capitals* decorated with *volutes* and *acanthus* leaves.

The *Gothic* cathedral has been called "a roof of stone with walls of glass," and justly so, for with the introduction of the *ribbed roof vaulting,* massive walls of masonry which characterized Roman and *Romanesque* structures became unnecessary. *Gothic vaults* composed of intersecting surfaces and resting on *pointed arches* distributed the weight of the roof in such a fashion that it became concentrated at a few points. At these points the necessary support was furnished by *buttresses* and the spaces between the *buttresses* were then filled with light masonry and large windows. The windows were ornamented with *molded mullions* decorated with *sculptures* and *carvings* fulfilling both esthetic and didactic purpose. The vertical lines of the structure, calculated to carry the eye of the beholder heavenward, were accentuated by tall towers and numerous sharp *spires.* The waterspouts on the sloping roof were made in the shape of *grotesque,* diabolical figures— *gargoyles,* placed there to remind man of the temptations that must be overcome before Heaven is reached.

No one has expressed with greater *empathy* the spirit of the French *Rococo* than Antoine Watteau. A consumptive, a slowly dying man, he loved to paint in pastel shades the *fêtes galantes* of the gracefully perverse, genteelly decaying age, which Voltaire, its greatest ornament and scourge, called *le siècle des petisses.* With delicate strokes of his brush, Watteau recorded in minute detail the coiffures and gowns of the ladies, the spangles, ruffs and ribbons of the cavaliers. The enervation of the *Rococo* is well reflected in its architecture. The preceding age had been pompous and imposing; each monument—an apotheosis of the Great King, each interior or garden—an expression of the geometric, Cartesian spirit of the Late *Baroque.* The *Baroque façades* had been almost forbidding in their simplicity; the *Rococo* architect, smothered his *bonbonnières* in shell-work and garlands, covered the interior walls with *flamboyant arabesques,* and filled the rooms with *porcelain* and *chinoiserie.* China had just been 'discovered,' and Chinese silks and paintings, *cloisonné* and *lacquer* kept company with shepherds and shepherdesses of Dresden china. The gardens had a calculated informality and were crowded with miniature *pagodas* and *pavilions;* peacocks, *bizarre* and theatrical birds, strutted among the beds of delicately tinted flowers. Mixed, fading colors prevailed in everything. The garments were of light green and yellow, of apricot and lilac. The flea, a very familiar animal in those days, provided the artists with a whole *gamut* of shades of *puce,* or brownish purple. Flea-belly, flea-shank and flea-with-milk-fever, were some of the *nuances* used in toning the fabrics. The birth of the heir to the throne, the future Louis XVI, was celebrated by the introduction of a brownish yellow—*'caca Dauphin.'* A reaction against the eccentricities of the age began toward the end of the reign of Louis XV, and a slang phrase, *C'est du Rococo,* meaning "It's twaddle," became current and eventually passed into the idiom.

ASTRONOMY

aphelion, apogee of the moon, asteroid, astrolabe, astrology, astrophysics, azimuth, Cassiopeia, celestial mechanics, chronograph, comet, conjunction, constellation, Copernican system, cosmogony, cosmology, declination, double stars, eclipse, ecliptic, ephemeris, equator, equinox, galaxy, galactic latitude, geocentric, gravitation, great circle, heliocentric, Jupiter, light-year, luminosity, lunation, magellanic clouds, magnitude of stars, Mars, mean solar day, Mercury, meridian, meteorite, meteor, Milky Way, Moon, nebulae, Neptune, novae, orbit, parallax, perihelion, planetesimal theory, planetoids, planet, Polaris, precession of the equinoxes, quadrant, reflector, refractor, relativity, right ascension, satellite, Saturn, sextant, sidereal day, Sirius, solar day, solstices, spectroscope, spectrum, spiral nebulae, sun spots, telescope, transit, Ursa Major, variable stars, Venus, zenith, zodiac.

In 1543, the *geocentric* system of *cosmography* formulated by the Alexandrian astronomer and *astrologer* Ptolemy, received its first blow. In that year, the year of his death, Copernicus published his work on *planetary* motions. He showed that the sun was at the center of the *solar system* and that the earth and other *planets* moved about it in circular *orbits*. The earth had always occupied the honored central place among other *celestial* bodies and its dethronement was regarded as an abominable heresy. Even the greatest astronomers of the next few generations could not accept the *heliocentric* system. Tycho Brahe, the Dane, effected a compromise by putting the earth back in its central place and by making the rest of the *solar system* with the sun as its center, revolve about it. The first astronomer who accepted the Copernican system and elaborated it, was Tycho's assistant—Kepler. Kepler showed that the planetary *orbits* were *elliptical* and that the sun occupied one of the *foci* of the *ellipses*. This was a daring attack on the time-honored Aristotelian idea that the circle is the perfect figure, and that, therefore, *celestial bodies* must move in circles. Iconoclastic though this discovery was, it explained many puzzling phenomena such as the seeming loop in the *planetary orbits,* and the varying speeds of their motion. Kepler with his three laws of *planetary* motion laid the foundation of *celestial mechanics.* He was unable, however, to explain how the *planets* were kept in their *orbits* and conceding to tradition suggested that each *planet* had its guiding angel. It was not until Newton, in the later part of the XVII century, evolved his theory of *universal gravitation,* that this problem was clarified.

AUTOMOBILE

accelerator, ammeter, anti-freeze, axle, back-firing, battery, bearings, brakes, brake lining, cam, carburetor, chassis, chauffeur, choke, clutch, connection, crank, cut-out, dashboard, differential, drive shaft, engine, exhaust, fan, fuse, gaskets, gasoline, gear, gear-shift, headlight, ignition, lubrication, magneto, motor, muffler, non-skid, pedal, piston, piston ring, pump, puncture, radiator, shut-off valve, skidding, spark, spark plug, springs, starter, steering wheel, switch, throttle, tire, transmission, tube, valve.

AVIATION

aerodynamics, aerofoil, aeronautics, aileron, aircraft, altimeter, autogyro, aviator, aviatrix, balloon, biplane, blimp, cabane, camber, cockpit, contact, controls, dirigible, drag, elevator, fuselage, gap, glider, hangar, heavier-than-air, kite, landing gear, lift, lighter-than-air, longeron, monoplane, parachute, pilot, propeller, seaplane, stabilizer, stagger, stay, stick, streamline shape, tail fin, tail skid, zeppelin.

See also diagram of airplane on specimen page from *Winston's Simplified Dictionary* in Chap. III, *ante.*

BIOLOGY

abdomen, adaptation, alimentary, amphibian, annelida, anus, aorta, artery, asexual, auricles, bacillus, bacteria, bivalve, blastula, bladder, body cavity, botany, bronchus, calyx, capillary, carapace, carnivorous, cartilage, caudal, cell, cerebellum, cerebrum, chlorophyll, chrysalis, cilium, clavicle, cloaca, coleoptera, corolla, cranium, cytoplasm, deciduous, dentine, digestion, ectoderm, ectoplasm, embryo, endoderm, endoskeleton, entomology, epidermis, evolution, exoskeleton, extensors, femur, fertilization, fetus, fission, flexors, fungus, ganglion, gastric, gastrula, genus, gills, gland, habitat, heliotropism, hemoglobin, herbivorous, heredity, hibernation, hormone, humerus, immunity, integument, invertebrates, iris, larva, larynx, ligament, lymph, mammary, medulla oblongata, mimicry, mucous, nutrition, esophagus, organism, ovary, oviparous, palate, pancreas, parthenogenesis, pelvis, peritoneal, petal, photosynthesis, phylum, physiology, pistil, placenta, plasma, pollen, primates, protoplasm, protozoa, pupa, pupil, rectum, retina, rodent, scapula, secretion, sinus, species, spermatozoa, spinal, spleen, stamen, starch, sterile, sternum, suture, symbiosis, tarsus, tendon, testis, thoracic cavity, tibia, tissue, tonsil, trachea, tympanic membrane, urino-genital, ureter, vaccination, valve, variation, vein, ventral, vertebrates, virus, viscera, vitamin, viviparous, zoölogy.

A famous novelist has used many of these in two short passages:

". . . Under the impulsion of a central organ and of the *motor nerves* originating in the *spinal marrow,* chest and *abdomen* functioned, the *peritoneal cavity* expanded and contracted, the breath, warmed and moistened by the *mucous membrane* of the *respiratory canal,* saturated with *secretions,* streamed out between the lips, after it had joined its oxygen to the *hemoglobin* of the blood in the *air-cells* of the lungs." p. 351, and:

". . . He saw the *single-celled organism* of the fructified egg on the point of being transformed into a *multiple-celled organism,* by *striation* and *division;* saw the *cell-bodies* attach themselves to the *lamellae* of the *mucous membrane;* saw the *germinal vesicle,* the *blastula,* close itself in to form a cup or basin-shaped cavity, and begin the functions of receiving and digesting food. That was the *gastrula,* the *protozoön, primeval* form of all animal life, *primeval* form of flesh-borne beauty. Its two *epithelia,* the outer and the inner, the *ectoderm* and the *endoderm,* proved to be the primitive organs out of whose foldings-in and -out, were developed the *glands,* the *tissues,* the *sensory organs,* the *body processes.* A strip of the outer *germinal* layer, the *ectoderm,* thickened, folded into a groove, closed itself into a *nerve canal,* became a *spinal column,* became the *brain.* And as the *fetal* slime condensed into fibrous *connective tissues,* into *cartilage,* the *colloidal* cells beginning to show *gelatinous* substance instead of *mucin,* he saw in certain places the *connective tissue* take *lime* and fat to itself out of the *sera* that washed it, and begin to form bone. *Embryonic* man squatted in a stooping posture, tailed, indistinguishable from embryonic pig; with enormous abdomen and stumpy, formless extremities, the *facial* mask bowed over the swollen paunch; the story of his growth seemed a grim, unflattering science, like the cursory record of a *zoölogical* family tree. . . ." THOMAS MANN. *The Magic Mountain.* p. 354. (Alfred A. Knopf, Inc.)

CHEMISTRY

acids, albumin, alloy, analysis, aqua regia, argon, atom, base, bicarbonate, Brownian movement, carbohydrate, carbon, catalysis, celluloid, cellulose, chemical, chlorine, coagulation, colloid, combustion, compound, diffusion, dispersion, distillation, effervescence, efflorescence, electrolysis, electrolyte, element, enzyme, ethyl, fats, fermentation, fluid, gaseous, glucose, helium, hydrogen, ion, isotope, liquid, melting point, molecule, monoxide, neon, nitrogen, non-metal, nucleus, oxidation, oxygen, ozone, periodic law, protein, radium, salts, silica, sodium, solid, solubility, solution, starch, substance, sulphur, synthesis, valence, vitamins.

Substances that may be resolved into two or more constituents or *elements,* are called *compounds.* Water is a compound of *hydrogen* and *oxygen;* table salt, or *sodium chloride,* is a compound of *sodium* and *chlorine.* The elements cannot be *decomposed* into simpler substances by means of *chemical analysis.* It is known, however, that they consist of very small particles called *atoms.* All *atoms* of a given *element* are identical in size and other properties, but different from those of any other *element.* According to the *electron* theory, an *atom* may be visualized as a miniature solar system, with a compact central *nucleus* made up of *electrons (negative charges of electricity)* and a larger number of *protons* (positively charged particles), and enough *planetary electrons* to balance electrically the excess of *protons* in the *nucleus.* Although the *electrons* are attracted by the *nuclear* mass, some of the *planetary electrons* are known to escape from the paternal *atom.* Metals such as *potassium* and *sodium* have a great tendency to throw off outer *electrons,* while *non-metals* like *chlorine, fluorine,* etc., are reluctant to part with their *electrons;* but are eager to take in new ones. If an active *atom* and an inert one come together, a *reaction* takes place, and a new *molecule* is formed. The loss of a *negative electric charge* from the active *element* leaves in that *atom* an excess of *positive electricity,* while the inert *element* gains a *negative* charge in its *atom.* The two *atoms,* therefore, are held in the new *molecule* by electric attraction. The *atoms* of such *elements* as *neon, helium,* and *argon* are so stable that they neither throw off, nor gain *electrons* from other *atoms,* and consequently they never form compounds.

The process of decomposing a chemical solution by passing a *current* of electricity through it is called *electrolysis.* When a solution of *copper sulphate* is so decomposed, copper appears on the negative *electrode* or *cathode,* and *sulphuric acid* and oxygen at the positive *electrode,* or *anode.* The important process of *electroplating* is based on the phenomenon of *electrolysis.*

Carbohydrates are compounds of *carbon, hydrogen,* and *oxygen.* They form the largest proportion of the solid constituents of plants. The *crystalline,* sweet carbohydrates are called sugars; the *amorphous,* tasteless ones are known as *starches* and *cellulose.* *Cellulose* is used in manufacturing paper, rayon, *celluloid* and other useful materials.

Catalysis is the changing of the *velocity* of a *chemical reaction* by certain substances which themselves do not appear in the final products of the reaction. *Enzymes,* or ferments, are organic *catalysts.* *Yeast* is an *enzyme.*

ECONOMICS

agricultural stage, amortization, bank, bimetallism, boycott, business, capital, capitalism, clearing house, commerce, communism, consumer's surplus, consumption, coöperation, corporations, cost of production, credit, currency, customs duties, direct taxation, distribution of wealth, division of labor, economics, excess-profit tax, Federal Reserve system, finance, gold standard, indemnity, interest, internal revenue, labor, land nationalization, Malthusian, margin, market, Marxism, medium of exchange, money, monopoly, paper money, par of exchange, personal property tax, private property, production, profit, profiteering, purchasing power, rationalization, *rentier,* sales tax, single tax, socialism, speculation, supply, syndicalism, tariff, taxation, trades-unions, trusts, vested interests, wealth.

Karl Marx calls his brand of *socialism* 'scientific,' to distinguish it from the so-called 'rationalistic' socialism of Saint-Simon, Robert Owen and others. The *Utopian,* or rationalistic socialism, draws a picture of an ideal society whose members behave 'reasonably,' so that unhappiness and injustice are banished. This, of course, presupposes a radical change in human nature, and belongs, therefore, to the realms of fancy. *Marxism,* on the contrary, is devoid of idealistic coloring; it merely states, that the *private capitalistic system* is breaking down, and that the next step in *social evolution* must inevitably be a *collective ownership* of the means of *production* by the *proletariat.* *Socialists* say that *labor* creates all values. As values, goods are nothing but crystallized work, and are worth the number of hours of work that has gone into their production. The cost of work is determined by the wages of labor. Under capitalistic system, the wages are minimal, and the value of what a worker produces is in excess of what he gets for it. This is *surplus value* and constitutes the profit of the employer. The fact that part of this surplus value goes to pay *ground-rent, middleman's cost,* etc., does not bother Marx, for, he says, it makes no difference how many members of the *bourgeoisie* split the profit,—the worker is cheated of what is due him. The antagonism between the *bourgeois* and the *proletarian,* arising from the former's self-interest and injustice, Marx calls the *class struggle,* and regards it as the basis for his *economic* interpretation of history. As the gulf between the employer and the worker increases, and as the latter comes to the realization of his desperate position, a violent upheaval becomes inevitable, the proletarian revolts, dispossesses and destroys the bourgeois, and gathering all property into his hands, creates a *communistic* state. Under *communism,* the means of production are common property, and production and *distribution* of goods is in the hands of the government consisting of workers.

Lewis Mumford writes on economic subjects, using a minimum of technical terms.

The Elements of Social Energetics

In the course of *capitalistic* enterprise, which accompanied the widespread introduction of machines and machine-methods in the fifteenth and sixteenth centuries, the focus of industry shifted from the craft guild to the merchant guild or the livery company or the company of merchant adventurers, or the special organization for exploiting patent *monopolies.* The *means of exchange* usurped the function and meaning of the things that were exchanged: *money* itself became a commodity and *money*-getting became a specialized form of activity. Under *capitalism* profit reigned as the main economic objective; and *profit* became the decisive factor in all industrial enterprise. Inventions that promised *profits,* industries that produced *profits,* were fostered. The reward of *capital,* if not the first claim upon productive enterprise, was at all events the dominating one: the service of the *consumer* and the support of the worker were entirely secondary. Even in a period of crisis and breakdown, such as that *capitalism* is still in the midst of at the moment I write, dividends continue to be paid to *rentiers* out of past accumulation while the industry itself often operates at a loss, or the mass of workers are turned out to starve. Sometimes *profits* were obtained by lowering the costs and spreading the product: but if they could be had only by offering inferior or adulterated goods—as in the sale of medical nostrums or the slum housing of the underpaid worker—health and wellbeing were sacrificed to gain. The community, instead of receiving a full return for its goods and services, permitted a portion of the product to be diverted for the private gratification of the holders of land and *capital.* These holders of land and *capital,* backed up by the law and all the instruments of government, determined privately and solely in accordance with the canon of *profit* what should be produced and how much and where and how and by whom and on what terms.

In the economic analysis of the society that grew up on this basis, the three main terms in industrial activity were production, distribution, and consumption. Profits were to be increased by cheaper production, by wider and multifold distribution, and by a steadily rising standard of consumptive expenditure, with—sometimes in lieu of that, sometimes accompanying it—an enlarging market of consumers. Saving labor, or cheapening labor by a superiority of bargaining power—obtained by withholding land from the laborer and *monopolizing* the new instruments of production—were the two chief means, from the capitalist's standpoint, of increasing the margin of profits. Saving labor by *rationalization* was a real improvement which bettered everything but the position of the laborer. The stimulation of the demand for goods was the chief means of increasing the turnover: hence the problem of *capitalism* was essentially not to satisfy needs but to create demands. And the attempt to represent this process of private aggrandizement and class-advantage as a natural and socially beneficent one was perhaps the main labor of political economists during the nineteenth century. MUMFORD, LEWIS. *Technics and Civilization.* 1934, pp. 373-374. (Harcourt, Brace and Company.)

THE DUTY TO INVENT

The principles that had proved effective in the development of the scientific method were, with appropriate changes, those that served as a foundation for invention. *Technics* is a translation into appropriate, practical forms of the theoretic truths, implicit or formulated, anticipated or discovered, of science. Science and technics form two independent yet related worlds: sometimes converging, sometimes drawing apart. Mainly empirical inventions, like the steam-engine, may suggest Carnot's researches in thermodynamics: abstract physical investigation, like Faraday's with the magnetic field, may lead directly to the invention of the dynamo. From the geometry and astronomy of Egypt and Mesopotamia, both closely connected with the practice of agriculture to the latest researches in electro-physics, Leonardo's dictum holds true: Science is the captain and practice the soldiers. But sometimes the soldiers win the battle without leadership, and sometimes the captain, by intelligent strategy, obtains victory without actually engaging in battle.—MUMFORD, LEWIS. *Technics and Civilization.* p. 52.

GEOLOGY AND GEOGRAPHY

alluvial, alp, anticline, Archeozoic, arctic, atoll, bar, basalt, bed-rock, breccia, caldera, cambrian, canyon, Carboniferous, conglomerate, corrosion, crater, crevasse, crust, debris, delta, diastrophism, dike, dinosaur, dip, equator, erosion, era, fault, fold, formation, fossil, geyser, glacier, gneiss, gorge, granite, igneous, inlet, isostasy, isotherm, latitude, lava, limestone, longitude, magna, mammoth, moraine, mastodon, Mesozoic, metamorphic, mica, orogenic, paleontology, Paleozoic, peneplain, placer, Pleistocene, porphyry, quartz, ravine, reef, rock, sandstone, schist, sedimentary, seismic, shale, silt, slate, stratification, stratum, strike, subtropical, trilobite, tropical, tundra.

Paleontology studies the life of past ages, as shown by the remains of plants and animals, called *fossils,* which have been preserved in the *sedi-*

mentary rocks. The degree of perfection in *fossils* may vary from a mere imprint of a leaf in *shale* or *sandstone* to an entire carcass of an elephant, as in case of the extinct *mammoth* frozen in the Siberian *tundras*. As *species* and *genera* have a span of life, and usually a short one geologically speaking, and are constantly changing, their degree of evolution is more or less indicative of the time of their existence. In other words, each *stratum* has *fossils* or combinations of *fossils* peculiar to itself; these can be used in correlating the *strata* from place to place and in establishing a geologic column or chronology. For instance, a tooth of a s*abre-tooth* tiger or of a *mastodon* indicates *Pleistocene* period; a dinosaur indicates *Mesozoic era,* and a *trilobite, Paleozoic era.* Besides dating the rocks in which they occur, *fossils* also afford testimony as to the *environment* in which they lived. Every *species* of plant or animal has a certain *habitat* which may be land, rivers and lakes, or seas and oceans. Moreover, *climate* varies between the *poles* and the *equator,* and therefore, organisms are cold, *temperate, subtropical,* or *tropical,* in their adaptations. These differences in *habitat* are reflected in *fossils.* For example, we know that *corals* make *reefs* or *atolls* only in warm seas. Hence, when we find *fossil* coral reefs in ancient rocks in the *arctic* regions, we must conclude that the climate of those regions must have at one time been warm.

The word *rock* is used by *geologists* to designate the materials which compose the solid *crust* of the earth. In ordinary usage a rock is something hard and rigid, but, geologically speaking, a *rock* may be a soft and unconsolidated substance; thus a *bed* of *silt,* or *volcanic ash* is a *rock,* as well as a mass of *granite* or *basalt.* According to the mode of their origin, *rocks* are divided into three groups: the *sedimentary rocks (sandstones, shales, limestones)* formed by deposition of *sediment* chiefly by water; the *igneous* rocks *(granites, diorites, basalts, lavas)* made by the solidification of molten materials, or *magmas,* originating in the depths of the earth; and *metamorphic* rocks formed from the preceding two groups by various processes which completely destroy their original character. *Gneiss* and *schist, marble* and *slate* belong to this group.

Because of the sorting activity of running water, *sedimentary deposits* show *stratification,* i.e., they are arranged in layers or *strata.* *Sediments* which form these deposits are products of *erosion,* of the *bed-rock* by the action of rivers, *rain-wash,* glaciers and air. The rock *debris* is transported by these agents and eventually deposited in various places such as, the *deltas* and the *flood-plains* of the rivers, the beaches of seas and oceans, the *moraines* of the glaciers. Other, chiefly marine, deposits are built up of the shells of minute organisms called *diatoms* and *foraminifera.* Most *sedimentary* rocks contain remains of organic life of past geological ages, these are called *fossils* and are very useful in determining the relative age of different *formations.* The newly deposited *strata* are more or less flat, but they soon become deformed by the continuous movement of the earth's *crust (diastrophism)* the beds are thrown into *folds* and fractured by *faults.* The *diastro-*

phic processes are of a paramount importance in shaping the face of the earth.

LAW

abeyance, abrogate, abstract of judgment, accessory before the fact, acquittal, action in personam, action in rem, adjudicate, admiralty, adverse possession, affidavit, agency, appellate, arraignment, assizes, attestation, bailiff, bill of attainder, bill of certiorari, burden of proof, causa mortis, civil, code, codicil, color of title, common law, complaint, conveyance, corpus delicti, corpus juris, covenant, criminal, decision, declaratory judgment, decree, defendant, demur, disseisin, docket, double jeopardy, due process, duress, easement, equity, estoppel, evidence, fee simple, felony, fiduciary, freeholder, grand jury, habeas corpus, in chancery, indenture, indictment, intestacy, jointure, judiciary, jurisprudence, jury trial, malfeasance, modus operandi, motion, multifariousness, non sequitur, nonsuit, opinion, peremptory challenge, plaintiff, pleading, probate, prosecution, replevin, supreme court, tort, true bill, verdict.

HOUSMAN *v* PETERSON

Supreme Court of Oregon, 1915. 76 Or. 556, 149 p. 538

This is an *action* for damages for personal injuries resulting from *assault and battery*. The *complaint* charges, in substance, that on March 24, 1914, *defendant*, without cause or provocation, willfully and maliciously *assaulted* and beat the *plaintiff;* that the blows so received caused the blood to settle in and around *plaintiff's* eyes and cut and wounded *plaintiff's* nose, causing a permanent scar thereon; that by reason thereof *plaintiff* suffered bodily pain, humiliation, and distress to his damage in the sum of $2500. Then follows a *claim* for special damages for loss of time, medical attention, and nursing, in the sum of $75. *Defendant's* answer admits striking *plaintiff* in the face, but denies all the other allegations of the *complaint*. Then follow two affirmative *defenses* in the nature of *counterclaims,* but these were abandoned at the *trial* and no *evidence* offered in support thereof. From a *verdict* and *judgment* for *plaintiff, defendant appeals.*

MATHEMATICS

abscissa, algebra, analytical geometry, arc, area, average, asymptote, binomial, calculus, coefficient, continuum, coördinates, cube, curve, cycloid, denominator, derivative, diameter, differentiation, dimension, divisor, ellipse, equation, equilateral, exponent, exponential, fraction, function, geodesy, helix, hexagonal, hyperbola, hypothenuse, increment, infinitesimal, integration, invariant, isosceles, limit, locus, logarithm, magnitude, mean, minus, multiplicand, numerator, non-Euclidean, ordinate, parabola, parallelogram, parallelepiped, perimeter, periodic, periphery, perpendicular, plane curve, plus, polygon, prism, quadratic, quantity, quotient, radius, ratio, rate of change, rectangle, sector, segment, sine, sinusoidal, spiral, summation, tangent, trapezoid, trigonometry, variable, vector, volume.

Calculus, or *infinitesimal* analysis, is that branch of higher mathematics which deals with constantly changing quantities or *variables.* When two *variables* are so related that the value of the first *variable* depends on the value of the second *variable,* then the first *variable* is said to be the *function* of the second *variable.* For instance, the *area* of a square is a function of the length of its side; the *volume* of a *rectangular parallelepiped* is a function of its three *dimensions.* The fundamental problem of the *differential calculus* is the determination of the *rate of change* in a function corresponding to the changes in value of the *independent variable.* This rate of change of a function is called its *derivative,* or *differential coefficient,* and is defined as the *limit* of the *ratio* of the *increment* of the function to the *increment* of the independent *variable,* when the latter *increment* approaches the limit zero. *Calculus,* called the 'method of fluxions,' by its inventor Isaac Newton, provides an accurate method for measuring infinitely small and imperceptibly varying *magnitudes.* Since all matter is in a state of continuous flux or change, *infinitesimal calculus* is the most perfect instrument devised by man for studying the manifold phenomena of nature.

Analytical geometry enables a mathematician to express the properties of any *plane curve* (the commonest being the circle, the *parabola,* the *hyperbola,* the *trigonometric curves,* the *cycloid,* and the *spirals*) in an *equation* whose main constituents are formed out of two *variable quantities,* the *coördinates.* The system of coördinates most commonly used consists of two straight lines *perpendicular* to each other. The vertical line is called the *ordinate,* the horizontal—the *abscissa.*

The second and third paragraphs of the following are capital examples of the difficult art of translating abstruse mathematical symbols and formulae into language intelligible to the lay reader:

MARTIAL MATHEMATICS

Last week Japan was again threatening China while Italy was mobilizing 45,000 more men for possible war service against Abyssinia. Also last week Lewis Fry Richardson, D. Sc. F. R. S., principal of Paisley Technical College, showed in the British journal *Nature* how the approach of any two nations toward war can be reduced to mathematical equations:

$$\frac{dx_{(1)}}{dt} = k_{(1)(2)} \cdot x_{(2)} - \gamma_{(1)} \cdot x_{(1)} + \Delta_{(1)}$$

$$\frac{dx_{(2)}}{dt} = k_{(2)(1)} \cdot x_{(1)} - \gamma_{(2)} \cdot x_{(2)} + \Delta_{(2)}$$

The symbol *d,* common in calculus, operates to make the left side of the equation a quantity containing the element of change. The suffixes (1) and (2), explains Dr. Richardson, identify the symbols which they follow as the opposing nations or groups of nations; x denotes preparedness for war, a variable; t is the length of time during which the nations have been coming together as enemies; k is a "defense-coefficient"; γ is a "fatigue and expense" coefficient; Δ "represents those dissatisfactions-with-treaties, which tend to provoke a breach of the peace."

Thus the first equation simply means that the approach of Nation (1) toward war with (2) is equal to the product of the defense-coefficients of both nations multiplied by the preparedness of (2), minus the preparedness of (1), multiplied by its fatigue-and-expense coefficient, plus the dissatisfactions-with-treaties of (1). The second equation can be translated conversely. *Time* 10 June '35, p. 30.

MEDICINE

adrenals, ague, alcoholism, anaesthesia, analgesia, anatomy, antiseptic, appendicitis, astigmatism, atropine, bacteriology, beri-beri, black death, bloodletting, blood-poisoning, bubonic plague, cancer, cataract, chemotherapy, cholera, clinic, consumption, contagious, cretinism, cytology, delirium, diabetes, diarrhea, diphtheria, dysentery, epidemic, epilepsy, goitre, gout, hygiene, hypodermic, iatrochemistry, iatrophysics, immunology, infantile paralysis, infantile poliomyelitis, innoculation, insanity, leprosy, lesions, lockjaw, malaria, Materia Medica, measles, mysoedema, obstetrics, ophthalmic, pathology, pharmocology, phthisis, physiology, preventive medicine, prognosis, prophylaxis, quarantine, rheumatism, sanitation, surgery, scurvy, smallpox, stethoscope, syphilis, tetanus, therapeutics, therapy, thyroid gland, toxin, trepanation, trephining, tuberculosis, typhoid fever, typhus, vaccination, venereal diseases, yellow fever.

A recently evolved, still uncertain, but promising method of *therapeutics,* is *colloidal therapy.* An organism, as is well-known, is a system of *colloids,* each tissue, in other words, is a loose aggregate of *molecules* and *atoms.* A healthy organism is characterized by a certain degree of *colloidal dispersion;* in disease, the *colloids* become either *coagulated* or abnormally dispersed. *Coagulation* is caused, for instance, by habitual use of drugs—*morphine, cocaine,* and other *alkaloids,* by alcohol and by certain *cerebral* diseases. The treatment in such cases consists of bringing the *colloids* to the normal state by means of *dispersion* agents—*potassium thiocyanate* being one of them. *Senility,* it has been found, is also due to *coagulation* of bodily *colloids* and should *colloidal therapy* prove efficacious in curing the infirmities of old age, mankind will have found at last its Fountain of Youth in the shape of a *hypodermic syringe* filled with *potassium thiocyanate.*

MOVIES

adaptation, angle shot, animated cartoon, camera, camera angle, cinema, cinematograph, close-up, cut-back, cutting, director, dissolve, double exposure, fade-in, fade-out, feature, film, flash shot, flicker, glass-shot, location, long shot, motion picture, panning, photoplay, projection, reel, register, release, scene, scenario, screen, set, setting, shooting a scene, silver screen, soft focus, sound-on-film method, still, studio, superimpose, synchronization, talkie, technicolor, travelogue, vision, vitaphone.

If you look at the above fragment of *continuity* analytically you will see that it contains the following elements: each *shot* (or *camera set up*) is separate; the kind of *shot* or *camera angle* is indicated; the *location* is indicated ("interior kitchen," "exterior façade of house," etc.); a description of each character as he or she appears is given; for each *shot* the stage is completely set, the properties are listed, the person who speaks and that person's dialogue are set down; where it is necessary the mood or tone in which words are spoken is noted; every sound aside from human voices which occurs in the motion picture is stated; the end of each scene is described as, a *dissolve* or a *fade*—but if there is no such description it is understood that the scene is *cut*—i.e., it is to have the effect on the screen of an instantaneous jump from place to place or person to person.

Not only is each *camera set up* separated from the one that precedes and the one that follows, but the *continuity* is divided into two columns. In the left-hand column are all the camera directions, all the stage directions and all the descriptions of people and of *action*. In the right-hand column is all that is to be caught on the *sound track*.

Of course, when the picture is *shooting,* the director may make changes in our *camera angles* or our *set ups*. In the great majority of *motion pictures,* however, he follows the *script.* So does the camera man. So do the actors. So do the technical department and the department which designs the sets. Thus, it may be seen that it is usually the writer who makes the *motion picture,* and the director and stars merely follow him sedulously. WYLIE, PHILIP. "Writing for the Movies," in *Writer's Digest,* vol. XIV, No. 3.

MUSIC

accelerando, accent, accompaniment, adagio, allegro, alto, andante, animato, aria, bar, baritone, basso, bassoon, baton, beat, brass band, cantata, canto, 'cello, choir, chord, chorus, chromatic, clef, concerto, contralto, crescendo, decrescendo, dolce, finale, flat, fortissimo, largo, mezzosoprano, moderato, motif, obbligato, octave, opera, overture, parlando, pianoforte, pitch, prelude, presto, rhythm, saxophone, scherzo, sharp, solo, sonata, soprano, staccato, stanza, symphony, syncopation, tempo, tenor, tone, treble, trio, tremolo, trombone, two-four, unison, violoncello, violin, volume, waltz, wind, operetta.

NAUTICAL

barge, bark, barkentine, boatswain (bosun), boom, bow, brig, bulkhead, capstan, chips, clipper, companion-way, coxswain (cox'n), craft, cutter, dhow, dingy, doldrums, ease the helm, fiddle, fiddley-deck, forecastle (foc's'l), full ahead, galleon, galley, gig, hard a-port, heave to, junk, keel, lead-line, lugger, main-deck, make fast, marlin-spike, mast, mizzen-mast, pirogue, poop-deck, port, privateer, rigging, rowlock, schooner, scuppers, scuttle, sloop, square-rigger, starboard, stern, supercargo, swing the lead, tug-boat, vessel, watch, winch, yacht.

PHYSICS

aberration, acceleration, achromatic, alternating current, ampere, anode, astigmatism, calory, cathode, centrifugal, conductor, cosmic rays, cycle, density, dielectric, direct current, ductility, dynamics, dynamo, dyne, elasticity, electric, electrode, electromotive, electron, energy, equilibrium, erg, focus, force, frequency, friability, fulcrum, gravity, hydraulic, hysteresis, induction, inertia, insulator, kinetic, lever, lines of force, magnetic field, magnetism, malleability, matter, mechanics, moment, momentum, negative, ohm, pendulum, permeability, phosphorescence, plasticity, potential, positive, radiant energy, reflection, refraction, relativity, resistivity, resonance, solenoid, space-time, specific gravity, spectrum, strain, stress, thermodynamics, thermopile, velocity, viscosity, volt, voltaic cell, watt, X-ray.

Electric *conductors* are those substances through which an electric *current* can flow freely. Copper is one of the best *conductors,* but even it offers a *resistance* to the passage of electricity. *Electric resistance* varies *directly* as the length of the *conductor, inversely* as its *cross-section,* and directly as the *resistivity* of its material. The longer and thinner the wire, the greater the *resistance.* The force that drives an *electric current* along a *conductor* is called *electromotive force.* A storage battery is one of the sources of electricity, and will produce *electromotive force* so long as a *difference of potential (electric pressure)* is maintained between its terminals or *electrodes. Electromotive force* is measured in units called *volts.* The amount of current *(amperes)* sent through a *conductor* is equal to *electromotive force,* or *voltage,* divided by *resistance,* the latter being expressed in *ohms.* In a *voltaic cell,* a battery, or a *direct current generator,* electricity flows in one direction only, namely, from the *positive* terminal to the *negative;* in *alternating current circuits,* the direction of the flow is rapidly and *periodically* changed. The *current* in this case builds up gradually in one direction, reaches a *maximum,* then falls down to zero, builds up to a *maximum* in the other direction, returns to zero, and so on. This double swing is called a *cycle* and may be *diagrammatically* represented by a *sinusoidal* curve. The number of *cycles* per second is called the *frequency* of the *alternating current.*

That which occupies space is *matter. Matter* exists in one of three states of aggregation, the *solid, liquid,* or *gaseous.* The last two states are sometimes called *fluid.* The constituents of *matter, molecules* and *atoms* are never at rest. If two different gases are placed together in a vessel, they tend to mix: this is called *diffusion.* Even many *solids* show *diffusion;* thus when a block of gold is placed on a block of lead and left there for several weeks, the particles of gold will be found to have wandered into the lead and vice versa. The *hypothesis* which assumes that the particles of *matter* are in motion is called the *hypothesis* of the *kinetic* constitution of *matter*. All *matter* has *density*. *Density* is measured by the *mass* per unit volume. The *ratio* of the *density* of a given body to that of some standard substance (usually water at 4° C.), is called its *specific gravity*. One of the most important properties of *solids* is *elasticity*, i.e., the tendency to recover original shape after having been distorted. The forces which tend to distort a body are called *strains*. The reaction of the internal forces of the body to *strain* is called *stress*. *Solids* also possess in varying degree such properties as *malleability, ductility, plasticity, friability,* and *hardness*. A *fluid* differs from a *solid* in that it has no permanent resistance to the forces tending to change its shape. The rate of yielding varies with the nature of the *fluid* and is called its *viscosity*.

PSYCHOLOGY

abnormal, aboulia, affect, afferent, algolagnia, amnesia, anesthesia, aphasia, association, audition, automatism, azone, character, clairvoyance, cognition, conation, consciousness, delusion, dementia, dendrite, efferent, emotion, empathy, euphoria, extravert, feeble-mindedness, gestalt, gustatory sensations, hallucination, hypnosis, hysteria, id, illusion, introspection, introvert, intuition, mania, manic-depressive, masochism, melancholia, mesmerism, neurasthenia, neurone, neurotic, neurosis, olfactory experiences, paranoia, perception, personality, phobia, psychopath, psychopathology, psychiatry, psychosis, rationaliztion, reaction time, response, sadism, schizophrenia, sensory, somnambulism, stimulus, subconscious, symbolism, threshold of consciousness, volition.

The most common *abnormal* phenomena, which are functional in their origin, and not constitutional, are: *hallucinations* and *illusions, automatisms, abnormal suggestibility,* and *dissociations of personality*. All these experiences may occur to a normal individual; dreams, for instance, are characterized by at least three of the four *abnormal* phenomena. Dream images are essentially *hallucinations* and *illusions;* dreams may be accompanied by motor reactions, as sleep-walking, or other *automatisms* grouped under the general name of *somnambulism; dissociation,* that is, interruption of habitual *associations* is also found in dream *consciousness*. Nor, does occasional occurrence of any of the *abnormal* phenomena in waking life, constitute a dangerous deviation from the normal. *Hallucinations,* especially, are much commoner than is usually thought. According to a questionnaire sent to 30,000 persons by the Society for Psychical Research, one out of every twelve persons had experienced a *hallucination*. The phenomena of *synesthesia*— 'colored hearing' and 'mental forms'—are also fairly common. Finally, *automatisms* and the closely connected momentary *dissociations of personality* are found in otherwise normal individuals. Should, however, these experiences become frequent and intensive, the sufferer is well-advised to consult a *psychiatrist*.

PSYCHOANALYSIS

ambivalence, anxiety dreams, censor, complex, daydream, death instinct, defense mechanism, dream analysis, Electra complex, extroversion, fixation, fixed symbols, free association, Freudian wish, id, infantile sexuality, inferiority complex, inhibition, introversion, libido, narcissism, Œdipus complex, phantasy, preconscious, pleasure principle, repression, resistance, sublimation, super-ego, superiority complex, suppressed desires, transference, trauma, unconscious, wish fulfillment.

The theory of *repression* is the cornerstone of *psychoanalysis*. Certain emotions and wishes, chiefly of sexual character, are withdrawn from *consciousness* because of their unethical, unsocial character. They are relegated to the *unconscious* mind, which is a kind of lumber room for all sorts of unseemly things. The pleasure-loving *libido* strives to carry out these instinctive, *infantile sex impulses*, but is thwarted by the individual's social personality. The result is the formation of *complexes*. Normally, these are *sublimated*, i.e., they are turned into socially acceptable channels—a *narcissist* becomes a movie star, an *anal-eroticist*—a banker or a lexicographer. But frequently, failing to find a suitable outlet, the *complexes* manifest themselves in various *neurotic* symptoms. *Neurotic* symptoms are substitutes for what is *repressed*. The purpose of psychoanalysis is to discover the emotional experiences, or *traumata* responsible for these symptoms. It is necessary, in other words, to explore the *unconscious* and to bring to light the disturbing factors. *Hypnotism* is one method, but since the state of *hypnosis* cannot always be induced, Freud searched for other means of exploration and found that *free association* used in conjunction with *dream analysis* answered his purpose to perfection. Dreams are expressions of *repressed* wishes; *libido*, a veritable hell of lust and hate and egotism, finds a vicarious satisfaction in dreams. But even in sleep the vigilance of the *censor* which guards the gates of the *unconscious* is not completely relaxed, the disturbing, abhorrent wish is disguised in complex symbolism, and the dream when recalled is frequently distorted and elaborated. To interpret dreams, therefore, requires much skill and more ingenuity.

BEHAVIORISM

behavior, conditioned reflex, discriminatory responses, explicit behavior, habit formation, habit integration, implicit behavior, language habits, response, stimulus.

Behaviorism discards *consciousness* with its elements of *sensation*, perception, imagery, desire, etc., as being insusceptible of objective study. *Behavior*, on the other hand, can be studied and measured in terms of *stimulus* and *response*. *Behavior* is 'what the organism does and says,' and all *mental phenomena* can be explained in terms of behavior, i.e., in terms of *conditioned responses* to various *stimuli*. *Sensations* and *perceptions* are *discriminatory responses;* emotion a *visceral* and *glandular* activity set up by certain *stimuli;* thought—a form of bodily activity involving the muscles of the *larynx,* throat and chest. Thought is almost always verbal, it depends on *language habits* and the chief organ of thought is, therefore, the organ of voice—the *larynx.* The *behaviorist* rejects *instinct* and all *hereditary mental traits,* and asserts that with proper *conditioning,* he can make any normal child a lawyer, a doctor, or any other kind of specialist. The process of training will consist in producing a chain of *conditioned reflexes.*

MENTAL TESTS

ability groups, achievement quotient, age curves, analogy test, aptitude, Army Alpha test, association tests, Binet scale, Binet-Simon scale, coefficient of intelligence, correlation, delinquency, intelligence quotient (I.Q.), mental age, norm, vocational guidance.

RADIO

aerial, air condenser, alternator, ammeter, amplifier, antenna, atmospherics, audibility, audio frequency, broadcast, B-battery, capacitance, circuit, code, coherer, condenser, continuity, crystal detectors, dead spot, dialer, direct current, directional antenna, double-circuit receiver, double-circuit transmittor, earth connection, electro-magnetic waves, electromotive force, frequency, grid, ground connection, hard tube, heterodyne, hook-up, insulator, interference, kilocycle, lead-in, loud-speaker, microphone, mike, ohm, plug, radio-telegraphy, radio-telephony, radio waves, receiver, rectifier, rheostat, selectivity, SOS, soft tube, static, short wave, sign off, tickler, tone frequency, vacuum tube, variocoupler, wave length.

STATISTICS

array, average, binomial distribution, boundary, Charlier check, chart, class, closest fit, correlation, curve fitting, deck, deviation, diagram, dispersion, double entry, forecasting, frequency, geometric mean, graduation, graph, histogram, interpolation, kurtosis, least squares, logarithms, mantissa, mean, median, mode, ogive, organic growth, pictogram, price relative, probability, probable error, quartile, ranks, regression coefficient, regression lines, sampling, saturation point, skewness, smoothing, standard deviation, variation, weighted mean.

The methods used to evaluate *group phenomena* by an analysis of data supplied by enumeration and measurement comprise the science of *statistics.* . . . The distribution of the *frequencies* among the different intervals must often be expressed in a much more summary way. For this, two type of *statistical* numbers are employed. One type is designated as *statistical averages.* In general, these indicate what may be called the position of the distribution, the value around which the different items center. The second type is designated as *dispersion* or *deviation* numbers. They indicate the extent of *variation* of the items with respect to one of the averages. For two sets of items may have the same central tendency although the amount of *deviation* of the two sets is very different. Thus in the two sets of numbers 3, 4, 5, 6, 7, and 1, 3, 5, 7, 11, the amount of the *dispersion* around a common center of distribution is different. Other types of *statistical numbers* may also be used to characterize a distribution, for example, the symmetry of the distribution around the center; but we shall not be concerned with them. (MORRIS R. COHEN and ERNEST NAGEL, *An Introduction to Logic and Scientific Method*, p. 303. (Harcourt, Brace and Company.)

But these be dry matters, as the old Elizabethan schoolmaster said. Still, it would have been cavalier to dismiss the vocabularies of science and technology as mere jargons. The modern world is too diverse and colorful to tolerate an adherence to the strict old literary canons of diction. The split which occurred long ago between the humanists and the scientists was unfortunate; it would be still sadder to perpetuate it. The modern student of words must become something of a scientist, whether he wants to or not. He should not, however, give himself quite over to the mercies of technical language; the illustrative passages above have shown quite clearly the necessity for using sparingly the learned jargons; while a thoughtful consideration for the general reader requires the translation of technical terms into the literary vernacular. The general reader in turn owes it to the hard-working scientist to familiarize himself to some degree with the language of the expert. By necessity, indeed, the general reader of today needs to become something of a "generalist" in knowledge, and so give new meaning to his familiar title.

So far as the acquisition of new words is concerned, this work on special and technical vocabularies marks the end of our task, within the limits which were set at the start of this project. It is time to turn from mere acquisition to the consolidation of vocabulary, and to double back on our tracks to complete the second, and perhaps more beguiling part of the undertaking: the employment of words both new and old in the familiar and everyday situations which we encounter in conversation, occasional speaking, letter-writing, and the like. Here, at the end of our work in the enlargement of vocabulary, it is perhaps well to recall Chesterfield's injunction: that a man should wear his learning, like his watch, in his pocket, and only take it out when asked. Yet it is only as words become galvanized into life through social use that they become truly significant; and only in their social context that they become an integral and organic part of their possessor. Hence the need for further work to assure that our command of words will be not only wide, but ready and sure.

TEST ON LITERARY TERMS

71) On the following pages you will find seventy-five terms used in the study of literature, with four definitions after each term. One of the definitions is the correct meaning of the term as it is applied in literary criticism. You are to read the definitions, choose the one which you think states the correct meaning in a literary sense, and put a circle around the number of that definition. For example:

precious—1. of great price; 2. of great non-material value; 3. affectedly refined in language or workmanship; 4. scrupulous in the observance of rules.

The first two definitions are correct meanings of the word, but they do not state the meaning of the word as it is used in the study of literature. The fourth is a definition of *precise*, not of *precious*. The correct choice is number three.

Sometimes you are asked to make distinctions between incomplete and inclusive definitions. Be sure to choose the definition which includes *all the meanings of the term*. For example:

trope—1. personification; 2. simile; 3. figure of speech; 4 refrain.

The third definition is correct and inclusive; the second is incomplete. A simile is a trope, but not all tropes are similes. There are other figures of speech such as metaphor, and personification, included in the term. Therefore the correct definition is the most inclusive one, number three.

(Used by permission of the University of Oregon Committee on the Appreciation of the Fine Arts; one of the studies financed by the Carnegie Corporation of New York.)

1. critic	1. one who says unpleasant things; 2. one who says pleasant things; 3. one who points out qualities; 4. another poet.
2. trite	1. overworked; 2. fish; 3. inside of calf's stomach; 4. attempted.
3. hackneyed	1. pulled by horses; 2. wornout; 3. legs bending inward; 4. written for pay.
4. sonnet	1. form having strict requirements; 2. same as rondeau; 3. form used in Italy only; 4. chronological period.
5. melodramatic	1. concerning horse racing; 2. mellow; 3. containing rural scenes; 4. containing heightened emotions without good cause.

6. parody — 1. equality; 2. sequel; 3. humorous imitation; 4. balanced structure.

7. epic — 1. a masterpiece; 2. a period characterized by a definite literary movement; 3. a long narrative poem concerning the exploits of one or more heroes; 4. a style of writing characterized by many figures of speech.

8. rhythm — 1. correspondence of terminal sounds in poetry; 2. movement marked by irregularity; 3. pattern; 4. symmetry of movement as determined by reoccurrence of heavy and light accent.

9. hexameter — 1. six feet; 2. event of ancient Olympics; 3. clothing used by Spenser while writing; 4. name of a newspaper.

10. criterion — 1. basis for judgment; 2. group of judges; 3. list of faults; 4. climax.

11. metaphor — 1. allegory; 2. comparison of unlike objects; 3. calling a spade a spade; 4. a kind of theater.

12. climax — 1. turning point in the action of a story; 2. point where the main plot and sub-plot come together; 3. the point at which the action ceases; 4. the solution of the plot.

13. aesthetic — 1. inclined to scorn pleasure; 2. stimulating; 3. pertaining to the beautiful; 4. inclined to indulge in pleasure.

14. style — 1. the personality of a writer's thought and expression; 2. dignity of thought; 3. elegance of expression; 4. the study of sentence structure.

15. pastoral — 1. nature poem; 2. religious poetry of the ancient clergy; 3. poetry for old English dance tunes; 4. idyllic poem of country life.

16. stanza — 1. division of a poem; 2. four lines rhyming abba; 3. a line of poetry; 4. text of a hymn.

17. occasional poem — 1. one every now and then; 2. verse for a special event; 3. poem celebrating birth; 4. poem celebrating death.

18. quatrain — 1. stanza of four lines; 2. person with one fourth Negro blood; 3. storm; 4. ancient kind of rhyme.

19. catharsis — 1. pity; 2. purgation; 3. fear; 4. tragic.

20. technique — 1. plot; 2. personal skill; 3. attitude of author; 4. effect.

21. realism — 1. a natural style; 2. ugliness; 3. unimaginative treatment of real life; 4. a style which portrays things as they are.

22. archaic — 1. out of date; 2. having the qualities of a keystone; 3. romantic; 4. foreign.

23. assonance — 1. stubborn foolishness; 2. resemblance in sound; 3. forceful sound; 4. improper position.

24. connotation — 1. with notes; 2. poetic arrangement suggested by the laws of harmony; 3. overtones of meaning suggested by a word; 4. a step in the process of making a bibliography.

25. irony — 1. that which has stern quality; 2. saying one thing, meaning another; 3. having the hero win; 4. having the hero lose.

26. epigram — 1. inscription on a tomb; 2. measure of weight; 3. condensed remark; 4. geometric figure.

27. analogous — 1. identical; 2. symbolical; 3. resembling in certain respects; 4. soothing.

28. medium — 1. kind of steak; 2. fortune teller; 3. form through which an idea is expressed; 4. average.

29. alliteration — 1. rhyme within a line of poetry; 2. method of printing; 3. understatement; 4. repetition of sound at the beginning of succeeding words.

30. iambic — 1. kind of line; 2. kind of foot; 3. kind of column; 4. geometric figure.

31. manuscript — 1. mimeographed copy; 2. original writing; 3. sample of penmanship; 4. collection of good themes.

32. sensuous — 1. fleshly; 2. soothing; 3. appealing to the senses; 4. voluptuous.

33. synthesis — 1. without plan; 2. putting together; 3. dissertation; 4. kind of drink.

34. vers libre — 1. free verse; 2. book of verse; 3. sonnet; 4. foreign poetry.

35. context — 1. parallel reading; 2. meaning; 3. preceding paragraph; 4. matter preceding and following, determining meaning.

36. image — 1. form; 2. the semblance of an object reproduced or suggested by words; 3. idea; 4. sense impression.

37. restraint — 1. lack of emphasis; 2. awkwardness; 3. avoidance of excess; 4. plainness.

38. poet laureate — 1. one who writes of the woods; 2. poet chosen by the king to write commemorative verse; 3. Edgar Guest; 4. a beginner.

39. Puritanic — 1. belonging in New England; 2. religious; 3. rigid; 4. name of ship.

40. patron — 1. one who attends plays; 2. one who aids authors; 3. customer; 4. an old man.

41. blank verse — 1. free verse; 2. verse without rhyme; 3. verse without meter; 4. verse with particular meter but no rhyme.

42. onomatopoeia — 1. echoic words; 2. too many words; 3. affected style; 4. use of inoffensive word to express unpleasant idea.

43. concrete — 1. concise; 2. solid; 3. recognized by the senses; 4. allegorical.

44. ambiguous — 1. wordy; 2. illogical; 3. of uncertain meaning; 4. of doubtful origin.

45. paradox — 1. an illogical comparison; 2. a falsification of the truth; 3. a statement seemingly contradictory, but possibly true; 4. a humorously ridiculing imitation of a writer's work.

46. subjective — 1. intuitive; 2. imaginative; 3. pertaining to the subject; 4. colored by personal feeling or opinion.

47. couplet
1. hero and heroine together; 2. a pair of rhymes; 3. small couple; 4. stanza in which every other line rhymes.

48. abstract
1. cannot be recognized by the senses; 2. profound; 3. something material; 4. a selection.

49. elegy
1. a religious poem; 2. a song of lamentation for the dead; 3. a poem commemorating a great battle; 4. a poem in praise of a friend.

50. cosmic
1. concerning life; 2. of the earth; 3. deeply philosophical; 4. of the universe.

51. verbose
1. jumbled; 2. unnecessary repetition of verbs; 3. using more words than are wanted; 4. characterized by broad, general statements.

52. sentimental
1. having a happy end; 2. insincerely sympathetic; 3. sarcastic; 4. prudish.

53. satire
1. ridicule; 2. irony; 3. burlesque; 4. parody.

54. dénouement
1. unraveling of a plot; 2. intervention of the gods in Greek drama; 3. turning point in the action of a story; 4. triumph of the hero over the villain.

55. antithesis
1. exaltation of person or ideal; 2. opposition or contrast of words or ideas; 3. a part of a poem answering a previous part; 4. argument against a certain doctrine.

56. denotation
1. literal meaning of a word; 2. principal meaning of a word; 3. the sound of a word; 4. emphasis at the end of a sentence.

57. art-epic
1. period productive of great art; 2. a conscious imitation of the old epics; 3. a long poem in high-flown language; 4. a masterpiece.

58. romance
1. a fictitious, often fanciful story of adventure; 2. a love story; 3. an imaginative story with historical characters; 4. a tale of mystery.

59. neo-classic
1. modern imitation of the classics; 2. writing in a tradition opposed to the classical tradition; 3. a work pertaining to the classics; 4. a work based upon the classics.

60. objective
1. not influenced by personal opinion or feeling; 2. objectionable; 3. argumentative; 4. characterized by precise statements of purpose.

61. mystic
1. a very religious person; 2. one who believes in the divinity of Nature; 3. a very spiritual person; 4. one who believes in the intuitive knowledge of divine will.

62. ballad
1. a poem about the Troubadors; 2. a narrative poem in short stanzas, often with refrain; 3. a French poetic form; 4. a poem written to be sung.

63. sensibility
1. reasonableness; 2. delicacy of feeling; 3. keenness of mind; 4. practicalness.

64. Victorian
1. restrained; 2. stuffy, decorous, sentimental, and proper; 3. unemotional; 4. celebrating.

65. unique
1. only one of its kind; 2. under; 3. new; 4. unusual.

66. euphuism	1. soft-pedalling; 2. elaborate, artificial diction and structure; 3. being well-bred; 4. stanza-formation.
67. tautology	1. unnecessary repetition of a word; 2. repetition of the same idea in different words; 3. excessive coördination; 4. excessive use of relative pronoun.
68. periodic	1. at regular intervals; 2. characteristic of a period; 3. descriptive of the movement running through a poem in couplets; 4. descriptive of a statement whose meaning is incomplete until the end.
69. lyric	1. romantic poem; 2. a short poem expressing author's feeling; 3. a love song; 4. words for music.
70. folio	1. house in which Shakespeare wrote; 2. sheet of paper folded three times; 3. particular size of sheet and binding; 4. letter holder.
71. aphoristic	1. inclined to fleshly desire; 2. bubbling forth; 3. full of witty remarks; 4. full of wise sayings.
72. conceit	1. an egotistic statement; 2. a far-fetched comparison; 3. a flattering biography; 4. a French form of poetry.
73. picaresque	1. pretty; 2. relating to rogues; 3. quibbling; 4. that which piques the imagination.
74. epithet	1. a curse; 2. an inscription on a tomb; 3. slang phrase; 4. an adjective fitly applied to a noun.
75. pantheism	1. worship of Pan; 2. God is everything; 3. spontaneous atheism; 4. worship of idols of natural objects.

(Of thirty third-year students in a college class in Literary Criticism, the best score was 67, the poorest 38, mean 52.)

HIGH CEILING TEST

72) How many of the following words can you define? Sixteen of them are taken from the preceding technical lists. The rest are words which will be found in reading learned works in history, science, technology, and art; except that there are a few words included which describe objects or living things found only in out-of-the-way places. These are words which may fairly be described as belonging to the learned vocabulary. Nearly all of them, however, could be used in formal literary prose.

transcendentalism	irrefutable	sub-maxillary
insouciance	indissoluble	anaphrodisiac
redaction	redintegration	cellarer
irredentist	palimpsest	sedative
ultramontanist	recondite	ichthyosaurus
irrevocable	diocesan	megatherium
catalytic	archiepiscopal	isogony
argot	icosahedron	mezzotint
allergic	salaam	fasces

lictor
moribund
detonator
guava
daguerrotype
phthisis
salacious
ribald
askance
dandiacal
addendum
cirrhous
antipodal
antithetical
onomatopoetic
circumvallation
logistics
terrain
sarcoma
divagation
quintessence
serrated
pyrrhic
anacoluthon

metathesis
satyr
hylozoism
cataleptic
exegesis
writ
caduceus
pursiness
monolithic
mnemonic
graminivorous
neo-classic
mitigate
succulent
apiary
apices
cherubim
humus
humoristic
sarcophagus
succubus
lithography
incandescence
asininity
sic

anacreontic
sylph
sulphide
bromide
cryptic
elliptic
trapezium
sardonic
eroticism
blatant
osseous
obfuscate
uxorious
periodic
conciliar
consular
praetorian
noumenal
schizoid
psychogenic
abecedarian
ousel
didoes
circumlocutory

CHAPTER IX

THE ART OF CONVERSATION

No monologues, no asides, say the French, who have developed conversation as a fine art. They dread a bore who monopolizes the talk, and rightly consider that listening is the better half of conversing. Any little eddy in the circle, where two of the group whisper behind their hands, will interrupt the main current of talk, and break that fine rapport which is so necessary to summon up good spirits in any company.

A real *conversazione* should be like easy high comedy, in which the tension is maintained, yet there is no constraint. In conversation, to be sure, the players are their own audience; but all the more need for playing up to one another. An easy give-and-take is what is wanted. Everyone should feel that he can join in when he pleases: no hurry, no striving for the floor, above all, no cutting in on a speaker before he has finished. So much for the social situation which is conducive to spirited, witty, and lively talk.

The gift of judicious silence is really the first need for good conversation. In a talkative company, one man's rests are another man's music. So it is not hard to see that most of us badly need a condenser when we start in talking. Compression, said Goethe, is the first sign of a master, and nowhere is this truer than in social talk. It is no accident that in the great ages of conversation the epigram flourishes; and that repartee, a polished form of back-chat, if deftly managed, is one of the most enjoyable resources of any company,—or at least it is the most amusing for the rest of the group who are listening. 'Wisecracks,' or 'witcracks,' as Shakespeare called them, may grow tiresome if labored or over-persistent, but they are a grateful spice to any talking match. They have the merit of brevity. The speaker must be quick on the up-take, ready to fence at close quarters, and, once he has made a touch, glad to turn his foil over to another. It is no trick for other speakers to cut in, if the rules of fence are observed. And once a talker has made a

215

witty point, he should give way to others. They will hear him all the more gladly, when he joins in again.

To be sure, if sustained and serious discussion is the aim, these principles do not wholly apply. But even for such occasions the lighter touch is welcome at the start. A sprightly phrase now and then will not mar the solemnity of tone. Why not admit a trace of that quality for which the French have a name, and we have none,—*légérité*, a kind of light and nimble lift? Before one rises high into serious matters, it may be well to find out the drift of opinion in the company on the subject, by flying a few kites or trial balloons. The bumbling talker who drops an anchor instead, when he starts out some serious discourse on religion, politics, or sex,—the only three subjects, says Bernard Shaw, which intelligent adults discuss with fully awakened interest,—may find that he has fallen foul of a good many of the company's pet aversions, and incidentally added himself to the number. That is why a kite is better than an anchor as a conversational opening.

Nothing so puts a damper on easy interchange of ideas as a blunt and over-assertive tone on the part of one speaker. Often this is heard in the heat of debate. Now in social company, a persistent argument is diverting only if it is carried on with a certain degree of light good humor, the disputants exchanging short, quick strokes. We have all experienced the sinking sensation which comes when two men, each with a one-track mind, move into action with heavy trains of argument. How to switch them is the question. Chesterfield suggests one answer.

Avoid as much as you can in mixed companies, argumentative, polemical conversations; which, though they should not, yet certainly do, indispose, for a time, the contending parties towards each other; and if the controversy grows warm and noisy, endeavor to put an end to it by some genteel levity or joke. I quieted such a conversation hubbub once by presenting to them that, though I was persuaded none there present would repeat out of company what passed in it, yet I could not answer for the discretion of the passengers in the street, who must necessarily hear all that was said.

There is only one worse fate than argument that can befall a group who have decided on conversation instead of bridge. That is to have a practiced orator inflicted upon them. His diction alone would be the death of the conversational spirit.

Words which would adorn a formal speech or an essay are in fact quite out of place in off-hand, spontaneous talk. Here ease and naturalness are much to be desired. These qualities depend on the choice of "language such as men would use." There is much greater freedom in talk than in writing. Words labeled 'colloquialisms' in the dictionary are often very well suited to the familiar intimacies of conversation among friends. If the talker, in fact, knows everybody present, he may safely use slang current in the circle. If there are strangers listening, they may conclude he knows no better; or they may not understand. As always, slang limits the range of intelligibility.

As for profanity, it is a careless method of punctuating speech; and unless it is fluent, varied, pungent, and original, it is usually annoying, except to an audience so habituated to it as to fail to notice it at all. In that event, why use it? It is a poor way to gain force, and argues a lack of ability to achieve emphasis without it. It is interesting to note how clearly Conrad can convey the effect of profanity without actually setting down words barred from polite company:

". . . began by calling me Pig, and from that went crescendo into unmentionable adjectives."

". . . a lusty voice blasphemed."

"May he be everlastingly blanked for a swab-headed deck-hand."

If one must indulge in strong language, it is perhaps better to follow the advice of Keith, in Douglas' *South Wind*: Cultivate a faculty for saying atrocious things in elegant and impeccable English. But mostly there is little occasion for either profanity or slang, in the speech of vigorous and engaging conversationalists. They command a style which enables them to give graphic definition to their ideas and images, without a resort to these stereotyped forms of expression.

All these cautions are essential, for anyone who wants to set up in business as a good talker. But when we sum them up, we find that we have mostly negative doctrine: No monologues, no asides; no long-winded arguments; no oratory; no launching out on heavy subjects unless the company clearly desires sustained discussion; no 'cutting in' or demanding the floor; no overdose of profanity or slang; and above all, no tall words or bookish language which smacks of pedantry or affectation. But after all, it is conversation we want, not a timorous hesitancy lest we fall into conversational

error. May not all these prohibitions be summed up as *the art of
not becoming a bore?* When it comes to positive doctrine on conversation, the problem is much harder.

No man can tell another how to converse. There are no cook-
book recipes. The old Ollendorf manuals tried to teach conversation
in a foreign language by furnishing discreet and agreeable formulas
for all occasions. These formulas have been the target for ribald
mirth, and 'Ollendorfian' a term of amused contempt:

> The uncle of my grand-aunt is gathering pineapples in the garden, and
> desires to know if you would care to join him.

> Let him rest assured that when I have completed the onerous task of
> cataloguing the collection of shells, nothing would be more consonant with
> my desires.

Nobody wants to talk such stilted stuff as this. The ornamental
formality of the speeches in Disraeli's and Miss Edgeworth's novels
now affords us derisive amusement, largely because the characters
talk in this fearful and wonderful style. Clearly, no one in his senses
would risk setting down patterns or forms for the conversationalist,
lest he fall into such traps as these. The safest way is to look at
the practice of the great masters of the art.

The Extractive Method: Socrates

Socrates, as Plato has recorded him in the *Dialogues,* is perhaps
more fully known than any other talker, ancient or modern, unless
it be Dr. Samuel Johnson. Socrates was preëminently a master of
the art of the question, using it to draw out the ideas of others,—a
trick of discussion little practiced by those who merely desire to
shine themselves. It may be called the extractive method of conversation. Socrates could weave his way into the most difficult subject, leading his pupils on from one question to another. He chose
homely illustrations by preference, setting them forth in a tentative
tone. Irony, that humorous form of understatement which the
Greek thought the mark of the superior man who had no need to
boast, was Socrates' regular weapon when he had to put some self-
righteous and cocksure disputant in his place. He remarked of the
sophist Protagoras, for example:

Protagoras gives a long winter course for forty drachmas, but he covers much the same material in a short summer course for ten drachmas. I think I would choose the short course.

This is a neat method of deflation. It does the work better than a flood of invective. The deceivingly simple, naïve phrasing represents the final term of sophistication. Socrates has passed through subtlety and come out on the other side.

His irony is, in fact, the resource by which he expresses any distasteful views which a tendencious and pig-headed debater, lacking irony, must bring plop out in blunt and tactless language. Socrates' opponents were often so amused at the ironic turn by which he undermined them, that they forgot to be annoyed. If one must be insulted, there is nothing like being insulted by an expert.

To be sure, there were many Philistines who did not understand how much positive conviction lay behind Socrates' eternal questioning; and at the end of his twenty years of informal teaching, "the archons of Sinn Fein with their naggin of hemlock" finished him off, as Joyce says. But Socrates' refusal to truckle to the Athenian jury, or to make any gesture of obeisance to the conventional prejudices of the middle-class moralist, stands to his eternal credit. For all his quiet, questioning, ironic conversational style, he had dauntless public courage, as became an old soldier and craftsman.

FIRESIDE AND TAVERN STYLE

For fireside, club, and tavern talk, Ben Jonson had a hardy vigor and forthright thrust, not to mention a sledge-hammer, iron-biting wit. Unluckily, the only uncensored record we have of Jonson in full cry, is found in the pages of the Scotch poet Drummond of Hawthornden, whose cellar Jonson had spent three weeks in drinking dry. But even these fragments from a none too friendly hand are sufficient to show why Jonson dominated the company at the Mermaid, or in the Devil's Room of the Apollo Tavern. His style is perhaps too truculent for any except the hardiest masculine company. But who would want the language softened in the following?

The Earl of Licester Gave a botle of liquor to his Lady which he willed her to use in any faintness which she after his returne from court not knowing it was Poison gave him & so he died [a perfect Jonsonian plot in miniature: The biter bit.]

Queen Elizabeth never saw her self after she became old in a true Glass. they painted her & sometymes would vermilion her nose, she had allwayes about Christmass evens set dice, that threw sixes or five, & she knew not they were other, to make her win & esteame her self fortunate.

Owen is a pure pedantique Schoolmaster sweeping his living from the Posteriors of litle children, and hath no thinge good in him, his Epigrames being bare narrations.

RECEPTIVE LISTENING: DRYDEN

The next of the great literary dictators was much more soft-spoken, suave, and restful. Dryden, in fact, while he presided gracefully over the famous suppers in the upper room of Will's Coffee House, where those famous talkers Sedley, Rochester, Congreve, and Prior repaired, was not himself renowned in conversation. But he was a celebrated and receptive listener. And if he could not talk conversation, he could certainly write it. Here is a passage from *Marriage à la Mode,*

Melantha (to her maid Philotis): O, are you there, minion? And, well, are not you a most precious damsel, to retard all my visits for want of language, when you know you are paid so well for furnishing me with new words for my daily conversation? Let me die, if I have not run the risk already to speak like one of the vulgar, and if I have one phrase left in all my store, that is not threadbare *et usé,* and fit for nothing but to be thrown to peasants.

Philotis: Indeed, madam, I have been very diligent in my vocation; but you have so drained all the French plays and romances, that they are not able to supply you with words for your daily expense.

Melantha: Drained? What a word's there? *Epuiseé,* you sot you. Come, Come, produce your morning's work.

Philotis: 'Tis here, madam. (Shows the paper.)

Melantha: O, my Venus! fourteen or fifteen words to serve me a whole day! Let me die, at this rate I cannot last till night. Come, read your words: Twenty to one, half of them will not muster neither.

Philotis: Sottises.

Melantha: Sottises: bon. That's an excellent word to begin withal; as, for example, he or she said a thousand *Sottises* to me. Proceed.

Philotis: Figure: As, what a *figure* of a man is there! [Properly, *figure* in French means 'face.'] *Naïve* and *naïveté.*

Melantha: Naïve! as how?

Philotis: Speaking of a thing that was naturally said, it was so *naïve;* or such an innocent piece of simplicity 'twas such a *naïveté.*

Melantha: Truce with your interpretations. Make haste.

Philotis: Foible, chagrin, grimace, *embarrassé, double entendre, équivoque, éclaircissement, suite, bévue, façon, penchant, coup d'ètourdi,* and *ridicule.*

Melantha: Hold, hold; how did they begin?

Philotis: They began at *sottises,* and ended *en ridicule.*

Melantha: Now, give me your paper in my hand, and hold you my glass, while I practise my postures for the day. (Melantha laughs in the glass.) How does that laugh become my face?

Philotis: Sovereignly well, madam.

Melantha: Sovereignly? Let me die, that's not amiss. That word shall not be yours; I'll invent it, and bring it up myself.

Incidentally, was there ever penned a more amusing satire on the affected habit of outlining social conversation in advance? Or a better laugh at the expense of those who dish up warmed-over phrases,—without quotation marks? It is amusing to note that many of the French words mentioned, which were not yet Anglicized in Dryden's day, are now in good use; most of the others are a part of society jargon.

No less in his verse than in his comedies did Dryden possess an effortless mastery of the colloquial turn of phrase. The apparently careless negligence of his lines on Zimri (The Duke of Buckingham) in *Absalom and Achitophel* represents not only the high point of English verse satire, but a most carefully managed blend of conversational informality and form:

> A man so various, that he seemed to be
> Not one, but all mankind's epitome:
> Stiff in opinions, always in the wrong;
> Was everything by starts, and nothing long;
> But, in the course of one revolving moon,
> Was chemist, fiddler, statesman, and buffoon:
> Then all for women, painting, rhyming, drinking,
> Besides ten thousand freaks that died in thinking.

Even the lazy click of the end rhymes does not disguise, still less retard, the very rhythm and accent of felicitous after-dinner talk,— say about the time Dryden started on his second bottle of port.

The Polished Style: Chesterfield

Probably the greatest theorist on the art of conversation, and one of its most polished practitioners, was the Fourth Earl of Chesterfield. Writing as he did for his young son, without any notion that the letters would ever be published, he tells the boy in the frankest and most detailed manner all the techniques, cautions, and positive 'graces' which mark the finished conversationalist, one who can commend himself to all companies, young and old, gentle and simple, and particularly to the ladies. The Earl does not disdain such elementary matters as clear enunciation and a well-placed voice. He warns against loud laughter,—or indeed, against laughing at all, since its disfigures the face and jars on the company! (It should be added, as will soon appear, that Chesterfield had a rare sense of humor, and a polished though slightly deliberate wit; the prohibition of laughter is part of a long social tradition, which goes back to Castiglione: laughter was an upset to public decorum, and not becoming in a man of birth and position, always under the need of playing a part in public.) He cautions the boy against rallying (American: *kidding*) even a close friend on any one of three points: his religion, his ordinary competence in his profession, and his taste in women. These, the Earl rightly remarked, are dangerous subjects.

As to religion, the Earl continues, it is not a safe subject for general conversation. Passions run too high on it. Above all, he tells young Philip, do not be guilty of beroguing the professions; for, adds the Earl, in what many would thing a crowning piece of cynicism, but which he did not intend as such, "I think it likely that a man will be neither the better nor the worse for wearing the cloth."

His famous letter on conversation is full of sound counsel and inimitably phrased.

Talk often, but never long; in that case, if you do not please, at least you are sure not to tire your hearers. Pay your own reckoning, but do not treat the whole company; this being one of the very few cases in which people do not care to be treated, every one being fully convinced that he has wherewithal to pay.

Tell stories seldom, and absolutely never but where they are very apt and very short. Omit every circumstance that is not material, and beware of digressions. To have frequent recourse to narrative betrays great want of imagination.

Never hold anybody by the button or the hand, in order to be heard out;

for if people are not willing to hear you, you had much better hold your tongue than them. . . .

Above all things, and upon all occasions, avoid speaking of yourself if it be possible. Such is the natural pride and vanity of our hearts that it perpetually breaks out, even in people of the best parts, in all the various modes and figures of the egotism. . . .

The only sure way of avoiding these evils is never to speak of yourself at all. But when historically you are obliged to mention yourself, take care not to drop one single word that can directly or indirectly be construed as fishing for applause. Be your character what it will, it will be known; and nobody will take it upon your own word. Never imagine that any thing you can say yourself will varnish your defects or add lustre to your perfections; but on the contrary, it may, and nine times in ten will, make the former more glaring and the latter obscure.

In spite of Horace Walpole's unkind remark that of all the great character [we would say *reputation*] which the Earl of Chesterfield erected at such infinite pains, little now is left worth remembering but a few *bon mots,* the Earl's reputation is a steadily growing one. And who that cherishes freedom of speech but will be delighted by Chesterfield's famous *bon mot* in the Lords, in opposing Sir Robert Walpole's censorship of the stage:

Wit, my lords, is the property of those who have it. Often, indeed, it is the only property they have. We, my lords, thank God, have other means of subsistence.

And anyone who doubts that Chesterfield implied by 'other' that the House of Lords was not too long on wit, simply does not know his man. The Earl, like Gibbon, could not pass by such a wonderful chance for an urbane, back-handed flick! He did not see why great lords who lived on their unearned increment, and on their ancestors' reputations, should censor men of wit out of their livelihood. It is sad to record that Walpole's censorship bill nevertheless passed!

Chesterfield's doctrines on conversation slide insensibly over into the field of manners; but it is hard to draw the line, for a man's manner is in large part his way of talking, if one includes the accompanying gestures and facial expressions, and the impression formed as to his social attitudes. The Earl is particularly concerned with the outward figure which his son will cut. He reminds him that it never pays to be ungracious or churlish. The Duke of Marlborough, he says, could refuse a favor more graciously than most men could grant it. This urbanity of manner is worth cultivating; it is a vital item in the command of 'the graces,' which are always a way of commending oneself to any company. Above all, says the Earl, a man should be more careful and considerate in his manner toward inferiors, than in dealing with his equals or superiors. He has the true spirit of social democracy, found at its best in the old Whig *grands seigneurs*.

The real essence of Chesterfield's doctrine, on manners and conversation alike, is that one should have profound consideration for the feelings of others. He has been accused of insincerity, of setting too much store on the public mask of a man, too little by the inward character. But as Washington once remarked, it is necessary not only to be virtuous, but to appear so. And Chesterfield after all was simply insisting that a man should extend his imagination to a point where he could see himself as others saw him; and that while he gauged their estimate of himself, he should in turn take great account of the temperaments and notions of his fellows. Only so, thought the Earl, could conversationalists maintain that tone of good company which was his ideal.

THE BLUNT AND ORACULAR STYLE: DR. JOHNSON

Chesterfield's enemy, Dr. Samuel Johnson, commanded a conversational style which stressed, not social polish, but truth to fact, honesty of opinion, and crushing finality in judgment. "I always talk for victory," said Johnson; and he usually won it. There is a widespread legend that Johnson invariably spoke in the ponderous Latin polysyllables in which he often wrote; but this is far from true. He did sometimes imitate his written style in talk, but he more often spoke a vigorous, blunt, idiomatic English. Yet he could be most genial on occasion; and when he came down early to breakfast at Mrs. Thrale's to hear "the little Burney" prattle, he could unbend to indulge in gallant small talk. Even when heading the table of the Literary Club, at the Turk's Head in Soho, he rarely roared or thundered, unless he was crossed, or moved to set Goldsmith right on one of the latter's foolish opinions. With Burke and Reynolds, whom he regarded as equals, he took always a civil and courteous tone. Toward Garrick, who was to him his pupil still, he might be a little condescending; and he was apt to speak in oracular accents to other writers. Not for nothing was he 'Dictionary' Johnson. When he dealt with what he considered impertinence, or presumptuous ignorance, he could be blunt beyond measure. Boswell was discussing with him the famous comic actor and playwright Samuel Foote:

Boswell. —Foote has a great deal of humour?
Johnson.—Yes, sir.
Boswell. —He has a singular talent of exhibiting character.
Johnson.—Sir, it is not a talent; it is a vice; it is what others abstain from. It is not comedy, which exhibits the character of a species, as that of a miser gathered from many misers; it is a farce, which exhibits individuals.
Boswell. —Did not he think of exhibiting you, Sir?
Johnson.—Sir, fear restrained him; he knew I would have broken his bones. I would have saved him the trouble of cutting off a leg; I would not have left him a leg to cut off.
Boswell. —Pray, Sir, is not Foote an infidel?
Johnson.—I do not know, Sir, that the fellow is an infidel; but if he be an infidel, he is an infidel as a dog is an infidel; that is to say, he has never thought upon the subject.—*Life of Samuel Johnson* I 395 (London, Froude, 1904)

Again, when Johnson said of Sterne's *Tristram Shandy,* "Nothing odd will do long," he made a bad prophecy, but he showed his turn for spare and curt phrasing. Johnson early determined to think before he spoke, and to say what he had to say in the most cogent and finished style at his command. Hence the trenchancy and finality of his utterance. There is no drama or novel in the English language which gives so much of salient, forthright dialogue as Boswell's *Life of Johnson.* All of Johnson's speeches are in character, and even when they are detached from their context, they require no identifying mark.

THE WHIMSICAL STYLE: LAMB

No less personal in his utterance, but far less oracular, Charles Lamb was a master of the whimsical style of conversation. He had read Browne and Burton, and, one suspects, Sterne, until he was full of archaic phrases and quaint, out-moded notions. But he had no need to look into odd authors to reinforce his peculiar way of regarding things. He always struck in at an oblique angle, seeing out of the corner of his eye some aspect to which Dr. Johnson, for instance, would have denied existence, or at least, any importance. Lamb was charmed by oddity, and he could convey the charm by his stuttering talk. He had a way of seeing the absurdity in statements which seemed quite unambiguous to prosaic minds. So when his doctor told him "to take a long walk on an empty stomach," Lamb asked, "On whose empty stomach?"

He was fond of telling outrageous yarns at the expense of his friend's foibles. Coleridge, for instance, was given to monologues of inordinate length. Lamb claimed that once when he was on his way from the East India House to luncheon, he saw Coleridge coming along the Strand, and bearing down upon him. "I shall get no luncheon," Lamb thought. Coleridge caught him by the lapel-button, as he feared, and, closing his eyes and leaning back his head, launched out in ever-widening circles on his monologue. Lamb, according to his own story, pulled out his penknife, cut off the button, and went on to luncheon. Two hours later, returning, he saw Coleridge still holding onto the button, and still talking! This story is artistically, if not historically, true. It is in Coleridge's character; and still more is it like Lamb to invent the anecdote.

It is tempting to trace the line of whimsical humorists from Lamb. Lewis Carroll, W. S. Gilbert, and James M. Barrie have continued in the vein which Lamb enjoyed. Indeed, English humor generally owes much to the genial, diffused whimsicality which so leavens and lightens any discourse. But it is not safe to analyze whimsy too far.

No more would it be kind to expand on the famous monologuists in English annals. Probably Carlyle in his old age could have out-talked Coleridge; certainly he had more force, more volcanic violence, and a finer collection of crotchets. Conversation, not monologue, is the matter in hand, so these long distance talkers lie outside the present limits of discourse. The mid-nineteenth century was not too favorable to animated drawing-room talk; there was an atmosphere of stuffy decorum about the Victorian assembly which was not conducive to conversational ease. George Eliot sat as stiffly as if she were on a throne, when she received. Free talk does not prosper on such solemn occasions.

THE EPIGRAMMATIC STYLE: WILDE

Toward the end of the century, as the Gay Nineties set in, the lost art of conversation began to be revived. The French influence, so widespread in the arts, began to make itself felt. Among the writers of the '90's, the most famous talker was Wilde. He aimed quite consciously, especially after he became an admirer of Whistler's, at holding the center of the stage in every social gathering

which he frequented. And it was by his conversation that he succeeded. He had long been a precisian in the use of words. His
extensive contacts with Greek and Latin literature had given him a
feeling for compactness of phrase, finish of style; he liked sentences
chiseled out and then put together with a proper architectonic effect.
He soon became a devotee of epigram and paradox, appropriating,
too, the startling methods of Whistler's *Gentle Art of Making Enemies,* but adapting them to making friends.

He aimed deliberately at an artificial style. Yet his phrases in
the plays are always lively, and have the ring of the spoken word.
This is no matter for wonder. His comedies, like his articles on
The Decay of Lying and *The Critic as Artist,* were really the result
of months of good talk, mainly his own, occasionally what he drew
from others by his brilliance. Frank Harris has some illuminating
comments to make on his talk, at a time just before the first comedy
was written: "At this time he was a superb talker, more brilliant
than any I have ever heard in England. . . . There was an extraordinary physical vivacity and geniality in the man, an extraordinary charm in his gaiety and lightning-quick intelligence. His
enthusiasms too, were infectious . . . he was indeed what the
French call a *charmeur.*" Again, "The extraordinary thing about
Oscar's talent was that he did not monopolize the conversation: he
took the ball of talk wherever it happened to be at the moment and
played with it so humorously that everyone was soon smiling de-
lightedly . . . at his best Oscar Wilde never dropped the tone of
good society: he could afford to give place to others; he was
equipped at all points: no subject came amiss to him: he saw everything from a humorous angle, and dazzled one now with word-wit,
now with the very stuff of merriment."

Here was a happy conjunction for high comedy: the greatest
dandy since the Restoration times, ready to make "the Pagan reply
to the Puritan"; equipped with a pointed, piquant style and inimi-
table charm of manner, his epigram and wit varied by a humour
which played like a lambent flame about his talk; gifted with an
urbanity which enabled him to be pleasantly rude to great London
hostesses and make them like it; yet for all his artificiality, more
than a celebrant of dandyism and the minor arts, possessed, indeed,
of a certain feeling for human nature—though preferably in high
places, and blessed with territorial titles, always, he said, "a cachet

of distinction." And it is chiefly through his comedies that we have his best epigrams.

On the vexed subject of gossip, Graham, in *Lady Windermere's Fan,* remarks:

> Oh! Gossip is charming. History is merely gossip. But scandal is gossip made tedious by morality. Now, I never moralise. A man who moralises is usually a hypocrite, and a woman who moralises is invariably plain.

Wilde has some amusing digs at Americans. In *A Woman of No Importance* there is a conversation between Mrs. Allonby, a married coquette, and a tired young man of fashion, Lord Ilingworth.

> *Mrs. Allonby*—The American girl has been giving us a lecture.
> *Lord Ilingworth*—All Americans lecture, I believe. I suppose it is something in their climate. What did she lecture about?
> *Mrs. Allonby*—Oh, Puritanism, of course.

Later we hear this American girl talking with a genteel snob, Lady Caroline Pontefract.

> *Lady Caroline*—In my young days, Miss Worsley, one never met anyone in society who worked for their living. It was not considered the thing.
> *Hester*—In America those are the people we respect most.
> *Lady Caroline*—I have no doubt of it.

There is an amusing passage in *The Importance of Being Earnest* in which Wilde, whether consciously or not, satirizes himself. Algernon and Jack are talking about an epigram.

> *Algernon*—It is perfectly phrased! and quite as true as any observation in civilized life should be.
> *Jack*—I am sick to death of cleverness. Everybody is clever nowadays. You can't go anywhere without meeting clever people. The thing has become an absolute public nuisance. I wish to goodness we had a few fools left.

In effect, Wilde admits the dangers of artificiality; and while we may read Wilde for the tune, most of us nowadays will not take any great stock in his manner, and still less in his content. But who would not like his polish?

The Provocative Style: G. B. S.

After Wilde's unhappy exit, the stage was clear for the most redoubtable of living talkers. George Bernard Shaw has made no secret of his aim: to say what he has to say with the most exasperating levity at his command. The provocative style in conversation is his forte. He aims to bedevil, and if it is a measure of success for forty years to have the world by the ear, tweaking it quite persistently, Shaw has succeeded. Take this specimen of his conversational attack. He had been invited to be the lion of the occasion at a tea given by the wealthy Mrs. Snowden for the wives of Labor M.P.'s. A few days earlier she had had her maid arrested for stealing her jewels. Shaw came in, looking for whom he might devour. His eye lit on the hostess. He walked up to her, held out his hand, and said in his strongest platform voice, "Hello, Mrs. Phil, where'd you get the fifty pounds worth of jewels your maid pinched?" The Labor ladies enjoyed the stroke; what Mrs. Snowden said is not reported.

Shaw has not often been worsted. Lady Randolph Churchill once had the last word, however. She had written asking him to dinner, and Shaw replied, "I should have thought, before asking me to dinner, that you would have gone to the trouble of finding out that it is not my *habit* to eat dinner. And besides, we have never met; and I wonder at your presumption in asking me to dinner just on the strength of my public reputation." Lady Randolph Churchill wrote back: "My dear Mr. Shaw, I know nothing about your habits, but I hope they're not as bad as your manners."

Comedy and Conversation

It is noteworthy, in glancing back over this list of past masters of the conversational art, that three of them practiced the writing of comedy. Besides Dryden, Wilde, and Shaw, there have been several other comic dramatists who commanded in their plays the very accent of living talk, and that tone of good company which Chesterfield thought so essential. Recall Benedick's "Idea of a Wife" in *Much Ado About Nothing*, II iii; or Millamant's terms for marriage, in Congreve's *Way of the World*, IV i; or the many lively discourses on marriage in Farquhar's *Beaux' Stratagem*—which rather recalls the Manchester schoolboy's definition of *acrimony:* another name for marriage, often called 'holy'; or that spirited rebuke which Mr. and Mrs. (by courtesy) Peachum administer to their daughter Polly, in Gay's *Beggar's Opera*, I viii; and see what an ingenious and resourceful talker can do by way of amusing embroidery upon an old subject. There is no better way to acquire an ear for the right cadence of good talk, than reading the best comedies.

Yet all the reading in the world will not make anybody a gifted conversationalist. Add up Socrates' quizzing method, Ben Jonson's offhand tavern delivery, Chesterfield's polish, Dr. Johnson's bluntness, Lamb's whimsies, Wilde's epigrams, and Shaw's provocativeness, and the result would be more apt to be a headache than a sprightly and individual style in conversation. One must finally live on his own wits in this field.

A pre-War American author, given to sweet sentiment, was convalescing at an inn up in the Adirondacks. As he began to take an interest in life, he noticed a beautiful pink-and-white milkmaid, and asked her to go for a stroll. They sat down in the shade of an orchard; the author pulled out a book of verse, and began to read aloud. After ten minutes the girl yawned, and said, "Oh, I ain't never been much on book-readin'. Why don't you talk out of your own head?" Who would want to risk a like indictment?

Yet a knowledge of the methods and the table-talk of the masters will insensibly affect one's own conversational delivery; and a really workable style should finally result. A sense of the occasion and a feeling for the audience can be built up by extensive reading. And to learn by contraries, nobody would want to set up as a bore,— and Coleridge and Carlyle did not quite escape that imputation, brilliant monologues though they delivered. Even Bernard Shaw has held the stage a little too long for some of his hearers. Arnold Bennett tells of a luncheon he attended at the Café Royale at which Shaw talked all the time—"which," says Bennett, "is the same thing as saying that he talked a damn sight too much."

Probably the strongest case that can be made out for studying the talk of the great writers is that we can thus acquire variety; and if we cannot reach their heights, we can at least avoid some of the mannerisms and gaucheries which now and then annoyed their friends. The final reason for reading them is that there is no more amusing entertainment than literary gossip, unless it is gossip about people we know. "What would our friends be good for if we couldn't talk about them?" asked Dr. Johnson. And the customary warning against gossip in company is so much idle rumble-bumble; though we owe it to public decorum to keep this gossip within the limits of amused and tolerant comment, free from self-righteousness and condescension toward the absent. It is safer to include oneself in any derogatory remarks; if they are repeated, there will be less sting.

In the last analysis, the way to learn to talk well is to go where good talkers are, whether in books or in life, first listen to them, and then join in the conversation on your own account. Even more than the pleasures of the cellar and the table, conversation is among the gayer arts of life; and while there may be something to be said for bridge as ending free speech for morons, there is nothing which so enlivens a company as the fine art of conversation.

73) There are many ways of going wrong in conversation. The following collection of horrible examples has been made with loving care. The faults exemplified may be tentatively labeled as conversational

1. rudeness	8. jolly-doggism
2. condescension	9. ghastly gayety
3. snobbery	10. blatant egotism
4. cuteness	11. fatuity
5. schoolgirl coyness	12. pedantry
6. false modesty	13. gush
7. bastard elegance	

Can you fix the appropriate label upon each of the following passages?

1. "Now tonight I am not at all well. Been dining with my people. Wonder why it is one's people are always so tedious? My father would talk morality after dinner. I told him he was old enough to know better."

2. "Awful manners young Hopper has."
"Ah! Hopper is one of Nature's gentlemen, the worst type of gentleman I know."

3. A young man, on taking leave of his hostess, says: "May I inveigle you, madame, into disclosing the whereabouts of my overcoat?"

4. "Whatever station in society I attain, through the medium of the learned profession of which I am about to become an unworthy member, I shall endeavour not to disgrace, and Mrs. Micawber will be safe to adorn. Under the temporary pressure of pecuniary liabilities, contracted with a view to their immediate liquidation, but remaining unliquidated through a combination of circumstances, I have been under the necessity of assuming a garb from which my natural instincts recoil—I allude to

spectacles—and possessing myself of a cognomen, to which I can establish no legitimate pretensions." Mr. Micawber in *David Copperfield*.

5. Babbitt, entertaining the millionaire McKelveys at dinner:
"I suppose you'll be going to Europe pretty soon again, won't you?"
"I'd like awfully to run over to Rome for a few weeks."
"I suppose you see a lot of pictures and music and curios and everything over there."
"No, what I really go for is: there's a little *trattoria* on the Via della Scrofa where you get the best *fettucine* in the world."
"Oh, I—Yes. That must be nice to try that. Yes."
SINCLAIR LEWIS, *Babbitt*. (Harcourt, Brace and Company.)

6. Actual conversation reported by an Englishman:
"And were you born in England, Mr. Cholmondeley-Pitt?"
"Oh, yes. Quite."
"You know—some of my mother's people—one of the best families in Boston—were related to a Lord Brown of London? Did you know him, perhaps?"
"Afraid not. Quite a plain man, myself."
"Really? Well, I always feel that a little drop of blue blood makes *such* a difference to one's standing in the community. . . ."

7. She put on her robes of philosophy to cloak discouragement. "I am glad the writing pleases you."

"The characters are as true as life!" cried Arthur Rhodes. "The Cantatrice drinking porter from the pewter at the slips after harrowing the hearts of her audience, is dearer to me than if she had tottered to a sofa declining sustenance; and because her creatrix has infused such blood of life into her that you accept naturally whatever she does. She was exhausted, and required the porter, like a labourer in the cornfield."
GEORGE MEREDITH, *Diana of the Crossways*, p. 228.

8. "I chose Bach especially for you, General Knoyle," said Lady Edward. . . . "Well—er—really, that was very kind of you." . . . "I hesitated," Lady Edward went on . . . "between Handel's *Water Music* and the B minor Suite with Pongileoni. Then I remembered *you* and decided on Bach." . . . "That was very kind of you," he protested. "Not that I can pretend to understand much about music. But I know what I like, I know what I like."
ALDOUS HUXLEY, *Point Counter Point*. (Copyright 1928 by Doubleday, Doran & Company, Inc.)

9. *Voltaire*. "Have you written many sonnets?"
Casanova. "A dozen which I value, and two or three thousand, perhaps, which I have forgotten. . . ."
We spoke no more of literature, and I remained silent until after Voltaire had retired, when I then left, thinking, fool that I was, that I had reduced this intellectual athlete to reason. But I cherished an enduring

spite against him, and for ten years criticised everything he wrote. *The Memoirs of Jacques Casanova,* New York, The Modern Library, Inc. 1929, pp. 190, 199.

10. "Have another cocktail," he suggested.
"Why you big bad mans!" she giggled. "I believe you're trying to make little Gertie squiffy!"
"We've been married a year, and I haven't done that yet."
"S'matter of fact, little Gertie needs all her courage to tell her candy-lamb the big news! Little Gertie's going to have a b-a-b-y!"

11. "Oh, Mr. Jevons, I'm afraid you must be terribly bored here!"
"Really, no, madame, I assure you. It takes a great deal to bore me."

12. "She was my daughter," said the old woman, nodding her head in the direction of the corpse; and speaking with an idiotic leer, more ghastly than even the presence of death in such a place. "Lord, Lord! Well it *is* strange that I who gave birth to her, and was a woman then, should be alive and merry now, and she lying there: so cold and stiff! Lord, Lord!—to think of it; it's as good as a play—as good as a play!"
CHARLES DICKENS, *Oliver Twist.*

13. Your achievement has thrilled me through, oh! brave men of my heart.
If this does not make the government sit up, nothing will.
Sleep well and feel proud of yourselves, as we all are.
Rule Britannia! God bless you both.

14. "This Mrs. Arrowsmith? Well, say, this is old Clif."
"I'm afraid I didn't quite catch it."
"Clif! Old Clif!"
"I'm frightfully sorry but—Perhaps there's a bad connection."
"Why, it's Mr. *Clawson,* that's going to feed with you on—"
"Oh, of course. I am *so* sorry."
"Well, look: What I wanted to know is: Is this going to be just a homey grub-grabbing or a real soirée? In other words, honey, shall I dress natural or do I put on the soup-and-fish? Oh, I got 'em—swallow-tail and the whole darn' outfit!"
"I—Do you mean—Oh. Shall you dress for dinner? I think perhaps I would."
"Attaboy! I'll be there, dolled up like a new saloon. I'll show you folks the cutest lil line of jewelled studs you ever laid eyes on. Well, it's been pleezhure to meet Mart's Missus, and we will now close with singing 'Till We Meet Again' or 'Au Reservoir.'"
SINCLAIR LEWIS, *Arrowsmith.* (Harcourt, Brace and Company.)

15. Suggested form for a reply to a banquet of Ph.D.'s on a college campus.
"I will be there oke-doke for 6 bits (a bargain)."

16. "Lovely, lovely, lovely—of you to have us. Such a nice party."

CHAPTER X

THE AFTER-DINNER TOUCH

A good after-dinner speech should be simply heightened conversation. But it must be heightened. Not only should the voice be lifted, without seeming to be; but the content of the talk should be artfully ordered, since it must reach a larger audience, and command their amused interest. The stories—and whoever heard of an American after-dinner speech without stories?—must begin in the middle, move rapidly toward a point, and come to an end with the climax. Also, the stories call for a certain care. Old wheezes will not do. The wit should arise from the occasion. If the musty, flat odor of an old joke book is detectable, the speech—and the audience—will suffer. It takes an Aristophanes or a Mark Twain to ring a new turn on an old jest, so that it lives again. Most humorists cannot dispense with novelty. If it is a choice between a broad joke and a long one, most companies will take more kindly to the broad joke,— if the wording is felicitous. One hesitates to recall Sir Robert Walpole's remark that he always talked bawdy at his table, so that everybody could join in; but probably in club and tavern talk, this is sound wisdom. For a mixed audience, it will never do.

An after-dinner speech should be tailored to measure, not ready-made; for if it is the latter, there will always be a suspicion that it is second-hand, or a hand-me-down,—and it may not fit. The speaker should first take account of the particular audience which he is addressing. Chesterfield's counsel on conversation applies with double force when an after-dinner speech is in question. One must know what to leave out. "The art to blot" is all essential. For if the prejudices of the audience are affronted, they will not respond; or if the subject is too serious, they will be bored.

The technique of delivery is a little beyond our province, but a few observations may be made. As in all public speaking, what the actors call a broad base will help to give an air of confidence. One should stand firm on both feet, refrain from leaning on the table, and look the audience square in the eye. Although the tone should be conversational, that is no excuse for being inaudible. Often in a banquet hall with pillars, it is essential to project the tone in a carrying voice, so that it will reach those guests who are at the far corners of the room. By throwing the voice high in the head, so that the vibrations of the vocal column of air are felt against the E-bridge in the nose, this needed amplification of tone can be achieved.

In general, the pace should be easy and deliberate. Wait for the points to sink in, and give ample time after each laugh. Here the actor's rule should be remembered: never hurry an audience. Once they catch a point, and want to enjoy it, give them free rein. In fact, feeling out the mouth of an audience is an essential part of the after-dinner speaker's trade. To this end, the phrase-groups in the sentence should be short, the timing rhythmical and leisurely. Above all, the speaker should appear at ease in Zion, even if he does not feel so; and it is curious what self-confidence will follow from the attempt to appear composed.

If the audience is to find the speech beguiling, the opening words should have an artful and arresting turn. The casual, easy attack, —to use the musician's term,—is the best. One should warm up to the subject by gradual stages. Let the hearers once be convinced that the speech will add to the sprightliness of the occasion and the battle is half won.

The late Master of Balliol, A. L. Smith, wearing his crumpled gray suit and bedraggled black gown, once came into the dining hall of the College to introduce Dean Roscoe Pound of the Harvard Law School. "I feel like the Queen of Sheba," said the Master. When the laughter had died down, he went on, "Though I admit I don't much look like her." (prolonged laughter) "You recall that when the Queen of Sheba was on her way to visit Solomon she was skeptical of his wisdom and magnificence. In the same way, I sometimes have felt a few doubts about American stories regarding their great men. But, like Sheba when she finally saw Solomon, I felt upon meeting Dean Pound, just now at dinner, that the half had not been told! (Laughter and applause)—And Mr. Pound will now tell it!"

It is easy to see why this introduction was a roaring success. The opening chord is magnificent. The strokes are short. After each laughter-provoking thrust, there is a sequel which is funnier still. The blend of audacity, genial good humor, and quizzical wit is irresistible. While the Master rallied Dean Pound, and took a sly dig at the American habit of "tall talk," he included himself as a target for mirth, always a disarming trick.—It all looks easy, until you try it.

Once at a Western college alumni luncheon, John H. Finley, editor of the *New York Times,* was to give the main address. His introducer mentioned that, while Dr. Finley was not an alumnus, if the class were to choose anyone to adopt, they would say, as Nausicaä did to Ulysses, "that they would rather have a man like him." Dr. Finley rose to reply: "I shall certainly be like Ulysses in one respect: my speech will be wandering,"—which of course it was not. But the alumni at once felt mellow, and settled back to hear him out.

As he launches into the main body of his remarks, the after-dinner speaker should never forget that his talk must serve as a *digestif.* That is why serious thought or exhortation is rarely in keeping. The Gilbertian advice, to say nothing in particular and say it very well, is perhaps a little too cynical; but it is better to risk running into the shallows than to sink into the depths. Keep one finger on the pulse of the audience, and if they seem to be settling into a lethargy, vary the pace and the tone, and bring in by the left hand a lively anecdote. As to the kind of jest, and the limits of raillery, one must never forget Shakespeare's injunction: The prosperity of a jest lies in the ear of him that hears it. By that glint in the eye of the beholder, the speaker can tell whether he has gauged the taste of his audience aright.

There used to be in Seattle a luncheon group called the Kind Words Club. It was composed of young lawyers, doctors, and municipal clerks. It was the rule of the club that the members should tell the truth about one another—even in public session. When a visitor was to be presented, after luncheon, somebody would move a vote of welcome. With a roar the Club would vote it down; upon which the President would explain to the guest that it was nothing against him personally: had he only come in with anyone else except his sponsor—! This reversal of the usual ghastly gayety and jollydoggism which prevails in luncheon clubs would perhaps be dangerous in most quarters. How many casual guests would appreciate the joke? But the Club at least had the nerve to break the usual pattern of Polyannanias procédure: the habit of telling pleasant and polite lies to gloze over the facts. Provided the break with this tradition is made without too much fuss, and the new method of polite insult is maintained with effortless bonhomie, the resultant feeling-tone should be gayer than ever. At least, such a departure would vary the monotony. To be sure, the technique of the Kind Words Club would never do among strangers, or in a large public gathering; but among intimate associates, it is perhaps closer to the American habit of rough jesting than the usual forced optimism.

The art of the toastmaster, of the master of ceremonies, or of the radio announcer, is largely a matter of good openings, such as the Master of Balliol's, or Dr. Finley's. No sooner has this ceremonial officer begun, than he must come to a quick end. Like a good ringmaster, he should get out of the way of the performers.

The Mayor of Bristol was once to present Bernard Shaw, who was in turn to introduce G. K. Chesterton. The Mayor talked forty minutes, finally giving way to Shaw. G. B. S. stepped briskly to the front, jerked his thumb over his shoulder toward Chesterton's massive roast-beef-and-Merry-England bulk, and said, "Fatty will now speak to us." The joke was also on the Mayor.

The master of ceremonies or announcer has also the task of weaving a plausible continuity between acts, speeches, or 'turns' which may not at first glimpse have much more relationship to each other than successive acts of vaudeville. Here, like the toastmaster, the announcer must have the power to pick up catchwords or short bits from each number, and playfully work them into his off-hand comments. He needs the art which conceals art. It can be achieved only if he has the seemingly easy negligence which is really the last achievement of the impresario. He must exhibit his performers with an air of genial relish and entire aplomb. Anyone who has heard M. Balieff of the Chauve-Souris, or Will Rogers on the air, or Frank Fay as master of ceremonies, will see what is meant. These seasoned maestros, as the radio artists and musicians call them facetiously, add a great deal to the show without making any attempt to steal the limelight. The trick of blending himself into the scene is an equally necessary one for the toastmaster.

Since by the nature of the case the toastmaster cannot prepare much more than his opening remarks, and must trust to his wits for the interludes, he needs perhaps more resourcefulness than the ordinary after-dinner talker. The latter may very well have his speech worked out in advance. But it should not sound like it. It must have the air of impromptu, or it will be like champagne which has stood over night,—that is, granting there was any sparkle in the speech to begin with.

One idea and three facts are enough, even for a full dress after-dinner speech. As for the stories, which will make up the filler, taste and tact must be employed in choosing them. Most Americans would quarrel with De Quincey:

> Of all the bores whom heaven in its merciful kindness and man in his utter folly have forborne to hang, the teller of good stories is the worst.

From Artemus Ward and Mark Twain down, we should most of us be hanged higher than Haman, if De Quincey had had his way. We should have to admit also a half-truth in the unkind remarks of a visiting Englishman, who said that in America, conversation is a tyranny of anecdote, tempered by interruption. To such criticism, we can pay this much deference: we can select stories which are fresh and timely. No anecdote should be dragged in by main force. The greatest risk is involved in transporting a story from one circle to another, for tastes may not be the same. That is why the speaker must first, last, and all the time compose with the particular audience in mind. The problem of writing out an occasional speech leads naturally to the question, when,—and how far—is a man to write as he talks.

CHAPTER XI

There are many occasions when a man should write as he talks,—assuming that he has a command of words that enables him to talk reasonably well. Many find it hard to write, simply because they do not boldly set down in script what they would say in face to face conversation. To be sure, there are certain differences between the two modes of expression, to which we shall return shortly. But there is a large common ground between the spoken and written word, and there is no reason that a man who speaks well should not write acceptably.

In writing out anything which is to be delivered orally, it is essential to catch the tone of one's own talk. An after-dinner speech, a radio broadcast, or the like, calls for an easy, colloquial note; so does the dialogue for a story, a radio script, or a talkie. A familiar essay or interpretive article should bear the imprint of an individual style, while a personal letter depends for full flavor on a direct, unmistakable rendering of the temperament and attitudes of the writer, set forth in a way free from self-consciousness and affectation.

THE FAMILIAR LETTER

The closer the spoken word to pure act, the better. So, too, with the written word, on those occasions where it is appropriate to write as one talks. Who needs a signature to identify the writer of the following letter, answering a request to contribute a foreword to a play about Lenin?

DEAR SIR,

I am sorry; but I can't write forewords. A preface by me is now a standard article in the literary market. It takes many weeks—sometimes months—to write, and is, in fact, a treatise on the subject with which it deals. Mr. _____ must try some author who does not specialize in prefaces if he insists on having one; but his play must finally stand on his own legs.

If the Labor Publishing Company, which has strong Bolshevik sympathies,

were to take the play up, it could find a preface for it. But Mr. ——————
would not in my opinion be well advised in allowing such a thing. If he
wants a preface, let him do as I do: write it himself.

This has the ring of the spoken word. It combines readiness of
phrasing with a steam-hammer sureness of stroke. If it has in it
the art to shock, a trace of that exasperating levity on which G. B. S.
resolved early in his writing career, what of it? The letter does its
work. No one could mistake its meaning. It is an admirable specimen of the finished style which has become second nature to its
writer, even in everyday correspondence. How well he has bridged
the gap between talk and writing, is evident. We can hear the voice,
almost follow the gestures, of the speaker. Has anyone, since Swift,
Cobbett, and Hazlitt, struck a happier balance between colloquial
and formal diction? Such a letter is within the power only of a
writer the range of whose vocabulary is equalled by his readiness
and sureness in commanding it; and whose habitual courage in
speaking out his real mind is carried over into his writing, so that
thought, speech, and written utterance are all one to him.

Not that we should all play sedulous ape to Bernard Shaw: he has
written many a cooling card for his would-be idolaters, and has laid
a solemn curse on anyone who should force helpless school-children
to study his plays,—for then, he adds, "I will be hated as Shakespeare is hated." But we can take a leaf out of his book when it
comes to shifting from oral to written expression.

The great letter-writers, in fact, are the best source from which
to acquire a feeling for natural, easy, informal writing. Chesterfield, whose letters have preserved much of the charm of his conversation, and the secret of his graceful style in oratory, remarks
about the letters of two famous French correspondents, Madame
Sévigné and Count Bussy de Rabutin: "They are so natural that
they seem to be the extempore conversation of two people of wit
rather than letters." And a famous bluestocking, who thought
Chesterfield slightly scandalous, sets forth her doctrine on letter
writing in a way to reveal the possibilities of the form as a guide for
the writer who wants to acquire conversational ease:

> If I want wisdom, sentiment or information, I can find them much better
> in books than in letters. What I want in a letter is a picture of my friend's
> mind, and the common sense of his life. I want to know what he is saying
> and doing: I want him to turn out the inside of his heart to me, without
> disguise, without appearing better than he is, without writing for a charac-

ter. I have the same feeling in writing to him. My letter is therefore worth nothing to an indifferent person, but it is of value to my friend who cares for me.—HANNAH MORE.

Horace Walpole, the greatest letter-writer in English annals, practiced the art as a deliberate literary form; but he kept to the tone of good company, and his letters never lose the informal, familiar touch. For over sixty years, he was an indefatigable correspondent, giving at once a backstage view of English politics, a gossipy account of social life among the great Whig and Tory families, and an intimate picture of his own domestic life at the curious Gothic mansion which he built at Strawberry Hill on the Thames. His goldfish, which he feared would drown in a flood; the cat which *was* drowned in a tub of goldfishes; the doings of Tonton, Mme. du Deffand's little poodle which he inherited when that redoubtable old lady, one of his chief correspondents, died at a great age; the chalkstones in his knuckles, and gout in his every joint: these interest him no less than public events and high politics. His account of the funeral of George II, with the Duke of Newcastle playing the comic relief, is a classic:

This grave scene was fully contrasted by the burlesque Duke of Newcastle. He fell into a fit of crying the moment he came into the chapel, and flung himself back in a stall, the Archbishop hovering over him with a smelling-bottle; but in two minutes his curiosity got the better of his hypocrisy, and he ran about the chapel with his glass to spy who was or was not there, spying with one hand, and mopping his eyes with the other. Then returned the fear of catching cold; and the Duke of Cumberland, who was sinking with heat, felt himself weighed down, and turning round, found it was the Duke of Newcastle standing upon his train, to avoid the chill of the marble. WALPOLE, HORACE. *Select Letters.* p. 125.

The coronation of George III is no less amusing. The Lord High Steward, Talbot, taught his horse to back, so that he could retire in proper fashion from the royal presence; but the horse had learned his lesson so well that he backed into the Coronation Hall, to the great joy of the assembled peerage in their full (and hot) regalia! What a rout pass through Walpole's pages! He shows to the full the possibilities of writing as one talks. He developed gossip to a fine art, an achievement which is another prize evidence that it is silly to rule it out either from conversation or letter-writing. The point is that gossip should be tolerant, amusing, and free from self-righteous condescension or malicious scandal.

Some of Walpole's contemporaries, notably Lady Mary Wortley Montagu and William Cowper, wrote capital letters, while Charles Lamb is without doubt the prince of humorous correspondents in the English line, unless it is Laurence Sterne.

Of American letter-writers, Mark Twain is perhaps the most famous, and the most characteristically American in his humor. His travel-letters, especially in *A Tramp Abroad,* are rare things of their kind; while his more personal letters furnish perhaps better models for the tyro, since they are not so full of Mark's platform humor. No one can read him without feeling more at ease in the world; and that is a distinct gain for the apprentice hand who is starting out to form a lively, facile style in letter-writing.

A letter is somewhat like one end of a telephone conversation. When it comes to inventing dialogue, the problem is a little harder, for one must differentiate between the speakers, at the same time maintaining a fairly consistent texture of style. But dialogue is only one step removed from the familiar letter, and the man who can write a good letter can invent dialogue, if he will set his mind to it. Since a number of specimens of conventional dialogue have already been given in the chapter on conversation, it may be well to turn to a novel form of dialogue-writing: the radio script.

THE RADIO SCRIPT

The radio script-writer faces a peculiar problem. Since he must convey effects to the ear, and until television comes in, to the ear alone, he must translate the imagery of the other senses into auditory form. Everything that the movie or stage play conveys to the eye, must be woven into the conversation of the radio players. And this must be done without slowing up the action; for the first law of script writing is to maintain the continuity, and that implies a continuous forward thrust toward action and feeling. Mere static description will never do. The dialogue must give the very feel of the scene. Notice in the following typical script the way in which these requirements are maintained.

Script No. 1: "THE THIRD PARTY"

Characters: George Raftery. *Clear, incisive, well-bred, but sporty voice.*
    Vickie Lane. *Lush, throaty, 'blues' voice, full of conscious, slightly animal coquetry.*

Props: Motorman's foot-gong, as used on street-car; sound effects for approaching street-car.

Musical Signature: A few bars of Gershwin's *American in Paris,* heard in the distance.

Announcer: Next follows a little drama of the streets, comedy or tragedy, or what you will. It is called "The Third Party," but she's a blond, not a political party.

Biz: (radio jargon for sound 'business' or any effect produced by props, not by the performers.)

Motorman's foot-gong heard sounding as if far off.

George: Is that the ferry car?

Vickie: (Nastily and flatly, as if to close the conversation before it began.) No!

George: You don't sound too bucked up with life?

Vickie: Why should I? My feet are friz, standing on this cold cement, and me with thin pumps.

George: Is that all that's worrying you?

Vickie: Well no, if you will ask. I just had a row with my man. I hit him with my handbag, and look at it (slight pause). Just my luck, when I cracked him I broke the handle off.

George: Hm. What with no bright lights here to cheer you up, and nothing but that drug-store night light there behind us, to take your mind off your troubles, sounds as if you needed a little consoling.

Vickie: Consoling, did you say, big boy? Not on your life I've had enough loving to last me a lifetime.—And besides, you sound too hopeful to me. Kinda pleased with yourself. I can't see you, by that dim light you mentioned; but I don't know I want to.

George: Well, I can't see you either, but you sound pretty nifty. How are you gonna forget your troubles, anyhow?

Vickie: Oh, I got a lady bootlegger friend across the Bay, and I guess I'll go across and take a little of her forget-me-quick.

Biz: Motorman's gong again, this time coming nearer. It continues for several seconds, finally there is the whirr and the grinding of brakes as a street-car approaches and comes to a stop.

George: Well, how about my tagging along, too?

Vickie: Oh, well, you can come along and pay for the drinks if you like,— but that'll be about all.

Biz: Street-car stars up, and motorman's gong is heard again, a little more exultantly.

Music: Spanish dance passage from Gershwin's *American in Paris,* played with a good deal of abandon.

The sound of the foot-gong, and the opening remarks of the dialogue, establish the fact that the couple are waiting for a street-car,
and a ferry-car at that; the girl's complaint that her feet are 'friz'
makes it clear that the night is cold; while the remark about the
dim light in the drug-store behind them is evidence that they are
on a street-corner which is otherwise dark. The fact that the two
have never met should be clear almost from the beginning; and the
unconventional situation is in keeping with the rather casual ending.
So far as the voices and dialogue can convey character, the disclosure
of the personalities of the two speakers is rapid, as it must be within
the brief limits of a skit of this kind.

It is a sudden ascent, but it should be remarked that Shakespeare,
working on a stage with very little scenery, had to convey the visual
aspect of the setting, and much of the atmosphere, in the verse
spoken by the characters. The Greek dramatists also created
scenery and mood by the poetry; they were aided by the convention
of the chorus, through whose lyrics and recitative they could add
description and comment to the line of action in the play proper. So
the radio author is in good company, if he only knew it. But he
must never forget the basic requirement of his craft: to translate all
the senses into a notation for the ear.

TALKIE DIALOGUE

The writer of talkie dialogue confronts a contrary situation. He
must contrive dialogue which, far from being the whole show, as in
radio, will only orchestrate or accompany the visual line shown on
the screen. Talkie dialogue must be crisp, condensed to the last
notch, and must serve at once to characterize the speakers and advance the action. Only what cannot be acted out in pantomime
should be conveyed by talk; for the eye is quicker than the ear, and
the art of the cinema is basically a visual art. Producers will eventually learn that it is bad business to photograph and phonograph
stage plays, and palm them off as movies.

What is really needed for the talkies is quick back-chat, so that
the reactions of the characters are rendered at a tempo which will
not retard the rapid succession of tableaux on the screen. It is not
unthinkable that a play which depends largely on its dialogue might
succeed as a movie, if it were by such a master of staccato talk as
Bernard Shaw; but it is significant that Shaw has never been willing

to permit the producers to put on his plays. His ostensible reason is that they are so stupid that he cannot trust them. The fact is that Shaw is too good a showman, and far too good a critic, not to realize that a play written for one medium will require extensive modification to be suited for another and entirely different mode of production. So much for these newer forms.

Limits to the Causerie Style

There are, of course, limits to writing as one talks. With the accompaniment of gesture, intonation, and lively facial play, a good many things can be said that would sound flat or inept in print; while, as Beaumarchais remarked, what is too silly to be said can be sung. Above all, in the maintenance of an easy personal tone in writing, one should avoid posturing and gesturing, or the repetition of eccentric mannerisms. The over-insistence upon mere personal vagaries of style is a glaring fault. Havelock Ellis has indicated in a happy passage the need for striking a balance between the personal and impersonal:

Every writer has his own music, though there are few in whom it becomes audible save at rare and precious intervals. The prose of the writer who can deliberately make his own personal cadences monotonously audible all the time grows wearisome; it affects us as a tedious mannerism. This is a kind of machine-made prose which indeed it requires a clever artisan to produce; but, as Landor said, 'he must be a bad writer to whom there are no inequalities.' (*The Dance of Life*, p. 155 in the Modern Library Edition.)

In writing up a diary, for example, no one with any sense of humor would dream of posing for his own benefit; and a familiar letter is, in a way, an extension of the diary, written for only one other eye, that of an intimate friend. Our friends do not mind us in slippers and dressing gown; but they can usually detect, with unerring eye, when we have put on more style than the occasion warrants.

One reason for attending so closely to the demands of familiar and easy writing, is that the taste of our age demands it, even on occasions which would once have called for full dress. We have already, in discussing conversation, noted by horrible example the danger of falling into jolly-doggism and fatuity, in an effort to maintain the familiar tone. But it is better to run this risk than to use words which are too elegant or too elaborate for the occasion. A piece of casual writing should never appear like a splendid façade with nothing behind it. And that leads naturally to the question as to the use of the American language in writing, for American is an undress style.

AN AMERICAN LANGUAGE?

We all talk American, but should we write it? That is the question. The differences between American and British English are a matter of common knowledge. There are about six hundred words and phrases which distinguish American from British usage. An *automobile* becomes a *motor* in England. A *street-car conductor* becomes the *guard* on a *tram;* a *railway engineer* is an *engine-driver.* A *taxi* is a *cab,* though a chauffeur is a chauffeur in either country. Other amusing contrasts are:

American:	English:
bug	insect
'charge it'	'put it down'
cracker	biscuit
delicatessen	Italian warehouse
dime novel	shilling-shocker
excursionist	tripper
garters (men's)	sock suspenders
girl for general work	cook-general
grain	corn
haystack	haycock
hello (over the phone)	Are you there?
peanut	monkey-nut
proof reader	corrector-of-the-press
soft drinks	minerals
street cleaner	crossing sweeper
to miss a train	to lose a train
typhoid fever	enteric

The English usage on prepositions differs somewhat from American. 'Different to' is good English, though impossible American. The English take more precise account of the meaning of a Latin derivative, in choosing which preposition shall follow it. They still keep the 'u' in *labor, honor,* and the like; and *jail* they spell *gaol.* But these are minor points, hardly more significant than the variation among different American dictionaries on disputed points of usage.

The really salient differences between spoken English and spoken American do not hinge on diction or spelling. There is a difference in tune, in the sentence rhythm, in the permitted limits of variation from good form, in the whole 'feel' of the two dialects. This is glaringly apparent if a passage of American vernacular is compared with a specimen of genteel, donnish English prose from the shades of Oxford,—though Cambridge style is often somewhat more barbarous, approximating American, as an Oxford man might say. But such a sharp and accentuated contrast is not needed to establish the difference. Take a passage at random from *Time*, whose editors go the whole hog in writing American:

By noon the sun was shining and the 60-piece 16th Infantry Band from Governor's Island was tootling a patriotic concert, including "American Medley" and "Under the Double Eagle." Then portly Mrs. Tubman, who looks something like old Mme. Schumann-Heink and boasts that she "can sing with or without a 60-piece band," mounted the stone platform in front of Washington's statue, launched into "The Star-Spangled Banner" while the band blared mightily and the crowd of 1000 looked on, munching their lunches. (*Time* XXII. 19, 13 May 1935, p. 40.)

"Tootling," "munching their lunches," and the rather unnecessary epithet "old" would not be found in a civil English newspaper. To be sure, *Time* means to be vulgar; but it succeeds without much effort. The music of its sentences is modernistic.

Set this off against a chance selection from the *Manchester Guardian Weekly*:

John Binney was sentenced last July to seven years' penal servitude for demanding money with menaces from the manageress of a Derbyshire hotel. He had been singled out in an identification parade as having visited the hotel just before the first of the threatening letters was received. His home was in Sheffield, where the letters were postmarked. Handwriting experts found strong similarity between his writing and that of the letters. He admitted that the name "Aix les Bains" had stuck in his memory, and unfortunately for him it occurred in the letters. On evidence of this sort the jury found him guilty. He protested his innocence, but was refused last August leave to appeal. He might still be serving his sentence but for the fact that the real culprits continued their threats. His petition to appeal had hardly been dismissed when a further threatening letter was received with which he could obviously have had nothing to do. That was nine months ago, but the law is slow to retrace its steps. Additional letters this spring decided the matter. The Crown on Wednesday admitted its error and Binney's conviction was quashed. (*Manchester Guardian Weekly*, vol. 32, No. 19, 10 May 1935.)

The *Guardian*, without resorting to the clipping, foreshortening, and portmanteau words which *Time* uses, can tell about the same amount of story in a given space; and there is no question that to anyone with a sensitive ear, the English cadences are preferable. An American, reading the English newspaper, would not sense any particular strangeness in the style, except for the phrase "leave to appeal," the word "manageress," and the reference to the Crown. In fact, the passage might appear in the *Springfield Republican* or the *Boston Transcript*, with these three items modified, and pass muster as literate and proper American (which the editors of the *Guardian* may or may not take as a compliment). Evidently, then, there is a ground common to literary English and literary American; in fact, at the level of the *Guardian* and the *Boston Transcript*, there is little to distinguish the two. If the two variant forms of the language are represented by intersecting circles, about ninety-five per cent of the area is common to the two. But the case is altered if one is considering the ordinary run of American newspaper and magazine writing, as set off against the more orthodox and formal expression in English journals of similar scope.

The difficulty which arises from the difference in tune between English and American is felt more strongly by Americans. Most of them are bilingual: that is, they can write, at a pinch, formal literary English; but from their constant contact with the freedom and novelty of cadence in spoken American, they feel a strong thrust toward writing "their own, their native tongue." The result is a mixed style, by all odds the most abominable macaronic jargon of English and American to be found. It is as if an orchestra, playing chamber music, mixed jazz with a Bach rondo, or imported a saxophone to help a Schumann concerto. The combination of rather literary diction with barbarous phrase patterns is noticeable in the following, from the hand of *Time's* cinema critic:

Fully as preposterous as it sounds, the story of *The Scoundrel* is at once a childish presentation of the theory that virtue is its own reward—which Hollywood producers outgrew years ago—and an attempt to disguise this fact by presenting Manhattan's neurotic literati as bogeymen equipped with malevolence in heroic quantities. . . . *(Time* XXII. 19, 13 May 1935, p. 38.)

H. L. Mencken and George Jean Nathan furnish many examples of the mixed style. Yet both these writers can write at will straight English or straight American. They command American more perfectly, and should stick to it. Sinclair Lewis, Ring Lardner, and John Dos Passos write the American vernacular without any corrupt reminiscence of literary English; and the result is humorous and pleasing, to American ears, if not to English sensibilities.

The logical compromise, then, is to use American on those occasions when you would naturally write as you talk. In an informal address to a luncheon club, or a speech before a trade union audience, formal literary English would sound stilted. Why forego the piquancy, the inventiveness, and the racy idiom which the American language affords? We have always lived with a leaning toward comedy, sometimes high and sometimes low; so why not keep, on informal occasions at least, the free and easy privilege of the comedian, to make up our lines as we go along?

In this work, we have devoted more attention to the reading vocabulary, the only one manageable in print, and the only one which can be acquired by systematic study. But the extension of our stock of words depends on the ear no less than the eye; and the alert student of words will attend to the spoken language no less than to the written. "Why not read in the book of life?" Casanova asked Voltaire, and the question is one which every writer and speaker should ask himself. Voltaire's answer is no less timely counsel: "The book of life? Ah, but it is so unwieldy!" Remembering this, the writer or speaker who wants to be completely equipped will not neglect his reading, or the constant and selective enlargement of his vocabulary. Only as his phrases are easily transferred from the memory to the tongue or pen, will the command of words be complete.

STYLE RULE

STYLE RULE

The STYLE RULE is designed to serve the writer in the way that a slide rule serves an engineer: as a quick check on the correctness of his work. The rules are all cast in question form, so that every writer can become his own critic. Of the eight or nine hundred technical terms usually used in grammar and rhetoric, only forty are retained, and these are all defined in section X of the device. No attention is paid to the formal divisions between grammar and rhetoric, since the writer at work is little concerned with them. This RULE has been checked against forty of the leading handbooks and rhetorics in common use, and it covers in condensed form most of the ground which they traverse. After a writer has finished his rough draft, he can turn to a section of the STYLE RULE to check on any point in regard to which he is in doubt. A rapid reading will quickly familiarize him with the organization of the RULE:

I. The Whole Work

II. The Paragraph

III. The Sentence

IV. The Sentence

V. The Fine Points of Diction

VI. Common Errors in Diction

VII. Capitalization

VIII. Punctuation

IX. Hyphens. Numbers

X. Forms and Terms

STYLE RULE

When you check copy, to all questions containing underlined words (as in Sections V and VI) you should be able to answer "No."
To all other questions you should be able to answer "Yes."

I. THE WHOLE WORK

1) Is the title brief? expressive? delimiting?
2) Do the topic sentences by themselves
  a) follow one out of the other?
  b) each relate clearly to the subject?
  c) include the significant phases?
  d) mark off clear divisions?
  e) show, by their spacing, proper proportion?
  f) furnish: the first, a strong opening;
  g) the last, signs of a rounded ending?
  h) serve as a condensed version or précis?
3) Does the table of contents or outline
  a) show both structure and content?
  b) divide the subject consistently?
  c) put important items in emphatic places?
  d) show proper subordination of the parts?
  e) keep a similar form for parallel headings?
  f) preserve a consistent notation?
    I) Main Headings in Topical Outlines.
      A) Chief Division, under main head.
        1) Sub-division, under A.
        2) Another item parallel to 1.
          a) supporting detail.
          b) similar detail.
      B) Another Chief Division.
    II) Analytical outlines, like briefs for argument, demand
      A) complete sentences in each main division;
      B) the maintenance of order based on
        1) time sequence;
        2) spacial relationship; or
        3) logical relationship: a movement
          a) from particular to general,
          b) from general to particular;

C) greater rigor than the topical outline;
D) subdivisions which shall always be indented as this one is, never running out to left margin.

4) Does the work convey a single total impression?
5) Is the point of view consistently maintained?
6) Is the style reasonably consistent?
7) Have you included all necessary steps in rendering
   a) thought?
   b) feeling?
   c) reasoning?
8) Is the whole work logically consistent?
9) Does the work communicate your precise meaning?
10) Have you put yourself in the reader's place?

II. The Paragraph

11) Has the paragraph a single purpose, stated either
    a) in a topic sentence?
    b) in a topical word or phrase? or
    c) in its whole content?
12) Does every sentence relate to the topic? advance it?
13) Is the treatment complete? is it
    a) long enough for intelligibility and smoothness?
    b) the right length for the relative importance of the topic?
14) Is the paragraph consistently developed
    a) by definition—logical, restrictive, or amplifying?
    b) by illustration?
    c) by presentation of details or particulars?
    d) by comparison or contrast?
    e) by reasons or proof?
    f) by causes, effects, or cause and effect?
    g) by a judicious combination of methods?
15) In narrative, is there forward motion in time?
    a) or, if "cutbacks" are used, is the time relation clear?
16) In description, is there an order based on
    a) spacial contiguity?
    b) order in which details are seen?
    c) contrast?
17) In exposition and argument, is there order based on
    a) time sequence?
    b) logical progression?
    c) climax?
18) Have you made the connections between the sentences evident, through
    a) parallel construction for like ideas?
    b) repetition of a key word?
    c) the use of connective words?
    d) careful use of pronouns of reference?

e) avoiding shifts of tense?
f) avoiding shift in point of view?
19) Is there variety in the sentences, as to
  a) length?
  b) form—simple, complex, compound?
  c) structure—loose or periodic?
  d) mode of beginning?
  e) rhythm and ring?
20) Are you sure it is a paragraph, i.e.
  a) is it a true thought unit?
  b) is it properly indented?

III. The Sentence

21) IS THERE A MAIN VERB? Is the sentence complete, i.e.
  a) not a phrase?
  b) not a dependent clause?
  c) not a coordinate clause without its twin?
  d) not minus personal pronouns?
  e) not minus other necessary words?
  Exceptions to the requirement of completeness:
  Command or request: *Make ready. — Please stop.*
  Question: *What next?*
  Exclamation: *Watch out! What rubbish!*
  Conversation: *"Ready?" "Not yet."*
  Transition: *Enough of this.*
22) Do the subject and verb agree?
  a) When a phrase with a plural comes between a singular subject and the verb, is the verb singular, as it should be?
  b) When the subject comes after the verb?
  c) After *each of us, everybody*, etc., are possessive pronouns and verb singular?
  d) If *either . . . or, neither . . . nor* join two singulars, is the verb singular?
  e) For *committee, jury*, and like collective nouns, is the verb plural if the individuals are meant? singular if the group is taken as a unit?
23) Are related ideas only combined in one sentence?
24) Have you avoided sentences which are
  a) choppy, needing to be combined into one?
  b) stringy, needing to be broken up?
  c) rambling, needing to be condensed?
  d) awkward, needing to be recast?
  e) marred by wrong subordination?
  f) marred by wrong coordination?
25) Are the parts of the sentence arranged
  a) to express the ideas in logical sequence?
  b) to place together elements alike in function?
  c) to eliminate tagged-on details or after-thoughts?

26) Have you avoided shifts in construction, except with good reason,
   a) from active to passive voice?
   b) from one person to another?
   c) from one tense to another?
   d) from singular to plural or vice versa?
27) Are similar thoughts and elements indicated by parallel structure?
   a) *and which:* does another *which* clause precede the *and?*
28) Have you avoided making unlike elements improperly parallel?
29) Are modifiers rightly placed
   a) so that there is no doubt what they modify?
   b) so that no participle is left dangling?
   c) so that they are as close as feasible to the word modified?
30) Have you used any word in a double capacity?

IV. The Sentence, *Continued*

31) Do reference words refer to a particular antecedent? Have you avoided leaving the antecedent
   a) doubtful?
   b) merely implied?   (If so, rewrite.)
   c) expressed only in the title?
   d) marooned too far from a relative pronoun which stands for it?
32) Does the pronoun agree with its antecedent
   a) in number?
     Each, every, either, neither, one, anyone, everyone, anybody, no one, nobody, somebody: all call for the singular possessive pronoun. (Cf. 22c.)
   b) in gender?
   c) in person?
33) Are your comparisons
   a) completed?
   b) made between comparable things, persons, or qualities?
   c) based on a definite standard?
   d) quite clear, with only one possible meaning?
34) Have you avoided contradictory or inconsistent statements?
35) Does one main idea emerge from the sentence?
36) Have you secured emphasis by
   a) periodic structure, for suspense?
   b) balanced structure, for close comparisons?
   c) climactic structure, for increasing tension?
   d) placing important items first or last?
   e) judicious repetition when needed?
   f) cutting down unnecessary repetition?
   g) cutting out surplus words?
   h) simple, direct, brief, lucid, plain wording?
   i) altering normal sentence order to throw some element in relief? BUT
37) Are unimportant items *kept out of* emphatic positions?

38) Have you kept to the normal order except for good reason?
NEVER: *Came the dawn.*
39) Does the sentence fulfil its function, as
   a) topic sentence?
   b) transition sentence?
   c) isolated statement?
   d) summary sentence?
40) Has the sentence an easy, natural ring?

V. THE FINE POINTS OF DICTION

Errors underlined

41) Have you preferred
   a) the familiar word to the far-fetched?
   b) the concrete word to the abstract?
   c) the single word to the circumlocution?
   d) the short word to the long?
   e) the Saxon word to the Romance? (3 times out of 4)
42) Have you avoided words unsuited to the context, as
   a) slang: "a peculiar kind of vagabond language, always hanging on the outskirts of legitimate speech, but continually straying or forcing its way into the most respectable company." (Greenough and Kittredge. *Words and Their Ways.* p. 55)
   b) jargon: technical words inappropriate in prose addressed to the general reader.
   c) a foreign word or phrase, when English has a word for it?
   d) home-made coinages?
   e) infinitives in *ing* when the usual noun would do?
   f) colloquial words in formal prose?
   g) bookish words in informal writing?
   h) vulgarisms: words that have come down in the world, e.g., *hot, lit, lousy, sunk, swell.*
   i) genteelisms: over-polite words where common words would be better, e.g., sales*lady*, the *élite.*
43) Have you used words in
   a) present use? i.e., not archaic.
   b) national use? i.e., not local.
   c) reputable use? i.e., none of those listed in 42a-d above.
44) Have you used such worn-out words as
   a) *awful, fine, grand, ideal, intriguing, lovely, outstanding, weird?* (and similar girls' boarding school language and vile journalese).
   b) *appreciate, appeal, intrigue, thrill,* in an ecstatic tone?
   c) *proposition, line, angle, slant,* figuratively?
45) Have you used a synonym needed for variety? but kept the same word where explicitness requires it?
46) Have you confused
   a) *affect* with *effect?*

b) *allusion* with *illusion?*
c) *capital* with *capitol?*
d) *continuous* with *continual?*
e) *deprecate* with *depreciate?*
f) *demean* with *debase?*
g) *principle* with *principal?*
h) *elemental* with *elementary?*
i) *genius* with *talent?*
j) *transpire* with *happen?*

47) Have you avoided rhyming or echoing words in prose? *"The latter is no matter." "Thence he went to the fence."*

48) Have you used the idiomatic preposition?
See Weseen's *Dict. of Eng. Grammar,* (T. Y. Crowell) pp. 491-514.
Are your words and phrases otherwise in accord with English idiom?
Idioms: phrases which . . . transgress . . . either the laws of grammar or the laws of logic, but which are yet approved English.—See L. P. Smith. *English Idioms.*

49) Have you avoided mixed metaphors?

50) In employing *shall* and *will,* have you,
   a) for simple futurity, used *shall* in the first person, *will* in the second and third persons?
   b) for command or promise, used *will* for the first person, *shall* for the second and third persons?
   c) for questions, the form expected in the answer?

VI. Common Errors in Diction

Errors underlined

51) Have you made one of the very common errors?
   a) *don't* after *he, she,* or *it? doesn't* is the contraction
   b) *due to* for *on account of* or *because of?*
   c) *is when* or *is where?* (Both are barred.)
   d) *it's* for *its? (it's=it is; its=*possessive of *it)*
   e) *kind of a* for *kind of* (so with *sort of a* for *sort of)*
   f) *like* for *as?*
   g) *there* for *their* or *they're?*
   h) *those kind* for *that kind?*
   i) *to* for *too* or *two?*
   j) *while* for *whereas* or *although?*
   Have you written (or said)
52) *among we friends* for *among us friends?*
53) *between you and I* for *between you and me?*
54) *no one but I* for *no one but me?*
55) *They asked him and I* to come? or *Come with John and I to the dance?* (*me,* as object.)

BUT
They said he and I were to blame is CORRECT.
56) *They favored me coming* for *They favored my coming?*
    BUT   (possessive before gerund)
They saw me coming is CORRECT. (objective before participle)
57) Have you written (or said)
a) *set* for *sit* or *sat?* (*set* takes an object, except when used of the sun, moon or stars)
b) *laid* for *lay* or *lain?* (*lay, laid, laid* takes an object; *lie, lay, lain* requires no object)
c) *raise* for *rise?* (*raise, raised, raised* takes an object; *rise, rose, risen* requires no object)
d) *came* for *come*, or *come* for *came?*
e) *would of* for *would have? should of* for *should have?*
f) *had ought* for *ought to have? hadn't ought* for *ought not to?*
g) *was* for *were?*
58) Have you written (or said)
a) *any* for *at all?*
b) *but what* for *but that?*
c) *can't hardly* for *can hardly?* or other *double negatives?*
d) *can't seem to* for *seem not able to?*
e) *different than* for *different from* (NEVER *than* after *different*, except in British English)
f) *inside of* for *inside?*
g) *myself* when you mean *I?* (*myself* is reflexive)
h) *off of* for *off?*
i) *outside of* for *outside?*
j) *quite* for *quiet?*
k) *quite* for *rather?* (*quite* means *entirely*)
l) *where* for *that?*
    I see by the paper *where* he won. WRONG.
    I see by the paper *that* he won. RIGHT.
59) Have you used legal jargon in ordinary prose, as
a) *party* for *person?*
b) *said* for *previously mentioned?*
c) *same* or *the same* for *it?*
60) Have you used *humans* for *human beings?*

VII. CAPITALIZATION

HAVE YOU CAPITALIZED

61) the first word of a sentence?
62) the first word of a line of poetry?
    (except in verse originally begun in lower case?)

63) the first word of a complete direct quotation?
64) the first word, and all important words, in titles of books, plays, magazines, and newspapers?
(but do not capitalize *the* in newspaper titles.)
65) personifications?
66) proper names and proper adjectives of all kinds

when used in a proper sense, e.g.,	BUT	*not* when used in a common sense, e.g.,
a) geographical names, as India, China, Brussels, Paris, the East.		ax) *india* ink, *china* ware, *brussels* sprouts.
b) names of races, used ethnically: Polynesian.		bx) a *negro* song.
c) political parties: the Farmer-Labor Party.		cx) a *republican* form of government.
d) religious sects and orders: Puritans, Roman Catholics.		dx) a *puritan* code, a *catholic* taste.
e) philosophical, literary, and artistic schools: Stoics, Romantics.		ex) a *stoical* temper, a *romantic* episode, a *symbolist* device.
f) historical and geological epochs.		
g) periods of art or literature: Decadence of 1890.		gx) the onset of *decadence*.
h) official titles of organizations and institutions: the University of Oregon, the Library of Congress.		hx) a *university* charter, a *federal* form of government, a *library*.
i) bureaus of government: the Census Bureau.		ix) taking the *census*.
j) fixed ceremonies.		
k) important historical events.		
l) titles of treaties, acts, and laws ratified or passed.		lx) *bills* not yet passed.
m) religious, military, and civil titles, when preceding the name, or standing alone to denote a definite person.		mx) peers above the rank of *baron*, and one *bishop*.
n) names of holidays, creeds.		
o) all names of the Bible and its divisions.		
p) nouns and substantives referring to the Deity.		
q) abbreviations of titles and degrees.		

67) *street*, when used in addresses, as Third Street?
68) *river, mountain, strait, sea, school,* when used as part of a proper name? (Newspapers often use lower case.)
69) *age* when the sense requires it, as the Age of Elizabeth?
70) HAVE YOU CAPITALIZED AS SPARINGLY AS POSSIBLE?

VIII. Punctuation

71) In punctuating clauses in compound sentences, have you put
   a) a comma before *but* and *for*?
   b) a comma before *and*, except in short sentences?
   c) a semicolon between clauses of equal rank, which are not joined by conjunctions?
   d) a semicolon between independent clauses, if there are internal commas in the various sections?
72) Have you put a comma after a clause or phrase modifier which precedes what it modifies?
73) Have you set off by commas a non-restrictive relative clause?
74) Have you used commas to set off parenthetical matter, such as
   a) *of course, on the other hand, however?*
   b) *oh, yes, no?*
   c) appositives?
   d) *I think, I believe, as it seems to me,* etc.?
75) Have you put a comma
   a) before and after a vocative?
   b) between the day of the month and year, in a date?
   c) between city and state, in addresses?
   d) before *and, or,* and *nor,* connecting the last two elements in a sequence of three or more?
      e.g., *the fifth, sixth, seventh, and ninth verses.*
   e) always before *etc.*?
76) Have you put quotation marks
   a) around direct quotations? *but omitted them around indirect quotations?*
   b) around titles of chapters when they are cited?
   c) around titles of periodical articles cited?
77) Have you put a period
   a) at the end of each declarative sentence?
   b) after all abbreviations except *per cent*?
78) Have you used a colon
   a) to introduce a series?
   b) to separate two balanced or antithetical statements?
79) Have you put an apostrophe
   a) before an "s" signifying the possessive case? (For words ending in "s," either put the apostrophe after it, or add an apostrophe "s," as euphony requires.)
   b) to mark contractions: *won't* for *will not,* etc.

80) HAVE YOU USED THE LEAST PUNCTUATION NEEDED FOR
CLEARNESS AND CERTAINTY? HAVE YOU USED
   a) a question mark after direct questions, but *not after indirect
   questions*?
   b) a dash only where no other punctuation mark will do?

IX. HYPHENS   NUMBERS

81) In hyphenating a word at the end of a line, have you refrained from
dividing
   a) any group of letters representing a single sound?
   b) any monosyllable?
   c) any syllable that does not contain a vowel? NEVER *schis-m.*
   d) any word of four letters? (preferably not five or six)
82) Have you refrained from dividing any word on a single letter? NEVER
a-round, o-mit, stead-y; and preferably do not divide any word on
two letters: *ac-cept* is BAD.
83) Have you kept from dividing compound words except at the hyphen
already there?
84) Have you hyphenated the ff. terminations only at the point indicated
herewith: *-cial, -tial, -cion, -sion, -tion, -cious, -geous, -gious*?
85) Have you divided between the similar letters, when a consonant is
doubled in inflected verbs? (*admit-ted;* but *profess-ing*)
86) Have you divided a word (as you should)
   a) after a single consonant, when the preceding vowel is short?
   b) before a single consonant, when the preceding vowel is long?
87) Have you divided a word (as you should)
   a) between two or more consonants not capable of beginning a word
   or syllable, coming between two sounded vowels? (*myr-tle, accom-
   modate*; *rt, mm* could not begin a word)
   b) between two or more consonants capable of beginning a word or
   syllable, if the preceding vowel is short? (*gas-tric, mas-ter*)
   c) before two or more consonants capable of beginning a word or
   syllable, if the preceding vowel is long? (*re-script, neu-tral*)
   d) between two vowels coming together, but sounded separately?
   (*curi-osity, sci-ence*)
88) Have you used a hyphen
   a) between the elements of a compound adjective preceding the noun
   it modifies? (a *red-headed* woman)
   b) between the parts of a compound noun when the elements are
   distinct, or of equal importance?
   c) in words compounded with prefixes, adverbs, or prepositions which
   are felt as distinct elements? e.g.: a *non-restrictive clause.*
   d) between cardinal numbers from twenty-one to ninety-nine? and
   corresponding ordinals?
   e) between parts of compounds one member of which is *fellow, father,
   mother, brother, sister, daughter, parent,* or *foster*?

89) Have you spelled out
 a) isolated statements of numbers under one hundred?
 b) numbers over one hundred which can be written in one or two words?
 c) approximations expressed in round numbers?
 d) numbers in dates of formal social communications?
90) Have you used figures
 a) for numbers greater than one hundred which take more than two words?
 b) for sums including both dollars and cents?
 c) for grouped numbers, as in statistics?
 d) for cardinal numbers referring to house addresses, room numbers, pages in books, numbers in dates?

X. FORMS AND TERMS

91) In a book-list, are your entries as follows:
 Author's surname. *Book title.* Place publ., Publisher, Date.
 Partridge, Eric. *Slang.* London, Routledge, 1933.
92) In a list of periodical articles, have you kept to the form:
 Author's name. "Title of Article" in *Periodical,* vol., no., pp.
 Sinclair, Upton. "The Future of Epic," in *The Nation,* 139, no. 3621; (or, in *The Nation,* Nov. 28, '34, pp. 616-17).
93) In referring to a chapter in a book, is the entry:
 Author's name. "Title of Chapter" in his *Title of Book* as in 91.
 Partridge, Eric. "Gangster Slang" in *Slang,* London, Routledge, 1933.
94) Are your footnotes consecutively numbered, and their sources added as in 91-93 *supra?* Are page numbers given?
95) Have you checked your references after the MS. is complete?

DO YOU HAVE A FIRM GRASP OF THE TERMS USED IN THIS *STYLE RULE?*

96) SENTENCE: a purposive expression of thought or feeling by means of a word or words.—Can you distinguish sentences which are
 a) simple?—one principal clause.
 b) complex?—one principal clause, and one or more dependent.
 c) compound?—two or more principal clauses.
 d) loose?—meaning fairly complete before the end?
 e) periodic?—meaning complete only when the end (period) is reached.
 f) balanced?—two principal clauses parallel in form.
 g) antithetical?—same, but with an opposition in thought.
 h) topic?—stating the subject of a paragraph.
 i) transition?—a bridge between other sentences.
 j) summary?—summing up the section or whole work.

97)—CLAUSE: any group of words containing subject and predicate. Can you distinguish a clause which is
a) independent or principal? It can stand alone.
b) dependent? It cannot stand alone.
c) restrictive? It narrows and limits the meaning; it is essential to establish the reference.

98) PRONOUN: a word used in place of a noun. Do you know which pronouns are
a) personal? *I, me, we, us; you; he, she, it, they.*
b) possessive? *my, mine, our(s); your(s); his, her, its; their.*
c) relative? *who, what, which, that,* and their compounds.
d) reflexive? *myself, yourself,* etc. (these are also intensive.)
e) indefinite? *one, both, anyone, everyone,* etc.

99) Do you know the following general terms?
a) parallelism: correspondence in form and arrangement, in two or more parts of a sentence or paragraph.
b) logic (in composition): the absence of internal contradiction; the parts of a logical statement hang together.

100) ABBREVIATIONS; *cf.*—compare; *i.e.*—that is; *e.g.*—for example; *pp.*—pages; *op. cit.*—work referred to; *ibid.*—in the same place; *sp.*—spelling; *gr.*—grammar askew; *w.w.*—wrong word; *ff.*—following; *MS.*—manuscript, as distinct from printed form.

A DESK-SET FOR THE STUDENT OF WORDS

1. Any one of the college dictionaries described in Chapter III of this work.
2. *Roget's Treasury of Words* or *Roget's International Thesaurus,* (Thomas Y. Crowell Co.)
3. Fernald, James C. *English Synonyms, Antonyms and Prepositions.* N. Y., Funk & Wagnalls, 1896.
4. *Thorndike Century Junior Dictionary* (for finding word frequency).
5. Greenough and Kittredge. *Words and Their Ways in English Speech.* N. Y., Macmillan, 1925.
6. Fowler, H. W., & Fowler, F. G. *The King's English.* Oxford, Oxf. Univ. Press, 1919.
7. Smith, Logan Pearsall. *English Idioms.* S. P. E. Tract No. XII. Oxford, Clarendon Press, 1923.
8. McKnight, G. H. *English Words and Their Backgrounds.* N. Y., Appleton, 1923.
9. *Modern English in the Making.* N. Y., Appleton, 1928.

BIBLIOGRAPHY:

FURTHER STUDY ON WORDS

1. Burke, Kenneth. *Permanence and Change.* N. Y., *New Republic,* 1935.
2. Fowler, H. W. *Dictionary of Modern English Usage.* Oxford, 1926.
3. Horwill, H. W. *Dictionary of Modern American Usage.* Oxford, 1935.
4. Krapp, G. P. *Modern English.* N. Y., Scribner's, 1909.
5. Mawson, C. O. Sylvester. *International Book of Names.* N. Y., Thomas Y. Crowell Company, 1933.
6. Mencken, H. L. *The American Language.* N. Y., Knopf, 1921.
7. Ogden, C. K. *The System of Basic English.*
8. *Basic for Science.* London, Orthological Institute.
9. Partridge, Eric. *Slang / Today and Yesterday.* N. Y., Macmillan, 1933.
10. Skeat, Rev. W. W. *Etymological Dictionary of the English Language.* Oxford Press.

   (It is now safer to consult the etymologies in the OED; but Skeat's is a pioneer work, and still worth reading for its flavor and point, and particularly for the *furor scholasticus* with which its author belabored fanciful, far-fetched, and mistaken etymologies.)

11. Thorndike, E. L. *The Teacher's Word Book of 20,000 Words.* N. Y., Teachers' College, 1932.
12. Trench, Archbishop. *On the Study of Words.* N. Y., Macmillan.
13. *English Past and Present.* N. Y., Macmillan.
14. Weekley, Ernest. *The Romance of Words.* London, N. Y., Dutton.
15. *Etymological Dictionary of Modern English.* N. Y., Dutton.
16. Weseen, Maurice H. *Dictionary of American Slang.* N. Y., Thomas Y. Crowell Co., 1934.
17. *Words Confused and Misused.* N. Y., Thomas Y. Crowell Co., 1932.

KEYS TO EXERCISES

Exercise No. 1

1. (1)	34. (3)	67. (3)	101. (1)	134. (1)	167. (1)
2. (2)	35. (2)	68. (3)	102. (3)	135. (1)	168. (2)
3. (3)	36. (1)	69. (2)	103. (4)	136. (1)	169. (1)
4. (4)	37. (4)	70. (1)	104. (3)	137. (2)	170. (4)
5. (1)	38. (2)	71. (1)	105. (1)	138. (2)	171. (4)
6. (3)	39. (3)	72. (2)	106. (2)	139. (4)	172. (1)
7. (3)	40. (4)	73. (4)	107. (2)	140. (4)	173. (3)
8. (4)	41. (1)	74. (1)	108. (1)	141. (1)	174. (4)
9. (1)	42. (3)	75. (1)	109. (4)	142. (1)	175. (3)
10. (2)	43. (1)	76. (4)	110. (1)	143. (4)	176. (3)
11. (3)	44. (2)	77. (1)	111. (2)	144. (4)	177. (4)
12. (4)	45. (4)	78. (4)	112. (3)	145. (2)	178. (4)
13. (4)	46. (3)	79. (1)	113. (4)	146. (4)	179. (2)
14. (4)	47. (4)	80. (4)	114. (1)	147. (4)	180. (4)
15. (4)	48. (3)	81. (1)	115. (1)	148. (1)	181. (1)
16. (1)	49. (4)	82. (2)	116. (3)	149. (2)	182. (2)
17. (1)	50. (4)	83. (2)	117. (2)	150. (4)	183. (1)
18. (3)	51. (3)	84. (1)	118. (1)	151. (1)	184. (4)
19. (3)	52. (2)	85. (2)	119. (4)	152. (3)	185. (4)
20. (1)	53. (2)	86. (1)	120. (1)	153. (1)	186. (4)
21. (2)	54. (1)	87. (2)	121. (2)	154. (1)	187. (1)
22. (3)	55. (4)	88. (3)	122. (4)	155. (4)	188. (3)
23. (4)	56. (4)	89. (2)	123. (3)	156. (1)	189. (4)
24. (2)	57. (1)	90. (2)	124. (4)	157. (2)	190. (2)
25. (2)	58. (3)	91. (3)	125. (4)	158. (3)	191. (2)
26. (3)	59. (1)	92. (3)	126. (1)	159. (3)	192. (4)
27. (1)	60. (3)	93. (2)	127. (3)	160. (4)	193. (1)
28. (3)	61. (2)	94. (3)	128. (1)	161. (2)	194. (4)
29. (3)	62. (4)	95. (2)	129. (1)	162. (3)	195. (1)
30. (1)	63. (3)	96. (3)	130. (2)	163. (1)	196. (1)
31. (2)	64. (2)	97. (4)	131. (4)	164. (4)	197. (1)
32. (3)	65. (4)	98. (1)	132. (2)	165. (3)	198. (4)
33. (4)	66. (4)	99. (3)	133. (2)	166. (1)	199. (2)
		100. (2)			200. (4)

Exercise No. 4

1. agreement
2. comparison
3. competition
4. direction
5. metal
6. conversation

267

7. misery	13. invention	20. memory
8. frail	14. office	21. hook
9. insects	15. development	22. imagination
10. history	16. inevitable	23. current
11. discovery	17. suggestion	24. solvent
12. request	18. slope	25. organization
	19. facts	

EXERCISE No. 5

Kipling—waddled
Stevenson—bloodless
Stevenson—arduous, labors
Stevenson—pathetically
Conrad—interminably culminating, excessive, penetrates, sadden, incorrigible
Stevenson—laden with showers, ran riot

EXERCISE No. 6

Mistakes	Correct Usage
1. invite	invitation
2. humans	human beings
3. irregardless	nevertheless
4. all enthused	enthusiastic
5. intrigued	interested
6. lot	great deal
7. nice, grand and elegant turn-out	charming, very well-dressed
8. in back of	behind
9. previous to me	before I did
10. Haven't you had no raising?	Around 1910, the popular form of this insult was "Were you born in a barn?" How can one correct what should never have been said in the first place? If you must say it,—"What was wrong with your up-bringing?"

EXERCISE No. 8

Colloquialisms: 3, 4, 6, 9
Slang: 2, 10, 11, 13, 17, 18
Good Use: 1, 5, 7, 8, 12, 14, 15, 16, 19

EXERCISE No. 9

Obsolete in Prose: 1, 2, 3, 4, 5, 6
Genteelisms: 7, 8, 9, 10
Vulgarisms: 21, 23, 25, 26, 27
Good Use: 11, 12, 13, 14, 15, 16, 17, 18, 19, 20, 22, 24,

EXERCISE NO. 10

Jargon: 3, 5, 6, 9, 12, 13

EXERCISE NO. 12

1. proposition
2. evergreens
3. affairs
4. Blake wrote *bow*
5. griffin

6. breath-bereaving insolence
7. luxuries, necessities
8. the biter bit
9. rusty cannon balls
10. artist

EXERCISE NO. 13

1. cousins
2. ape
3. peck
4. incoherence
5. bellyful

6. part and parcel
7. Joyce wrote *apple-pie*
8. flowers
9. cessation
10. voltage

EXERCISE NO. 34

Common: 5, 9, 14, 20, 36
Literary: 4, 8, 19, 27, 28
Colloquial: 6, 13, 21, 30, 31
Scientific: 1, 11, 18, 24, 34

Foreign: 2, 12, 16, 25, 35
Dialectal: 3, 15, 29, 37, 40
Slang: 22, 26, 32, 38, 39
Technical: 7, 10, 17, 23, 33

EXERCISE NO. 40

a) djinn, jinn, inn, in, id, I
b) eyeless, eye, eyes, yes, less, eel, lee, lye, else, lees
c) trotter, otter, rotter, rot, trot, to, tort, retort, or, tot, tote, tor, toe, roc, ret, err, rote
d) mammal, ma'am, lam, ma, am, la, ala, lama
e) April, pul, rip, lip, la, rap, par, air, pair, lair, pa, la, lira

EXERCISE NO. 46

AG: 1. agitation 2. litigation 3. agenda 4. mitigate 5. variegated.

APT: 1. adaptability 2. aptitude 3. inept 4. attitudes.

ART: 1. inert 2. artifact 3. artless 4. artificial 5. artful 6. artifice.

AUD: 1. inaudible 2. audience 3. obedience 4. disobedience 5. audit.

CAN: 1. enchantment 2. accentuated 3. canto 4. recant 5. accented.

CAP: 1. anticipation 2. capacious 3. recipient 4. susceptible 5. incapable.

CAPIT: 1. recapitulation 2. precipitate 3. precipitous 4. precipitant 5. capitulation.

CED: 1. intercession 2. decease 3. predecessor 4. accession 5. accessories 6. accessible.

CERN: 1. discretion 2. discernible 3. secrecy 4. secretive 5. discreet.

CLAM: 1. proclamation 2. acclaim 3. exclamatory 4. claimant 5. declamation.

CLAUS: 1. recluse 2. excludes 3. conclude 4. inclusion 5. inclose.

COR: 1. courageous 2. accord 3. discord 4. concord 5. cordial.

CRED: 1. creditable 2. incredible 3. credulity 4. discredit 5. creed.

CUR: 1. assurance 2. procure 3. security 4. curate 5. curator 6. accuracy 7. reassures.

CURR: 1. precursor 2. cursory 3. occurrence 4. concur 5. discursive.

DAT: 1. antedates 2. data 3. editorship 4. extradition 5. absconded.

DIC: 1. diction 2. contradict 3. malediction 4. contradict.

DIGN: 1. dignitary 2. indignity 3. disdain 4. indignation.

DUC: 1. education 2. inducing 3. duke 4. produce 5. introduction 6. duchess 7. seduced 8. ducats 9. abducted 10. induced 11. conduct 12. duchy 13. traduced.

EQU: 1. adequate 2. equivalent 3. equinoctial 4. equator.

FAC: 1. defeated 2. feat 3. difficulty 4. benefactor 5. surfeit 6. fact 7. infected 8. forfeiture 9. difficulty 10. artificial 11. proficient 12. certificate 13. efficient 14. official 15. manufactory 16. efficiency 17. benefactor 18. factions 19. facilitate 20. forfeit 21. fashionable 22. counterfeit 23. feasible 24. factitious.

FER: 1. referee 2. proffered 3. different 4. delay 5. prelate 6. related 7. correlation 8. fertility 9. relative 10. vociferous 11. relations 12. floriferous 13. fructiferous 14. coniferous 15. different 16. conference 17. sufferance 18. ferry 19. delayed 20. circumference 21. pestiferous.

FORM: 1. deformity 2. transformation 3. reformer 4. conform 5. informalities 6. form 7. information 8. uniform 9. conformable.

FRANG: 1. fragment 2. suffrage 3. frail 4. infringements 5. fractures 6. frailty 7. fraction.

GER: 1. belligerent 2. gerunds 3. jester 4. suggested 5. indigestion 6. congestion 7. gesticulations 8. registration 9. vicegerent.

GRAT: 1. disgrace 2. gratification 3. agreed 4. grace 5. congratulation 6. disagreed 7. gratitude 8. gratuity.

HAB: 1. debility 2. inhibitions 3. habits 4. debt 5. habitation 6. habiliments 7. enable 8. disabled 9. exhibition.

JECT: 1. rejection 2. dejection 3. abject 4. jetty 5. ejaculation 6. jetsam 7. ejected 8. adjacent 9. injection 10. conjectured.

JUNG: 1. joints 2. joiner 3. jointly 4. conjugal 5. subjugate 6. injunction 7. adjoined.

LEG: 1. collector's 2. intellect 3. eligible 4. selection 5. Legion 6. legacy 7. elegance 8. neglected 9. lecture 10. dialectics 11. recollect 12. dialects 13. legends 14. illegible 15. collection.

MAN: 1. managed 2. manoeuvre 3. amanuensis 4. manifesto 5. emancipation 6. manacles 7. manner 8. manager 9. maintained 10. manufactory 11. manual 12. manuscript.

MITT: 1. promised 2. admit 3. emissary 4. permit 5. remit 6. remittance 7. commission 8. submit 9. missile.

MOD: 1. modish 2. modest 3. commodious 4. modern 5. modulations.

MOV: 1. motion 2. automobile 3. momentum 4. commotion 5. movie 6. mob 7. mobilized 8. removal.

NOT: 1. noblemen 2. incognito 3. ignorant 4. not 5. notary 6. notifying 7. recognition 8. annotations 9. ignorance 10. ignoble 11. notorious 12. denoted.

PAND: 1. passage 2. passengers 3. trespassed 4. compass 5. pass 6. pace 7. expanse.

PAR: 1. apparatus 2. irreparable 3. repair 4. severing 5. preparations 6. prepare 7. several.

PART: 1. party 2. partner 3. partial 4. department 5. parcels 6. particle 7. departed 8. apartment 9. particular 10. portions 11. compartments 12. partition 13. parse 14. parts.

PET: 1. petitions 2. petulant 3. impetuous 4. incompetent 5. impetus 6. appetite 7. competent 8. competitors.

PLAC: 1. please 2. pleasant 3. implacable 4. pleasure 5. placid.

PLIC: 1. reply 2. application 3. employment 4. simple 5. apply 6. comply 7. employer 8. employs 9. multiply 10. displayed 11. simplicity 12. plait 13. simplify 14. complications 15. replica 16. supple 17. plexus.

PON: 1. deposits 2. impostor 3. propound 4. positivists 5. imposition 6. opponents 7. exponents 8. duplex 9. juxtaposition.

PORT: 1. deportation 2. port 3. sport 4. imported 5. important 6. report 7. support 8. comport.

PREHEND: 1. apprentice 2. surprised 3. comprehension 4. enterprise 5. prize 6. prehensile 7. prison 8. impregnable.

QUER: 1. conquest 2. conqueror 3. inquisitive 4. questions 5. disquisition 6. requirements 7. perquisites 8. requisition 9. acquisition.

RAP: 1. rapt 2. rapids 3. ravishing 4. ravenous 5. surreptitiously 6. ravaged 7. rapine.

REG: 1. regime 2. corrective 3. reign 4. ruler 5. insurrections 6. incorrigible 7. rector 8. dressed 9. erection.

RUPT: 1. eruption 2. disrupt 3. routine 4. incorruptible 5. bankrupt 6. irruption.

SAL: 1. assailed 2. desultory 3. salmon 4. salient 5. exultation.

SCRIB: 1. circumscribed 2. ascribed 3. manuscript 4. postscript 5. Scriptures.

SED: 1. assiduous 2. president 3. insidious 4. possessed 5. residues.

SENT: 1. sensible 2. consent 3. nonsensical 4. sentiments 5. sententious 6. resent 7. scent 8. presentiment 9. sentence 10. resentful 11. senseless.

SEQU: 1. persecution 2. sued 3. executors 4. pursuance 5. suitable 6. obsequies 7. executive 8. suit 9. suite 10. obsequious.

SERV: 1. conservative 2. unobserved 3. conservatory 4. observers 5. reserve 6. unreserved 7. preserve 8. reservoir 9. preservative.

SIGN: 1. assignation 2. resign 3. significance 4. signet 5. signal 6. designer 7. consignment.

SPEC: 1. spectacle 2. auspices 3. spectators 4. spyglass 5. expect 6. inspector 7. prospect 8. inauspicious 9. prospective 10. specimen 11. respectable 12. perspicacity 13. perspicuity.

STA: 1. substantial 2. constable 3. arrest 4. circumstantial 5. circumstances 6. estate 7. destitute 8. assistance 9. existence 10. constant 11. restitution 12. distant 13. stately 14. station 15. institution 16. stationery 17. stanza 18. restive 19. irresistible 20. desist 21. insist.

STRING: 1. distressing 2. restricted 3. strait 4. strainer 5. restraint 6. constricts 7. constrained.

TANG: 1. contingent 2. contagious 3. contagion 4. tact 5. tangent 6. contact 7. integrity 8. integration 9. attainments.

TEN: 1. discontent 2. continued 3. maintain 4. tenacious 5. impertinent 6. retinue 7. continual 8. sustenance 9. abstain.

TEND: 1. subtend 2. pretender 3. attendants 4. ostentation 5. portents 6. pretense 7. tendency 8. superintendent.

TRAH: 1. subtrahend 2. portray 3. distraught 4. attract 5. trace 6. trail.

UT: 1. utensil 2. utility 3. misuse 4. perusal 5. useless 6. abuse.

VEN: 1. advent 2. convention 3. adventure 4. avenue 5. event 6. venture 7. circumvent 8. covenant 9. inventory 10. revenue.

VID: 1. evident 2. evidence 3. advice 4. revisit 5. revise 6. survey 7. surveillance 8. visitant.

VOC: 1. equivocation 2. advocate 3. revoke 4. vociferous 5. vocation 6. avocation 7. convocation 8. vouch.

EXERCISE No. 47

ARCH: 1. architrave 2. oligarchy 3. monarchy 4. anarchy 5. archangels 6. hierarchy.

AGON: 1. protagonist 2. agonizing 3. antagonist.

ALLOS: 1. allotrope 2. allegory.

ASTER: 1. astrolabe 2. astrology 3. astral.

BIBLOS: 1. Bible 2. bibliomancy 3. bibliography 4. Biblical.

DEMOS: 1. democracy 2. demagogue 3. epidemic.

DRAO: 1. dramaturgy 2. dramatize 3. melodramatic.

DUNAMIS: 1. dynamics 2. hydrodynamics 3. aerodynamics.

EIDOS: 1. anthropoid 2. geoid 3. spheroid.

ERGON: 1. ergometer 2. energy 3. ergs 4. metallurgy.

GE: 1. geology 2. geomorphology 3. geodetic 4. geometry.

GRAPHO: 1. historiographer 2. graphic 3. autographed 4. biography 5. photographs 6. typographer's.

HUDOR: 1. hydrant 2. hydrophobia 3. dehydrated.

HOMOS: 1. homonyms 2. homographs.

IDIOS: 1. idiosyncrasy 2. idiom 3. idiocy 4. idiot.

ISOS: 1. isotherms 2. isobars 3. isosceles.

KOSMOS: 1. microcosm 2. macrocosm 3. cosmic 4. cosmogony 5. cosmos 6. cosmography.

METRON: 1. hexameters 2. geometry 3. symmetry 4. anemometer 5. barometer 6. thermometer.

MONOS: 1. monarch 2. monocle 3. monotony 4. monogamy 5. monogram 6. monomania.

NEOS: 1. neophyte 2. neon 3. neolithic.

NOMOS: 1. gastronomy 2. economy.

PHOBOS: 1. claustrophobia 2. phobias 3. hydrophobia.

PHOS: 1. phosphate 2. photosynthesis.

PHILOS: 1. philosophy 2. philharmonic 3. philanthropy.

PHONE: 1. symphony 2. euphonious 3. phonograph 4. phonetics.

PHUSIS: 1. physic 2. physician 3. physicist 4. metaphysics 5. physiography 6. physiognomy.

POIEO: 1. poetry 2. onomatopoeia.

PROTOS: 1. protomartyr 2. protoplasm.

PSUCHE: 1. psychoanalysis 2. psychotherapy.

SKOPEO: 1. stethoscope 2. bishop 3. episcopal.

TECHNE: 1. architect's 2. technique 3. pyrotechnic.

THESIS: 1. hypothesis 2. epithets 3. anathemas 4. synthesis.

TOPOS: 1. toparchy 2. topic 3. topography.

ZOON: 1. zodiac 2. protozoan 3. zoölogy.

Exercise No. 61

None of them is of Anglo-Saxon origin. Most of them are clipped forms from Latin, or in a few cases, Greek derivatives. Yet they sound like good old Anglo-Saxon words. *Verbum sap.*

Exercise No. 63

1. report
2. deed
3. adaptation
4. aggregate
5. entertainment
6. praise
7. reason, reasoning
8. care
9. pull
10. equilibrium
11. low
12. nativity
13. respiration
14. cremate
15. break
16. reason
17. hazard
18. transform, alter
19. ease
20. assembly
21. authority, check
22. lid, shelter
23. stream
24. injury
25. decease
26. measure
27. land
28. boundary, margin
29. consequence
30. mistake
31. trade
32. sensitivity
33. falsehood, story
34. regulation, rule
35. consonance
36. loathing
37. record
38. wit
39. growth
40. underwriting
41. occupy
42. unite
43. erudition
44. even, flat
45. confine
46. fluid
47. privation
48. weight
49. extent, degree
50. center
51. impel
52. melody
53. folk
54. want
55. tender
56. sentiment
57. system
58. ache
59. delight, satisfaction
60. dot
61. potency
62. charge
63. yield
64. gain
65. objection
66. discipline
67. shove
68. inquiry
69. scope
70. pace, velocity
71. response
72. recompense
73. law
74. ascend
75. ego
76. sensibility
77. gender
78. shadow
79. concussion
80. edge
81. bulk
82. slumber
83. slant
84. kind
85. asseveration
86. elasticity
87. intimation
88. prop
89. astonish
90. organization
91. object
92. duration
93. business
94. difficulty
95. spiral
96. manner
97. script
98. term
99. toil, labor
100. injury

Exercise No. 66

ABLE:

1. proficient 2. competent 3. qualified 4. adroit 5. dexterous 6. adequate 7. apt 8. cogent.

ADDITION

1. annexation 2. accretion 3. accumulation 4. augmentation 5. increment 6. supplement 7. addendum 8. appendage 9. adjunct 10. reenforcement 11. agglomeration.

ANGRY: 1. irascible 2. exasperated 3. virulent 4. acrimonious 5. irritable 6. infuriated 7. maddened 8. wrathful.

ATTENTION: 1. observance 2. vigilance 3. scrutiny 4. surveillance 5. heedfulness 6. circumspection 7. cognizance 8. alertness 9. inspection 10. solicitude.

AUTHORITY: 1. authority 2. predominance 3. corroboration 4. ascendancy 5. prestige 6. credential 7. jurisdiction 8. prerogative 9. supremacy 10. voucher.

AUTOMATIC: 1. unintelligent 2. unintentional 3. unthinking 4. impulsive 5. mechanical 6. unwitting 7. spontaneous 8. instinctive 9. involuntary.

BAD: 1. pernicious 2. depraved 3. onerous 4. malignant 5. detestable 6. detrimental 7. noxious 8. unsatisfactory 9. deplorable.

BEHAVIOR: 1. bearing 2. demeanor 3. breeding 4. deportment.

BELIEF: 1. dogmas 2. assurance 3. predilection 4. vagaries 5. credence 6. supposition.

BROKEN: 1. disconnected 2. collapsed 3. ruptured 4. severed 5. shattered.

BUSINESS: 1. functions 2. vocation 3. profession 4. employment 5. pursuit 6. crafts 7. mission 8. career.

CARE: 1. adversity 2. discretion 3. prudence 4. solicitude 5. anxiety 6. precaution 7. circumspection 8. vigilance 9. forethought.

CERTAIN: 1. inevitable 2. indisputable 3. infallible 4. incontestable 5. positive 6. undeniable 7. definite 8. reliable 9. established 10. secure.

CHIEF: 1. salient 2. cardinal 3. vital 4. essential 5. significant 6. paramount 7. weighty 8. influential 9. momentous 10. consequential.

COMMON: 1. trite 2. hackneyed 3. habitual 4. widespread 5. normal 6. customary 7. rife 8. conventional 9. accustomed 10. prevalent.

COMPARISON: 1. ratios 2. parable 3. identification 4. metaphor 5. simile 6. similitude 7. allegories 8. similarity 9. parallelism 10. relationship.

COMPETITION: 1. rivalry 2. tournament 3. antagonism 4. contest 5. contention 6. disputation 7. opposition 8. competition.

COMPLETE: 1. achieved 2. compete 3. fulfilled 4. dispatched 5. intact.

COMPLEX: 1. labyrinthine 2. tangle 3. intricate 4. complicated 5. involved 6. entangled.

CONDITION: 1. stipulation 2. predicament 3. plight 4. state 5. category.

CONNECTION: 1. consanguinity 2. relationship 3. kinship 4. relationship 5. junction 6. affiliation 7. alliance 8. adherence.

CONSCIOUS: 1. rational 2. intelligent 3. cognizant 4. realizing 5. discerning.

DECISION: 1. conclusion 2. verdict 3. arbitrament 4. estimation 5. deduction 6. determination 7. decision.

DELICATE: 1. fragile 2. exquisite 3. unsubstantial 4. frail 5. delicate 6. scrupulous 7. discriminatory.

DEPENDENT: 1. enthralled 2. contingent.

DESTRUCTION: 1. abolition 2. disorganization 3. extermination 4. eradication 5. annihilation 6. demolition 7. obliteration 8. sabotage 9. devastation 10. cataclysm.

DEVELOPMENT: 1. construction 2. formation 3. extension 4. unfoldment 5. evolution 6. expansion.

DIFFERENT: 1. heterogeneous 2. variegated 3. incongruous 4. diversified.

DIRECTION: 1. tendency 2. bearings 3. regulations 4. management 5. auspices 6. supervision 7. tutelage.

DISTANCE: 1. aloofness 2. extension 3. remoteness 4. span 5. separation.

DISTRIBUTION: 1. appropriation 2. allotment 3. radiation 4. dissemination 5. broadcasts.

EDUCATION: 1. guidance 2. attainments 3. training 4. inculcation 5. scholarship 6. breeding.

ELASTIC: 1. rebounding 2. elastic 3. expansive 4. flexible.

EQUAL: 1. tantamount 2. identical 3. synonymous 4. equal.

EXISTENCE: 1. vitality 2. subsistence 3. reality 4. entity 5. essence.

EXPANSION: 1. inflation 2. enlargement 3. dilation 4. amplification 5. aggrandisement.

EXPERIENCE: 1. cognizance 2. insight 3. sophistication 4. enlightenment 5. comprehension 6. recognition.

FALSE: 1. counterfeit 2. perjured 3. imitation 4. pseudo- 5. fallacious 6. invalid 7. illusory 8. perfidious.

FERTILE: 1. copious 2. life-giving 3. generative 4. prolific 5. fecund.

FOOLISH: 1. misguided 2. frivolous 3. injudicious 4. maudlin 5. asinine 6. foolhardy.

FORCE: 1. goad 2. coercion 3. vehemence 4. necessitated 5. regiment 6. soldiery.

FREQUENT: 1. habitual 2. prevalent 3. inveterate 4. reiterated 5. incessant.

GENERAL: 1. catholic 2. customary 3. widespread 4. encyclopedic 5. accustomed 6. panoramic.

GROWTH: 1. luxuriance 2. vegetation 3. dilation 4. growth 5. development.

HELP: 1. assistance 2. avail 3. succor 4. coöperation 5. weal 6. ministrations.

IDEA: 1. ideas 2. concept 3. reflection 4. supposition 5. sentiment 6. impression.

IMPORTANT: 1. momentous 2. eventful 3. vital.

IMPULSE: 1. impetus 2. instigations 3. momentum 4. spurt.

INDUSTRY: 1. exertion 2. assiduity 3. perseverance 4. constancy 5. persistence 6. sedulous.

INSTRUMENT: 1. operator 2. implements 3. apparatus.

KNOWLEDGE: 1. scholarship 2. lore 3. erudition 4. learning 5. apprehension.

LANGUAGE: 1. expression 2. barbarism 3. vocabulary 4. diction 5. vernacular 6. idiom.

LIKE: 1. homogeneous 2. similar 3. uniform 4. similar 5. resembling.

PROCESS: 1. routine 2. performance 3. process 4. disposition 5. evolution 6. transition.

QUALITY: 1. traits 2. endowments 3. faculties 4. quality 5. peculiarities.

REGULAR: 1. invariable 2. consistent 3. undiversified 4. symmetrical 5. unbroken.

RELATION: 1. relations 2. affinities 3. consanguinity 4. alliance 5. lineage 6. similarity.

RELIGION: 1. conversion 2. religion 3. piety 4. regeneration 5. veneration 6. theology.

REPRESENTATIVE: 1. exponent 2. trustees 3. legate 4. emissary 5. deputy 6. delegates 7. nominee.

RESPONSIBLE: 1. accountable 2. prudent 3. veracious 4. conscientious 5. regardful.

SELECTION: 1. selection 2. option 3. preference 4. specification.

SEPARATE: 1. insular 2. asunder 3. bisect 4. partition 5. disintegrating 6. dismembered 7. rupture.

SOCIETY: 1. civilization 2. humanity 3. syndicates 4. society.

TRUE: 1. mathematical 2. demonstrable 3. infallible 4. incontrovertible 5. indisputable 6. unimpeachable.

UNIT: 1. integer 2. companionless 3. isolated 4. ace 5. solitary.

USE: 1. expediency 2. recourse 3. manipulation 4. exploitation 5. etiquette 6. prevalence 7. disposal.

VALUE: 1. assessment 2. value 3. estimation 4. productiveness 5. utilization 6. expenditure.

VIEW: 1. contemplation 2. survey 3. prospects 4. discernment 5. scrutiny.

WASTE: 1. prodigality 2. overplus 3. squandering 4. dross.

WEIGHT: 1. lading   2. cargo   3. ballast   4. preponderance
     5. emphasis   6. weight   7. potency.

WISE: 1. sagacious   2. perspicacious   3. judicious   4. erudite   5. provident.

EXERCISE No. 68

1. lawyer   2. literary critic   3. phony legal style with a trace of the logician   4. professor of education   5. advertising man   6. medico.

EXERCISE No. 69

1. vibration	34. combustion	67. cartilage
2. velocity	35. buoyancy	68. carbon dioxide
3. transmission	36. battery	69. capillary
4. thermometer	37. barometer	70. bacteria
5. solution	38. artesian	71. absorption
6. saturated	39. alkali	72. variations
7. resonant	40. acid	73. tubercles
8. resistance	41. germination	74. tilth
9. reflection	42. embryonic	75. subsoil
10. radiation	43. perennial	76. Grafting
11. neutral	44. chlorophyll	77. silo
12. negative	45. Botany	78. pruning
13. meter	46. sterilize	79. propagation
14. magnetism	47. skeleton	80. pollination
15. lever	48. secretes	81. Nitrogen
16. Isothermic	49. Saliva	82. mold
17. insulate	50. respiration	83. mildew
18. indissoluble	51. pasteurize	84. hybrid
19. incandescent	52. oxygen	85. humus
20. hydrogen	53. nutrition	86. Horticulture
21. hydraulic	54. inhale	87. blight
22. humidity	55. infection	88. biennials
23. filter	56. heart	89. succulent
24. fermentation	57. glands	90. sediment
25. erosion	58. germ	91. nutritive
26. elements	59. gastric	92. laboratory
27. electricity	60. fumigate	93. evaporation
28. dynamo	61. exhale	94. coagulation
29. distillation	62. disinfect	95. cellulose
30. density	63. digestion	96. Carbohydrates
31. decompose	64. corpuscles	97. conductor
32. contraction	65. circulation	98. fulcrum
33. compression	66. cell	99. solvent
		100. protoplasm

All but ten are in general literary use, though not always in the scientific sense.

EXERCISE No. 71

1. (3)	20. (2)	39. (3)	58. (1)
2. (1)	21. (4)	40. (2)	59. (1)
3. (2)	22. (1)	41. (4)	60. (1)
4. (1)	23. (2)	42. (1)	61. (4)
5. (4)	24. (3)	43. (3)	62. (2)
6. (3)	25. (2)	44. (2)	63. (2)
7. (3)	26. (3)	45. (3)	64. (2)
8. (4)	27. (3)	46. (4)	65. (1)
9. (1)	28. (3)	47. (2)	66. (2)
10. (1)	29. (4)	48. (1)	67. (2)
11. (2)	30. (2)	49. (2)	68. (3)
12. (1)	31. (2)	50. (4)	69. (2)
13. (3)	32. (3)	51. (3)	70. (3)
14. (1)	33. (2)	52. (2)	71. (3)
15. (4)	34. (1)	53. (1)	72. (2)
16. (1)	35. (2)	54. (1)	73. (2)
17. (2)	36. (2)	55. (2)	74. (4)
18. (1)	37. (3)	56. (1)	75. (2)
19. (2)	38. (2)	57. (2)	

EXERCISE No. 73

1. condescension 2. snobbery 3. bastard elegance 4. bastard elegance
5. condescension 6. snobbery 7. pedantry 8. fatuity 9. blatant egotism
10. schoolgirl coyness 11. rudeness 12. ghastly gayety 13. fatuity 14.
jolly-doggism 15. jolly-doggism 16. gush.

INDEX

INDEX

A, an, 71
Abbreviations, dictionary, 43, 46; style rule, 264
Able, 149, 274
Accentuation in dictionaries, 42
Act, ag, 75
Adams, Sir John, quoted, 178
Addition, 149, 274
Adjectives, synonyms, 140, 149-164
Affixes, 68, 72; in active use, 69
After-dinner speeches, 234
Agon, 95, 273
Aim, 147
Ain't, 23
Alfred, King of Wessex, 61
Allen's *Synonyms,* 55
Allos, 95, 273
Alpha privative, 71
American and British English, 246
Amoral, 71
Anagrams, game of, 58
Anatomy of Melancholy, The, 63
Anglo-Saxon Chronicle, 61
Anglo Saxon words, 57, 60, 61, 64, 65; prefixes, 68, 109; suffixes, 110; synonyms, 132
Angry, 150, 275
Announcer, radio, art of, 237
Anthropology, terminology, 189
Antonyms, 38; dictionaries, 55
Apt, 75, 269
Arch, 95, 273
Architecture, terminology, 191
Aretino, Pietro, quoted, 51
Argument, art of, 216
Aristophanes, 172
Art, 75, 269
Art, terminology, 191
Ash, John, dictionary, 124
Aster or astron, 95, 273
Astronomy, terminology, 192
Attention, 150, 152, 275
Aud, audit, 76, 269
Authority, 150, 275
Authors, masters of diction, 31
Automatic, 151, 275

Automobile, terminology, 193
Aviation, terminology, 194
Ayres, vocabulary estimate, 13

Babu English, 112
Bad, 151, 275
Balieff, M., 237
Balzac, Honoré de, 177
Barham, Richard Harris, *Ingoldsby Legends,* 177
Barrie, James M., 226
Bartlett's *Familiar Quotations,* 55
Basic English, 39, 136; common words from list of, 136; verbs, 136; nouns, 137, 149; suggested by Pidgin English? 177
Beaumarchais, Pierre Augustin Caronde, 245
Beauty vocabulary, 15
Bedlam, 127
Behavior, 151, 275
Behaviorism, terminology, 206
Belief, 151, 275
Bennett, Arnold, 17, 230
Bethlehem Hospital, 128
Bible, vocabulary, 64
Bibliography, 265-266
Biblos or biblion, 95, 273
Bind, 143
Biology, terminology, 194
Blake, William, 182
Bluff, 147
Book of Common Prayer, 64
Boswell, James, quoted, 225
Bottomly, Horatio, 128
Brewer, *Dictionary of Phrase and Table,* excerpt, 167
Broken, 152, 275
Brown, Ivor, 34
Burton, Robert, 63, 169
Business, 152, 275
Butler, Samuel, quoted, 35, 37, 179

Cabal, 129
Can, cant, 76, 139, 269
Cap, capt, captus, 76, 269

Capit, 76, 269
Capitalization, style rule, 259
Care, 152, 275
Carew, Richard, 170
Carlyle, Thomas, 14, 112, 124, 226
Carroll, Lewis, 172, 226
Causerie style, 245
Ced, cess, 77, 270
Celtic words, 60, 63
Century Junior Dictionary, Thorndike's, 47, 53, 59; specimen page, 52
Cern, cret, 77, 270
Certain, 152, 275
Cervantes, 21
Chamberlin, William Henry, quoted, 44
Chancellor, 127
Character, 45, 46, 119
Chaucer, 62, 64
Chemistry, terminology, 195
Chesterfield, Lord, quoted, 208, 216, 222; as conversationalist, 222; on manners, 223
Chesterton, Gilbert K., 240
Chief, 153, 275
China, Pidgin English, 177
Chisel, 175
Churchill, Lady Randolph, 229
Clam, clamat, 77, 270
Classical derivatives, 57, 60-63, 65; *see also* Greek words: Latin words
Classical word families, 66-111
Claus, 77, 270
Clause, style rule, 264
Clemens, Samuel L., *see* Twain, Mark
Cohen, Morris R., 208
Coleridge, Samuel Taylor, 45, 226
College Standard (dictionary), 53
Collegiate Dictionary, Webster's, 42, 45, 46, 51, 58
Colloquialism, definition, 25
Come, 138
Comedy and conversation, 215, 229
Comic compounds, 172
Common, 153, 275
Comparison, 141, 153, 275
Competition, 153, 275
Complete, 154, 275
Complex, 154, 275
Compound words, 172
Concise Oxford Dictionary, 47, 48, 51
Condition, 154, 275
"Confusions" in vocabulary tests, 12, 15
Connection, 154, 276
Connotation, 36

Conrad, Joseph, 20, 21, **217**
Conscious, 154, 276
Context, defined, 35
Contrast, 141, 142
Conversation, average vocabulary, 1, 12; art of, 215-233; extractive method, 218; fireside, club, and tavern talk, 219; receptive listening, 220; polished style, 222; blunt and oracular style, 224; whimsical style, 225; epigrammatic style, 226; comedy in: provocative style, 229; faults in, examples, 231-233; speeches: introductions: announcements, 234-238; oral and written expression, 239-249
Crabbe's *English Synonyms,* 55
Crack down, 175
Crawl, 138
Cred, credit, 78, 270
Cret, cern, 77, 270
Cooper, Fenimore, 131
Cor, cord, cordi, 78, 270
Cowper, William, 242
Cur, curat, 78, 270
Curmudgeon, 124
Curr, curs, 78, 270

Dat, 79, 270
Decision, 155, 276
Defoe, Daniel, 2, 64
Degradation of meaning, 120-123
Delicate, 155, 276
Demos, 95, 273
Denotation, 35
Dependent, 155, 276
De Quincey, Thomas, 238
Derivation of words, 44, 56, 60-111
Derogatory metaphor, slang as, 169
Destruction, 155, 276
Development, 155, 276
Diacritical markings, in dictionaries, 42
Dialogue, for radio, 242; talkie, 244; *see also* Conversation
Dic, dict, 79, 270
Dickens, Charles, 125, 232, 233
Diction, masters of, 31; oral and written, 239; fine points, 257; common errors, 258; *see also* Words
Dictionaries, number of word-entries in Webster, 40, 56; use of, 42-59; accentuation-markings, 42; symbols: abbreviations, 43, 46; derivation of words, 44; most comprehensive, 47-51; desk sets, 51-53, 265; special

kinds, 53-58, 59, 265; games and recreations, 58-59
Dictionary of American Slang, 56, 176
Dictionary of Modern English Usage, 59, 189
Dictionary of Phrase and Fable, Brewer's, excerpt, 167
Die, slang synonyms for, 175
Different, 156, 276
Dign, 79, 270
Direction, 156, 276
Disraeli, Benjamin, 218
Distance, 156, 276
Distortion of words, 172
Distribution, 156, 276
Do, 139
Dog-Latin, 177
Don Quixote, 21
Dos Passos, John, 248
Doublets, 62, 133
Douglas, Norman, 32, 36, 42, 50, 217
Drao, 95, 273
Drummond of Hawthornden, 219
Dryden, John, 37; quoted, 169, 220; conversation, 220
Duc, duct, 79, 270
Dunamis, 96, 273

Economics, terminology, 196
Edgeworth, Maria, 218
Education, 156, 276
Eidos, 96, 273
Elastic, 157, 276
Eliot, George, 226
Ellis, Havelock, 129, 245
Elton, Oliver, 168
Emerson, Ralph Waldo, 2, 32
English Idioms, 167
English language, number of words, 39; multiple meanings, 45; vocabulary of, chart and description, 49; linguistic origin, 57, 60-111; compared to geological strata, 64; chart, 65; preserved by mountaineers, 112; difference between American and British, 246; see also Basic English
English Past and Present, 173
English Synonyms, Crabbe's, 55
English Synonyms, Antonymes, and Prepositions, Fernald's, 55
Epigram, in conversation, 215, 226; quotations from Oscar Wilde, 228
Equ, 80, 270
Equal, 157, 276

Ergon, 96, 273
Errors of the learned, 124
Etymological Dictionary of the English Language, Skeat's, 56
Eupeptic, 13
Euphemism, 121
Evelyn, John, 14
Example, 148
Existence, 157, 276
Expansion, 157, 276
Experience, 157, 276
Expression, differences between oral and written, 239-249
Extension of meaning, 114

Fac, fact, factur, 80, 270
False, 157, 276
Fay, Frank, 237
Fer lat, 81, 270
Fernald, James C., English Synonyms, Antonyms, and Prepositions, 55
Fertile, 158, 276
Fielding, Henry, 21
Figurative extension of meaning, 44
Finley, John H., 236
Flaubert, Gustave, 20
Fly, 138
Folk etymology, 123
Foolish, 158, 276
Force, 158, 276
Foreign Friends of the Emerald Isle, 172
Foreign origins, see Linguistic origin of words
Foreign words and phrases, use of, 122
Form, 81, 270
Forms and terms, style rule, 263
Fowler, H. W., Dictionary of Modern English Usage, 59, 189; quoted, 120; definition of jargon, 178
Fowler, H. W. and F. G., 167; The King's English, excerpt, 26; wit, in Concise Oxford Dictionary, 51
Frank, fract, fractur, 81, 270
Freeman, R. Austin, 183
French words, 62, 64, 65
Frequency numbers of Thorndike, see Thorndike, E. L.
Frequent, 158, 276
Funk and Wagnall's dictionary, see Standard Dictionary

Galsworthy, John, 173
Games and recreations, dictionary, 58

Ge, 96, 273
General, 159, 276
Generalization of meaning, 114
Genteelism, definition, 25
Geology, terminology, 198
Ger, gest, gestur, 82, 270
Germanic element in English, 57, 58, 61, 65
Get, 138
Get, got, 167
Ghost-words, 124
Gilbert, W. S., 226
Give, 138
Go, 137
Goethe, 45, 215
Going, 138
Gossip, 230
Got, 167
Graph, 67
Grapho, 67, 96, 273
Grat, 82, 270
Greek words, 57, 61, 63, 65, 72, 119; roots, 66, 105-107; stems, 67, 95-100; prefixes, 68, 70, 109; suffixes, 68, 70, 71, 109
Greeks, use of irony, 123
Greenough and Kittredge, *Words and Their Ways in English Speech,* 28, 113, 118; excerpts, 25, 128
Grog, 126
Growth, 159, 276

Hab, habit, 82, 270
Harmony, 144
Harris, Frank, 227
Have, 139
Have got, 167
Hazlitt, William, 2; quoted, 36
Help, 159, 277
Henry, O., slang, 165, 168
"High-ceiling" tests, 29, 213
History of words, 47, 123-130
Homos, 96, 273
Hudor, 96, 273
Human nature, terms relating to, 119, 126
Humor, 125
Huxley, Aldous, 32; quoted, 232
Huxley, Julian, 32
Huxley, Thomas Henry, 32; quoted, 33
Hyperbole, 122
Hyphenation, 43
Hyphens, style rule, 262

Idea, 159, 277
Ideas, and words, 17; indispensable, 39; words classified under key-ideas, 53
Idioms, 27, 167, 168
Idios, 97, 273
Image, 146
Important, 159, 277
Impulse, 160, 277
Indispensable ideas, 39
Indo-European roots, 57, 67; number of, in English, 56
Industry, 160, 277
Inge, Dean, 31
Ingoldsby Legends, 177
Instrument, 160, 277
International language, 39
Introducing speakers, 235
Irony, 123, 218
Isos, 97, 273

James, Henry, 20
Jargon, 40; defined, 25, 176, 177; use of, 168, 176; special and technical vocabularies, 181-214
Ject, 83, 271
Jingo, 128
Johnson, Hugh, 175
Johnson, Dr. Samuel, 124; quoted, 24, 225, 230; conversation, 218, 224
Jonson, Ben, quoted, 21, 125; conversation, 219
Journalese, 51
Journalistic, 51
Joyce, James, 60, 112, 172, 219
Jump, 138
Jung, junct, junctur, 83, 271

Keep, 138
Kent, Roland G., *Language and Philology,* 57
Key-ideas, words classified under, 53
Key-words in Basic English, 39
Keys to exercises, 267-279
Kind Words Club, 236
King's English, The, excerpt, 26
Kipling, Rudyard, 20
Kittredge, Professor, 167; *see also* Greenough and Kittredge
Knowledge, 160, 277
Kosmos, 97, 273

Lamb, Charles, 120, 242; conversation, 225
Language, 160, 277

Language and Philology, Kent's, 57
Languages, mixture of, in jargon, 176; difference between American and British English, 246
Lardner, Ring, 248
Latin words, 57, 64, 65, 120; first layer, 60; second layer, 61; third and fourth layers: present-day use, 63; roots, 66, 100-105; stems, 67, 75-95; prefixes, 68, 69, 107; suffixes, 68, 69, 108; synonyms, 132
Laughter, prohibition against, 222
Law, terminology, 200
Leg, lect, lectur, 83, 271
Leonardo da Vinci, quoted, 15; notebooks: modes of expression, 19
Let, 139
Letter-writing, 239; number of words used in, 1, 12
Lewis, Sinclair, 232, 233, 248; quoted, 180
Lexicographers, mistakes, 124
Life of Samuel Johnson, 225
Like, 160, 277
Linguistic origin of words, 57, 60-111; chart, 65
Listening and conversing, 215, 220
Literary terms, 178, 209-213
"Little languages," 177
Logos, 67, 97
Lousy, 169

Macaronic language, 176
McKnight, Professor, on slang, 176
Make, 139
Malapropisms, 174
Man (Latin stem), 84, 271
Manchester Guardian Weekly, excerpt, 34, 247
Mann, Thomas, quoted, 195
Manners, Chesterfield's doctrine, 223
Marriage à la Mode, excerpt, 220
Master of ceremonies, art of, 237
Mathematics, terminology, 200
Maupassant, Guy de, 20
Mawson, Sylvester, 53
May, 139
Meanings, *see* Word-meanings
Medicine, terminology, 202
Mencken, H. F., 32, 112, 248
Mental conceptions, words dealing with, 119, 126
Mental tests, terminology, 207
Meredith, George, quoted, 232

Metaphor, slang as, 169
Metron, 97, 273
Misfortune, 145
Mispronounced words, 43
Mistakes of the learned, 124
Mitt, Miss, 84, 271
Mod, 84, 271
Monos, 97, 273
Montagu, Lady Mary Wortley, 242
More, Hannah, quoted, 241
Mountaineers, phrases used by, 112
Mov, mot, 84, 271
Movies, terminology, 202
Mumford, Lewis, 197; quoted, 198
Munson, Gorham B., quoted, 179
Murray, Sir James, 49
Murray's Dictionary, 47; *see also Oxford English Dictionary*
Music, terminology, 203

Nagel, Ernest, quoted, 208
Names, nouns derived from, 126; from literature or history, 126, 127
Nathan, George Jean, 248
Nautical terms, 203
Neilson, William Allen, 51
Neos, 98, 273
New English Dictionary, 47; *see also Oxford English Dictionary*
New International, Webster's, 51; number of words in, 10, 56; excerpts, 51
Newcastle, Duke of, 241
Newman, John Henry, 31
Newspapers, number of words needed to read, 1, 12
Nomenclature of objects, processes, etc., methods of acquiring, 18, 66; *see also* Jargon
Nomos, 98, 273
Norman—French languages, 62
Not, 85, 271
Nouns, from proper names, 126; in Basic English, 137, 149; synonyms, 140, 149-164
Numbers, style rule, 262

OED, 49; *see also Oxford English Dictionary*
Ogden, C. K., Basic English, 39, 136
Ollendorf manuals, excerpts, 218
Omnibus words, 140
On the Study of Words, 28
"Operators," Basic, 137
Oral and written expression, 239-249

Oregon, University of, Committee on the Appreciation of the Fine Arts, 209
Orthological Institute, 39, 136
Oxford English Dictionary (OED.), 45, 47-50, 69, 71, 124, 166, 169, 173

Pand, pans, pass, 85, 271
Par, parat, 85, 271
Paragraph, style rule, 254
Parker, Dan, quoted, 174
Part, 86, 271
Partridge, Eric, *Slang*, 56, 176
Pater, Walter, 21, 22
Pathetic fallacy, 118
Pet, petit, 86, 271
Philos, 98, 273
Phobos, 98, 273
Phone, 98, 273
Phos, 98, 273
Phrasal verbs, 136; use in slang, 175
Phrasing, 27
Phusis, 98, 273
Physics, terminology, 204
Pidgin English, 112, 177
Plac, placit, 86, 271
Plato, quoted, 41, 45
Plic, plicat, plicit, 86, 271
Poetry, word-meanings, 36, 120
Poieo, 99, 273
Pon, posit, postur, 87, 271
Port, portat, 87, 271
Porter, William Sydney, *see* Henry, O.
Portland Oregonian, excerpt, 179
Portmanteau words, 172
Preachers, masters of diction, 31
Prefixes, Anglo-Saxon, 68, 109; Greek, 68, 70, 109; Latin, 68, 69, 107
Prehend prehens, 88, 271
Prepositions, dictionary, 55
Process, 161, 277
Profanity, 217
Projection of feeling, 119
Pronoun, style rule, 264
Pronunciation, 42, 43
Protos, 99, 273
Psuche, 99, 273
Psychology, terminology, 205, 206
Punctuation, style rule, 261
Put, 139

Quality, 161, 277
Quer, quisit, 88, 271
Question, art of, in conversation, 218
Quiller-Couch, Sir Arthur, 177

Quiz, 171
Quotations, books of, 55

Rabelais, comic compounds, 172
Rabutin, Count de Bussy, 240
Radiation, meaning extended by, 117
Radio, terminology, 207
Radio announcer, art of, 237
Radio scripts, 242; sample, 242-243
Ralegh, Sir Walter, quoted, 120
Rap, rapt, raptur, 88, 272
Reading for enlargement of vocabulary, 31
Reading vocabulary, 1, 12
Record, 145
Reg, rect, 88, 272
Regular, 161, 277
Relation, 161, 277
Religion, 161, 277
Repartee, 215
Representative, 162, 277
Responsible, 162, 277
Restriction of meaning, 114, 116, 121
Ride, 138
"Right-word," doctrine of, 21
Rogers, Will, 237
Roget, *Thesaurus*, 53, 55; *Treasury of Words*, 53; sample page, 54
Romance element in English, 64, 65, 66
Romance of Words, 126, 128
Roosevelt, Franklin D., 175
Roots, Indo-European, 57, 67; number of, in English, 56; defined, 66; Latin, 100-105; Greek, 105-107
Run, 138
Rupt, ruptur, 89, 272
Ruskin, John, quoted, 35, 118

Sal, salt, 89, 272
Sandwich, 126
Satire of Dryden, 221
Saxon words, *see* Anglo-Saxon words
Say, 139
Scandinavian element in English, 61
Science, terminology, *see* Jargon: Technical vocabularies
Science of word meanings, 113
Scott, Sir Walter, 21
Scrib, script, scriptur, 67, 89, 272
Secrecy, language used to maintain, 165, 178
Secut, sequ, 90, 272
Sed, sess, 90, 272
See, 139

Seem, 139
Selection, 162, 277
Semantics, 113
Send, 139
Sensations, terms describing, 119
Sent, sens, 90, 272
Sentence, style rule, 255, 263
Separate, 162, 277
Sequ, secut, 90, 272
Serv, servat, 90, 272
Sess, sed, 90, 272
Sévigné, Madame, 240
Shadwell, Thomas, 125
Shakespeare, 21, 57, 116, 138, 173, 175, 236, 244
Shaw, George Bernard, 13, 32, 71, 129, 216, 237; conversation, 229, 230; letters, 240; excerpt, 239
Shop talk, 178
Shrinkage of vocabulary, 39
Sign, 91, 272
Simplified Dictionary, Winston's, 46, 53, 194
Sist, sta, stat, 91, 272
Skeat, W. W., *Etymological Dictionary of the English Language*, 56
Skopeo, 99, 273
Slang, 165-176; definition, 25; dictionaries, 56; uses, 165; O. Henry's use of, 165, 168; a living language, 166; sources, 169, 176; malapropisms, 174; use of, to minimize solemnity, 175; described, 176
Smith, A. L., 235
Smith, Logan Pearsall, 167
Smith, S. Stephenson, 253
Snowden, Mrs. Philip, 229
Society, 162, 277
Socrates, 41; conversational method, 218
Solecisms, 166
Spec, spic, spect, 91, 272
Special vocabularies, 40, 181-214; *see also* Jargon
Specialization of meaning, 114, 116, 121
Speeches, after-dinner, 234
Spencer, 126
Spic, spec, spect, 91, 272
Spooner, Canon, 174
Spoonerisms, 174
Sta, stat, sist, 91, 272
Standard Dictionary, 12, 51
Statistics, terminology, 207
Stein, Gertrude, 131

Stems, defined, 66; word-compounding, 72; confusing of, 73; Latin, 75-95; Greek, 95-100
Sterne, Laurence, 242
Stevenson, Burton, *Home Book of Quotations*, 55
Stevenson, Robert Louis, 71; quoted, 20, 21, 169
Stories, after-dinner, 234
String, strict, stricture, 92, 272
Style rule, 251-264
Suffixes, Anglo-Saxon, 110; Greek, 68, 70, 71, 109; Latin, 68, 69, 108
Swift, Jonathan, 31, 64; words condemned by, 171
Swim, 138
Syllabic divisions, 42
Symbols, of dictionary, 43, 46; abstract, 140
Synonyms, 131-164; dictionaries, 55; importance of study of, 129, 131; words of Anglo-Saxon or classical origin, 132; doublets, 133; synonyms for common words, 135; verb-synonyms, 136; nouns and adjectives, 140, 149-164; words with widest meaning: differentiation in use, 141-148

Take, 139
Talkie dialogue, 244
Talking, *see* Conversation
Tang, tact, 92, 272
Tatler paper, words condemned in, 171
Teacher's Word Book of 20,000 Words, The, 1, 2, 10, 266
Techne, 99, 273
Technical vocabularies, 40, 181-214; *see also* Jargon
Ten, tent, 93, 272
Tend, tens, tent, 93, 272
Thesauri, 53
Thesis, 99, 273
"Third Party, The," excerpt, 242
Thompson, Francis, 21
Thoreau, Henry David, 32
Thorndike, E. L., *The Teacher's Word Book of 20,000 Words*, 1, 2, 10, 266
Thorndike, E. L., word-frequency studies, 1, 29, 38
Thorndike's *Century Junior Dictionary*, 47, 53, 59; specimen page, 52
Time, excerpts, 247, 248
Toastmaster, art of, 237
Tolerate, 143

Topos, 99, 273
Trah, tract, 93, 272
Transference of meaning, 119
Treasury of Words, Roget's, 53, 54
Trench, Archbishop, *On the Study of Words,* 28; *English Past and Present,* 173
True, 162, 277
Turgenev, Ivan S., 20
Twain, Mark, criticism of Cooper, 131; as letter-writer, 242

Ulysses, 60, 172
Unit, 163, 277
Unmoral, 71
Use, 163, 277
Ut, us, usur, 94, 272

Value, 163, 277
Van Dine, S. S., 182
Ven, vent, ventu, 94, 272
Verbal facility, dangers, 15, 27
Verbs, in Basic English: synonyms, 136; phrasal, 136, 175
Vernon, Admiral, 126
Vid, vis, 94, 273
View, 163, 277
Vizetelly, Frank, 12, 39
Voc, 94, 273
Vocabulary, range of active: of passive or reading, 1, 12; time-honored modes of building, 31-38; recent methods, 38-41; shrinkage, 39; special and technical, 40, 181-214 (*see also* Jargon); of English language, chart and description, 49; *see also* Diction: Words
Voltaire, 249
Vulgarisms, 25, 169

Walk, 138
Walpole, Horace, 24, 223; letters: quoted, 241
Walpole, Robert, 234
Washington, George, 224
Waste, 164, 277
Webster's Collegiate Dictionary, 42, 45, 46, 51, 58
Webster's New International, 51; number of words in, 40, 56; excerpts, 51

Weekley, Ernest, 124, 165; *Romance of Words,* 126, 128
Weight, 164, 278
Weseen, Maurice E., *Dictionary of American Slang,* 56, 176
Whimsicality in conversation, 226
Wilde, Oscar, epigrams, 134, 228; conversation, 226
Will, 139
William the Conqueror, 62
Winston's Simplified Dictionary, 46, 53, 194
Wise, 164, 278
Wisecracks, 215
Wit, dependence upon words, 15; in conversation, 215, 229, 234
Word-meanings, 112-130; science of, 113; generalization, 114; specialization, 114, 116, 121; radiation, 117; transference, 119; degradation, 120; word histories, 47, 123; fine shades: synonyms, 131-164
Words, number of, understood by readers: in active use, 1, 12; Thorndike word-frequency studies, 1, 29, 38; 50 most often used, 12; and ideas, 17; learned by contact with object or process, 18, 66; careful selection of, 19; doctrine of "the right-word," 21; sureness in use of, 22; contextual aspect: denotation, 35; connotation, 36; number of, in English: in Basic English, 39; as part of a pattern, 40; word-entries in largest dictionaries, 40, 56; division and pronunciation, 42; figurative extension of meaning, 44; historical treatment of, 47; linguistic origin, 57, 60-111; chart, 65; 100 common words, 136; compound, 172; *see also* Diction: Vocabulary
Words and Their Ways in English Speech, 28, 113; excerpts, 25, 128
Work in Progress, 60, 172
Writing as one talks, 239-249
Wylie, Philip, quoted, 203

You was, 24

Zoon, 100, 273